Too Much to Ask

ELIZABETH HIGGINBOTHAM

Too Much to Ask

BLACK WOMEN IN THE ERA OF INTEGRATION

The University of North Carolina Press   Chapel Hill & London

Set in Minion by Keystone Typesetting, Inc.
Manufactured in the United States of America

The paper in this book meets the guidelines for permanence
and durability of the Committee on Production Guidelines for
Book Longevity of the Council on Library Resources.

The publication of this volume has been aided by generous
support from the Z. Smith Reynolds Foundation.

Selection from Langston Hughes's "I, Too," is from *The
Collected Poems of Langston Hughes*, copyright © 1994 by
The Estate of Langston Hughes. Used by permission of
Alfred A. Knopf, a division of Random House, Inc.

Library of Congress Cataloging-in-Publication Data
Higginbotham, Elizabeth.
Too much to ask: Black women in the era of integration /
Elizabeth Higginbotham.
    p.   cm.—(Gender and American culture)
Includes bibliographical references (p.   ) and index.
ISBN 0-8078-2662-6 (cloth: alk. paper)—
ISBN 0-8078-4989-8 (pbk.: alk. paper)
1. African American women—Education (Higher)—Longitudinal studies.
2. African American women—Social conditions—Longitudinal studies.
3. African American college students—Longitudinal studies. 4. College
integration—United States. 5. Educational surveys—United States. I. Title.
II. Gender & American culture.
LC2781.H545   2001
378.1′9829′96073—dc21   2001027543

05 04 03 02 01   5 4 3 2 1

To the memory of my grandparents,

David Alfred Thompkins (1903–2000) *and*

Helen Belle Miller Thompkins (1908–1993)

I am grateful for what they taught me about

responsibility, community, and caring.

CONTENTS

Preface ix

Chapter 1. The Women and the Era 1

Chapter 2. Family Social Class Background 20

Chapter 3. What Money Can Buy:

   Social Class Differences in Housing and Educational Options 42

Chapter 4. The Ties That Bind: Socialized for Survival 63

Chapter 5. Public High Schools: Surviving or Thriving 86

Chapter 6. Elite High Schools: The Cost of Advantages 116

Chapter 7. Adult-Sponsored and Child-Secured Mobility 141

Chapter 8. College: Expectations and Reality 163

Chapter 9. Survival Strategies in College 185

Chapter 10. Struggling to Build a Satisfying Life in a Racist Society 204

Epilogue 233

Notes 241

Bibliography 265

Acknowledgments 277

Index 279

TABLES

1   Occupations of Parents by Social Class 28

2   Parents' Expectations for Daughters' Educational Attainment
      by Social Class 67

3   College Attendance by Social Class and Type of High School 166

4   Life Plan Preferences during Senior Year in College by Social Class 199

5   Women's Occupations in 1976 by Social Class Background 208

6   Women's Marital Status in 1976 by Social Class Background 208

7   Women's Life Plan Preferences in 1976 by Social Class Background 224

The experience of Black women in colleges and universities during the era of integration presents a complex, rich, and varied history. It is a history of racial pioneers. It is also my own history. Beginning graduate school in the fall of 1971 was a significant experience for me. I was crossing boundaries that few of my friends from City College of New York attempted. While most friends who had recently graduated from college were working in jobs as teachers and caseworkers in New York City, I was preparing to continue my education at a private university in Massachusetts. Living in Boston with middle-class White people was part of that boundary crossing. At Brandeis University, I was the only African American in my cohort. Attending graduate school with students from privileged backgrounds was a challenge.

I was somewhat overwhelmed with the many changes in my life and by the everyday details involved in attempting the next educational level. Much of my energy that first year was devoted to mastering a new environment and sorting out my own place within it. I was different from my cohort in terms of race, social class, and urban residence, which meant I had not had the "privileged college experience" of most of my fellow students. Most had lived on a campus and devoted the majority of their time to studying and socializing with peers.

A commuter student in college, I integrated course work and studying with much paid employment. While in college, I tutored elementary school students at a community agency, tutored Upward Bound students in high schools in Manhattan and the Bronx, and worked in after-school programs in community centers for elementary school children. In addition to regular part-time employment, for two years I worked for a CBS News polling operation that conducted national surveys for elections and other news-related programming. Those experiences did not count in this new environment where how much one had read and the ability to discuss these books were prized instead. In time I learned to value my experiences and look at my new peers with my own eyes. Many in my cohort with limited work experiences had a vision of the world that was shaped by books. While I was initially intimidated, I learned over the course of that year to trust my life experiences, especially in terms of what scholars had to say about the people I knew. Much of the 1960s scholarship on White working-class people did not capture the experiences of many of the people whom I knew growing up, yet my classmates were willing to grant legitimacy to such portrayals because they were published in books. It took years to formulate a position that reflected my perspective as a Black person raised in the working class negotiating a predominantly White academic world.

A month into my second year of graduate study, I had my first meaningful discussion with Elizabeth, another Black woman who had just entered the program. The daughter of professionals, Elizabeth talked about her background and began to complain bitterly about how little Brandeis University had done to help her solve her many relocation problems. In contrast, I had felt privileged to be in this space where people recognized me and where I could conduct business without giving my social security number. As Elizabeth complained, I asked, "What made you think that Brandeis would do these things for you?" Apparently, her elite college had made many such accommodations. However, I am sure that the college was pushed into such activities by people who felt entitled to them, just as Elizabeth had pushed for services at Brandeis.

The encounter haunted me. Elizabeth was a Black woman, close in age, but I was struck by our very different expectations of what the world owed us. I was clearly working class and she was middle class. I was prepared to enter this educational environment, just as I had entered others, by fending for myself. After this discussion, I began to think more systematically about social class background, particularly how it "stamps" individuals, including people who are members of an oppressed racial group. I questioned how the intersections of race and social class would influence how Black people operate within predominantly White spheres and within their own communities. This core investigation (and the many related questions it spawned) culminated in the study here, which examines the race, social class, and gender constraints on fifty-six Black women who graduated from predominantly White colleges in the late 1960s. Developing, conducting, and analyzing this research was a twenty-year project. In 1980, when I completed my dissertation, "Educated Black Women: An Exploration into Life Chances and Choices," based on my initial investigation, my advisor said there were a hundred ideas in the work. Over the years since then, I have thought about the many themes in the data and have crafted a book that seeks to highlight the negotiations that achieving educational success requires and the different resources that women bring to the task.

In 1980 much research on Black Americans, men and women, was viewed as occurring within a cultural framework, and the findings were considered unique to the Black population and marginal for the rest of U.S. society. Many scholars now recognize that race is both a social construction and a key feature of the stratification system in the United States (McKee 1993; Omi and Winant 1994). Scholars focus on the power dimensions of race rather than limiting themselves to a language of racial differences. These changes have helped to make race and social class, as well as gender, central analytic categories in the social sciences. Thus insights from scholarship on Black women now have a more profound impact on the state of general knowledge. I have also come to a greater appreciation of the significance of this cohort's experiences. These fifty-six Black women, who all attended colleges in a single city, were among the first major wave of Black students in predominantly White colleges in the mid-1960s. Other Black women encountered similar situations in other northern cities during this era of integration. We can learn much from them that can help us understand the shifting issues that face Black students in predominantly White settings.

The lives related in this book are complex and intricate. These women came from different regions as well as different social classes. There were Black women from the South who graduated from segregated high schools as well as women who grew up in the North in overwhelmingly White suburban communities. There were women from working-class communities who struggled in comprehensive high schools where their talents were unrewarded and who then found more support and encouragement in colleges, and there were others who found college to offer experiences similar to their previous schooling. There were middle-class women from highly ranked high schools where they were encouraged to attend college, but not prestigious ones. The nuances in the interactions these women had in educational settings structured the varied paths and patterns of their lives. There is no easy way to present the findings. As a sociologist, my task was to examine these complex lives and develop a perspective that can help readers ask a series of questions to better understand the alternatives these women faced and to examine how people move within varying social structures.

What did being a Black person in a time of shifting racial dynamics mean for the course of these women's lives? What was it like to be a pioneer in a predominantly White college as the college attempted to change how it operated? What obstacles *and* supports did social class differences create for the women in their journeys through childhood, into college, and into their early adult lives? How did gender impact Black women raised with certain expectations within the Black community and exposed to different expectations in predominantly White colleges? The answers will vary for women who traveled along different educational paths. There are no charts that map out a neat course. However, we know that race is central. Membership in a disadvantaged racial group shaped aspects of these women's lives, especially as they struggled to scale barriers. Social class was always an issue in terms of the women's own expectations for their lives, the material resources available to surmount racial barriers, and their reception by people in mainstream institutions. Gender also played a critical role, especially since their parents' gender expectations shaped how they reared their daughters. Further, as the women interacted with mainstream institutions, they found conflicting visions of their futures based on others' views of oppressed racial groups as inferior. Social class shaped these images of their futures; some Black women coming of age at this time were expected to be schoolteachers and social workers, while others were expected to be service and clerical workers. But these women shared the common experience of being outsiders, looking for a way through the institutional and interpersonal obstacles to their successful passage through the educational system.

This study provides an opportunity to look anew at the integration of educational institutions, both secondary schools and the predominantly White colleges that these fifty-six women entered in the 1960s. While school principals, college presidents, and many other educational officials put forward plans to increase the numbers of Black students in particular settings, these women did the actual desegregating. They were active in the process, making choices about their own educational settings and often working for years to attain their goals. As smart people entering those educational systems, they saw much more than those who were already established in positions of power could see. As members of oppressed groups, they saw much that those entrants with racial privilege did not see. Thus they have much to say about how institutions are structured and what does and does not change when minor alterations are made to their racial composition. By listening to their stories, we can develop a more nuanced understanding of what social change requires of institutions. That vision can help us develop institutions that are truly welcoming, where everyone can thrive.

As part of this age cohort, I shared their historical moment and was also a pioneer in many respects. My own working-class family moved out of Harlem so that the children could attend better schools in a racially and ethnically integrated working-class community in Manhattan, where we were one of only a few Black families. Both in and out of the classroom, I learned much about the racial and ethnic peoples who make up New York. This learning enabled me to cross borders between Black, ethnic White, Puerto Rican, and Asian American peoples, and it still shapes how I do sociology. When I was in junior high school, my family moved to the racially and economically mixed Upper West Side of Manhattan. After one year in a genuinely integrated seventh grade class, I was again pushed to be a pioneer as one of three Black working-class students in an enrichment class. Attendance at an all-girls public high school meant even more learning about how working-class and middle-class students think about themselves and their options.

This background gave me an understanding of the experiences of the women I studied. And in turn, their stories helped me to put into perspective what I had often viewed as the odd behavior of my own parents. I found other Black women whose parents had moved out of the ghetto to ensure quality schooling, even if that meant social isolation. I spoke with other Black women whose working-class parents were avid readers who made sure there were books and magazines in the home. Most important, the experiences of other Black women taught me to look closely at what had been invisible to me, particularly the work that I performed daily as a pioneer throughout my educational experiences. While I often had only a few Black allies in those settings, I was fortunate to have had many working-class compatriots. Thus at each educational level I had close ties with other students as we set about exploring the city's cultural institutions and mastering our academic tasks. The experiences of these other Black women gave me the impetus to categorize and make visible much of the tacit knowledge I already had about pioneers by race, class, and gender in the educational system.

In the ten chapters of this book I hope to help readers understand the times and the work of integration for these Black women. The first four chapters provide a context for understanding the era and the resources that Black women brought to the task of navigating educational environments to reach goals often nurtured in their families. Careful attention is paid to the meaning of being working class and middle class in the 1950s and 1960s (Chapter 2). Chapter 3 extends that discussion to explore how the differences in families' economic resources translated into residential and educational options. Black families during this era shared the need to prepare their daughters to survive in a world where they would encounter racial prejudice and discrimination (Chapter 4). The majority of the women I studied desegregated educational settings long before attending college. Some faced social isolation as young children in predominantly White settings, while others entered integrated or predominantly White high schools after junior high. Family lessons and resources influenced how the women faced the specific challenges in either comprehensive high schools (Chapter 5) or elite high schools (Chapter 6). As they were planning for college and scaling new barriers in their schools, their families offered very different kinds of support (Chapter 7). We also find that social class shaped their expectations for college as well as the adjustments they all had to make in their predominantly White colleges in the mid-1960s (Chapter 8). Chapter 9 turns our attention to how the women balanced their academic pursuits and their social lives and explores their thinking about their lives beyond college. Chapter 10 presents the women as they were in 1976 and provides a way to look at the achievements of these racial pioneers as well as their costs. By examining the lives of Black women who challenged racial barriers before the rise of affirmative action and special programs, we not only begin to unravel the complexity of race, social class, and gender interactions, but we learn about the energy and creativity within people that is essential for integration to happen. In that way, we can see the institutional barriers and can commit ourselves to doing the work that really addresses our legacy of injustice.

CHAPTER 1 : THE WOMEN AND THE ERA

I didn't really see too much prejudice until I entered high school, which was at a seventh grade level. That was a mind blower. It was a time when people were beginning to get into "Black is beautiful" and recognizing their Blackness more. It was the same time when there were freedom schools. So I don't know if it was a reaction to my being involved in some of that, that brought out prejudice in the [White] people around me. Or if it was that I was all of the sudden in a school that was majority White. Teachers were reacting very differently. I had always been in the top of my class; there was never any hassles and then all of the sudden I was being given Cs when I felt there was nothing wrong with the composition. I was also competing with a group of people who were the tops from all across the city. So it might not have had anything to do with it, but when people were making remarks to my parents about my not belonging there [in the school] and that I wasn't going to work [out] there—different attitudes which would come through, that my father picked up on—then he started on how I was not going to let White people tell me that I didn't belong here. "We know you can do better." That really sort of started me being aware and these hassles became personal, instead of being something that was happening to someone else.

—Denise Larkin, respondent from working-class background

As part of the baby boom cohort, Denise Larkin and many other African American youth came of age during a shifting racial climate in the United States.[1] Black youth born after World War II, especially those residing in the North, benefited from the lifting of some racial barriers in the 1950s and 1960s. This shift was most evident in the realm of education, especially for young people living outside of the South. In Denise's case, attending a prestigious public high school that uniformly sent the majority of its graduates to college was a clear benefit. Denise graduated in 1964 and proceeded to a predominantly White college in her native city. As young Black people desegregated schools, they might have gained in terms of educational preparation, but access to these environments was not without a cost.[2]

As they desegregated schools, Denise and many young people learned to negotiate two worlds. Armed with life skills from their families, Black women and men moved between predominantly Black settings and newly desegregated, yet still predominantly White settings. In the former, they were seen as full human beings and treasured for their unique talents and energy; in the latter, the reactions were quite mixed. While some White people might have celebrated their arrival, others viewed these new students through a lens of racial inferiority. In these new settings, the Black people drew upon the nurturing of their families to maintain positive self-esteem. They also used skills acquired to fight different forms of racism to hold on to their own sense of purpose and get the education they needed to achieve their goals. As this study illustrates, many women would master negotiations that would be part of a lifelong pattern of coping in predominantly White settings.

In *Black Feminist Thought*, Patricia Hill Collins (1990) noted that "Black women's lives are a series of negotiations that aim to reconcile the contradictions separating our own internally defined images of self as African-American women with our objectifications as the Other" (p. 94). Denise Larkin was recognized by her parents as very bright. In a long tradition of resistance to oppression, her parents wanted her to go as far as she could. Her potential was clear to many in her predominantly Black community. However, as a Black woman she would encounter people and settings where her talents would not be recognized and treatment would be based on race/gender stereotypes. In the Black community, the family is not just a site for reassurance, as daughters confront other images of their abilities, but also the place where children learn the critical importance of not letting White people define and set limits for them. Denise was to achieve not just for herself, but as a representative of a racial minority.[3]

How do people master such negotiations to ensure their success? The young women in this study rejected notions of Black inferiority; instead, they saw limited opportunities and racial prejudice as the real reasons that Black people may not be successful. Black families traditionally have equipped young people with alternative frameworks to meet the various forms of institutional racism they may encounter throughout their lives. Moving through the doors that previous generations had worked to open, Black youth had to hold their own and not let White people tell them where they belonged. These battles are serious business and tax the individuals, especially as young people like Denise became aware that such hassles were happening to them and not to someone else. Raised in families that held higher educational goals for their children, young women like Denise internalized these goals and then confronted educational systems that held different expectations for them as Black women. Relying upon stereotypical notions of Black women's abilities and inclinations, many White teachers and school officials would challenge the aspirations nurtured at home. However, the women in this study held on to their own definitions of themselves as they scaled institutional barriers in educational settings.

Undertaking this task requires one to learn to live with a certain degree of tension as one negotiates between the two worlds of home and school. These negotiations are not in vain; they contest the established racial order. For example, the actions of these women as they pursued their educational goals meant they rejected what White people had defined as their place. Personal and group challenges within social institutions produce social change (Omi and Winant 1994). As the racial climate shifts, Black women gain access to new spheres where their negotiations with racism likely continue. Students like Denise who desegregated schools paved the way for other students of color, especially by how they defined themselves in these settings.

The lives of the fifty-six Black women in this book were shaped by the significant social structural changes of the post–World War II era. The college-educated women featured here came of age in the 1950s and early 1960s. They personally witnessed a transformative period in U.S. history and were profoundly affected by a legacy of struggle. This group of women was not homogeneous; some were raised working class and some middle class. In the Black experience, social class is related to power in occupational settings, economic resources, information, expectations, and the strategies employed to overcome obstacles. The women from middle-class families grew up with high expectations as well as many resources to help them achieve their goals. The working-class women's families also had high expectations, but fewer material resources to secure their goals.

In this study, social class is determined by using a professional-managerial/ working class division that is based on the mental/manual dichotomy developed by Harry Braverman (1974) and Nicos Poulantzas (1974). The parents in middle-class families were either professionals or managers, while the parents in working-class families were manual workers, including clerical, sales, and service workers (see Chapter 2). Braverman's mental/manual dichotomy captures critical differences between the families that speak not only to the parents' level of control in the workplace, but also to the economic resources they could employ to express their values, needs, and priorities. For these families, supporting their daughters' educational attainment was a priority. Parents' economic resources and awareness of middle-class institutions, especially schools, would shape their daughters' paths to college (see Chapters 3 and 7).

The adaptation of new strategies to challenge racial discrimination would shape these women's lives (see Chapter 4). Their parents initially stressed the personal importance of battling prejudice to prepare them for playing a role in the struggle for equality. Over time, the women would come to appreciate the role of institutionalized racism in their lives. However, their struggles, even with the successes that merit celebration, cannot be fully appreciated without attention to the costs. This book presents the social structural obstacles faced by Black women in this new era of race relations, the negotiations and creative strategies developed to scale the barriers that existed within integrated settings, and the costs of these achievements.

Four Women Go to College

To Jennifer Taylor, a respondent who was raised working class, leaving her home in a mid-Atlantic city to enter East City University in 1964 was like a dream come true. Neither of Jennifer's parents had graduated from high school, but, like the majority of the Black community, they valued higher education. Mr. Taylor worked hard over a lifetime in different service jobs. Mrs. Taylor left domestic service after the birth of her second child to devote more time to her family. The Taylors were determined to save money to give their children advantages they never had, including a college education. Mr. Taylor promised Jennifer the funds to attend the college of her choice. The family's hard work and the shifting racial climate in their city made it possible for the Taylors to move to a townhouse in a predominantly White, central city neighborhood. Jennifer, who was nine years old at the time of the move, remembered, "It [the move] meant a better house and better schools."

Mr. and Mrs. Taylor had attended segregated schools in their youth, but the 1954 *Brown v. Board of Education* Supreme Court decision created new options for their children. The changing climate gave more Black Americans living in the North access to predominantly White educational institutions.[4] But gaining access to school was just one stage; Black parents then had to advocate for their children to ensure fair treatment. They regularly visited the schools to question the treatment of their children and to monitor the activities of teachers. Parents made sure their children were in the appropriate courses to reach their goals of college attendance.[5] The advocacy of the Taylors was critical to making the most of new opportunities. Hence, Jennifer attended an excellent high school where she was one of the few Black students in the honors program.

Once in the honors program in her integrated high school, Jennifer accepted the challenge and worked hard to turn an opportunity into a real advantage. In her school, Jennifer was close friends with Black peers who shared her aspirations of attending college. Perhaps one of the most difficult adjustments she made was learning to deal with pressures of competition. Jennifer recalled, "I had to recognize the fact that competition is omnipresent, and yet, can be enjoyable if not taken to a life-or-death extreme." She excelled in high school, and her grades earned her a partial college scholarship. In 1964, with her scholarship and the family savings in hand, Jennifer left home to attend a private college in East City.

Robin Washington, also raised working class, did not have the benefits of a two-parent family. After her husband left, Mrs. Washington, a high school graduate, raised five children on welfare and sent them all to college. When Robin, the second oldest, was ten years old, the family moved into a public housing project in East City, which meant a better neighborhood for the family. The Washingtons were the first of many Black families who would reside there. As Robin grew up, this housing project slowly became more integrated. In her adult years the majority of residents were Black Americans. Coming of age, Robin observed that "most families were on welfare or dependent upon a single, maybe sporadic, low wage." Robin attended the local elementary school, which reflected the social class and racial composition of her neighborhood.

Mrs. Washington combined community work with child rearing, and she was diligent about both. While she could not earn additional money to provide her children with many material resources, she used the means within her reach to encourage her children in academic pursuits.[6] Robin recalled her years growing up: "I lived through reading. It was a strong influence on me. My mother was in book clubs, record clubs, and other things. . . . There were always lots of books, magazines, and records [in the apartment]. We were never dressed as well as others, even though we were all on welfare. But my mother had thirteen magazine subscriptions. We always had books and I was reading more than other children in the housing project." Mrs. Washington also closely monitored her children's educational progress.

Robin did very well in elementary school and attended an all-girls college preparatory high school, where high grades were a requirement for entrance. This public high school, like its all-boys counterpart, sent the majority of its graduates to college, many to prestigious institutions.[7] Robin performed well in high school and was encouraged by school officials to apply to prestigious colleges. Upon graduation in 1964, scholarships and plans to work part-time during college enabled Robin to proceed to a private university.

Allison Cross's parents both held advanced degrees. In the 1960s only about a quarter of Black college students had parents with a college education, and an even smaller percentage had parents with advanced degrees (McGhee 1983). Mr. Cross, a public sector scientist, advanced within his occupation as his family grew. Mrs. Cross initially worked as a librarian and teacher when Allison was young. She left paid employment when she had her second child, devoting her time to raising her children, who eventually would number six. Mr. Cross was also actively involved in the rearing of his children.

Increasing economic opportunity for the Black middle class and the changes in the racial climate of the nation influenced Allison's route to college. As the family's economic situation improved, they could translate these gains into improved housing and new educational opportunities in their mid-Atlantic city. When Allison was an infant, her family had lived in an apartment; they moved to a small home in a Black community when she was a toddler. They moved again when she was ten years old, this time to a larger home in a predominantly White neighborhood. This move was meant to give the children access to schools with an excellent reputation. Allison's high school was initially integrated and then became predominantly Black. It offered a high level of academic preparation, especially for middle-class students. In 1964 Allison went to East City to attend a private university.

While making college a reality for Jennifer and Robin required many family assets and much energy, the transition from high school to college appeared seamless for Allison. All her life, it was assumed that Allison and her siblings would at least attain their parents' level of education. Allison mostly enjoyed her social experiences in high school, and academics were secondary. However, neither Allison nor her parents ever doubted that she would attend college. Allison's Black friends, who were either in honors or the college preparatory program, were also college bound. Allison recalled her friends as "middle- and upper-middle-income students who aspired to professional positions like doctor or lawyer. Our aspirations were generally vague, but involved making money and having high status."

Both of Helene Montgomery's parents were professionals. Mr. Montgomery was a health professional and Mrs. Montgomery, a librarian, worked continually outside the home while she raised four children. The Montgomery family moved into a White section of their Midwest city when Helene, their oldest child, was five years old. This area quickly became majority Black, but Helene remarked that it remained a "stable middle-class and white-collar neighborhood."

In the Montgomery family, as in many Black middle-class homes, there was the expectation that all the children would attend college. To ensure that goal, Mr. and Mrs. Montgomery carefully monitored their children's schooling. The children went to a Catholic grammar school, but their parents then placed them in the public high school. Helene's integrated high school offered an excellent college preparatory program in which she participated. She recalled, "College was taken for granted just like grade school and I was expected to achieve this at a minimum and then get an advanced degree of some type." Helene and her Black college-bound peers took these aspirations seriously. After her high school graduation she entered a university in East City in the fall of 1964.

Elementary and secondary teachers saw Allison and Helene, the daughters of college-educated parents, as attractive candidates for college. On the other hand, Mrs. Washington and Mr. and Mrs. Taylor knew that education was important, but they had less control over neighborhood schools, were limited in the financial support they could provide their daughters, and knew little about the world of higher education. These limitations meant that the working-class daughters felt pressured to have excellent grades and had to assume much of the responsibility for navigating the world of higher education to make decisions about colleges themselves. While the strategies were different, both working- and middle-class parents prepared young people to enter a more integrated world. Changes within predominantly White higher educational institutions made the entrance of Black students possible, but the paths to these institutions were complex. Black families in the United States had to challenge many biased institutions that made it difficult for their children to secure the secondary schooling essential for college.

It is important to look at the Black students of the 1960s who were ready for admission to predominantly White colleges and universities. College attendance is based on solid secondary educational preparation. We see evidence of extraordinary efforts in the lives of the women in this study, because in the mid-1960s there were few affirmative action or remedial programs in colleges to compensate for the effects of institutional racism in high schools. Colleges made new efforts to attract minority students, but they were seeking Black and other students of color who met all the regular requirements for admission. Therefore social class background, regional educational options, and family composition were key factors in how these fifty-six Black women gained access to majority White colleges in the era of integration.

Racial Transformations

Race relations in the United States, and thus the opportunities for African Americans and other people of color, changed dramatically over the twentieth century. Geographic mobility in response to regional and national shifts created new opportunities as well as new challenges. "The severe labor depression in the South in 1914 and 1915 sent wages down to 75 cents per day and less. The damage of the boll weevil to cotton crops in 1915 and 1916 discouraged many who were dependent on cotton for their subsistence. Floods in the summer of 1915 left thousands of blacks destitute and homeless and ready to accept almost anything in preference to the uncertainty of life in the South" (Franklin and Moss 1994, p. 340). As these factors pushed Black people out of the South, stories in the Black press and labor agents' promises of new jobs pulled them north. Legal restrictions on European immigration meant industrial employers were looking internally for new workers (Takaki 1993). In their new region, Black Americans entered manufacturing and service industries, found new educational opportunities, and participated in local and national politics (McAdam 1982; Pohlmann 1990). The Black population's involvement in World War I also meant more interaction with mainstream institutions. While there were many setbacks during the Depression, there were also some gains. Scholars acknowledge that the New Deal did much to reinforce patterns of racial segregation (Quadagno 1994), but it also provided a forum for challenging the established order.

Within the South, the Black population also shifted. More African Americans moved into urban areas and enjoyed greater occupational diversity, enabling many to increase their earnings. In urban areas, Black Americans experienced greater freedom to establish and expand their own social organizations, especially churches, schools, and civic groups (McAdam 1982; Marks 1989; Morris 1984). These political and economic gains provided the backdrop for additional challenges to the racial hierarchies of the 1950s, 1960s, and 1970s.

The protracted struggle for full equality in this country and the many published testimonials by middle-class African Americans about continued racism up to the present time makes it difficult for many to appreciate the measure of change brought about in the post–World War II era and through the 1950s and 1960s (Carter 1991; Cose 1993; Gates 1994; Nelson 1993; Parker 1997; Williams 1991). There were expanding opportunities in those years as Black Americans, especially in the North, participated more fully in American institutions. Black World War II veterans had access to the many benefits of the G.I. Bill (Kiester 1994). This cohort was the first generation of Black veterans who could get educational, medical, housing, and insurance benefits for their families, and preferential hiring for veterans increased their own access to jobs.[8] Yet these rights and privileges were often curtailed by continued racial discrimination.

Black Americans systematically built upon the political, employment, and educational gains made during the New Deal and World War II. These gains were translated into new resources for continuing the struggle for even greater rights, particularly working for equity within the political system (Harding 1987; McAdam 1982; Omi and Winant 1994; Payne 1995). Every year brought new gains in employment, with increasing numbers of Black people employed in industrial jobs and growing numbers holding political positions, either citywide or statewide (Franklin and Moss 1994; Harris 1982; Pohlmann 1990). There were also increases in per-pupil expenditures for Black children in public schools and in the admission of Black students to predominantly White graduate programs (Billingsley 1992). The most dramatic victory, in many respects, was the *Brown v. Board of Education* decision of the Supreme Court in 1954 that declared segregated schools to be unconstitutional (Tushnet 1987). It would be ten years before the passage of the Civil Rights Act, but the court decision paved the way for changes in educational options for young people of color in the North and border states. This victory also inspired grassroots social protests that involved major segments of Black communities in both the South and the North (McAdam 1982; Morris 1984; Payne 1995; J. Williams 1987).

NEW EDUCATIONAL OPPORTUNITIES

The 1950s and 1960s witnessed significant upward social mobility for Black Americans along with other social changes. Funding for education, inspired by the Cold War and the need for educated workers, meant increased access to higher education. Unlike the World War II veterans in college in the late 1940s, a majority of the middle- and working-class students in this later cohort were traditional college age and not already married with children. Members of the earlier group were eager to complete their college degrees and enter the workforce (Kiester 1994). The college students in the mid-1960s were more inclined to participate in a range of school activities. This new cohort was also gender and racially diverse.

In 1960, 141,000 Black and other students of color between the ages of eighteen and twenty-four were enrolled in colleges (the census data for this year combines Black people and other people of color). The majority of African American youth at that time attended traditionally Black colleges and universities; scores of public and private institutions served their needs. But the G.I. Bill and the expansion of public colleges and universities after the war had resulted in increasing enrollments of Black students in majority White colleges outside the South. As the baby boomers came of age, Black college enrollments expanded during the 1960s. In 1970 the number of Black students had grown to 437,000 (American Council On Education 1990). By that year the majority of Black students in higher education were enrolled in predominantly White institutions (McGhee 1983). However, Black students were a small percentage of those attending majority White public and private institutions across the nation (Berry 1983; Mingle 1981).

Besides reflecting the growth of the pool of potential Black college students, increases in attendance indicated the enhanced economic stability among some Black families in the 1950s and 1960s (Coontz 1992; Ginzberg 1967). These families could support their children's completion of secondary school and even college. Many families were aided by scholarships and loans, including federal support for higher education (Berry 1983; McGhee 1983). Women in this study are representative of the expansion of higher education among Black Americans. For Black women, however, college attendance was far from the norm; in 1970 less than 4 percent of Black women between the ages of eighteen and thirty-four were enrolled in colleges.[9] To reach their educational goals, Black families had to work within an educational system that had a social class and gender bias as well as a racial one.

White colleges in the North created new options as they opened their doors to African American students in the wake of the 1954 *Brown* decision, the direct-action phase of the Civil Rights movement, and in response to federal and local antidiscrimination initiatives. In the 1960s a few private White colleges began actively to recruit high-achieving Black high school seniors; some began summer programs as recruiting tools. Public institutions were also changing. Northern state colleges and universities, responding to political pressure from officials and legislators who were sensitive to Black constituencies, did more outreach to Black students. Many state universities developed urban campuses to better serve many working-class constituencies, including Black citizens. Beginning in the 1960s, Black enrollments in southern institutions of higher education, formerly all White, also began to increase (Willie and Cunnigen 1981).

Other new programs were contributing to increasing Black enrollments in White colleges by actively recruiting high school students. For example, the National Scholarship Service and Fund for Negro Students (NSSFNS) directed many Black students to northern White colleges. Initially, in the 1950s, NSSFNS targeted students in segregated high schools; later it reached out to Black students in all types of schools who were identified as college bound by their scores on standardized tests. Such programs and desegregation trends were in place as the baby boom cohort came of age. Consequently, for a range of reasons, more Black women and men elected to attend predominantly White colleges and universities by the 1960s.

A number of African Americans in this baby boom cohort, especially those who lived outside the South, had already desegregated other settings before college: their elementary schools, junior high schools, and/or high schools. Motivated by their parents and by the time, these students took part in the great experiment of integration. The unique perspective of the Black women who were pioneers in this process provides insight into the circumstances of others who cross racial boundaries. Entering these majority White settings created tensions in their lives, but college degrees from predominantly White institutions also meant significant advantages for them in the larger society. This is an important story in the history of United States race relations that teaches us much about the complexities of these relations, strategies for social change, and the tenacity of racial ideology in the society.

As Denise, Jennifer, Robin, Allison, Helene, and women like them came of age in the 1950s and early 1960s, there was a sense of optimism within the Black community, especially among the middle class and those stable working-class families who could afford to send their children to college (Ginzberg 1967). This optimism was grounded in the significant gains achieved as the Civil Rights movement proceeded and as new legislation passed on the federal level and within many states. The decisions these African American families made about where their daughters would attend secondary schools and colleges reflected that optimism.

When discriminatory barriers began to shift in elementary and secondary schools, especially in the North and border states, many African American families were eager to have their children take advantage of these new opportunities. As a consequence, young people like Denise, Jennifer, Robin, Allison, and Helene had greater educational options than had been available to generations of Black youth before them. They were part of a new era, witnessing changes in their own lives as well as gains for Black Americans on the national scene. In 1957 they watched as nine young African American students made social change by integrating Central High School in Little Rock, Arkansas. These women's stories are not as dramatic as those of the Little Rock Nine. There were no mobs of White people protesting the arrival of these young Black girls at their new schools, and their actions were not covered by the media, but the young women still faced traumas as they learned to work and play in integrated and predominantly White settings. Going to such schools meant entering complex interactions with White peers, teachers, and school officials, as well as negotiations with members of their own racial groups in these new settings and within their African American communities.

When it came time to select colleges, many of Allison's and Helene's middle-class Black peers decided to attend traditionally Black institutions, while a minority would venture into predominantly White colleges around the country. Working-class women like Denise, Jennifer, and Robin were restricted by funding considerations. Many Black students, especially those raised in the working class, could not afford to relocate to attend college. College attendance might have been dependent upon living at home and working part-time. If they did not live in areas with predominantly Black colleges, then regional, predominantly White, state-supported colleges were often their only options. In order to go away to school, Black working-class students were dependent upon scholarships to either predominantly White or Black colleges.

The lives of these five women reflected a new era in American race relations. They, and many of the other women in this study, made educational history in several respects. However, changes in discriminatory patterns did not signify the end of racism. As they came of age and went to elementary school, junior high, high school, and college, Denise, Jennifer, Robin, Allison, and Helene were affected by racism that intersected with social class and gender.

Rethinking Racism

For much of the twentieth century, racist ideologies were the rationale for policies and practices of exclusion (Omi and Winant 1994). In the area of education, people of color were routinely either denied access to schools or relegated to segregated schools. The majority of African Americans who did receive an education prior to the Civil Rights movement did so within institutions that were segregated, either de jure or de facto (Kluger 1977). Within these settings, educational options and treatment were also influenced by gender: Black men often had greater access to higher education than Black women. Black women's educational futures were shaped by gender restrictions both within their own community and within the larger society. Thus, until the challenging of gender restrictions by the women's movement, the majority of educated Black women were prepared for traditionally female occupations such as teaching, nursing, social work, and library science (Higginbotham 1987; Hine 1989; Shaw 1996; Wallace 1982). These positions lacked the financial rewards and independence of many traditionally male occupations (i.e., medicine, dentistry, ministry, and business) open to educated Black men.

Securing an education was just one obstacle to practicing a profession or skill, because educated Black men and women still faced racial discrimination when looking for a job or position (Althauser, Spivack, and Amsel 1975; Dill 1988; Glenn 1992; Jaynes and Williams 1989). While both women and men had to maneuver in a work environment with prescribed racial barriers, gender barriers made educated Black women more dependent upon securing work from others; educated Black men were more able to establish themselves as independent entrepreneurs (Higginbotham 1987). Education gave people of color an additional resource in the struggle for racial equality, but there were still structural limits to individual advancement.

To support a system of economic exploitation of African Americans and other people of color, the dominant group had established and maintained patterns of disenfranchisement, blocking access to political and independent economic power. This system was held in place by an elaborate ideology of negative images of people of color that influenced how even members of the White working class, many of whom were new immigrants to this nation, perceived African Americans (Fields 1990; Goings 1994; Holt 1995; Roediger 1991; Takaki 1993). Efforts to isolate people of color were successful in some respects, as patterns of segregation in residential location, employment, and educational and religious institutions remain the rule even today. However, within these settings, people of color continually negotiate with members of the majority about their assessments of self and place in society.

Stephanie Shaw (1996), in *What a Woman Ought to Be and to Do*, noted that "family members provide the first lessons on the social and cultural values of the groups of which they are a part" (p. 13). Her social history of educated Black women in the era of Jim Crow documented the key role that African American parents played in preparing their daughters for formal education and the wider world. With goals of expanding their daughters' employment options and the expectation that their daughters would also play a role in the betterment of the race, these parents stressed "appropriate behavior, dedicated preparation, hard work, and community consciousness" (p. 13). These lessons would later be echoed in Black educational institutions. Like Shaw, Patricia Hill Collins (1990) also demonstrated that family support and the institutions within the Black community are sites for Black women to create their own perspectives of themselves. These are places where individual Black women learn to contest the mainstream ideologies that objectify "the Black woman as the Other" (Collins 1990, p. 85) that are readily found in schools, the media, corporations, and government agencies. The socialization of Black youth to withstand the impact of negative controlling images and discriminatory treatment is well documented. This training is often a collective effort involving "other mothers," community members, and ministers as well as parents. Even in poor families, socialization can provide expectations and experiences supportive of success for young people (Clark 1983; Jarrett 1995).

Family support is essential for young people's development. However, it is frequently as an individual that one has to face stereotypical expectations within mainstream institutions and learn to negotiate within those spheres. The values and expectations stressed in families were critical to how the women in this study held on to their aspirations when confronted with very different visions of their futures (see Chapters 3, 5, 6, and 7). Across social class lines, Black girls and women experience controlling images and limited expectations in majority White settings. In their predominantly White and integrated schools, these women faced White individuals who held culturally sanctioned beliefs that Black students were inferior or at least different from White students in some critical ways. These individuals also held beliefs about the appropriate futures for Black women. Thus many White teachers were obstacles to their enrolling in college preparatory programs, and the young women and their parents had to insist upon access to such programs. Even when Black women had solid grades, they faced teachers who held assumptions about their career options that were based more on racial prejudice than on the young women's abilities. Thus as girls and young women, they learned to operate and stand up for themselves within institutions constructed in ways that either actively or passively discouraged their advancement (Collins 1990; Higginbotham 1985; St. Jean and Feagin 1998; Turner, Singleton, and Musick 1985).

It is important to look at the family and other institutions in the Black community as sources of values and orientations that would serve these women as they encountered mainstream messages that often devalued them. Alternative perspectives, sensitive to how Black Americans' life options are limited by political and economic restraints, helped them to identify racist ideological frameworks. These understandings, nurtured in families and Black institutions, are the foundation for alternative self-definitions that are sustained in the face of negative mainstream visions. As Black students entering predominantly White colleges in East City in the mid-1960s, these women had to undertake critical negotiations between their images of self and the majority White visions of them. Examining the stories of their paths to college and early careers enables us to see the operation of racism within desegregating institutions, the strategies developed by Black women to cope with the legacy of racism in these settings, and the costs for those who have weathered the storm. This investigation into their educational strategies tells us much about how Black women might still be negotiating between the vision of themselves in their communities and mainstream perspectives of them. It also examines how a strong foundation from family and community can be a source of resilience as Black women cope in predominantly White environments.

Today African Americans are no longer routinely denied access to all major institutions on the basis of race. However, it is only recently that a majority of Black people have experienced some freedom of movement to enjoy educational and employment opportunities. There is no denying that access to employment for this population is still restricted (B. Williams 1987), even for members of the middle class (Collins 1997; Cose 1993; Feagin and Sikes 1994; Oliver and Shapiro 1995; Pattillo-McCoy 1999), that many of our communities are highly segregated (Massey and Denton 1993), and that the ability to exercise civil rights is influenced by economic means (Franklin 1991). Our nation's schools continue to be plagued with problems that are barriers to the social mobility of children of color. Many White students have left urban public school systems, resulting in new patterns of resegregation, and inequalities in funding public schools persist (Anyon 1997; Kozol 1991).

Regardless of recent U.S. congressional and Supreme Court efforts to deny the centrality of race in contemporary life for all citizens, "racial inequality is still the unsolved American dilemma" (Oliver and Shapiro 1995, p. 193). Race remains a critical dimension in the lives of all U.S. citizens, shaping not only our expectations but our treatment within public and private institutions. Yet the problem of race today is not the same problem that plagued the United States at the beginning of the twentieth century. The dominant racial order of that era was challenged throughout the century in many respects, resulting in a more complex interplay of race with other factors in our social fabric (Omi and Winant 1994; Takaki 1993). Thus we have to become more sophisticated in our analysis, rather than more simplistic. A contemporary analysis addresses race within a context that is sensitive to the social class and gender dimensions of inequality that operate simultaneously to influence material conditions of life, how individuals think about themselves, and how they are perceived within small groups and institutions.

When the women in this study left high school and entered college in the 1960s, they were an optimistic group ready to accept the challenges of integration. Their struggles were critical ones, and we can point to individual successes. However, we have not seen the institutional change that many of the women thought their actions would bring about. Many secondary high schools and institutions of higher education are still sites of routine and periodic trauma for African American and many other students of color (Feagin, Vera, and Imani 1996; Kozol 1991; McDonald 1999; Sidel 1994; Suskind 1998). We have desegregated, but we have not uniformly altered the mainstream assessment of racial minorities. As a consequence, many African American young people continue to feel like racial pioneers.

In 1990 two young Black women students at Spelman College in Atlanta were interviewed on the National Public Radio news program *All Things Considered* as part of a featured segment on Johnnetta Cole, the first Black woman president of Spelman. The two young women discussed their experiences in high school and their decisions to attend Spelman College, one of the nation's most highly regarded Black educational institutions. They had grown up in integrated communities, attended suburban schools, and said they chose Spelman College because they wanted an intermission from the subtle racism they had experienced in their high schools. As they described incidents that took place in public schools in the late 1980s, their tales sounded familiar. They were the same words I had heard or read in reply to questions I posed to Black women who attended public and private integrated and predominantly White high schools in the early 1960s.

Much had happened in this nation in the twenty-five years that separated these women's high school experiences. Yet these younger Black women talked about being discouraged by teachers who doubted their abilities and having to be aggressive to get the attention that their educational performance merited. Aretha Hankenson, then a senior at Spelman, said: "I remember one time I was in an advanced English class and then from the 11th grade to 12th grade, we had the option of choosing an advanced placement English class. I remember asking the teacher specifically, timidly, 'Do you think I can handle this [class]?' And she told me, 'No, I think you should just better stick with the English class that we will put you in.' Two other Black girls who were also told this went ahead and took that class and told me that the advanced placement class was no problem. It was no more difficult, it just had a few different reading assignments. Little things like that." Another Spelman student, Lorie Robinson, added: "I can attest to similar situations—always getting the highest grades in the class, but never being asked to be tested for the honors class. It got to the point that I had to request that I be tested."[10]

Listening to these accounts, I knew that the complexities of the arguments in this book were still relevant and much needed, as we have to understand the nature of racial inequality within integrated settings and how it is mediated by social class.[11] Despite decades of research, there is still much to be learned about the nature of race, social class, and gender barriers in society. Perhaps most important, there is much to learn about how people cope and build meaningful lives in the face of these barriers. We have not achieved that color-blind society many politicians hint at, and we might never arrive at that mythical place.

However, a deeper understanding of what it costs for people to cope in a racist society might motivate us to address the problems that persist.

Methods

This book traces the paths to college traveled by fifty-six Black women who graduated from predominantly White colleges in East City between 1968 and 1970. These women, the majority born after World War II, were educated in the 1950s and 1960s and were among the first major wave of Black students to enter predominantly White colleges in significant numbers during the mid-1960s.[12] After deciding that I wanted to investigate a diverse population of educated Black women but control for some shared experiences, I began to gather the names and addresses of Black women who had graduated from one of nine area coeducational institutions in East City. These respondents were contacted six to eight years after their college graduations because I wanted women who could reflect on their educational experiences; I felt that time might provide the necessary distance to evaluate the benefits and costs.

To reach the women, I used informal contacts, newly emerging Black alumni chapters, yearbooks, and the women themselves to help me identify classmates. As a group, these educated Black women were cognizant of the paucity of research on women like them; thus they were enthusiastic about the study. After searching for more than a year, I located, either by telephone or letter, eighty Black women graduates. Four women refused to participate in the study. In April of 1976, I mailed seventy-six questionnaires to these graduates, and fifty-six women (or 73 percent) returned them by the end of that year.

The fifty-six women answered a detailed questionnaire that requested information on family background, schooling and college experiences, plans and ideals while in college, employment history, and educational and marital status since college. Many of the questions were open-ended, and the women were encouraged to write about their experiences. The questionnaire gave me systematic data on all the women, but some women also used its pages to write detailed descriptions of their feelings about their schools or impressions of specific periods of their lives.

At the time of the study, twenty-six of the women still resided in the East City area, and thirty lived elsewhere. In terms of social class background, thirty-one were working class and twenty-five were middle class (see Chapter 2 for details on the conceptualization of social class). The majority, twenty-one of the working-class and twenty of the middle-class respondents, either had secured or were working on degrees beyond the bachelor's; six (three from each social class background) had taken additional courses, and eight (six working-class and two middle-class women) had ended their formal education with college.

The subjects all responded affirmatively to a letter, telephone call, or personal solicitation to participate in a study of educated Black women; however, there was some diversity in their racial ethnic background. Fifty-five of the women were born in the United States. The majority, twenty-eight working-class and seventeen middle-class respondents, indicated that their racial background was either Black, Afro-American, or Black American. Five respondents indicated that one parent was of mixed Black American and Native American ancestry (if specified, it was Cherokee). As was common in the 1970s, there was broad identification with being a Black American. For example, one respondent indicated that her father was Black but added in parentheses that his mother was Native American and that he had spent his early years on the Cherokee Reservation. There were also women who had other ethnic backgrounds. Two had a Black American parent and a West Indian parent, one respondent had one Black Portuguese parent, and one said both parents were West Indian. One woman identified herself as biracial, with a Black father and Chinese mother. In their questionnaires and in interviews, the women all identified themselves as Black Americans (or some other term that signified such identification).

After receiving the questionnaire data on the fifty-six women, I interviewed a subset of twenty respondents in person, ten working-class and ten middle-class women. The in-depth interviews explored their early impressions and experiences growing up, including family values, residence, and how they were socialized. They talked about their families' educational strategies and about their experiences in schools, including their planning and thinking about colleges and careers. We also discussed their lives after college, including work, family and personal life, and assessment of their lives. Each instrument was tailored to the individual respondent, using her answers to the fifteen-page questionnaire.

In addition to social class background, women were selected for the interviews based on geographic location, the colleges they had attended, and their occupations and lifestyles, to capture the varied paths of educated Black women.[13] The twenty women varied in their marital status and included respondents who had pursued careers in traditionally male as well as traditionally female occupations.

The interviews complement the questionnaire data by providing insights into the ways Black families prepared their daughters for their roles in actively combating racial oppression and highlight some of the costs associated with survival and even success in a racist society. In the national effort to desegregate institutions of higher education, little thought was given to the consequences for the young Black people who entered overwhelmingly White settings where many people still believed in Black inferiority. Yet it was critical for young African Americans to accept this challenge and prove both to themselves and to others their ability to achieve in these settings. Their efforts meant that the doors to many institutions would open wider and remain open for others. These women's detailed accounts shed light on some of the costs of being a racial pioneer and further our thinking about the dynamics involved in challenging racial oppression.

CHAPTER 2 : FAMILY SOCIAL CLASS BACKGROUND

My father, who never went to high school, rose to [be] a foreman in the post office. He was a hardworking person. He reached level nine in the system, which was very good for him. My mother attended college for one year before she was married. She was home until I [the youngest] was school-age. Then she went to work for the tax department [IRS] as a key-punch operator. She was not crazy about the work, but she did it.
—Tracy Edwards, respondent from working-class background

My parents and grandparents were college educated. My grandfathers were a minister and a principal, and my grandmothers were teachers. That made our family part of the middle class. We were pillar of the community types. We had financial security, but it was a strain to send me to private school.
—Katrina Charles, respondent from middle-class background

In this new millennium, many citizens and even scholars see the Black American community as divided between a middle class and an underclass (Franklin 1991; Marks 1990). Now, as in the past, there is little public discussion about the working class, a group that struggles to achieve stability in a postmodern economy. In the 1950s and 1960s, the majority of the Black community was working class. Members of this group varied in their occupational situations, residences, and economic resources. The poverty rate in the Black community was quite high, but while many people had low incomes, many at least had jobs. That era is a contrast to the current high level of impoverishment among Black Americans in both urban and rural communities in the wake of deindustrialization, global markets, and the flight of capital (Kushnick 1999; Wilson 1996). The decline of industrial jobs pushes many working-class people into service positions. Increasing rates of unionization help those in service jobs survive and provide for their families, but many people either work part-time or hold more than one job to make ends meet. Members of the Black middle class of today also differ from their counterparts in the 1950s and 1960s. While the professional middle-class parents of the past were likely to be employed either within the Black community or in the public sector, women of this baby boom cohort are more likely to work for majority White private firms, institutions, and nonprofit agencies. This chapter provides a framework for understanding social class and what that meant in terms of a family's level of material resources and knowledge of educational institutions. We can then understand the various strategies families employed to secure a college education for their daughters. Social class will also influence the paths to integration and the negotiations young women engaged in along the way.

Defining Social Class for Black Americans

Many people in the Black community, as well as many citizens of the nation, are only comfortable with defining social class as a group that shares certain values. Objectively, working-class families that express mainstream values are often accepted as middle class. Indeed, when discussing social class in the interviews, two of the ten respondents identified as working class in this study thought that their own families of origin were middle class.[1] In the field of sociology, there are many practices for assessing social class that look beyond values to material conditions.

First, there is a middle mass model that is derived from the work of Max Weber, where the occupational division between the middle class and working class reflects critical differences in status and affluence. Used by many scholars, this categorization has a broadly defined middle class that is "characterized by a variety of white-collar occupations ranging from sales clerks and teachers to executives, professionals, and the self-employed" (Oliver and Shapiro 1995, p. 70). William J. Wilson (1978), in *The Declining Significance of Race*, even expanded this middle mass model to include white-collar and skilled blue-collar workers along with professionals and managers. This model makes the middle class, regardless of race, look very large, enabling Wilson to indicate that 35 percent of Black males held middle-class jobs in 1970, a major increase over the 24 percent that held such positions in 1960. In a nation where many celebrate our affluence and like to think that we are all middle class, it is not surprising that many scholars use this model.

Second, there is a model that differentiates between white-collar and blue-collar occupational positions. Recent scholarship on the Black middle class by Joe Feagin and Melvin Sikes (1994), Jennifer Hochschild (1993, 1995), and Bart

Landry (1987) uses this white-collar/blue-collar dichotomy, which recognizes all white-collar workers as middle class and all blue-collar workers as working class.[2] This social class model, which is also derived from Max Weber, sees the working class as larger than the middle class. By treating all white-collar employees and entrepreneurs as one group, this model does not attend to critical differences in material resources and influences among secretaries, clerks, and professionals such as teachers, lawyers, and college professors.

Third, there is a neo-Marxist classification of a professional-managerial/ working-class dichotomy that has power as its central focus. Nicos Poulantzas (1974) envisioned "the middle class within the larger context of the struggles between capital and labor" (cited in Vanneman and Weber Cannon 1987, p. 56). Rather than a distributional scheme for social class that attends to status and influence differences along a continuum, this model is relational and explores dimensions of control as they relate to opposing structural positions (Lucal 1994; Weber 1998). Power relations are key elements in this model. The scheme recognizes that the social relations of dominance and subordination derived from either economic, political, or ideological dimensions of control are critical to the analysis of social class. Members of the middle class are involved in accumulating capital by designing and controlling the work of others, even though they themselves receive wages and/or salaries. In contrast, members of the working class execute tasks designed by others and in many respects have lost control over the work process. They are more likely to lack power in the workplace and be supervised by others, often doing work defined by members of the middle class.

In this study I employed the third definition of social class, the professional-managerial/working-class dichotomy. In this conceptualization of social class the segment recognized as middle class is smaller than in the other two models and that of the working class is larger. The middle class is limited to those in professional, technical, administrative, and managerial positions, while the working class is defined as clerical workers, skilled craftsmen, and those in manual occupations (Vanneman and Weber Cannon 1987).[3] This narrow definition is most appropriate for capturing mobility issues and the ways Black women and their families negotiated mainstream institutions where attention to power relations was vital.

In *The American Perception of Class*, Reeve Vanneman and Lynn Weber Cannon (1987) empirically demonstrated that most Black Americans, like others in the nation, recognize social class divisions that relate to power in the workplace.[4] The authors conclude: "To be middle class in America is to own productive property, or to have supervisory authority, or to perform mental labor at the expense of manual workers" (p. 61). Employing either a middle mass model or a white-collar/blue-collar dichotomy would limit this analysis and fail to explore critical differences in the ways that families could affect their daughters' educational careers. In many cases, parents' occupations, which reflected their levels of educational attainment, directly translated into their ability to pass on advantages to their children. Therefore the women's families of origin were designated as middle class or working class along a professional-managerial/working-class dichotomy.

The differences in the social class backgrounds of the women proved critical in shaping their routes to college and the life expectations they held for themselves. The class categories reflect how differences in their families' relationships to the production process influenced levels of material resources, knowledge of how dominant institutions operated, and the ways that parents aided their children in attaining goals of higher education. Barbara Ehrenreich and John Ehrenreich (1979) noted that this definition of class signified a shared relationship to the economic foundations of society and a "coherent social and cultural experience" (p. 11). Distinctions in occupational and work roles, educational attainment, lifestyle, consumer habits, and kinship networks attest to the lasting aspects of social class as a cultural experience. The social class indicators used here reflect the power, authority, and ideology to influence institutions in both the Black community and the larger society.

In this study, respondents provided complete employment histories of their parents, and the occupational positions of both parents were used to assign a family to either the middle or working class. If either a father or mother held a professional-managerial occupation, the family was designated as middle class. As many studies have shown, Black women's contributions to the economic support of the family have always been substantial (Amott and Matthaei 1991; Baca Zinn 1990; Billingsley 1992; Jones 1985; Mullings 1997). And Black respondents in other studies have routinely used characteristics of both spouses to designate class categories (Sampson and Rossi 1975) and given women's and men's status equal weight when making social class placements (Vanneman and Weber Cannon 1987).

Social Class and the Families in This Study

The discussion below and in the following chapters explores what social class means in terms of families' day-to-day life and the abilities of Black parents to foster aspirations in their daughters and to aid them in achieving a college education. At times the respondents faced challenges that are shared across social class lines, but more often variations in class resources enabled families to meet those educational and residential challenges in very different ways.

THE BLACK WORKING CLASS

Even after decades of social science research, we still understand little about the Black working class, and few scholars investigate this group today. As with the White working class, contemporary scholars have often overlooked this population (Steinitz and Solomon 1986). Among the White population, it is the middle class that is frequently studied; among Black people, it is the poor. The research orientation on Black Americans has most often centered either on the problems of Black life or on how the Black community is problematic for the dominant group (McKee 1993). As a consequence, the subjects of most social science research are poor and impoverished Black people. In the 1980s and 1990s, much of the published social science research about Black families was devoted to the "underclass" (Marks 1990). The working-class families in this study will appear to be very different from the usual depictions of this population, since they range from stable working-class families to poor, single-parent families.[5] As a group, the working-class women saw their parents as hardworking, but these parents were negotiating in a labor market with fewer resources than were available to members of the middle class.

For example, in the Maxwell family, Darlene was the oldest of four daughters. Both of her parents had high school diplomas and were steadily employed for most of her life. Mr. Maxwell worked as a longshoreman when Darlene was born and continued in that occupation until she was twelve, when he began working as a machinist. Mrs. Maxwell was not in the labor market when her four children were young, but after Darlene was eight she worked as a typist and secretary. Katherine Howell was the oldest of two daughters. Katherine said, "My father was a carpenter. He did everything, he worked for a contractor and did buildings, then he was a foreman. He always worked—days and weekends. The work was unstable in carpentry, so he did the work when he had it." Mrs. Howell did not work outside the home. She was devoted to family life and consistently cared for everyone. Katherine recalled, "A family priority was seeing the two daughters through to maturity without something terrible happening to us or them." These parents were models of stable employment and dedication to work, yet they did so within a labor market where Black Americans had limited options.

Over the centuries, racial oppression has structured the occupational options open to the Black working class. Until the middle of the twentieth century, the majority worked under oppressive conditions in farming and service work (Blauner 1972; Omi and Winant 1994). In both the North and South, many Black men and women were routinely denied access to industrial, retail, and clerical positions. Relegated to service and domestic work, the majority of urban employed Black women and men survived on low wages. The paths to higher paying industrial work were thorny; often entrance for Black workers was only possible during strikes and wars (Harris 1982; Marks 1989). Such positions were rarely secure, as Black employees were the first fired when normal conditions resumed.[6]

Significant gains in industrial employment, at least in the North, characterized the era around World War II (Billingsley 1992; Franklin and Moss 1994; Harris 1982; Omi and Winant 1994; Takaki 1993; Wilson 1978). As a result of organizing efforts by the Congress of Industrial Organizations (CIO) and New Deal programs, Black workers made strides in many unionized industries (e.g., automobile, meat packing, mining, and steel). In these industrial positions, Black men received wages more adequate for supporting a family. In the face of fair employment and Civil Rights legislation, the traditional arenas of White women's work, clerical and sales positions, slowly opened to Black women in the late 1950s and 1960s (Amott and Matthaei 1991; Jones 1985; Wallace 1982). These openings translated into better wages and working conditions for Black women as well as men. Such employment gave families greater resources to provide for their children's immediate and future needs.

Black Americans are particularly vulnerable economically, given their position in the system of production and the continuance of racial discrimination. Nevertheless, there are important distinctions among jobs opened to the Black working class that directly influenced parents' abilities to provide for their families. Working-class occupations can best be characterized as either primary or secondary labor market jobs. The circumstances of the work in the same occupation, for example, factory operative, could be very different depending upon its location in the labor market. Primary labor market jobs are characterized by "high wages, decent working conditions, employment stability and job security, equity and due process in the administration of work roles, and chances for advancement" (Piore 1975, p. 126). Such jobs often enable a breadwinner to support a family on one income.[7]

In contrast, secondary labor market positions lack these advantages; instead, those jobs generally pay the minimum wage, offer poor working conditions, and have few benefits. The secondary labor market is also characterized by instability, where workers are easily fired or laid off during slow periods. Furthermore, there are few channels for redress of grievances. Even if people have stable jobs in the secondary labor market, they are likely to see few raises and can remain economically vulnerable while stably employed. Since discriminatory barriers limited the number of Black people who could secure positions in the primary labor market, most working-class Black Americans held secondary labor market jobs. However, in the 1950s and 1960s there were significant economic gains for Black families as men and women moved into industrial jobs and clerical positions in large firms (Coontz 1992). The parents who secured employment in the primary labor market were a small but significant segment of the Black working class.

THE WORKING-CLASS WOMEN

Fifty-five percent of the respondents (or thirty-one women) in this study were raised in working-class families. This group includes fathers and mothers who were clerical workers, sales persons, skilled workers or craftsmen, semiskilled and unskilled operatives, and service workers. The wide variation within this group has implications for the families' lifestyles. However, there are clear similarities among them with regard to educational strategies, so they will be treated as a group. Parents were most often working, since a pattern of stable employment was critical to raising a family and sending children to college. Although they worked hard, the working-class parents lacked the greater economic means and knowledge of higher educational institutions available to middle-class parents. Thus they had to take different steps to create conditions to achieve educational mobility for their children.

The majority of working-class parents were high school graduates. As a group, these parents had lower levels of educational attainment than the parents of middle-class respondents, but they reflected the educational attainment of the Black population at large. According to the respondents, eighteen parents had schooling beyond high school. One set of parents had bachelor's degrees but never translated them into professional occupations. Five fathers and eleven mothers had between one and three years of college or attended a technical school after high school. Eight fathers and nine mothers were high school graduates. Finally, thirteen fathers and ten mothers had less than a high school education, many with seven to nine years of schooling.[8]

Working-class parents with high school diplomas were found in both primary and secondary labor market jobs (see Table 1). This dispersion is evidence of the existing racial discrimination that limited employment options for Black workers. Thus, while a high school education enabled a majority of White men to secure primary sector jobs, the same schooling could not guarantee that goal for Black people. Of the fifty working-class parents (both mothers and fathers) for whom the respondents wrote occupational histories, eighteen were identified as having held primary labor market jobs. Some working-class Black men and women were able to secure employment in the public sector. Seven parents worked for the U.S. Postal Service. Many of them, including Tracy Edwards's father, spent their entire careers in the post office and were able to advance within the system. A few other working-class parents were employed in primary labor market jobs within the public sector. For example, Cynthia Butler's father worked as a conductor with an urban transit authority. These public sector jobs were unionized, and regular contract negotiations often meant significant wage increases, as well as career ladders and wage increases with seniority.

A few working-class parents secured primary labor market jobs in the private sector. For example, when Janet Sheldon was eight years old, her father moved from a low-wage factory job, as a packer of women's wear, to a better-paying position on an electrical assembly line for a major business machine company. With predictable employment and higher wages than his old job, as well as opportunities for advancement, Mr. Sheldon could adequately provide for his family, including securing a home in an integrated community. In a decent economy, this segment of the Black working class could create the conditions conducive to getting their children through high school and into college.

In contrast to the relatively high unionized wages of the primary labor market, the low wages and poor working conditions of the secondary labor market limited the economic security Black parents in those jobs could achieve, even though they worked equally hard. Many working-class parents in this sector held positions traditionally thought of as Black jobs. They found employment either in service work, as janitors, porters, or cooks, or as unskilled laborers in factories. Although these jobs varied in the nature of the work performed and the employers, they shared the above characteristics. Such jobs offered little opportunity for advancement, so fathers remained in these positions during most of their daughters' lives. For example, Elise King wrote about her father's job history: "My father was a custodian, gardener, and a chauffeur. He often worked all week, including Sundays. He held the same job for thirty-five years." Working-class parents caught in secondary labor market jobs could only pull themselves out of poverty if both spouses were employed. And even so, progress was never a certainty.

Several working-class mothers were employed as domestics or cooks during their working careers, and a few mothers did labor-intensive factory work. For example, Tracy Edwards's mother held a factory job from the time Tracy was two until she was twenty years old. Joanne Bell noted that her mother worked as a cook from the time Joanne was five years old, while her father was a machinist in a factory. Indeed, some involvement with domestic or other service or factory work was found in other mothers' work histories. A few Black working-class mothers worked as domestics when their daughters were young, but then held factory or clerical jobs as racial barriers shifted in the late 1950s and early 1960s. These new occupational positions paid higher wages and typically offered health

TABLE 1. OCCUPATIONS OF PARENTS BY SOCIAL CLASS

Working Class		Middle Class	
Fathers	*Mothers*	*Fathers*	*Mothers*
Carpenter	Assistant buyer	Administrator	Administrative assistant
Conductor (transit)	Caseworker	Architectural engineer	Certified public accountant
Construction worker	Clerical worker	Attorney	Clerical worker**
Electrician	Cook	Chemist	Director, social welfare agency
Janitor	Domestic, private household worker	Dentist	Editor
Laborer	Factory worker	Director, social work agency	Educators
Longshoreman	Fashion coordinator	Educators	Assistant principal
Mechanic	Keypunch operator	Assistant principal	College professor
Porter	Personnel worker (clerical)	College professor	Teacher
Postal clerk	Postal clerk	Principal	Homemaker**
Postal supervisor*	Public school aide	Teacher	Librarian
Real estate agent	Receptionist	Guard**	Nurse
Semiskilled factory worker	Salesperson	Journalist	Sales clerk**

and other benefits. Eight respondents noted that their mothers worked as secretaries or clerks, and six described their mothers' involvement with retail sales. During this era, more Black women were moving into clerical and sales positions, jobs that had traditionally been White female occupations. Linda Trott, Darlene Maxwell, and Stephanie Lawrence noted that their mothers always did clerical or sales work, while others noted that their mothers moved into such employment after engaging in either domestic service or factory work. For example, Sylvia Mason, who grew up in East City, said her mother did factory work from the time Sylvia was six until she was seventeen; then, in 1964, her mother started working in a bank. Natalie Small's mother worked as a cook until 1963, when she became a sales clerk in her small southern city.

The mothers' economic contributions were critical for the survival of their families. Linda Trott was accustomed to both her parents working, but when her

TABLE 1. CONTINUED

Working Class		Middle Class	
Fathers	*Mothers*	*Fathers*	*Mothers*
Taxi driver, chauffeur	Secretary	Minister	Social worker
Unskilled factory worker	Welfare recipient	Mortician	Secretary**
		Owner/manager	Owner, travel agency
		Parole officer	
		Pharmacist	
		Physician	
		Police department head	
		Police detective	
		Postal clerk**	
		Public relations	
		Social worker	

Note: This is an inclusive list of all the different occupations mentioned by the subjects in the work histories of their parents. Some parents had more than one occupation over their lifetime, and many of these occupations are mentioned by more than one parent.

*In the *Dictionary of Occupational Titles* (U.S. Department of Labor 1977) the postal supervisor is identified as a clerical supervisor. His/her duties include supervising and coordinating activities of workers processing the mail in the post office. This person also keeps records of processed mail, mail in progress, and changes in worker assignments. This person does not manage the office and is identified as working class in this study.

**These parents are members of the middle class by virtue of their marriage to a spouse who fits the study's criteria for membership in the middle class.

mother, who usually worked as a secretary, was ill, the family survived on Mr. Trott's wages as a factory operative. Linda remarked: "It was either feast or famine, depending upon my mother's health." Economic stability was uncertain for many working-class families, so the patterns of either fathers working two or more jobs or having two wage earners in the family was essential to achieve a reasonable standard of living.

The majority of the women raised in working-class families grew up with two parents in the home. However, this was the case for a smaller number (64 percent) than for the women raised in middle-class families (80 percent). Among the working-class respondents there were a total of nine divorces, separations, and mothers who never married. Three working-class respondents reported that a parent died before they graduated from high school.

Working-class mothers who were single heads of households were employed in both primary and secondary labor market jobs. Without a spouse to contribute to the family income, female heads of households with dependents were serious about advancing in their jobs to maximize financial rewards and enhance the economic support they could provide for their children. Mrs. Greene, the sole supporter of four children, was typical of this small group. Carolyn and Marion Greene's mother initially did factory work but then secured a job as a sales clerk in a major department store in East City. Mrs. Greene worked hard at her job, and her performance led to a promotion to floor manager. Francine Chambers's mother was also a single parent with a high school education. Over the years, Mrs. Chambers advanced in the recreation field to support her six children.

Beth Warren's mother also was a single parent, but their household included Beth's grandmother. This arrangement gave Mrs. Warren greater flexibility in scheduling her employment and pursuing additional education; thus she could devote time to advancing in the clerical, bookkeeping, and administrative support positions she held over the course of her career.

Two participants were raised by mothers who received Aid for Families with Dependent Children (AFDC). Their mothers left welfare when the youngest child in the family began public school. For example, Mrs. Washington, who did community work while she was raising her five children on welfare, found a stable job in a War on Poverty program when her youngest child was school-age.

The experiences of these single parents differ from the common images of Black female heads of household perpetuating a cycle of poverty. Descriptions of such cases may change this persistent stereotype and create an appreciation for the diversity of single parents and greater awareness of factors that affect their level of functioning. In his research, Andrew Billingsley (1992) notes the strong evidence of diversity among single Black parents. However, the stereotype of single parents as poor is a strong one. Family composition plays a significant role in family functioning, since single parents have to be responsible for all the breadwinning and nurturing activities (Edin and Lein 1997; Ellwood 1988). All single parents, those on welfare and those employed, face obstacles that not everyone can surmount. Many of the women who raise children alone are poor (Albelda and Tilly 1997; Stack 1973). Family composition is a major contributor to their poverty, but the family's economic status before pregnancy, the woman's level of educational attainment, and the availability of social supports are also determinants of the economic well-being of women who head families.

This study found that single mothers, like other parents, made the advancement of their children a priority, even though they faced an uphill struggle to realize their dreams. As single heads of households, most mothers found it difficult to acquire the additional education needed to enhance their own occupational mobility. With child care obligations and limited funds, they could not return to school. Thus the mothers who advanced economically did so the only way they could, through demonstrating competence on the job and receiving promotions. Mrs. Greene's experience, noted earlier, is illustrative of that path. These mothers might have advanced further if they had been able to acquire the educational credentials, but few were able to do so. Many single parents therefore strongly encouraged their daughters and sons to get sufficient schooling while they were still young.[9]

In both single-parent and two-parent homes, working-class respondents recalled their parents as hardworking. Because working-class earnings were lower than those of middle-class professionals and managers, providing for their families required some sacrifice on the part of one or both parents. The case of the Johnson family reveals the nature of these sacrifices. Karen, the youngest of three children, described her parents' employment:

> My father was the janitor of the building [where we lived]. He did the dirty work, the ugly work that other people didn't want to do. He had many other jobs; he used to work day and night. He worked for an auction gallery and when they had sales he would work for three or four nights. He used to take care of a school, when I was very young. He took care of the grounds and then he would also clean some stores at night. He was working all the time. . . . My mother used to sew in the house and then, when I was in the fourth grade, she worked in a store part-time, and then that [position] developed into a full-time job. But even when she worked full-time she still did some sewing at night for a small specialty shop.

The Johnson family's life was dominated by work. This pattern was the norm among many working-class families in this study.

Working-class respondents remembered their parents working even when they were sick. Karen Johnson's recollections of her father's actions were typical. She said: "Even if he didn't feel well, he always went to work, because that was what you had to do." Parents, especially those in non-unionized secondary labor market jobs, feared the consequences of lost income and therefore did not take any actions that would jeopardize their employment.

Another survival pattern involved fathers working more than one job. Mr. Johnson was one of six working-class fathers (of a total of twenty-one who lived with their daughters) who periodically or for extended periods of time worked two or more jobs to secure sufficient funds to support their families. This pattern of holding multiple jobs is also commonly found in other research on Black families (Lee 1961; Scanzoni 1971).

Holding more than one job enabled Black fathers to be better providers for their families, but such a work schedule also kept these men away from their families. Adele Lewis noted that her father's work schedule left little time for interaction with the family. Mr. Lewis got much of the information about his five children from his wife. He regularly worked two jobs and was on call for the waiter's union. Adele recalled her father as interested in their lives, but he was always one boyfriend behind when asking his daughters about their social activities. When she was growing up, the family had one meal together each week. On Sundays Mr. Lewis did not attend church with his family but cooked brunch when everyone returned from church in the afternoon; after eating, he went off to work. Upon reflection, Adele commented: "My father gave up a lot for the real costs of raising a family."

There was no item on the questionnaire about extended families; however, some of the women who were interviewed mentioned living either with or near extended families. This pattern was noted by women raised by both single parents and two parents. For example, when Mrs. Washington became a single parent, she and her children lived with her own mother and sister. The economic marginality of single-parent families often dictates housing choices, yet some working-class families prefer the lifestyle of the extended family. Katherine Howell grew up in a household with her parents and grandparents. "When my parents married, they moved into my grandfather's house. It was renovated and very comfortable," she recalled. Katherine also received a lot of attention. Thinking about the benefits, she said: "It was an ego boost. Emotionally, it gave me a healthy outlook on people. I am open to people. There are problems with me being too trusting, but I will take that risk." However, she was accustomed to many people looking after her and finds it "hard to cope when no one deals with what is happening to me." The love and support of other family members was helpful in terms of family functioning, but the arrangement meant a great deal of work for Mrs. Howell because she cared for most of those in the extended family.

It was also common for working-class families to live clustered near other family members. Tracy Edwards, the youngest of six children, lived in a community that had numerous children, many of whom were her cousins. They all played together, since she lived across the street from a park. Dorothy Wall also grew up surrounded by family. She said, "The majority of my parents' sisters had one or two children, so my first cousins were close. We grew up like brothers and sisters. I had aunts, uncles, a godmother, and close family friends. When you are the only child, you get love from them all. They were always supportive and I still have their love. They wrote me a letter and sent money when I was in graduate school in North City."

The working-class families had a wider variation in the number of children per family than the middle-class families had. The distribution of family size was bimodal, with the most common number of children being either one or four. Finding seven working-class respondents who were only children was surprising, but possibly parents were limiting the size of their families to provide the one child with many opportunities. This possibility is suggested by a comment from Linda Trott: "Being an only child made all the difference. Now, I understand that my parents could not have afforded more children. The dollar could not stretch that thin." In addition, there were five women with one sibling and two from three-children families. On the other hand, there were several respondents from quite large families; seven women were one of four children, and six had five children in their families. Four respondents grew up in families of six or more children. In the era of the baby boom such family sizes were the norm.

The respondents were asked their parents' ages at the time of their birth. We can compare the women who were only children with the respondents who were the first born in their families. As a group, the parents of only children were older when they became parents than most of the other working-class parents in the study. The youngest mother of an only child became a parent when she was twenty-seven years old. Among the eleven working-class women who were first of other children, five parents were in their late twenties or early thirties, like the parents of only children, but six were in the late teens or early twenties when their first child was born.[10] Parents of baby boomers were a diverse group that included adults who came of age during the Depression and the beginning of World War II, who were likely to postpone starting a family, as well as those who became adults at the end of World War II. One can therefore expect a wide age range among these parents, which also translates into varying abilities to provide for a family.

As a group, these working-class parents worked hard to provide for their families. They were models of stable employment and dedication to achievement. As we will see below and in Chapter 3, the working-class families frequently had fewer economic resources than their middle-class counterparts, yet these families were strongly committed to similar goals, particularly the education of their children.

THE BLACK MIDDLE CLASS

Historically, the Black middle class has had three different sources of financial support: the White elite, the Black community itself, and the public sector. In the late nineteenth and early twentieth centuries, the majority of middle-class Blacks earned their living by providing services to White people. Initially they owned service delivery enterprises, such as barber shops and catering businesses, or small retail establishments (Drake and Cayton 1970; Spear 1967). The increased earning power of urban Black communities during World War I created a second source of support for a Black middle class. Black men and women began to serve other Black community members both as professionals and as providers of commercial services, including newspapers (Billingsley 1992; Drake and Cayton 1970; Gaines, 1996; Shaw 1996). But for most of the twentieth century, segregation and racial discrimination permitted only a very small group to achieve a standard of living above the norm for the majority of the Black population (Oliver and Shapiro 1995). During this era, even a college and professional education did not ensure one a professional living, and the development of a professional class within the Black community was not achieved without major difficulties (Drake and Cayton 1970; Gaines 1996; Higginbotham 1987; Hine 1989).

Protest movements that began in the 1930s and increased access to the franchise, especially in northern urban areas, gave Black residents more political clout. Political pressure on elected officials opened the ranks of public sector jobs to Black people, especially in civil service positions (Billingsley 1992; Franklin and Moss 1994; Gaines 1996; Higginbotham 1987; Landry 1987; Shaw 1996). Urban political power also created employment opportunities for educated Black people, particularly as professionals and managers in the public sector. In the segregated South, a small Black elite of schoolteachers, public health nurses, and other public service employees provided services within the system of Jim Crow (Morris 1984; Shaw 1996). Many educated Black people in northern areas had access to professional public sector positions after World War II. Unlike their counterparts below the Mason-Dixon line, northern Black professionals, administrators, and managers employed in the public sector had fairly equitable wage scales.

The Black middle-class population described in this study is quite different from the images found in E. Franklin Frazier's (1962) *Black Bourgeoisie*. Frazier saw the "black bourgeoisie" as a group that had abandoned its Black heritage, while also being rejected by the White world. This, he claims, results in "an intense feeling of inferiority" and behavior such as "constantly seeking various forms of recognition in placing great values upon status symbols to compensate for their inferiority complexes" (Frazier 1962, pp. 11 and 184). According to Frazier, this inferiority complex, the overriding characteristic of the Black bourgeoisie, drove its members to live in a "make-believe world" composed of institutions over which they did have control (e.g., Black businesses, Black presses, and Black churches). The middle-class families in this study, however, were more in line with revisionist perspectives by scholars such as Sidney Kronus (1971),

Charles Willie (1976), and Bart Landry (1987) that document a Black middle class active in challenging persistent racial barriers and providing for their families.

Empirical research investigating the Black middle class since the late 1960s reveals the complex lives of people who, as central players in integrated settings, could not escape into a make-believe world (Billingsley 1992; Ginzburg 1967; Hochschild 1993; Kronus 1971; Landry 1987; Willie 1976).[11] Many members of the contemporary Black middle class are professional public sector employees who monitor activities within both the Black community and the predominantly White world as they face urban politics and shifting national agendas. Even those who own their own businesses have to deal with political realities. Many middle-class Black people are drawn into the White world because of their own occupations and their roles as key leaders in the Black community. Therefore their work spheres and housing situations differ from Frazier's earlier depictions.

In the 1970s, however, Frazier's picture of the Black middle class was still a powerful image, and a few Black middle-class respondents felt the need to comment that their families either did or did not fit the popular stereotype. For example, Allison Cross volunteered on her questionnaire: "We were economically more affluent than our lifestyle reflected. My parents were very thrifty and straight laced and our family was very child centered. We didn't socialize with other 'bourgeois' families despite the common ground of income and educational level." In contrast, Deborah Jones, the daughter of a physician and a social worker, talked about growing up as a member of the Black bourgeoisie: "Growing up we were very secure. We were in the Black bourgeoisie in [a Midwest city]. It was a kind of arrogance and sense of security which can be useful as a child. Our world was really self-enclosed. We pitied Whites who lived in the suburbs, since they were culturally deprived. It was very pleasant in a classical middle-class way." Deborah's parents were also politically active, and many family conversations were focused on issues of discrimination and civil rights. Her father faced the racial politics of health care in his practice, and her mother faced racial issues in her own work settings. While her parents' social world was focused within the Black community, their occupations kept them planted in the mainstream institutions where racism was rampant.

Like working-class Black women, wives and mothers in middle-class families were also employed. In the 1950s and 1960s, educated Black women were often found in traditionally female professions such as teaching, nursing, social work, and library science, initially earning less than White women who did the same work (Higginbotham 1987; Wallace 1982). Few Black women were high-status professionals during this period.

Twenty-five of the fifty-six participants were raised in middle-class families. In each family, either the father or mother was employed as a professional or manager. Most middle-class parents had some college experience. Four fathers and seven mothers had bachelor's degrees, and sixteen fathers and nine mothers had advanced degrees that provided them with essential credentials for the positions they held. However, ten parents had less education: two fathers and six mothers ended their schooling with high school, and two fathers and four mothers had either a technical education or between one and three years of college.[12] In twelve families both parents had completed college and/or advanced degrees. For example, in the Anderson family, both parents had doctorates; in the Cross family, both parents had master's degrees; and Mr. Montgomery had completed dental school, while Mrs. Montgomery had a master's in library science. There were also twelve families where one parent had completed college and/or an advanced degree while the other parent had not completed college.

In eight out of the twelve cases where parents' educational level differed, fathers had more education than mothers. Yet there were cases where the a mother's educational attainment did exceed her spouse's. Irma Dennis's mother had a master's degree and taught in the public school system, while her father had a bachelor's degree and worked in the post office. Most important for this study, each middle-class household had at least one parent, if not both, who had experiences in higher education that gave them access to either professional or managerial work and would help them chart a course for their daughters to attend college.

The study includes parents who were high-status professionals (eleven fathers and three mothers) such as physicians, dentists, attorneys, accountants, ministers, engineers, research scientists, and college professors (see Table 1). Only three families owned their own businesses (a pharmacy, a bar/entertainment club and a farm, and a mortuary). As was typical of the Black petty bourgeoisie, these establishments specifically served the Black community. In the past, these high-status professional and independent entrepreneurial parents were classified as upper middle class in many Black communities, but in this study they are recognized as a segment of the Black middle class.

Twenty-three of the Black middle-class parents (nine fathers and fourteen mothers) in this study were in professional managerial positions in the broad areas of education, health, human services, and criminal justice. In the 1950s and 1960s, Black professionals and educated workers were beginning to make serious inroads into public sector employment, especially in urban areas. Several parents held professional, clerical, and administrative support positions in the public sector. For example, Mrs. Tucker was an accountant who worked for two different employers, both of whom were part of the federal bureaucracy. Two other mothers worked in clerical positions in government agencies. A few parents were professionals in the nonprofit sector, especially in human service work. Most of these parents taught in public schools; a few even became administrators. Others worked in public libraries, interviewed welfare clients, and had regular meetings with parolees. Their success represents both their educational attainment and many years of hard work, often within one agency or system. For example, Brenda Reed's father was a special education teacher who became a vice principal. This ascendancy to a supervisory position is indicative of Black Americans' progress into municipal employment, especially in social service agencies and school systems.

The middle-class respondents described how their parents had lived within the racial restrictions of an earlier era. They also detailed how, as barriers were challenged, their parents owed their success in part to their own perseverance and hard work. Although intelligent and talented, these parents had to discipline themselves to continue to work toward their goals and to overcome some of the hurdles obstructing their progress. A few parents relocated to different cities, where they hoped to find less employment discrimination. Many of the middle-class parents began their careers when the respondents were very young, leaving the women with images of their parents as very hard-working people.

Indeed, their parents had worked hard to take advantage of the new opportunities that emerged in the wake of social movements and federal government actions. Karen Wright's father graduated from college with a B.S. degree in chemistry and started work as a lab aide in one department of a public sector hospital in a mid-Atlantic city. Over the years he moved up through the civil service system, from junior chemist to assistant chemist and finally to senior chemist. Karen recalled: "He was always studying for Civil Service exams, and I really couldn't say at what point in my life he was at what slot."

Other participants remembered the many occupational changes in their parents' lives, documenting a legacy of hard work, either on the job or in educational institutions. When Mary Knight was born, her father was a parole officer. When she was three, he completed his master's degree in social work and became a social worker, an occupation he remained in for several years. By the time Mary was ten, Mr. Knight was directing a social service agency for children.

In general, middle-class parents provided excellent models of people with a serious attitude toward work and a commitment to educational and career goals. In their teachings, parents communicated that they viewed such efforts as part of a larger struggle that would advance the race. Even in racially tense times, these

parents continued their personal struggles to improve their occupational prospects. Such efforts were especially true of fathers, who were remembered by
these middle-class women as providing them with significant models of career
commitment.

In the 1950s and early 1960s, the small number of Black professionals often
worked with African American clients. These parents' occupational positions
reflect that trend. As professionals, either as employees or entrepreneurs, these
middle-class parents worked either within segregated institutions or in public
sector settings where most of their clients were Black and other people of color.
Katrina Charles's mother, as well as a few other parents in this study, ran social service agencies that provided services primarily to Black clients. Parents
who were college professors taught in traditionally Black colleges. Ministers, like
Sabrina and Florence Powell's father, served Black congregations. Like many
other urban ministers in the South, Mr. Powell had advanced schooling and was
able to earn a reasonable salary (Morris 1984). And the health professionals,
typified by Olivia Stevens's and Deborah Jones's fathers, had predominantly
Black practices and worked in hospital settings where the majority of their
patients were people of color. Those middle-class parents who were employed in
the public sector as teachers, social workers, librarians, nurses, and other professionals worked in integrated or predominantly Black workplaces. Currently,
however, Black professionals and managers are found in a wider range of occupational positions and settings, including the predominantly White private sector
(Billingsley 1992; Jaynes and Williams 1989; Sokoloff 1992).

The occupational paths of Rosalind Griffin's parents represent a pattern common among the middle-class families in this study. Dr. Griffin, Rosalind's father,
was a dentist with a large practice in the Black community in an eastern city.
When Rosalind, the only child, was quite young the family moved to a suburb of
that city. Dr. Griffin continued to practice dentistry in the central city. However,
Mrs. Griffin was gainfully employed during most of Rosalind's childhood. She
began working as a secretary in the local public school system. She liked the field
of education and took courses to qualify as a teacher. She worked as an elementary schoolteacher and continued her own education as Rosalind grew up. In the
early 1970s, when Rosalind was an adult, her mother became an assistant principal of a public elementary school. Other respondents, like Katrina Charles and
Beverly Rawlins, also spoke of parents who were actively building careers in their
respective fields as their children grew.

In many respects, this is a self-selected population, identified by their support
of their daughters in attending predominantly White colleges in the mid-1960s
rather than traditionally Black colleges.[13] As Black professionals, these parents

had power and clout in the Black community, yet they still knew the limited parameters of that power when they crossed over into the dominant society. While their credentials carried weight in the White community, they were even more significant within the Black community. Nevertheless, these parents were determined not to escape or remain sheltered within a totally Black world; instead, they chose to struggle for greater recognition in the larger society. Attendance in predominantly White colleges would prepare their children for the same course.

In the examination of a family's ability to ensure a future for its children, both family size and family intactness are important variables. They are measures of both the level of family resources and the demands on those means. In this study, the majority of women were raised by two parents, but this pattern was more frequently found in middle-class homes. Twenty of the middle-class women grew up with both parents.[14] Only two middle-class women reported divorces in their families during their childhoods. Three women reported the death of a parent.[15]

I also found middle-class women who grew up in extended family networks. There is increasing attention paid in research to how commitment to kin differentiates the Black from the White middle class (Higginbotham and Weber 1992). Some suggest that such obligations can complicate the Black middle class's efforts at achieving and sustaining a better economic position (Billingsley 1992). The fact that many in the middle class have family and kin who are working class further suggests that extended families might work best for those who are poor and be problematic for those who have achieved (McAdoo 1997). Although limited, the data here suggest that extended families were helpful to single parents and an asset for their daughters, even when the mothers were college educated. Beverly Rawlins, for example, lived with her grandparents after her mother divorced her stepfather; this arrangement enabled Mrs. Rawlins to complete her advanced degree. Living with her grandparents also had a critical stabilizing effect for this small family. Even when the Rawlinses established an independent household, the grandparents were very involved in child care for Beverly and her brother.

Irma Dennis, an only child, lived within an extended family even when her mother remarried. The household also included Irma's grandparents, an aunt, and an uncle. Like Beverly Rawlins, Irma benefited from the arrangement because she was socialized by her mother and the other adults. "I couldn't do anything wrong in my mother's eyes, so other family helped balance the picture," she said. This family was not economically marginal but preferred this lifestyle. Family traditions, obligations to kin, and the protection of children are all rationales for extended families, even among the middle class (Taylor 2000). Other respondents indicated that family ties were strong, even if kin were not living in the same city.

When compared to their working-class counterparts, the middle-class women came from smaller families. Five of the women were only children; seven had one sibling; eight had two siblings; and three were in families of four. Only two middle-class respondents were from families of six or more children.[16] Small family size meant that the financial resources in middle-class homes were often sufficient to pave a road to college and the reproduction of a middle-class position for the children.

Like many parents of baby boomers, these middle-class parents varied greatly in the ages at which they began parenting. Like those in the working class, the five couples who had one child were slightly older (late twenties and early thirties) when they became parents than those who had larger families. The parents of the oldest daughters, on the other hand, were in their early twenties when their first child was born. The other middle-class parents varied widely in the age at which they started their families.

Even though many middle-class parents faced racial restrictions on their own development, they acquired the resources to maximize the options for their daughters and sons. These experiences reflect wider trends in which Black middle-class parents in this era were able to improve their own positions and to pass these advantages on to their children (Billingsley 1992; Hochschild 1993, 1995). These parents differed tremendously from working-class parents, for whom economic security was more elusive. Social class was a key factor in determining how Black families worked to achieve economic stability and provide a foundation for their children's educational careers.

Social Class and Race

Racial oppression is a reality for members of the Black community across social class lines, but there are class differences in how they experience and resist racism. Members of the middle class enjoy social class privileges, both within their communities and often in the wider society. Their positions enable them to secure educational goals for their children. Working-class families with similar goals face both race and class obstacles. Social class measures enable us to explore the varying degrees of control Black people have over their own lives, including their resources to challenge informal and institutionalized racism.

By completing college, middle-class respondents reproduced their social class position, building on the advantages accrued by their parents and perhaps their grandparents. As the daughters of middle-class parents, they were expected to acquire the education necessary to be employed. Their families also assumed they would socialize with other people at a similar social class level. Because middle-class parents held expectations that the women would marry and raise families, the social scene in college was important. While the majority of these Black women informants were in the labor force at the time of the study, those who were not gainfully employed were married to middle-class men. College attendance was meant to guarantee women access to specific social circles and help them acquire mates of appropriate social standing.

In contrast, the women raised in working-class families have been upwardly mobile, that is, they moved from the working class into the middle class because their educational attainment enabled them to enter professional-managerial occupations. Their parents stressed getting an education, and as young women they were intent upon acquiring the schooling that would enable them to be economically independent. Their parents were often narrowly focused on their pursuing an education to secure employment; they did not see college as a social setting. As working-class women, most faced barriers at junctures critical to the mobility process, especially during the selection of a high school curriculum and when applying to colleges.

The differences in the obstacles faced by middle-class and working-class Black women and the negotiations necessary to overcome them are central to this discussion. When these Black women graduated from college in the years 1968 to 1970, their accomplishments reflected both their individual efforts and the collective work of their families. All their achievements are worthy of praise, but there are significant differences in the social class–based strategies that enabled them to achieve their goals. Such an appreciation has to be grounded in an understanding of social class in the Black community as well as its meaning in mainstream institutions, such as public and private schools.

CHAPTER 3 : WHAT MONEY CAN BUY

Social Class Differences in Housing
and Educational Options

*Initially we lived in the Chester Houses [a low-income housing project]. It was a tight
Black community, since many of the men had been in the service [during World War II]
and they were temporarily settled there while going to school. People all knew each other
and their kids. I had a lot of friends. We moved to our own home, a two-family dwelling in
Southbury [a Black community], when I was in the fourth grade. I would take two buses
and go back to the old neighborhood because I had friends there. Eventually I made friends
in the new neighborhood.*
—Denise Larkin, respondent from working-class background

*From when I was born until I was five we lived in a low-income housing project. When my
father graduated from college and started working as an architectural engineer we moved
from the projects to a one-family house in the suburbs. Housing was segregated, so our
block was all Black, but the neighborhood and schools were majority White.*
—Marlene Turner, respondent from middle-class background

In this nation, housing and education are intimately linked, especially in
the neighborhood public schools. Thus securing quality housing and education
are related struggles for Black families. This chapter examines how social class
positions gave respondents' families different economic resources to negotiate
the racism in the housing market and educational facilities. The Black women
in this study all faced institutionalized racism as they grew up, but they did
so equipped with different tools and resources. Their social class backgrounds
played a key role in the educational strategies families developed. As a consequence the young women had very different experiences with integration and
institutionalized racism.

Residential segregation remains a critical problem in the United States (Goldberg 1998; Massey and Denton 1993; Pattillo-McCoy 1999), but it is important to put the efforts of these middle- and working-class Black families in historical perspective. All of these respondents attended elementary and secondary schools in the 1950s and early 1960s. In the face of general neglect of inner city areas and at a time when movements for either improving or integrating predominantly Black schools were making little headway, Black parents sought individualized solutions. Schooling for their children was an immediate need, and they acted accordingly. In the mid-1960s, when de facto segregation was more widely acknowledged as problematic and there was broad support for more collective solutions, these respondents were completing high school or already in college. The individualized solutions revealed here do not necessarily indicate preferences, but rather the options parents saw at the time.

Residential Segregation

The Black population is a decidedly urban one. Since World War II most Black Americans can be found living in the central city rather than in less populated areas.[1] An overwhelming majority of the respondents in this study were raised in urban areas (fifty-one of the fifty-six women) in the 1950s and 1960s. Thus the struggles of Black people for decent urban housing and schooling is very much a part of their lives. Ever since the first significant Black migration around the time of World War I, African Americans have been disproportionately clustered in specific sections of urban areas (Goings and Mohl 1996; Marks 1989; Massey and Denton 1993; Osofsky 1971; Spear 1967; Taueber and Taueber 1972). Black people were quite deliberately segregated from the White population in both northern and southern cities. Unlike White immigrants who disperse as their economic situations improve, working-class and middle-class Blacks are more likely to be restricted to the established Black community. Thus their housing history is distinguished by economically heterogeneous communities in which Black people of all strata resided (Blackwell 1985; Forman 1971). This pattern did not significantly change until the 1960s, when residential segregation decreased more for non-White professionals than for people of color in other occupations (Massey and Denton 1993; Pattillo-McCoy 1999; Roof 1979; Simkus 1978).

People often talk about housing choice purely in terms of whom one prefers as neighbors, but segregation is a deliberate policy that achieves many goals, including saving a city money. Segregation enables a city to provide unequal services to its residents. Typically ghetto areas are ill served by health care and educational facilities, fire departments, sanitation departments, park services, and other city agencies. Thus ghetto residents face major health and safety hazards that people living elsewhere in the same city do not.[2]

As the ghetto swells and Black people move into adjacent communities, private and public sector practices of delivering inferior services to Black people often follow them. Initially, Black families are successful in finding better rental units and even homes. But very quickly, landlords in both the private and public sectors (in the form of urban housing authorities who operate public housing projects) cease maintenance of their property as the color of residents changes. As the number of Black middle- and working-class homeowners increases in an area, that district becomes a lower priority for city services (Blackwell and Hart 1982; Forman 1971; Massey and Denton 1993; Valentine 1978). Thus, although African Americans can move, they often find it difficult to escape inner city neighborhood problems.

Perhaps the most troublesome problem created by segregation in the 1950s and 1960s was the ghetto school, a northern product of de facto school segregation that accompanied residential segregation. In such schools, often with predominantly Black student bodies and predominantly White faculty, pupils were systematically taught less than students in other urban schools. Ghetto schools were believed to have more inexperienced teachers, greater rates of teacher turnover, and fewer supplies and older equipment when compared with other primary and secondary schools in the same urban school system. Often ghetto schools were among the oldest—often unsafe—physical facilities in the public school system.[3]

Before scholars were talking about institutionalized racism in the mid-1960s, Black parents were well aware of its importance in shaping their children's lives. While Black students educated in predominantly Black schools in the South had sympathetic Black teachers, their northern counterparts often faced hostile White faculty. Even if teachers were not abusive in their racism, many still believed, as did much of White America, in the inferiority of Black youth. Narratives and research demonstrated that many White teachers accepted the status quo, while only a few challenged the institutionalized racism in urban public school systems (Kohl 1967; Kozol 1967, 1991).

Actions by northern school administrators and planners kept Black and White pupils segregated. New schools were routinely built in the center of predominantly Black or White communities rather than in areas between these communities. Institutional support for natural integration, especially when many cities were building new schools to accommodate the children in the baby boom, would have made a significant contribution to decreasing educational segregation. But officials reinforced segregation and even increased its levels by a deliberate policy that directed students from predominantly Black elementary schools into specific junior high schools, which then became predominantly Black. If possible, this practice was repeated at the high school level.

Residential segregation results in serious disadvantages for a majority of Black people and leaves them vulnerable to other forms of exploitation.[4] Not only did Black citizens have schools that lagged behind those available in other areas of the city, but in the ghetto they were more likely to be the victims of personal and property crimes, including arson. Furthermore, Black residents paid high prices for housing (whether renting or buying). In their communities, they were poorly served by food and retail stores, as well as by public facilities such as hospitals, health facilities, and other city services (Blackwell 1985; Clark 1965).

Segregation also limited the nature and degree of interaction between Black and White residents of the same city. It isolated Black people and stifled their developing alliances with other groups in the city. Most urban institutions were also class stratified, so racial segregation added an additional layer of obstacles for Black residents. Together, class and race segregation served to perpetuate the status quo.

In the 1950s and 1960s, many parties participated in the maintenance of segregation in housing. First, real estate agents discriminated against Black people by refusing to sell or rent them housing units located in predominantly White areas.[5] If African Americans were not openly refused, agents might steer them to housing in established Black neighborhoods (Blackwell 1985; Massey and Denton 1993; Forman 1971). If agents sold homes in predominantly White districts to Black people, it was often because such areas were targeted for expansion of the Black community. The expansion might have been a natural process, as Black people moved into areas adjacent to an established Black community, or it may have been fostered by practices of real estate agents.

In the 1950s, 1960s, and into the 1970s, the practice of blockbusting was common (Forman 1971; Massey and Denton 1993). Frequently, when a neighborhood had a few Black homeowners, real estate brokers would act in ways to destroy this gradual integration. Brokers would exploit the racial fears of White homeowners in the neighborhood by convincing them that property values would deteriorate. Brokers might actually call or visit White homeowners, tell them about declining property values, and encourage them to sell immediately before they lost all their investment. Often brokers would buy homes from White residents at very low prices, which were supposedly better than future prices. These same agents would then resell the homes to Black people at considerably higher prices (Forman 1971; Massey and Denton 1993). Many Black prospective homeowners accepted these inflated prices because there was a chronic housing shortage in the Black community, giving people few opportunities to improve their housing. Such practices sometimes resulted in a neighborhood changing from predominantly White or integrated to predominantly Black within one or two years. In this process the White sellers and Black purchasers of homes both lost money, and real estate agents made considerable profits. Through their abilities to direct people to housing options and their role in blockbusting, real estate agents played a major role in deciding the racial composition of neighborhoods.

Second, major lending institutions were active in maintaining segregation by not granting mortgages to Black people who wished to live outside of the established Black community.[6] The limiting of choices meant that mortgage lending was only available to Black people under certain circumstances, that is, if they wanted to buy a home in an existing Black community, where there were often only a limited number of homes for sale (Massey and Denton 1993).

Banks also played a supportive role in blockbusting by making mortgages available to real estate agents that enabled them to purchase the homes of White residents at below market values. Then the same banks might offer mortgages to new Black buyers. The practice of blockbusting could never have become so widespread without the cooperation of large financial institutions (Massey and Denton 1993; Oliver and Shapiro 1995).

Third, the use of restrictive covenants meant that many homeowners discriminated against Blacks when selling their homes. Covenants barred signers from introducing new populations into a neighborhood. If people did otherwise, they risked being sued in court by their White neighbors (Blackwell 1985; Forman 1971; Taueber and Taueber 1972). In 1948 the Supreme Court ruled that restrictive covenants were not enforceable in courts, but the practice and variations on it continued until the passage of fair housing legislation in 1968 (Blackwell 1985; Massey and Denton 1993; Vose 1959). Although discriminatory practices by real estate agents and banks persist and continue to make fair housing a struggle, the use of restrictive covenants has declined.

Until challenged in the 1960s, these actions were chiefly responsible for much of the segregation in the twentieth century. But while the private sector did much to keep most Black people closeted in ghettos around the country, the public sector also played a role, especially through federal government policies. The dismal record of the federal government in the area of housing has been discussed by many scholars.[7] Rather than providing leadership for integration, federal policies expanded racial discrimination into public housing projects and later into the developing suburbs (Massey and Denton 1993; Oliver and Shapiro 1995; Wright 1981).

Urban Black Americans faced more barriers in the housing market than any other urban group. The levels of housing segregation in metropolitan areas actually increased from 1940 to 1960, the era during which these respondents grew up (Taueber and Taueber 1972). Although many of the supports of the institutionalized dual housing market have been declared illegal in recent decades, housing in the United States continues to be highly segregated (Farley 1984; Goldberg 1998; Massey and Denton 1993; Pattillo-McCoy 1999).

Although segregation produced ghettos across the nation, the social class heterogeneity of many inner city communities has frequently been obscured. In fact, many people think "ghetto" and "slum" are two words for the same type of neighborhood, but this is not the case. A ghetto is a fairly homogeneous area in terms of the race, ethnicity, or some other characteristic of the residents. This term is also used to connote similarities in socioeconomic status, such as the "gilded ghetto." While "ghetto" refers to the characteristics of residents, "slum" is used to describe deteriorating housing stock, poor conditions of the streets, or other negative structural characteristics of a neighborhood. Thus a slum is a rundown area, regardless of the race or ethnicity of residents (Forman 1971). In the 1950s and 1960s, when the women in this study were growing up, many Black communities across the nation were heterogeneous, with both middle- and working-class Black residents as neighbors.[8]

Because Black communities received poorer city services than other urban neighborhoods, many Black parents tried to live outside the confines of recognized ghettos. While social class affected their degree of success in this quest, this strategy was common among middle- and working-class families. To many Black parents of this generation, both middle- and working-class, gaining access to integrated schools was an essential part of an educational strategy for their children. In an integrated school, their Black children, seated next to White children, were more likely to receive a level of instruction that would enable them to get into college. Also, predominantly White and integrated facilities were often newer, better equipped, and more adequately staffed. Black parents placed a great deal of importance on elementary and secondary schools because they were the route to college, and higher education would make a huge difference in the quality and shape of their children's lives. As this chapter demonstrates, their social class resources made a difference in how they secured these goals.

Escaping the Ghetto: The Black Middle Class

With schooling a high priority for Black parents, many looked to the racial and class composition of the neighborhood for clues to the quality of schools. The notion that the less segregated the facility the better the school was common among northern African Americans during the 1950s and early 1960s.[9] With this perspective in mind, many Black parents moved outside of the ghetto as new housing options developed in the post–World War II era. Middle-class families were far more successful than working-class families in navigating racist obstacles in urban areas, primarily because money enabled them to overcome many of the restrictions of ill-financed ghetto public schools. In their search for schools, middle-class families could either move out of the ghetto or send their children to private schools.

Even prior to the federal Fair Housing Law of 1968, some Black middle-class families found ways to overcome the restrictions of a dual housing market and find housing outside the established Black community. Their strategies are reflected in this study. The majority of the middle-class women, eighteen of the twenty-five, reported that they grew up in either integrated or predominantly White communities, while a minority of the working-class women, twelve out of the thirty, lived in such communities. In the 1950s and 1960s, the increased suburbanization of the White population and the legal end of restrictive covenants translated into additional housing options within the central cities for many Black residents, especially those in the North. Moving into these sections of the city meant improvements in the quality of housing for Black dwellers, because the rental units abandoned by White residents were often larger and better maintained than rental housing in the established Black community. For Black residents seeking to buy homes, this change meant wider options.

But even with the greater availability of a better stock of housing, poor and working-class Black people faced more obstacles in their quest for better housing and schools. During this era it was almost exclusively middle-class families who possessed the necessary economic resources either to relocate from or to avoid predominantly Black sections of the city.[10] While some Black parents might have preferred to remain in Black communities where they had family, friends, and social institutions (primarily the church), they were troubled by the poor services ghetto residents routinely received. With their eyes on the schools, middle-class parents selected predominantly White or integrated neighborhoods where their children would receive an education that the parents believed would adequately prepare them for college and also remove them from the temptations of ghetto streets.

The eighteen middle-class women who reported that they lived in neighborhoods that were integrated or predominantly White tell very different stories. As the examples below illustrate, the majority of these women began their lives in Black communities but moved early and therefore spent most of their childhood and adolescence in their new neighborhoods. Many moved into areas where there were few Black families or were themselves part of the initial movement of Black residents into a new section of town. Of the eighteen middle-class women in integrated neighborhoods, eleven reported that their families remained in the central city, and seven noted that their families relocated to the suburbs.

In both the 1960 and the 1970 censuses, Black people were only 5 percent of suburban residents.[11] Both the priority of education and the career mobility of parents made the suburbs an option for some Black families, but they needed substantial economic resources to effect such a move. Some of the respondents' families moved to the suburbs early in their children's lives to provide them with the benefits of a suburban elementary and secondary education. Others moved when the respondents were in their teens, which gave the young people access to high schools with solid college preparatory programs. Social relations in the new neighborhood depended upon whether the family was one of only a few Black families in the community or lived in a predominantly Black enclave. Rosalind Griffin's family moved to the suburbs early in her elementary school career; the Griffins were the only Black family in their area and never developed close ties with their neighbors. The Saunders family also moved to a predominantly White suburb, distant from their old community, when their daughter Joyce was in high school. Both respondents reported that their families were isolated in these new settings.

In contrast, two respondents, Evelyn Tucker and Marlene Turner, indicated that their families moved into majority Black sections, comprising often one or two blocks, of predominantly White suburbs. These families did not face the social isolation of life within a predominantly White suburb that the Griffin and Saunders families encountered. All of the families had access to the advantages of suburban areas, however, particularly excellent schools. Marlene Turner recalled that her suburban high school had many science and math programs. Participating in such programs gave her an edge over Black youth educated in the central city and some White youth in the inner city as well. In the end, her education made Marlene a very attractive candidate for college, and she won several scholarships. In Marlene's metropolitan area, quality schooling came with a suburban address.[12]

Both in interviews and on their questionnaires, many of the respondents indicated that the primary motivation for their families to relocate to integrated or predominantly White areas was the search for better schools. In this respect, these respondents were similar to participants in an earlier study by Oscar Handlin (1965). Handlin surveyed eighty-two Black families who moved out of a privately owned, middle-income apartment complex in Harlem in the years 1952 to 1956. The majority of Handlin's sample was middle class. While these Black families left the central city, they remained in the New York metropolitan area, choosing to reside in suburban communities. Concern about the education of their children motivated the parents to relocate, since the city did not make providing educational opportunities for Black children a priority. Like Handlin's subjects, the middle-class Black families in this study were tired of apartment living and wanted to be homeowners, but they also focused on the educational options available to their children in their new communities.

Black middle-class parents who remained in the central city but who had moved into integrated sections shared the concerns of suburban dwellers. Northern parents employed this strategy to secure improved schools and city services. Although southern parents had limited ways to challenge their region's segregated school systems, relocating to integrated neighborhoods gave them access to better municipal services. In both regions, African American families moved into middle-class communities where they shared class positions with the White residents. Relocation during their children's early school years could indicate that parents were reacting to the quality of schools in their predominantly Black communities. They sought the available alternatives by taking advantage of the decreasing racial barriers in the society. Escaping the ghetto meant access to better schools along with improvements in housing stock, sanitation, police and fire department coverage, and other services. Yet there were personal costs to this solution.

The price was particularly high for those token Black families in predominantly White suburbs. In their interviews, Rosalind Griffin and Joyce Saunders vividly described the isolation of their families in suburban settings in the 1960s. They recalled more pleasant times when they lived in predominantly Black communities, where family members had more friends and involved themselves in community activities. As an only child, Rosalind felt particularly lonely when the family moved out of the city. She recalled: "It was a shock to move from the city to Springdale. I went from a mostly Black environment into a predominantly White environment. I had lots of friends in my old neighborhood. In Springdale people were okay, somewhat friendly, but I felt like an outsider." Life was more complicated as Rosalind grew. She recalled the pain of isolation. "In the fourth grade, we had a party at one of the children's houses. All the boys were asked to pick girls, and no one picked me. It was very hard, and I was confused. My parents were not very helpful. I think I felt ashamed of being Black." Money could purchase a home in the suburbs and provide Rosalind with access to a school system with a national reputation, yet her parents' financial resources could not remove Rosalind from a national racist climate.[13] Regardless of class, Black people were viewed as inferior, and the majority of White residents kept them at a distance.

ALTERNATIVES TO PUBLIC SCHOOL SYSTEMS

Some middle-class families preferred to remain in the Black community rather than face the social isolation that often accompanied residence in a pre-dominantly White neighborhood. During the 1950s the ghetto was actually a protective setting for many middle-class Black families. Their class advantages contributed to developing a pleasant life in the Black community. They domi-nated local institutions and had control over their communities, especially if they were homeowners. The Dennis family provides an example of such a case. Irma Dennis was quite content in her predominantly Black community. She said: "I had no idea how White people grew up in Center City [a Midwest city]. I lived in an extended family and was more influenced by that than the city as a whole. I never saw people outside my neighborhood."

Middle-class parents who made the choice of remaining in a Black commu-nity were as concerned with the matter of schooling as their counterparts who moved to integrated or predominantly White communities. Financial resources enabled them to achieve independence from their local public schools. Instead of relocating, these families chose to pay private or parochial school tuition. Six of the middle-class respondents graduated from private or parochial high schools, while only one working-class respondent was a parochial school gradu-ate. Few working-class families could afford the burden of secondary school tuition payments.

Black middle-class families sent their children to private or parochial schools at different stages in their lives. Professional parents, like Dr. Jones, could afford private school tuition for their children. Therefore Deborah Jones lived in a pre-dominantly Black community until her teens but always commuted outside her neighborhood to attend private schools. Irma Dennis attended public schools because her mother was a teacher and was committed to this goal. But when the environment in her public high school became troublesome during school inte-gration, Irma's parents placed her in a private school. Wendy Anderson, from the

South, went to public schools at the elementary level and then went to a northern private boarding school for her secondary education. Overall, middle-class families recognized their options and used their leverage and resources to send their children to alternative school systems.

Because some of these middle-class families did not have to depend on a local public school system, they were able to consider other factors when choosing a neighborhood. When affluent families moved, their selection of a location could be made independently of schools. For example, Deborah Jones's family, which always used private schools, lived in a predominantly Black community until Deborah was fourteen years old. Reflecting on the change in residence, Deborah said, "We moved from an all Black neighborhood to an integrated one. There were no real consequences for me. I was closer to certain friends and to school. My parents were concerned because the old neighborhood was changing into a more working-class district." Apparently, her parents were concerned over the decline in services that could be a consequence of a changing neighborhood. They were not personally troubled by the quality of education in their area, having already addressed that issue. When the Jones family did decide to move, they had the resources to live in an integrated middle-class community.

The fact that six middle-class women graduated from private or parochial high schools is a significant finding, but these figures actually mask the schooling options of Black middle-class families and their relative independence of public school systems. Three of the women raised middle class indicated during their interviews that they had spent some elementary or secondary years in private or parochial schools. The personal interviews and comments on the questionnaires reveal a complex pattern of housing and schooling options employed by individual middle-class families to secure the best schooling available.

When middle-class Black women were in public institutions, these particular schools were often the best educational option their parents could locate. The educational history of Beverly Rawlins illustrates this point. Beverly frequently attended private schools while growing up:

> When I started school I went to a progressive, private school on the east side. I really enjoyed it. I went there from nursery school to third grade. I rode the bus, and it was an hour ride from home. When my parents divorced, I went to a neighborhood public school. It was one of the worst schools in the city. The faculty was predominantly White and the student body was predominantly Black. We were not allowed to talk and it was very rigid. My mother worked on getting us to move. Finally, we moved into one of the university-owned apartments. We were the first Black family in the building. The new neighbor-

hood school was one of the best public schools in the city. Many of the university faculty sent their children there, and it was a very good school. So I stayed in public school.

When Beverly's family moved to another region, she and her brother attended both private and public schools. In the end, Beverly graduated from a well-integrated public high school that had a solid college preparatory curriculum. But her mother and grandparents were prepared to spend the funds for a private school if the public schools were not adequate.

STILL A SACRIFICE

The fact that some of the middle-class families in this study successfully used private and parochial schools does not mitigate the effects of the racial discrimination of the day. Discrimination in public school systems pushed middle-class parents to seek schooling for their children outside of the Black community. The ability of some parents to afford private school tuition does not change the fact that people subjected to racial discrimination and segregation had to allocate an extraordinary proportion of their incomes for adequate education for their children, in addition to the tax dollars that they were contributing to urban public schools. Black parents employed as high-status professionals might have been able to afford this strategy, but most middle-class families were not so well situated. Many in the Black middle-class at this time were schoolteachers, social workers, nurses, librarians, and public officials (Althauser, Spivack, and Amsel 1975; Landry 1987; Sokoloff 1992). Because most of these families could not afford private school tuition, they frequently attempted to live in integrated or predominantly White neighborhoods where they did not have to spend additional funds for private schools. Two of the six middle-class families that sent daughters to private or parochial high schools were not affluent. These cases enable us to see how securing schooling outside the public school systems could impose a major financial burden on Black middle-class families. In one case, the family was able to use an employment connection, while the other family made financial sacrifices.

The education of their youngest daughter was a major concern for the Charles family. They worried about her educational options in their southern community. When a new employment opportunity developed, Mr. Charles relocated with his eye on the educational benefits. By working for a religious-based social advocacy group, he made his children eligible for partial scholarships to the religious school affiliated with this group. He could not have secured such schooling on his income alone.

Lacking employment benefits meant the North family had to pay full tuition for their daughter to attend a parochial school. Sherri North, the only child of two civil servants, lived in a middle-class housing development in the Black community. Their northeastern city did not make any special programs available to the middle-class residents of the ghetto. Families were expected either to attend the local public schools or to fall back upon their own resources. With education as a family priority, Mr. and Mrs. North were willing to make the economic sacrifices to pay school fees for their only child. Sherri attended a parochial school in her neighborhood for grades one through six and then went out of the community to a parochial high school. Sherri recalled her mother's frequent refrain, "When you're in college," and viewed it as a promise of a reward for studying hard in high school. Sherri described her parents as involved in advancing themselves and working to overcome the limited services of the surrounding community. Later, as a widow employed as a supervisor for a city human services agency, Mrs. North continued to pay tuition for Sherri.

Economic resources and such opportunities gave many middle-class families the freedom to live wherever they desired. Some chose to remain in predominantly Black communities, where they had support networks of friends and family; others ventured into predominantly White and integrated neighborhoods, opting most often for neighborhood schools. On the whole, these families were successful in getting their children into primary and secondary school classrooms where they received educations that would enable them to continue on to college, but the families paid in terms of economic resources and social relations.

Working-Class Options

Working-class respondents were more likely than the middle-class women to have resided in predominantly Black neighborhoods. In their search for better schooling and higher quality housing, many Black working-class families employed strategies similar to their middle-class counterparts. In this study, there were twelve working-class respondents whose families gained access to integrated areas or predominantly White neighborhoods. Many of these families lived in neighborhoods where integrated areas were becoming predominantly Black. Although some working-class families did leave the ghetto, more working-class than middle-class families remained in the Black community.

The questionnaires from the working-class respondents revealed that their families frequently moved into different neighborhoods during their childhoods. Some of the families moved around the ghetto, and others relocated to the fringes of other communities. Working-class housing options were almost totally limited to urban areas. In the 1950s suburban developments were made available to many White working-class people. Interest rates for FHA mortgages were low, and developers were asking for small down payments. But these developers were not selling to Black people. The discriminatory policies of Levittown and other suburban developments were notorious (Oliver and Shapiro 1995). Even Black families who had access to federal mortgage programs were barred from low-cost suburban housing (Massey and Denton 1993). Although the option of suburban living was routinely closed to them, many Black working-class families did reap benefits from the expansion of suburban housing. As middle- and working-class White people had greater access to modern and higher quality housing outside the central city, their urban apartments and houses "trickled down" to Black residents.

INTEGRATED HOUSING FOR BLACK WORKING-CLASS RESIDENTS

A few respondents indicated that their families considered themselves lucky because it took years for their integrated neighborhoods to become predominantly Black.[14] This meant they might succeed in a race with time before they faced declining services. Jennifer Taylor's story is typical of many working-class families who moved to find better housing and integrated schools. Jennifer recalled her housing history: "We moved once when I was nine, across town to a White neighborhood. We lived in what is now fashionably called a town house. It was a better house and the area had better schools. The neighborhood started off as predominantly White, then became integrated and finally predominantly Black within eight to ten years. It was a middle-class area and then became working class as the racial composition changed."

The timing of the neighborhood change enabled Jennifer to attend integrated schools. In fact, Jennifer's graduating class was the last well-integrated one in her high school. The shift in the racial composition was accomplished by official redistricting of the high school. School district lines were changed so that all the junior high schools that fed into Jennifer's high school were predominantly Black. Providing resources to this high school became less of a city priority. To Jennifer's parents, neither of whom had graduated from high school, living in an area with identifiable good schools was one of the few ways they could ensure an education to equip Jennifer to advance. As the racial composition of their neighborhood changed, the Taylors watched the neighborhood schools decline both in quality of instruction and in the state of the physical plant.

Unlike middle-class Black residents, these working-class families had less control over their own communities and lacked the financial resources to abandon the local public school system. In the case of the Taylor family, the strategy of moving out of the ghetto worked, but for Black families who later moved to this neighborhood, it was less likely that they could secure as high a quality of education for their children while pursuing this same strategy.

Working-class Black people did not have much freedom in selecting the predominantly White or integrated areas in which they would reside. They were frequently steered into areas targeted for expansion of the Black community by real estate agents and government policies. The Lewis family was one of the first Black families on their block. Then panic selling by White residents took place as this area was blockbusted. Adele Lewis recalled hearing her White neighbors asking her mother, "Do you know a nice colored family like yourselves who would want to buy our house?" Very quickly this neighborhood became predominantly Black.

Black residents who were overcrowded in the ghetto with few options of becoming homeowners were quick to move into new areas where they could buy, even though this meant paying high prices. Mr. Lewis held two jobs to pay the mortgage and other bills. Mrs. Lewis also worked outside the home to support the family financially. Paying high housing costs enabled the Lewis family to employ a strategy similar to middle-class Blacks for ensuring that their children had access to good schools. The Lewis family moved into a neighborhood in time for Adele to receive most of her schooling in integrated schools. But her neighborhood changed so quickly that by the time Adele's younger brother and sisters attended these same schools, they were predominantly Black. Thus the younger Lewis children faced some of the problems associated with ghetto schools.

Securing housing, integrated or predominantly Black, was not easy. The Trott family was intent upon moving but did not have the opportunities available to White working-class families. Linda described her family's search for better housing: "We lived in a row house in the ghetto. We needed a bigger house. My parents wanted to move to a new suburban development, but no Blacks were allowed there at the time. When I was seven we finally did move into West Hills, an integrated area in the city which was being developed. We got a house with a hill behind it, so there was enough play space. This neighborhood was integrated, but my section was mostly Black. In about five years the whole neighborhood was majority Black, except for one White family that did stay."

A few working-class families found unique solutions to their housing and education dilemmas. For example, the Johnson family was able to live in a predominantly White suburban community because they resided in the apartment building where Mr. Johnson was the janitor. This was not an option attractive to everyone, but it did enable these working-class parents with few economic resources to provide their children with access to one of the finest school systems in their area. On their income alone, they would not have been able to leave the ghetto. Even these success stories are touched with disappointments, however. Black members of the working class could rarely afford their first choice of schools or neighborhoods. In many cases, working-class families were able to reap only temporary benefits from living in areas in transition from predominantly White to predominantly Black.

STAYING IN THE GHETTO

In many cities, segregation by race and class was so intense that it was difficult for Black working-class people to move into integrated sections of the city. Therefore a more common pattern was for Black people to move within the established Black community or to the immediate fringes of the ghetto, which were generally areas in quick transition (Massey and Denton 1993; Taueber and Taueber 1972). Some Black community residents were homeowners, like the Larkin and Wall families, but many were renters. The housing history of Nancy Brooks's family illustrates the vulnerability of many people looking to rent decent housing. She recalled, "We first moved when I was ten, then at age eleven, then at twelve, again when I was fourteen and at age eighteen. We were always in Eastville [a Black community]. I was not aware of race until high school. In high school we moved to the edges of Eastville, and I was far away from my friends, but then we moved back to the center two or three years later. Moves were always difficult. I hate to move and that was one reason why I bought a house [as an adult]." Her family's search for improved housing was frustrating; they were like many Black working-class families who moved frequently only to achieve the same type of housing in another section of the Black community. While some working-class families like the Taylors and Trotts were able to achieve significant gains in the quality of housing and education available to their daughters by becoming homeowners, many others who were dependent upon the rental market could not easily achieve such gains by relocating.

Working-class homeowners also faced obstacles. Often it was difficult to secure home improvement loans, initially because banks favored suburban areas for lending. Eventually banks began to redline entire sections of the central city and to deny home improvement loans to residents in these communities (Massey and Denton 1993; Oliver and Shapiro 1995). Thus Black homeowners were left with few resources with which to maintain their community and fight the economic policies and political forces that could turn the community into a slum. Over time many integrated communities became predominantly Black, and neighborhoods that had been heterogeneous in terms of social class slowly became majority working-class and poor residents (Pattillo-McCoy 1999; Wilson 1996). Those who could escape, generally the Black middle class, did so. But Black working-class homeowners had fewer options. Many of them remained, because all their economic assets were tied to their home. The home that once represented security turned, in some ways, into a liability. The Wall family was such a case, as they sacrificed much to remain homeowners. Dorothy Wall described her family's plight: "We owned a home, but we were working class and had to pay high taxes. Our level of income was not really adequate, but we aspired to be middle class. . . . Until I was a teenager our neighborhood was integrated; then it began to change. Now it is Black and Spanish-speaking." If Black working-class homeowners, who have most of their assets tied up in their homes, cannot sell and relocate, their circumstances are far from the American Dream (Franklin 1991; Oliver and Shapiro 1995).

WHERE UNCLE SAM PUTS YOU: LIFE IN PUBLIC HOUSING

While working-class people had few options in the private housing market, residents of public housing had the least control over the composition and quality of their environment, especially as public housing became the lodging for the long-term poor. In the late 1940s, public housing was targeted to the submerged middle class. It was designed to help intact families where the breadwinners were employed (Wright 1981). The family of one middle-class respondent, Marlene Turner, fit into this category. The Turners used public housing while Mr. Turner was working full-time and completing his education. Residing in public housing enabled the family to save money and later to purchase a home in the private housing market when Marlene was five years old.

During the 1950s and 1960s, when these respondents were growing up, federal government and local housing authorities made policy decisions that changed the role of public housing. It ceased serving those who were striving to be middle class, especially White residents who found new opportunities as low interest rates made single-family homes in both urban communities and the suburbs affordable. As times changed, housing authorities increasingly operated public housing for poor people who had few options and dim futures (Kotlowitz 1991; McDonald 1999). This population was overwhelmingly composed of families headed by women; today, public housing projects in many urban areas are primarily occupied by women and children.[15] The four respondents who grew up in public housing were all in female-headed families.[16]

In the late 1950s and the 1960s, local public housing authorities offered clients little choice about where they would reside. On a waiting list for years, families were assigned to locations where units were open. If they declined, they lost their place on the list. Frequently they were offered units located outside of their communities and distant from their established support networks. It was a difficult decision for families to sacrifice personal and social ties to have better housing.

A variety of policies have maintained rigid segregation in public housing and wide gaps in the level of maintenance in White and Black facilities. The four working-class respondents who grew up in housing projects were not pleased with the quality of life there. These women, all residents of East City, were also caught in the middle of shifting patterns of racial composition in housing projects. For example, Robin Washington's family desegregated a facility and then, over the decade, watched the project change from predominantly White to Black. Another respondent, Crystal Robinson, also watched her low-income project, Perkins Houses, change from predominantly White to integrated. At age fifteen, her family was shifted to another predominantly White housing project, where the process of desegregation started again.

In the 1950s and 1960s, housing projects were increasingly used to house families relocated by city efforts to clear slums. Urban renewal, so labeled in the 1954 Housing Act, was a federal initiative that gave cities the ability to clear blighted areas and use public and private funds for redevelopment. The program was used by coalitions of politicians, businesses, and academic institutions to restructure inner city communities (Hirsch 1983; Sugrue 1996). After slum clearance, prime land near downtown areas often became the site of commercial establishments, large office complexes, cultural centers, and expensive residential units (Gans 1962). The former residents had to live elsewhere because there were few funds to replace low- and moderate-income housing. As urban renewal cleared sites of low-income housing in the private market, people were often directed to public housing. This housing was permitted to deteriorate, and it became even harder for working-class people to find decent rental housing in the private market.

This was the prospect facing Gloria McDonald's family when the tenement building where they had an apartment burned. After the fire, the family was relocated to an integrated public housing facility. This development very quickly became predominantly Black. In their new neighborhood, the McDonald family faced poor services and facilities. The local public school was inadequate and actually threatened to cripple Gloria by failing to prepare her for high school. The restructuring of metropolitan areas thus meant additional burdens for working-class Black families, particularly those in public housing.

THIS IS WHERE WE GO TO SCHOOL

The working-class families' lack of control over housing had dramatic implications for the schooling options available to their children. Even if they moved, they were more dependent upon public school systems than middle-class families. Too frequently, poorly supported schools were the norm for Black communities. Parents valued education and worked as best they could with the public school system. This partnership had different implications in the North and South. While southern African Americans had a measure of control over the education of Black children, because they were the teachers and often the principals of such institutions, this level of control was harder to achieve in many northern communities. Northern residential segregation gave birth to ghetto schools that survived in an environment of urban neglect. Nationwide, Black adults experienced racial disadvantages in employment, housing, and various city services, but the ghetto school had an especially deadening impact on Black children (Kohl 1967; Kozol 1967; Rist 1974).

Understandably, many northern Black parents failed to perceive the school system as a place where their children could reap any benefits. In schools where discipline was stressed over learning and where minimal attention was given to academic goals, Black children could become even more disadvantaged than they might have been when they entered. These school situations did not facilitate participation in the mainstream of American life. Rather, in the words of Kenneth Clark (1965), ghetto schools were "very effective instruments in widening socio-economic and racial cleavages in our society and in imposing class and caste rigidities" (p. 165).

Committed to having their children enter the mainstream of American society, Black working-class parents worked within their means to achieve this goal. As noted above, it was sometimes possible to relocate to new communities where schools would be integrated. Families varied in their degree of success with this strategy. They also sought other options. Three working-class families were able to use local parochial schools to ensure a quality education for their children. Two working-class respondents, Beth Warren and Katherine Howell, attended parochial schools at the elementary or grammar school level and then proceeded to public high schools. In Beth's case, a parochial school was selected for her education because it was an improvement over the local public school. Both Beth and Katherine later attended high schools that required entrance examinations.

Brenda Carter attended parochial schools for all her precollege education and was the only working-class respondent who did not graduate from a public high school. Brenda indicated that paying school fees was difficult for her parents, but they were determined to see her, their only child, advance. The Carters lived in an apartment complex in a predominantly Black community in an eastern city. Every day Brenda left her community to attend high school. She wrote about her experiences: "There were no Catholic high schools in my community and the public schools were not satisfactory; they were poor academically. My parents were working so I went to St. Bernard's Academy. It was predominantly White, with the majority of the students being college bound."

The Carters found a way to overcome the racial and class bias in the structure of urban areas. Their daughter was relegated to a public high school that school administrators shaped to be appropriate for Black youth, but the Carters doubted the ability of this facility to prepare their child adequately and took action to avoid that school. However, this was a rare case in this cohort of Black women college graduates. The majority of working-class families could not contemplate paying school tuition because they were already facing hardships in providing housing and meeting other basic needs. They were dependent upon the public educational facilities. While middle-class families could escape such ghetto problems, working-class families had to cope with them, including the schools available in the central city. These facilities could be problematic in both the level of educational preparation and the personal treatment shown to Black students.

Social Class and Resources

Black middle-class families were in a position to pass on class advantages to their children. Money was a major factor, but the possession of a recognized middle-class occupation also helped. If White homeowners or landlords were reluctant to sell or rent to Black people, the middle-class professional Black person was more acceptable to them than a working-class Black person (Simkus 1978). Thus middle-class Black families were more successful in escaping the ghetto. These families also had the economic resources to avoid public schools when they were viewed as inadequate by paying tuition for private and parochial schools.

When working-class families attempted the same strategy of living in areas with integrated schools, they were less successful in their pursuits. The ghetto problems they sought to escape frequently followed them into the communities where they relocated. Because few could afford the additional expense of secondary school tuition, they were more dependent upon the public school system and had to live within the policies of that system.

While the African American women in this study were all graduates of predominantly White colleges in East City, their routes to those colleges were very different. There were regional differences, but most important, the paths to particular outcomes varied by their class of origin. We have seen that to overcome the racist restrictions in public schools during this era, Black children often had to integrate predominantly White settings. Being in schools and neighborhoods with White students frequently meant greater opportunities to secure the learning essential for high achievement and to benefit from other amenities, such as excellent libraries, college counselors, and preparation for standardized tests. Middle-class Black families had more resources to combat the layers of obstacles fostered by segregated housing and facilities. They were more familiar with integrated and predominantly White settings, where their children were less likely to be disadvantaged in learning centers. For the respondents, early exposure to White peers helped them learn to navigate within predominantly White settings. This would be an asset when they moved on to predominantly White colleges.

What middle-class families could often buy, working-class families had to develop alternative means of achieving. Working-class respondents spent more time in segregated communities and schools, where they frequently received lower quality services than those in nonsegregated settings. As a consequence, they had to spend additional time compensating for these educational losses. This effort also required more energy on the part of parents to monitor public schools to ensure that their children were getting an adequate education. Thus, while racism was a constant and critical issue in the lives of all the respondents, class advantages could play a role in tempering the impact of institutionalized racism (Feagin and Sikes 1994). Money can buy a great deal when families are struggling in a racist and classist society.

CHAPTER 4 : THE TIES THAT BIND
Socialized for Survival

I learned to be satisfied with myself. This meant setting my own standards and always aspiring to them. You know, "Do the best that you can do." I'm not sure how I was taught, either by example or explicitly. Neither of my parents ever quit, but continued to aspire and encouraged me to do so.
—Linda Trott, respondent from working-class background

I was told to work hard at what you are doing and do a good job. My parents indicated that we had a certain set of obligations. You owe people who have been good to you. We were taught to do something, in terms of the work. If you are in a certain position, you have to give something back to the community.
—Deborah Jones, respondent from middle-class background

Today in the United States, as in the past, most African Americans have daily encounters with racism (Cose 1993; Feagin and Sikes 1994; Feagin, Vera, and Imani 1996; Hochschild 1993, 1995; Nelson 1993; St. Jean and Feagin 1998). This chapter explores how the Black families in this study raised their daughters to survive in a world that was changing in terms of race relations, but where they would encounter racial prejudice and discrimination. Across social class lines, women in this study overwhelmingly conceded that U.S. society is racist. This acknowledgment does not mean they accepted the racism, but that it forced them to prepare for the reality. Patricia Hill Collins (1990), in *Black Feminist Thought*, documents a tradition of resistance to negative controlling images and notes that there are several sites "where Black women construct independent self-definitions [that] reflect the dialectical nature of oppression and activism" (p. 95). The Black family is a major site where resistance is nurtured.[1] Teaching their children to live with racism places additional parenting burdens on Black families. Because parents operate with the knowledge of racism and its role in their lives, they must socialize their children and prepare them to be productive adults with that same awareness but without breaking their spirits (Tatum 1997b). If Black families had unlimited economic resources, perhaps they could shelter their children so that encounters with racist institutions might be delayed until their young people were teenagers. But because few African American families have such resources, they have to address the task of preparing their children to face the reality of racism. This task involves nurturing positive self-esteem, stressing appropriate values, and helping young people develop skills to negotiate complex environments.

Families traditionally promoted the socialization of values that would foster both success in the mainstream society and connectedness to the Black community, including a high achievement orientation, self-direction, and self-definition (Billingsley 1992; Collins 1990). Girls' socialization was influenced by the dominant stereotypes of Black women as lascivious and sexually easy. Such stereotypes created barriers for Black women to be taken seriously as students. Black families attempted to protect their daughters but in their teachings also insisted that the young women be responsible for their own behavior (St. Jean and Feagin 1998). These teachings were critical in helping this cohort of young Black women make their way in a society where class privileges and disadvantages made for varied interactions with peers, community members, teachers, and other gatekeepers.

These women's experiences illustrate how racism formed a backdrop against which Black parents made many life decisions (Collins 1990; Essed 1990; Feagin and Sikes 1994; St. Jean and Feagin 1998). The process of planning for their daughters' futures was complex because it had to anticipate institutionalized racism and dominant racist ideologies. The legacy of poorly supported segregated schools, race-based wage discrimination, and a racially segregated housing market limited the choices available to Black Americans in this era. Because of mainstream beliefs in Black inferiority, even money did not ensure safety from all racist encounters. Gaining access to either predominantly White or integrated neighborhoods, schools, or both did not mean that Black children would be sheltered from either deliberate or unaware racist treatment. Although these women varied in terms of their experiences with the racial composition of neighborhoods and of primary and secondary schools, they were all ready for potential encounters with racist individuals and institutional barriers.

Primary to these respondents' socialization were values and orientations that their parents hoped would be conducive to success in educational settings as well as in the wider world. The women recalled being instructed to be honest, to work hard, to remember their families, and to seek security. Tracy Edwards, who was raised in the working class, said she was taught by her family to "be forthright and honest" and "to be responsible for myself." She saw her parents as honest people, who devoted much time and energy to the family. They were significant role models for their children. Comments such as Tracy's were echoed in the interviews by the other nineteen women.[2]

Instructing children to survive in a racist society is a complex and cumbersome task with a long tradition in the Black community (Billingsley 1992; Collins 1990; Feagin and Sikes 1994; Gates 1994; St. Jean and Feagin 1998; Scanzoni 1971; Shaw 1996). As Black children learn at an early age that their group is devalued in the wider society, Black parents have to prepare their children both to recognize and to handle racist situations. Racism has the potential to limit life chances and choices of Black women and men; thus the expectations nurtured at home might reflect distant possibilities for individuals. Parents must also be ready to provide support and encouragement to contradict the negative feedback their children will most likely receive within schools and other mainstream institutions. Ideally, such encouragement and skills will enable Black children to become adults who have the capacity to love and work with others despite the crippling effects of racism. At times, these women had to stand up for their rights, while at other times they might have had to silently reject negative comments and attitudes. The women readily recalled the values and preparation that aided them in surviving in a racist society because, as adults, many continued to live by these tenets.

While racism makes the job of parenting extremely complex in Black families, the wider society does not necessarily acknowledge that racism invades and alters the shape of family tasks in this manner.[3] Without a keen awareness of the complex socialization that is taking place, scholars can easily misread the actions of Black parents. For example, in his study of middle-class Black families, the sociologist Sidney Kronus (1971) identified their actions around securing schooling for their children as an obsession with education. However, such activities might be the level of vigilance necessary to help Black children secure a solid education in public schools. Because Black parents were cognizant of their devalued status and its implications, even if they rejected mainstream definitions, they would be remiss if they had not worked to remedy settings where assumptions of inferiority could impact their children. Many parents of color long for the days when such actions will not be necessary, but we are not now a color-blind society. Thus it is important both to monitor educational settings and to teach children coping styles that help them to negotiate difficult situations.

Education Is the Way

As recalled by their daughters, the parents' primary teachings were in support of education. They explicitly stated such goals, demonstrated them in terms of their own behavior, and rewarded educational achievement. Research has long established education as a strongly held value in the Black community (Collins 1990; Feagin and Sikes 1994; Fichter 1967; Ginzberg 1967; Scanzoni 1971; Slevin and Wingrove 1998). The widespread acceptance of education as the most effective mobility strategy for Black people reflects the legacy of employment discrimination in working-class occupations (Billingsley 1992; Drake and Cayton 1970). Schooling enabled people to aspire to the small number of professional positions available in the Black community and the public sector. Patricia Hill Collins (1990) saw education as "a powerful symbol for the important connections among self, change, and empowerment in African American communities" (p. 147).

A common sentiment among the respondents was voiced by Jennifer Taylor: "My father wanted to give me an education, because that is something no one could take away from me."[4] This view acknowledged that other attributes could be removed, so the valuing of education was not just a mirroring of mainstream American values but the key to a mobility strategy linked to the realities of the economic, political, and ideological oppression of the race. An education was more than an avenue to a white-collar job; it enabled Black people to understand the society, achieve economic gains, and acquire knowledge and skills for self and community. Parents and, as a consequence, the respondents themselves valued education and assumed it would make a significant difference in the quality of their lives.

When asked, "When you were growing up, how far did your mother/father expect you to go in school?," the majority of these women responded that their parents thought they would complete college; they reported thirty-nine mothers and twenty-six fathers with this view (see Table 2).[5] Earlier studies also noted high educational expectations, but few indicated any differences in middle- and working-class families' educational goals for their children (Fichter 1967; Scanzoni 1971). In this study, the respondents' answers to open-ended questions about parents' educational aspirations for them reveal variations that are directly linked to their social class origin.

All the middle-class parents assumed that their daughters would go to college. The women from these homes knew higher education was inevitable, and it was only a question of which college to attend. The majority of working-class parents, or 81 percent (twenty-six mothers and sixteen fathers), also held goals of college

	Educational Attainment			
Social Class	High School	College	Advanced Degree	Total
Working class	19%	69%	12%	100%
	(10)	(36)	(6)	(52)
Middle class	0%	60%	40%	100%
	(0)	(29)	(19)	(48)

Note: Numbers in parentheses indicate the number of respondents in each category.

attendance for their daughters. Thus the overwhelming majority of women came from families where they were exposed to the idea of college attendance as a goal. Ten out of fifty-two working-class parents (five fathers and five mothers) expected their daughters to end their formal schooling with graduation from high school. Such working-class parents held what they saw as attainable goals for their daughters. For working-class parents who had only completed the sixth or eighth grade, watching their children graduate from high school was a major achievement. For parents who had just a high school education themselves, holding such goals was appropriate. Adele Lewis recalled her family's teachings: "My family believed education was the key to greater social and economic success." The educational futures of working-class respondents were nowhere near as certain as those of their middle-class counterparts. Furthermore, many working-class families lacked the resources to guarantee their children a college education, and they could not anticipate the major changes in the enrollment practices of predominantly White colleges and the financial assistance made available to college-bound students in the 1960s.

Although college was not an immediate family goal for all working-class families, the fact that forty-two parents set goals of college for their children suggests that working-class Black parents were following a traditional pattern of mobility for the Black community as well as for White ethnic and immigrant groups. Once these families achieved a level of economic security, they invested in their children's education (Coontz 1992).[6] Those families that were the most stable, particularly where a parent had a primary labor market job, were consistent in holding high expectations for their daughters (and, in fact, for all their children).

The majority of the middle-class women were raised to become professionals, so college attendance was expected. Women indicated that sixteen mothers and thirteen fathers expected their daughters to graduate from college. A smaller but sizable group of the middle-class parents (nine mothers and ten fathers) had aspirations of advanced degrees for their daughters. Many parents had traditionally female professions in mind, but a few encouraged their daughters to seek traditionally male occupations. Mary Knight, the daughter of human service workers, noted that she "was raised to be a professional. I saw my choices as medical school, graduate school, or law school. I picked law because it seemed to be the least difficult." Mary's middle-class advantages enabled her to build on her parents' foundation and train for a prestigious profession.

The differences in the initial goals for their children are reflective of both the parents' places in the social world and their assessments of their daughters' unique abilities. Most middle-class parents thought about college and/or advanced degrees for their daughters, while most working-class parents held goals of college attendance. Six working-class parents (three fathers and three mothers) expected their daughters to get advanced degrees. Cynthia Butler and Tracy Edwards each mentioned that a parent urged her to go to medical school. These parents thought their daughters were very bright and wanted them to go as far as they could.

On the whole, working-class parents were less sophisticated about higher education, because they had little direct experience with it. Many working-class parents learned about the world of higher education along with their daughters. Dorothy Wall recalled that education was the major family priority. Her father, who had a high school diploma, was always reading and seeking to improve himself. Her mother had started college when she was young but had to leave because of economic circumstances. Initially, the Walls wanted Dorothy, their only child, to attend college and saved money for that goal. When they found out about graduate school, they encouraged Dorothy to go. Discussing her parents' expectations, Dorothy commented: "My parents never set limits on the amounts of education I could or wanted to attain. They believed in me and never doubted my ability."

Parents in both social classes linked educational attainment to employment. Middle-class parents had expectations of high-status professional positions for their daughters, while the working-class parents, whose daughters would be the first generation in the family to complete college, often held goals of traditionally female occupations, like teacher. These Black women were raised in a tradition where securing an education made them employable and gave them a chance to be economically independent (Billingsley 1992; Noble 1956; Shaw 1996; Slevin and Wingrove 1998). A college education would enable them to be self-supporting, to aid their spouses in supporting a family, or, if the marriage ended, to be the major breadwinner. Such gender expectations differed from many of the expectations of White college women at the time (Angrist and Almquist 1975; Fichter 1967; Mednick and Puryear 1975; Turner and McCaffrey 1974).[7]

To ensure their daughters' futures, parents not only instilled a commitment to learning in their children, but also monitored their schools (explored further in Chapters 5, 6, and 7) and took actions that reinforced the value of education. Dorothy Wall indicated that her parents were highly visible in both her elementary and her junior high school. The principal and teachers knew her parents because they attended the parent-teacher conferences, were present for special events, such as student performances at school, and came to school whenever they were asked. Such actions, in addition to checking homework regularly and inquiring about school progress, were the major avenues of parental participation in urban schools in the 1950s and 1960s (Winters 1993). At that time, these actions were effective in communicating to teachers that these Black parents were serious about educational goals.

Parents reinforced the importance of education in various ways. Susan Thomas, from the middle class, wrote: "My mother lessened my household chores so that I could study more." This support enabled her to devote the time she needed to succeeding in the gifted classes. Karen Johnson, a working-class respondent, said, "When we didn't work [in the summers], my mother would send us to summer school. If you didn't work, you went to summer school. You had to keep busy; that way you didn't get into trouble." Summer school may have been intended for the students who failed during the school year, but Karen's mother had a different perspective.

Parents carefully reviewed report cards and monitored their children's progress in school. Carla Jenkins, the daughter of a postal clerk and clerical worker, remembered these occasions as times of praise. Her parents expressed pride in her performance. "My mother always told me that I was very intelligent and that I should be a psychiatrist." Education was stressed to all the children in the family, but differences in ability required parents to be balanced in their praise. As Adele Lewis noted, her mother "tried to equalize things and not have favorites." Denise Larkin, who learned early by listening to her parents tutor her older sister, recalled major differences in her parents' comments on report cards. Denise, who always got As in elementary school, was told "That's nice" by her parents, while her sister, who struggled to get Cs, was told that was her performance was wonderful. As an adult, Denise was aware that her sister needed such support to sustain her interest in school, whereas she had fewer needs at that stage.[8] Beverly Rawlins knew her mother valued education and won respect with her solid achievement in school, while her brother's experiences in school were more difficult. The interviews indicate that these parents understood the varied abilities of their children and tried to reward them appropriately in ways that would encourage achievement.

The values and patterns employed by these parents are similar to those identified by Reginald Clark (1983) among low-income families with high-achieving students. From his extensive observations and interviews with families, Clark identified how parents sponsored or groomed their children for the student role; he found that sponsored independence was a key trait in the socialization of high-achieving students. The respondents in this study talked about the trait as self-direction, which can be seen as a critical component of sponsored independence. Such teaching by parents not only supported their children in the mainstream role of student, but also prepared them to be "minority" students who at times could find themselves in conflict with established school practices.

READING WAS A FOCUS AT HOME

Across social class, all parents gave solid support for reading. In her household, Beverly Rawlins reported, "Reading was the one thing you could do to get out of chores or put them off." In many cases, parents attempted to supplement the schooling their children received and even to get children excited about reading before school. Joyce Saunders, a middle-class respondent, recalled getting her first library card: "My father took me to the public library when I was five. He told them at the desk that he wanted to get me my first library card. The librarian said that I had to be seven years old to get a card. Well, my father took me back the next day, and then the next until they finally gave me a card. After that I read constantly. When I was eight or nine I would come home with a whole pile of books and have them read in three days."

The public library was an important source of reading materials and activities for both working- and middle-class families, but especially for the less affluent, since their resources were limited. Cynthia Butler, who grew up in a major city, went to her two local neighborhood libraries as well as the main branch of the municipal library. Going to the library with a friend on Saturday could be an all day outing, including getting pizza or ice cream en route. Cynthia would get a stack of books and the librarian would ask, "Are you going to read all those books?" Cynthia always read them all. Visiting the public library was also essential for research projects throughout the school years. Karen Johnson even began working in her school library when she was twelve. She earned fifty cents an hour and was encouraged by the librarian to achieve in school. There were regional differences in the use of municipal libraries, however. In southern communities, where public libraries were still segregated, parents who had resources took pride in the family library. Florence Powell, a middle-class respondent, said, "Father spent a lot of money on books. We had a very good library."[9]

In the working-class families with the most limited resources, parental support for education might be expressed by encouraging children to excel in areas with which the parents were familiar, especially reading. These working-class parents, often single mothers, took actions to establish good reading habits in their children at an early age. Thus, while respondents from both social classes gave examples of how their families supported reading in whatever ways they could, it took on particular significance in some working-class homes, sometimes setting these families apart from others in their communities. Reading was a high priority in Robin Washington's family, more so than for other families in their housing project. The family had books, educational records, and magazines rather than new clothing. Working-class respondents frequently mentioned the presence of many books or even an encyclopedia in their homes. Middle-class respondents were more likely to take such items for granted and mention that their parents provided more expensive resources that supplemented their schooling, such as tutors and special lessons.

EDUCATION IS MORE THAN SCHOOLING

Black families had broad definitions of education. They valued formal schooling but also exposed their children to other enriching experiences. Many parents modeled this approach by their own behavior. For example, Dorothy Wall's father was eager to learn the views of other people. Therefore he talked with everyone he met and explored their thinking. This approach was typical, and most of the respondents, especially working-class women, were encouraged to learn from people as well as from books.

Both working- and middle-class parents sought to enrich their daughters' lives in ways that reflected their economic resources. Many middle-class families offered the children private lessons to supplement their schooling. Music and dance lessons, especially piano lessons, were common. The Powell sisters had music lessons, as did Katrina Charles, Cheryl Davis, Deborah Jones, and Joyce Saunders. When Joyce Saunders was born, her grandmother had the family piano shipped from another state. Joyce studied the piano through high school. Music lessons were a luxury, but a few working-class families, especially those with two incomes and few children, could provide their daughters with lessons. Linda Trott, an only child, had piano lessons because playing this instrument had been her mother's aspiration. The family made getting a piano a priority, but Mrs. Trott was relaxed about Linda's progress. Later Linda would use her skills to play the organ at her church. Cynthia Butler, the older of two children, began piano lessons when she was four years old with a teacher who lived down the street.[10] She studied until she was thirteen. Many children in her neighborhood took lessons from the same piano teacher. Music lessons were valued not just for the cultural exposure and the confidence that students gained from performing, but because mastering a musical instrument reinforced the value of learning itself. Reflecting on studying the piano, Deborah Jones said: "I learned discipline and a sense of what it really means to be devoted. I learned how to master something. I always worked hard, not for the end result, but because I was working at something that I enjoyed."[11]

Middle-class parents often had the resources to travel with their children and expose them to new environments. The Powell family resided in the South and traveled every summer. Florence Powell remembered the family piling into the car and taking off for different regions of the country. Rosalind Griffin, who grew up in the northeast, spent time in the different cities where her parents had relatives. Joyce Saunders visited family members who lived along the Atlantic coast. The ability to travel was also evident in the fact that many of the middle-class women visited college campuses before deciding where to attend.

Unlike the middle-class families, working-class families could not travel through much of the country and bordering nations. Travel for this social class group was mostly to see relatives and did not appear to be deliberately designed to broaden their children's experiences. Many working-class parents found inno-vative ways to enrich their children's lives, however. Typically they used the cultural resources of their cities. While segregation was still the dominant pattern in the South, limiting cultural access to public institutions for most African Americans, northern urban areas in the 1950s and early 1960s were rich cultural resources to which Black people could readily gain access. Denise Larkin recalled her family as active in exploring what her city had to offer. She said, "My parents were the type of people who would get out on family day and do things: go to the museum, the zoo, or whatever. We did take part in the cultural aspects of the city. We listened to concerts in the parks and other free events. There were lots of things to do in East City which were available and we took part in them."

Beth Warren, who grew up in another northern city, remembered exploring that city's cultural and educational resources with her mother. She said, "Living in a large eastern city, we were able to take advantage of many free and inexpen-sive cultural events, concerts, plays, and so forth. It was really exciting and my mother and I did many things. In high school I went to museums, was involved with discussion groups, and other things. Although we were not rich, we were clearly not poor." Perhaps the Larkins and Warrens attended cultural events more than other working-class people, but these parents had a broad definition of education and acted to ensure that their children were exposed to many different cultural and educational influences.

Other institutions played a role in reinforcing parental values and keeping young people involved in adult-directed activities (Jarrett 1995). In this study, participation in church and youth groups was encouraged by parents. The overwhelming majority of the women indicated that their families practiced a religion.[12] There were variations in family practices and in how young people were involved in church activities. As the children of a minister, the Powell sisters were very involved in church activities, including acting as role models for other young people. In the Turner family, also middle class, the children attended church regularly, while the parents went occasionally. Katrina Charles was very involved in church activities, as well as going to a church-affiliated school. Church and youth groups were important in many working-class families as well. The Washington children went to church often, especially to Sunday school and youth group, while their mother did not attend. Linda Trott was involved in a church youth group and regularly attended church. Later her parents would join this church. Carla Jenkins and her sister were in Young People's Fellowship, and in addition to regular Sunday services, they went to their church two or three times a week for a period of about three years. Cynthia Butler and her brother regularly went to Sunday school.

Organized youth groups and informal arrangements were important to working-class women growing up in central cities. When she was young, Robin Washington was a Brownie Scout. Later she participated in organized social activities in school and church. Dorothy Wall and Beth Warren participated in the Girl Scouts throughout their school years. A few parents in Cynthia Butler's Black community organized an informal neighborhood club. These mothers, who all had daughters, recruited other girls in the neighborhood. They did cooking, arts and crafts, and other activities. Many working-class families firmly believed in keeping young people busy, especially if they were involved in activities that reinforced educational and mainstream goals.

Striving for Excellence

In a racist society, members of racial ethnic groups are not readily rewarded or appreciated for memorable actions. Instead, negative stereotypes of target groups persist even in the face of contradictory evidence. With this problem in mind, African American children have to learn to work hard to achieve rewards. They might have to do A-level work at school to receive only B grades. They must persevere, even if they receive little positive feedback or recognition for their accomplishments from teachers. Therefore, once children had internalized the desire to learn and a commitment to going to college, parents had to teach other skills that would enable their daughters to pursue their educational goals in a social world that was more ambivalent about their abilities. Daughters needed skills and a perspective that would nurture an ability to persevere in the face of resistance. These additional lessons would prepare them for the many negotiations they would be faced with in the world. To prepare children for this reality, their parents encouraged them to strive for excellence. This was a major tenet found in parental teachings across social class. In fact, most of the twenty women interviewed actually used the phrase, and it also appeared in several of the questionnaires.

Even as young children, respondents were urged by their parents to do everything well: make their beds, clean house, and tend to household chores as well as do their homework and achieve in school. This orientation was stressed with the awareness that as Black children, and later as Black adults, they would have to be twice as good as White people to gain recognition and respect (Billingsley 1992; Slevin and Wingrove 1998). Common sayings from their parents were "If it is worth doing, do it well" and "Be the best that you can be." Striving for excellence was a major value these Black parents lived by and explicitly taught their children.

Joyce Saunders recalled her middle-class parents frequently instructing her to "do the best you can, whatever you do." She recalled the teachings in her family: "This attitude [striving for excellence] runs in the family—on both sides. I especially got it from my grandmother and my father. They taught me that no matter what kind of work you are doing, you do your best. That even meant housework. When I spent summers with my grandmother, I helped her clean houses. She would show me how to clean, making sure I got in the corners. . . . She always told me that there was no such thing as a lowly occupation." Even within restricted work roles, Black people who did their jobs well were respected because they were actively demonstrating the higher qualities of the race, including caring for their children (Dill 1980; Shaw 1996). In retrospect Beth Warren was able to see "striving for excellence" as a tenet that pervaded the life of "working-class and bourgeois Black folks."

This orientation not only prepared respondents for the long struggle to individual achievement but also initiated them into "doing for the race." The women learned at an early age to assume a personal level of responsibility for contradicting common racial stereotypes. In both their public and private lives they were expected to do everything well and therefore present a positive image of Black people. Dorothy Wall went to an integrated high school, where she had to make a good impression with White students. At the same time, she recalled that she was taught to handle slights that happen when White people fail to treat you like a human being. "I was told not to overlook them, but to face them head on." Her parents insisted that she be treated as a person, which meant setting limits and letting White people know when they crossed them. This behavior was also part of contradicting stereotypes.

Doctrines that expressed racial loyalty, doing for the race, and the notion that Black people had to advance as a group reflected the racial barriers uniformly faced by Black Americans in the 1950s and early 1960s. As children, these women, particularly those of the middle class, heard such views expressed in their homes.[13] Civil rights and health issues were often discussed at the dinner table in the Jones household. Deborah Jones was taught, both explicitly and by example, to be concerned with the larger Black community. Her father modeled this orientation by his involvement with the "politics of Black and White medicine." In his private practice and at the hospital, Dr. Jones advocated for the Black community. Joyce Saunders's father and other family members modeled working for racial uplift, and Joyce learned early that she was expected to do her part. Such a stance encourages Black people to use the power and resources of their middle-class positions for collective as well as individual ends (Collins 1990; Higginbotham and Weber 1992; Shaw 1996).[14]

A commitment to community was also learned in working-class families; however, the philosophy was not as explicitly stated. After living for ten years in the North, in 1976 Katherine Howell still appreciated her southern background. "In retrospect, I am grateful for my southern experience. For a long time I took for granted who and what you were, Black. People lived that way. [They did not question their race.] They kept in touch with the things Black people should be in touch with, like community. There was a feeling that Blackness was more than a label. People took care of each other. In the South, there is a community, a network, and people have roots." These sentiments are part of the reason that Katherine, as an adult, thought she should use her educational skills to help others.

Like other women, Deborah Jones was encouraged to contribute something to the Black community through her future employment. As a child and later as an adult, she was supposed to be both an example for White people of what Black people could achieve and a role model for other Black people. In her research on an earlier cohort of educated Black women, Stephanie Shaw (1996) documented the ethic of socially responsible individualism that was taught in African American homes and schools. Such tenets shaped women's involvement in community institutions that were either segregated public facilities or Black-initiated efforts. In contrast to the pronounced individualism found by research on mobile

White Americans, the development of a Black professional class was shaped by a strong ideology of personal responsibility for the betterment of the race (Gaines 1996). The majority of these respondents, born after World War II and outside the South, were not explicitly taught this ethic in schools. However, parents' teachings, along with those of churches and community organizations, continued to provide an alternative to mainstream ideas about mobility in that they stressed using an education and its consequent skills for the struggle against racial injustice.[15]

This socialization and support for an activist role was very important, but it should not detract attention from the reality that these women had to contradict negative stereotypes. They often had to do so within predominantly White and integrated settings where they had few social supports. Such pressure was an additional cost of being a racial pioneer. Having to be perfect left the women with little margin for error. Any straying from excellence could reinforce a negative stereotype of Black people. Although this fear was a source of pressure on the respondents, this strategy may have influenced their success. Certainly their continuous striving for excellence enhanced their chances of gaining recognition from teachers and other officials.

Self-Direction

One value most respondents remembered as central to their socialization was self-direction, as opposed to following the crowd and/or responding to pressures from one's peers. Andrew Billingsley (1992) saw the nurturing of skills as well as high aspirations as key to the protection of Black young people, especially adolescents. If parents can be sure that their children are in "supportive and demanding learning environments" (p. 61) that can also foster development, they are more likely to relax. Most Black parents had little control over public institutions. Once parents were assured that their daughters had internalized the values of honesty, hard work, and education, they encouraged a great deal of independence. As young women the respondents were expected to use the values they had been taught. Katherine Howell recalled that her father always wanted her to be something. He "promoted a great deal of independence. Perhaps I had to satisfy being [both] a son and a daughter. I made my own decisions and could do what I wanted as long as it was reasonable."

As young people, these women were expected by their parents to think through difficult situations and potential conflicts and then act responsibly. This path was particularly important for respondents who grew up in communities where their families' values were not shared by all residents. Denise Larkin recounted how her father stressed the importance of having principles, rather than following the crowd. In Denise's inner-city neighborhood, such encouragement was helpful in making decisions about actions that might have had undesirable consequences. At times when she was in conflict with her peer group, Denise knew her parents supported her efforts to follow her own thinking. For example, when her friends were smoking marijuana, Denise followed her father's advice and pursued her own path without directly confronting her peers. It is evident that self-direction is helpful in coping in poor and multiclass communities, where Black youth face competing value systems.[16] It is possible that Black parents stressed self-direction because they were aware of the limits on their abilities to shield their daughters from personal and institutional assaults. Yet, as we will see below, some parents were overprotective about dating.

The same tenet of self-direction was useful in helping women evaluate the behaviors of middle-class White students. To women raised in families where achieving for others was stressed over individual achievement, the competitiveness of predominantly White middle-class schools often came as a shock. Respondents had to sort out their feelings about this dominant culture trait. While some women accepted individual competition as the appropriate route, others distanced themselves from such activities. Several women recalled how their parents stressed the development of individual standards to counter the intense achievement orientation of their predominantly white schools. For example, Deborah Jones recalled comments from her middle-class parents: "My parents were not into competition or cheating. They told me not to worry about others, just do the best I can." Deborah remembered their support as critical. She noted: "My parents gave me the courage to not go with the crowd. They encouraged me to center on my own values and put my energy into those goals." Black students like Deborah still achieved, but they were not as overtly competitive or as invested in outdoing others, behaviors they frequently saw among many of their White school peers. Beth Warren, who attended a highly competitive public school, recalled that while her mother and grandmother wanted her to excel, "I was not pressured to do well like my Jewish friends."

Most of the respondents grew up with peers who were supportive of educational goals. The majority (thirty-nine of the fifty-six women) responded that either all or most of their friends also went to college.[17] However, this was not the case for all. As Black Americans in a racially polarized society, peer pressure could be a strong force in their lives, so it was important to learn to deal with it at an early age. Women from both social classes discussed how they reflected on their involvement in many activities and often chose different courses from their friends. At times they had to find sources of support when they were not readily available.[18] Self-direction aided respondents as they avoided activities that either contradicted their values or might jeopardize their futures.

Establishing their own standards helped these women to remain focused on their own goals. Equipped with their own means of evaluating themselves, the respondents could acknowledge the difficulties of the course they were pursuing. They did not achieve their goals without sacrifices, but their values gave them standards independent of their peers. The internalization of their own goals is evident in how some of the respondents accepted their failure to develop social lives in high school. As tokens in predominantly White high schools, some of the women had few social outlets. In such cases, parents helped them to see alternative ways of handling the adolescent years. Katrina Charles, a middle-class woman, discussed the support she received from her parents: "My parents never made me feel that not having a social life made me less of a person. . . . I had a lot of other things going for myself (school, musical ability, and church activities), and they helped me keep that in perspective." While her White high school friends had more active social lives, Katrina had to postpone dating until college. A working-class respondent, Katherine Howell, noted that her parents encouraged her not to follow the crowd. Katherine recalled: "My parents didn't make us [Katherine and her sister] feel like we should be like other people. They always stressed that it was important to find out who you are and deal with it."

All the parents, regardless of economic resources, faced limits on their abilities to shelter their daughters from personal and institutional assaults. Middle- and working-class families therefore valued and taught self-direction, but it was employed by these young Black women in different ways. Women in predominantly White and middle-class environments developed independent standards in a context in which peers were often overly focused on grades and individual achievement. Self-direction also helped those in predominantly White neighborhoods and schools adjust to the social isolation in these settings. Meanwhile, those women in predominantly Black communities and educational settings, especially in the North, remained focused on educational attainment even when faced with conflicting value systems. A solid grounding in values and continual family support helped young women establish and maintain their own standpoints for making decisions and evaluating themselves (Collins 1990). Linda Trott spoke about how her parents encouraged her when they could not give explicit lessons on what to do. "My parents could not protect me; therefore, they taught me to protect myself." She meant more than instructing her to walk down the center of the street when coming home late at night. Linda had to protect herself in school as well, not from physical violence, but from the neglect that could undermine her belief in herself. Linda had to take responsibility for her own life, including decisions about her education and social life. Her parents modeled and explicitly taught her to set her own standards and always to aspire. She, like other working-class women, would use her own judgment as she negotiated in high school and college.

THE DATING DILEMMA

Many Black families, both middle class and working class, were concerned that their daughters not engage in activities that might jeopardize their futures. This concern was especially keen in the area of dating and sexual activity. Parents were committed to curbing any potential sexual activity that might threaten their daughter's chances of completing school or limit future marital options. Mrs. Rawlins, who had married early and had two children, insisted that her daughter, Beverly, not get pregnant, even in college, and that her son not get any girls pregnant. While most parents trusted their daughters, often aided by explicit instructions, a minority attempted to tightly control their children's social activities. A few respondents from both social classes faced either open conflicts with parents or persistent tension around dating, socializing, and hanging out. In general, these parents were fairly tolerant of interactions with girlfriends, especially if such activities did not detract from homework and household chores, but they were very hesitant about supporting dating.

A few working-class women remembered their parents as overprotective. Nancy Brooks, an only child who grew up in a low-income Black community in the North, indicated that her father was very protective and gave her little independence, while her mother had a more permissive style. Karen Johnson said that dating was the only area of conflict with her parents during her high school years. She recalled: "I guess I wanted to be independent. When I was in high school I thought I was grown up and I wanted to be able to do things. I guess I wanted my parents to have more faith in me, to trust me when I went out with my friends." In retrospect, Karen saw her parents' protectiveness as "the care a parent should have." Furthermore, Karen remembered her parents as cool at times. She kept in perspective how her parents always encouraged her to invite friends over to the house. Interviews with a few other respondents indicate that many working-class parents, like Karen's and Nancy's, trusted their daughters, but not their communities and the wider world.

Reginald Clark (1983), in his research on Black families in urban Chicago in the late 1970s, also found that many working-class parents, identified by him as poor, tightly controlled their children's use of time and space and closely supervised their friendships. Clark found such practices in the families of high-achieving male and female students, especially those from single-parent families. Such tight control of young people was less an issue in this study, even for the working-class women. For this cohort, coming of age in the 1950s and 1960s, neighborhoods were diverse in terms of social class but were not seen as problematic for the raising of children in the way that they increasingly became in the latter part of the twentieth century (Anderson 1999; Billingsley 1992; Massey and Denton 1993; Wilson 1996). However, Clark's research speaks to the additional burdens of child rearing and reinforcing values when parents have to contend with a hostile community.

Perhaps the character of the neighborhood and the personalities of the individuals concerned were factors in producing these tensions. However, these parental concerns speak more directly to a strategy informed by a legacy of negative images of Black women. Collins (1990) notes that while Black families are important sites that nurture resistance, they are also places where Black women are subjected to the complexities of both internal and external controlling images of themselves. Parents wanted to raise their daughters to avoid being linked with negative stereotypes of Black women as sexually active at an early age. Although these women were not expected to uphold Victorian ideals of sexual restraint like their earlier counterparts (Shaw 1996), they still had to compensate for a negative image of Black women and be above reproach (Collins 1990; Morton 1991).

Such a strategy created tensions for the women of this baby boom cohort. They wanted freedom of mobility to participate in the youth culture of the 1960s, which they knew they had to maneuver in to have the futures both they and their parents desired. The doubts and concerns of their parents were interpreted as a lack of trust and even as questioning the degree to which these women had internalized values. For example, some parents voiced opinions about their daughters' friendship choices (especially the males) and the appropriate hour to return home. This parental stance was recalled as painful by these women, particularly since they were expected to be self-directed in other spheres. Florence Powell, a middle-class respondent from the South, testified to the difficulties with her parents. She was not permitted to date until she was a senior in high school. Prior to that time, either her mother or father acted as a chaperone when a young man would visit her at home. She recalled: "I didn't like the fact that I was treated as if I were not trusted. My mother was harder on us than she needed to be. We had to go through many changes to be allowed to do things. It was hard to have people over. I was never relaxed when I had guys over." Such tensions between parents and their teenage daughters are often assumed to be part of "growing up," but they were the source of special difficulty for women who had been socialized for self-direction. While respondents understood that such contradictory behavior on the part of their parents was related to parental fears, interactions were still stressful. The women who had to cope with overly protective parents were hurt because they felt that such interactions indicated their parents did not believe in them. These women valued attending college and would not jeopardize their own futures.

Overprotectiveness was not a characteristic of all the parents.[19] For every respondent who noted difficulties with parents around dating and social interactions, there were four who indicated that their parents genuinely trusted their judgment. Many of the respondents had social lives that were centered on high school activities and clubs, primarily with girlfriends. Thus many parents were not troubled by dating because their daughters were not dating at all. In such cases, the parents provided reassurance that socializing with the opposite sex would come in the future. The majority of respondents were in coeducational high schools, but a sizable group (nine of the fifty-six women) were in all-girl institutions. Linda Trott, one in that group, had to find other settings even to meet boys, which she did within a church youth group. Others were content to postpone dating until college, since many of their high school friends were also not dating.

HOLDING YOUR OWN AGAINST RACISM

Parents were conscious of teaching daughters to follow their own goals and values in the face of competing value systems within the Black community and the habitual competition of the White middle class, especially in schools.[20] But they had other ends in mind when they stressed finding your own direction and holding on to it. Self-direction helped Karen Johnson, a working-class respondent who grew up in a middle-class suburb, maintain clarity about her goals. She was frequently told by her elementary and high school teachers that her plans to go to college were unrealistic. In fact, school officials steered her away from the college preparatory program and encouraged her to take the commercial course in her high school. For the Johnsons, who located in this community to give their children access to an excellent school system, such maneuvers were rejected. Asked about such treatment, Karen replied:

> Oh, I laughed. My homeroom teacher and my guidance counselor were two fools. The homeroom teacher was a cooking teacher, which was great. I wasn't interested. But she used to always tell me that "you have to know how to cook, you have to know how to sew." I just thought it was degrading. I said that all Black people don't have to do that. My mother can teach me how to sew and cook; I don't have to learn it in school. I had a guidance counselor who did not

really guide me. My older sister did all the work with helping me apply to colleges. I just thought they [teachers and guidance counselors] didn't care since I was Black.

Viewing the comments from certain teachers as a response to her Blackness and not to her own potential gave Karen some distance from the negative feedback and poor guidance she received in high school.[21] Karen did have a few teachers who recognized her talent and encouraged her to go to college. In fact, she performed better in the classes where she received encouragement and respect. However, she received most of her support for higher education from her parents and older siblings. The family lessons of thinking and acting for yourself, and encouragement to define your own goals, constituted a lens to view the mixed responses that Black women might receive in high schools.

Identifying racist comments and individuals is one task; handling such encounters is another. Sometimes respondents had to tolerate racist teachers and keep focused on their own goals. Many students, especially working-class youth, recounted receiving Bs when they thought they deserved As. In educational settings where they lacked power because of their status as students, respondents typically avoided overt conflicts with teachers and school officials. Yet there were also times when students' educational experiences could be compromised if they did not speak up. To protect themselves, some young women had to confront racist teachers to assure appropriate education. For example, Joyce Saunders, a middle-class respondent, transferred from an integrated urban comprehensive high school to a predominantly White suburban high school when her father relocated for a job. In this new setting, Joyce had many battles with both teachers and students. Although she was a high-achieving student in her former high school, officials in her new school assigned her to a nonacademic track without informing either Joyce or her parents. Joyce was amazed at how easy the school work was in her new school. Other students told her that this was the "dumb" class. Upon discovering the type of class she was in, Joyce told her parents, who confronted the principal. After a long struggle that involved the local chapter of the National Association for the Advancement of Colored People (NAACP) working on behalf of the Saunders family, Joyce was placed in the college preparatory track.

Once she was in the appropriate classes, Joyce's difficulties with individual teachers continued. Daily interaction at school was very tense, and Joyce had to cope with these situations alone. She had her parents' support, but they could not attend school with her. Joyce recalled one teacher who particularly resented having a Black student in the classroom: "I went to the classroom and the teacher seated me two rows behind the rest of the class. I was in the last row in the last seat. I said to myself, 'Gee, this is like what I have been reading about in the newspapers. I'm being discriminated against.' When I went home, I told my mother. She told me to get another seat. So I told the teacher I could not see the blackboard. So she had to give me another seat. But I would hold up my hand in class, and she would not call on me. She called on me twice during the whole semester."

These respondents, like Joyce, learned early that confronting racial barriers was part of life. Parental teaching that stressed striving for excellence and self-direction gave them an edge in managing racist encounters, yet it was not easy to confront racist actions and to question authority figures. This was certainly a tall task for young Black women, but these women undertook the challenge because it was essential for their futures. Diligence was required of pioneers in new racial territories. They had to be alert to racial bias, as well as be exemplary young people and students. They would use the lessons learned in their families as they attended different high schools. Often their behavior was misconstrued as evidence that Black women do not have any problems with confidence, particularly because of their willingness to challenge injustice. This is a common perception held by White women, especially those in the middle class (Palmer 1983). Another interpretation is that these Black women's actions were motivated by a sense of personal responsibility for contradicting racism, a value explicitly taught in their families. By necessity, many people of color in this nation develop such skills to cope in hostile environments, but at a cost of alienation from the self (Collins 1990; Takaki 1989).

Further, controlling one's anger and mustering up the courage to confront a teacher or raise a question took a great deal of effort. When they did so, these women frequently felt as if they lacked options and had to handle their situations as best they could. They learned such behavior as young Black females and continued to practice this stance as adults. To outsiders these women frequently appeared to be more in control than they actually felt, but outsiders failed to grasp the complexity of their lives. For example, Robin Washington said, "People always told me that I was powerful. I was unsure about what to say. While I am powerful, I still have a negative self-image." It would only be later in life that Robin would build real confidence in herself. However, in high school she used her brilliance and determination to help her survive in often hostile educational settings.

Committed to the Struggle

As young people, these fifty-six women grew up with a sense that they would have to struggle to survive in this world. They watched their parents' efforts and were socialized to join in the struggle for individual and group respect. The encouragement to value education, lessons in striving for excellence, and instruction on being self-sustaining and self-directed were all part of that preparation. Of course, each encounter with a racist person or barrier would be trying and difficult—especially those involving both purposeful and unthinking assaults from White people. Parental teaching and instructions from other segments in the Black community, especially the church, helped to provide Black youth with a perspective on racism. At the same time, they were prepared to accept the challenge of combating racism in the society. Beverly Rawlins commented: "I think that one of the most important gifts that Black middle-class families give to their children is a high level of confidence in themselves. I think this is extremely important. If the child believes in herself and her ability to do the work, then her chances of doing so are much better. You have the security which is necessary to be able to ask questions and say you don't understand something without being embarrassed or whatever." Beverly's observations can be expanded to include many of the working-class women. This cohort of Black parents hoped that developing an independent stance, doing their best at all times, including in school, and being straightforward would enable their children to scale racial barriers in the society and take advantage of expanding opportunities.

These young women learned to quell their anger and work diligently toward personal goals. Yet there were limits on tolerance, and some acts of injustice required responses. Again, parental teachings that fostered a strong sense of personal responsibility helped women get through such periods. Linda Trott spoke about the learning she received from her parents: "My parents were into doing what was right, even fighting for what was right. This included your own thinking. They were not into open aggression, but if others aggressed against me, I was taught that I should stand up and fight for what is right. I was not encouraged to be a pacifist."

We see major similarities in the values taught to middle- and working-class women. Although social class would differentiate many areas of their lives, they were all prepared to struggle against the racism in the society, a racism that they would find expressed in different ways in segregated, integrated, and predominantly White schools. Parents taught a commitment to education and achieving. Striving for excellence would give Black youth an advantage and the opportunity for recognition. Family remained a source of strength and encouragement, but respondents were taught to be self-directed because they needed to be able to navigate the world beyond the family. As these young Black women entered various educational and community environments, there was the strong possibility that their families' goals for them would be questioned, even when the families had resources. The next chapters detail the complexity of their interactions in educational settings, both how the women used these family lessons to negotiate in different educational settings and the costs to them to do so.

Surviving or Thriving

In my high school, Black and poor White students were usually tracked into general or vocational programs, while the more affluent White students were in college preparatory. A guidance counselor usually helped to fill out your program and then your parents had to sign it. My eighth grade counselor tried to track me into the home economics curriculum, but my mother protested. So they put me in college prep courses.
—*Janet Sheldon, working-class graduate of a*
 predominantly White comprehensive high school

Several other Black students, about ten, were in an Honors group, but the rest of my friends were in the regular college prep group. I enjoyed high school. I liked my subjects and different activities. I had different friends and was in social groups. I particularly enjoyed math, glee club, the sciences, the newspaper, and sports—both ours and the men's school teams.
—*Michelle Clark, middle-class graduate of an integrated comprehensive high school*

High schools played a critical role in identifying students for colleges and directing students to specific colleges (Cicourel and Kitsuse 1963). In addition, high schools provided the educational preparation and social supports necessary for their graduates to meet the challenges of college (Walker 1996). During the high school years, parents and the young Black women themselves gave primary consideration to mastering academic materials. Yet this focus does not constitute the total high school experience. During this stage in adolescence, young people are developing socially and becoming emotionally prepared to assume adult roles. For these women, who would be among the first major wave of Black students to enter predominantly White colleges, social supports would be essential in scaling the barriers ahead. How did these Black women, of both social classes, fare in high school with regard to securing academic preparation and having positive social experiences?

Race, social class, and gender created very different barriers as the young women, with goals of educational attainment, entered high schools in the early 1960s. Parents stressed education, but as the women stepped outside of their families into the school environment, they found a range of receptions to their aspirations. It would be easy to think that all of these women, who are now college graduates, and in many cases hold advanced degrees, were encouraged by their teachers in high school. But in fact social class was a key factor in whether or not the women received encouragement to attend college from teachers and/or school officials. The majority of the middle-class women, twenty-four of the twenty-five, reported that they were encouraged, but only twenty-two of the thirty-one working-class women responded positively to that question. More-over, the women's stories reveal the complex interaction of institutional factors, like the racial and social class composition of the school, with an individual's social class. Some women faced institutionalized racism in the form of segregated schools, while others coped with informal racism in newly desegregated institu-tions, and still others enjoyed many of the social and educational benefits of an integrated school system. However, within the diversity of educational settings, the women's social class positions also shaped their experiences. These different educational settings required different strategies, as well as energy, to meet the women's goals.

This chapter examines the experiences of women who attended public com-prehensive high schools, the most common schooling experience for most U.S. youth, while Chapter 6 discusses the experiences of women who graduated from private, parochial, or selective public high schools. Our common distinction between public and private schools was not specific enough for the analysis of this generation of Black women's educational experiences. The distinction in the school's mission appeared to be the most critical factor in shaping the strategies necessary for meeting their educational goals.

Comprehensive public high schools are the backbone of the U.S. public sec-ondary educational system. Developed in conjunction with compulsory educa-tion laws, these schools offered the promise of equality. In reality, the operation of comprehensive high schools reveals much about the myth of equality of educational opportunities in this land. Comprehensive high schools serve stu-dents in designated school districts, but they vary in size and quality. All com-prehensive high schools serve a diverse population, offering programs to prepare some youth for college and other graduates for the world of work (Oakes 1985). Many schools offer specific vocational programs; in the 1950s and 1960s these were often sex-segregated, with home economics, clerical, or commercial courses for girls, while boys learned auto mechanics or printing. Ever since the publication of August Hollingshead's (1949) *Elmtown's Youth*, scholars have acknowledged that social class influences all aspects of high school life. The faculty plays a significant role in maintaining the status quo by directing working-class and middle-class students into courses that reproduce their social class positions (Bowles and Gintis 1977; Oakes 1985).

Educational institutions employ various mechanisms for preparing students for different futures. This goal is achieved by "tracking, that is, the process by which students are divided into categories so that they can be assigned in groups to various kinds of classes" (Oakes 1985, p. 3). It would be idealistic to assume that tracking is blind to color, class, and gender and that counselors and teachers are always able to identify, without their own prejudices affecting these judgments, the persons most appropriate for college and future professional careers and those who should aim for positions as secretaries, factory workers, and retail sales clerks. Instead, it is well documented that the classism, racism, and sexism of our society are replicated within our educational institutions (Bowles and Gintis 1977; Kozol 1991; Oakes 1985; Rist 1974). Comprehensive high schools, as well as primary schools, have consistently served the nation by preparing young people of different colors, classes, ethnicities, and regions for lives that closely resemble those of their parents. Most comprehensive high schools extend privileges to the children of the middle class and assist them in their routes to college, while they hamper the progress of those from the working class who hold such goals (Leacock 1969). This pattern is clearly demonstrated in this cohort of Black women, except for those who attended predominantly Black high schools.

Research demonstrates that factors other than academic ability influence the placement of students into specific tracks and courses of study, especially since the hard data of achievement test scores and grades are subject to interpretation and judgment by school personnel (Cicourel and Kitsuse 1963; Spade, Columba, and Vanfossen 1997). First, placement into different curricula is strongly correlated with social class background (Oakes 1985; Schafer, Olexa, and Polk 1970). Middle- and working-class students within the same building are following paths that lead to different futures, as schools aid the stratification process (Bowles and Gintis 1977; Colclough and Beck 1986; Larkin 1979; Leacock 1969). It is often just a minority of working-class students who are able to scale social class barriers to use schools as vehicles for upward mobility (Dews and Law 1995). School climate is an issue that merits greater exploration. In a recent study, Joan Spade, Lynn Columba, and Beth Vanfossen (1997) found that course offerings in science and math were related to the social class compositions of the student body, with high schools in more affluent communities offering not only regular and college preparatory math and science courses, but honors and advanced placement ones as well. However, the recruitment of students into the existing math and science courses was an independent factor. Schools that lacked many levels of courses might still be able to get students excited and interested enough to take the available science and math courses, even if they were not advanced placement or honors courses.[1]

Second, the racial inequalities of our society are more likely reinforced rather than challenged by educational institutions. De jure and de facto segregation keep Black Americans and other people of color in poorly supported and ill-equipped schools where their educational opportunities are limited. White students are offered better facilities and often higher quality curricula (Clark 1965). Within integrated facilities, race and ethnicity are factors in the assignment of students to different courses of study. Research in urban, rural, and suburban schools demonstrates that children of color and White children are unevenly distributed between academic and nonacademic programs (Anyon 1997; Kozol 1991; Larkin 1979; Leacock 1969; Oakes 1985; Schofield 1982).

Third, gender is a major construct in the structure of schools. In addition to a formal curriculum that directs women and men into different occupational and career paths, there is an informal or hidden curriculum that establishes and reinforces different expectations for boys and girls (Levine and Ornstein 1981; Lorber 1994). The hidden curriculum "consists of routine, everyday interchanges that provide students with information about the placement of persons of various race-gender groups" (Grant 1994, p. 43). Much of the scholarship on this hidden curriculum looks at gender issues, but it has relevance for race and social class as well. This informal curriculum is fueled by teachers' expectations, experiences, and personal beliefs about race, gender, and social class. Linda Grant (1984, 1994), who did pioneering work on first and second graders and teachers in desegregated classrooms, found central differences in how teachers treated Black boys, Black girls, White boys, and White girls. Grant identified the "complex, subtle processes in schools [that] encourage Black girls more than other students to assume distinctive roles: helper, enforcer, and go-between. These roles develop their social skills more than their academic abilities" (1994, p. 44). Grant's subjects are a later cohort than the one in this study; however, she directs our attention to how schools can be instrumental in encouraging Black girls toward service and helping behaviors that support traditional occupational roles for Black women. In our case, these expectations were also shaped by social class, as it was clear that some of the subjects were the daughters of professionals while others had working-class parents.

In addressing gender roles, we know that the gender beliefs found in Black families are different from those in mainstream society, particularly in the 1950s and early 1960s. These Black women were raised to anticipate long-term involvement in paid employment, as well as family life, and were urged to be academically prepared for such a future (Billingsley 1992; Fichter 1967; Shaw 1996; Slevin and Wingrove 1998). It is likely that within predominantly Black schools there will be more support for parental goals, since the gender beliefs are part of that community. Black women in integrated and predominantly White schools are more likely to encounter traditional U.S. gender roles and expectations and thus less support for college and career goals. These mainstream expectations, as Grant's work suggests, will be influenced by the respondents' race as well as their gender.

Nationwide, the majority of American young people receive their secondary schooling in public comprehensive high schools. The percentages were even higher in the late 1950s and early 1960s, when these women were in high school. Seventy percent of the women in this study, thirty-nine of the fifty-six, graduated from comprehensive high schools. Most of the women were graduates of either urban or suburban schools, while a few women graduated from rural high schools. Given the practice of tracking in comprehensive high schools, it was very important that the young women gain access to their schools' college preparatory programs because "college-preparatory courses cover more material, in more depth, and with more assigned homework and laboratory work than do non-college-preparatory courses" (Spade, Columba, and Vanfossen 1997, p. 114). A major factor in securing a place in the college preparatory program was the racial composition of the high school. Of the thirty-nine graduates of comprehensive high schools in this study, nine attended predominantly Black or segregated high schools, twelve went to predominantly White high schools, and eighteen attended integrated high schools. The racial composition of their schools created different climates of support for the women's aspirations. Those who attended majority Black schools found a positive reception to their goals, and they spoke highly of their social experiences. Those who attended majority White high schools had more varied receptions. The degree of institutional support they received was tied to their social class as well as to the specific racial composition of the school, either integrated or predominantly White.

In contrast to solid support for students of both classes in predominantly Black institutions, the working- and middle-class women fared differently in integrated and predominantly White high schools. The middle-class women had class privileges that enabled them to access college preparatory programs more readily than working-class women. However, the racial composition of the high school was a key factor in how that support for educational goals was expressed. Their goals of college attendance were accepted, but personal support and encouragement for careers was sporadic. Working-class women reaped many benefits in predominantly Black schools, but they were disadvantaged in the majority White settings. Lacking social class privilege, working-class women paid dearly for their education because they had to challenge directly or negotiate around race and class barriers. A few women, like Janet Sheldon, needed their parents' intervention to get into college preparatory courses. Once they gained entrance to these courses, they were not necessarily strongly encouraged in their goals. The existence of formal and informal barriers to their educational goals in majority White settings necessitated serious negotiations on their part as they sought to use these institutions to accomplish family goals. The kinds of negotiations required of the women to secure educational credentials in these varied circumstances, and the differing costs of that success, are explored as we look at predominantly Black, predominantly White, and integrated comprehensive high schools.

Predominantly Black High Schools

In the 1950s and early 1960s, the majority of Black children in this country attended secondary schools with other Black children because there were few options outside of predominantly Black public schools. In this study, nine of the women (or 16 percent) graduated from predominantly Black comprehensive high schools. Identifying a school as predominantly Black tells us little about the teaching staff, level of financial support for the school, or the overall quality of education that students received. The experiences of these nine women reveal regional variations in the level of academic preparation available in predominantly Black high schools. All the women reported their high schools as very supportive of them as individuals, as they reaped advantages in a majority environment. Their reports indicate that support was forthcoming for students regardless of social class background.[2] Their schools differed in that southern segregated schools had more limited budgets, while the predominantly Black schools in the border states were better equipped and offered students more educational opportunities.

The stories of these nine women all begin in segregated schools, both in the South and within the border states. Separate schools, along with other Jim Crow legislation, were supported by the *Plessy v. Ferguson* Supreme Court decision of 1896, which upheld the constitutionality of separate but equal facilities. Furthermore, separate schools were considered to be the foundation of a segregated society (Kluger 1977). Politicians and school officials in the Deep South were strongly committed to keeping their primary and secondary schools segregated, even if they were forced to bend to the federal courts and civil rights advocates with regard to higher educational facilities. Segregation required that the South, already a poor region, maintain dual school systems. As a rule, Black schools received less financial support than White schools. These differences were reflected in the physical plant (both the age of structures and quality of the facilities), educational supplies, requirements for teacher certification, and teachers' salaries (Bullock 1964; Coleman 1966; Kluger 1977; Slevin and Wingrove 1998).

Segregated schools proved to be problematic in many respects for Black Americans. In 1929, W. E. B. Du Bois noted that "separate schools would inexorably become less well housed, less well supported, less well-equipped and less well-supervised than the average public school" (Tyack 1974, p. 228).[3] According to the Supreme Court's *Brown v. Board of Education* decision in 1954, segregated schools, like other facilities, were inherently unequal. Psychological evidence identified the damaging impact of segregated schools on the self-esteem and egos of Black youth (Cross 1991). Yet, within these structural and social constraints, southern Black people worked to give their children the best education possible.

The nine women graduates of predominantly Black comprehensive high schools attended either traditionally segregated schools or schools that had desegregated in compliance with the law and became predominantly Black. Six respondents from the Deep South, two middle-class and four working-class women, graduated between 1964 and 1966 and therefore attended all-Black institutions for their primary and secondary schooling (Bullock 1964; Coleman 1966).[4] Although research has reported mixed impacts of segregated schools, these respondents, all excellent students, reported that they thrived in these social and educational environments. Natalie Small, a working-class respondent, was typical of this group. She remarked, "I enjoyed a variety of school activities: band, choir, language clubs, honor society, and more. Students, parents, and teachers all knew each other and cooperated to make the school (which was all Black) a very positive and meaningful experience. We never felt inferior or dejected because our school was all Black. We believed it was a good school with very concerned teachers and parents." While their schools were crippled by small budgets and restrictions shaped by all-White school boards, the graduates focused on their strengths. The racial composition of the teaching, counseling, and administrative staff helped mediate the impact of institutionalized racism. Even though funds were lacking, educators used their energies to compensate for a situation structured to produce disadvantage.[5] Within the shadow of Jim Crow, Black educators worked with supportive communities to create a humane learning environment for members of their own race (Bullock 1964; Hunter-Gault 1992; Reagon 1982; Shaw 1996; Walker 1996).

The other three graduates of predominantly Black high schools, one working-class and two middle-class women, graduated from institutions that desegregated in the years immediately after the Supreme Court decision of 1954. Once their district high schools in communities close to the Mason Dixon line desegregated, they very quickly became predominantly Black as many White families moved to the neighboring suburbs. According to the respondents, their high schools had student populations that were between 60 and 70 percent Black. They also noted that their high schools served both middle- and working-class Black communities as well as segments of the White community and other racial-ethnic groups. There was broad community support for these comprehensive high schools and a commitment to enhancing the lives of the students.

These three respondents' high schools had characteristics of both northern and southern public school systems. The legacy of segregation resulted in a cadre of Black teachers who, along with White teachers, were available to staff newly desegregated schools. The respondents reported having both Black and White teachers in their college preparatory courses. The women's experiences were most similar to those of Black youth in southern segregated schools, with two major differences: they were in schools with White youth and their institutions had more resources. In these border communities, per capita expenditures for public schools were higher than those found in states in the Deep South. With decent salaries for teachers, quality facilities, and sufficient materials, these schools provided the educational advantages routinely found in many northern communities.[6] The three women benefited from the support of both Black and White teachers. Their school officials encouraged them to participate in high school activities and to proceed on to college.

For example, Margaret Cooke, a working-class woman, recalled her school as an instructive and supportive environment that offered both a college preparatory program and high honors courses. In the high honors track, Margaret was well integrated into the student body. There were many Black students and other racial minorities as well as White students in her classes. Margaret enjoyed high school and found it academically stimulating: "I related well to both teachers and fellow students. There were good extra-curricular activities and I had an active social life. I had older Black teachers and some White teachers who knew their subject matter very well and were dedicated to teaching. Also they were supportive of students, at least those in the honors program." With strong encouragement in a well-financed high school, Margaret reaped many benefits. Unlike southern segregated schools, Margaret's high school had science laboratories and modern educational materials, making it a springboard for her interest in science. This unique educational background gave Margaret the preparation to do well in college and graduate school in the sciences. Since there are relatively few minority women in the sciences, her history is important (Malcom, Hall, and Brown 1976). Unfortunately, Margaret's experience is rare among the cohort in this study.

In contrast, a middle-class respondent, Florence Powell, in assessing the advantages and disadvantages of her segregated high school, noted the impact of the lack of resources. Like others, she was truly appreciative of the support and acceptance shown her, but Florence was also troubled by the school's limitations. She commented: "There was no exposure to things our teachers were not prepared for. For example, in my school there were few languages. Our teachers were from Black colleges in the South and we got a certain perspective from them. And there were huge differences between our school and the White high schools. The White schools had science labs, better facilities, especially in biology and chemistry. I never saw a science experiment performed. In my school the emphasis was on sports and music. I had a wide variety of music experiences teaching me to appreciate all kinds of music." Florence's sister, Sabrina, was critical of the way that music and sports were emphasized over academics. But the working-class women who graduated from segregated schools were not as critical.[7]

The frank comments by the Powell sisters caution against romanticizing this era of southern segregated schools by reminding us that these schools were a form of institutionalized racism that many people worked to end. The political economy of Black education was indeed harsh (Bullock 1964). Schools hampered by low budgets were limited in the educational exposure they could provide students, especially in the areas of math, science, and languages. Obviously, the lack of exposure to certain subjects can influence subsequent career decisions, as women are less likely to enter fields in which their level of preparation is poor.

Likewise, the graduates of predominantly Black schools at this same time also enjoyed an era that has passed, since the commitment to urban public schools has declined (Kozol 1991; Suskind 1998). In this earlier period, there were many advantages. In addition to White faculty, these schools were also staffed by highly qualified Black teachers who had been working for years in segregated school systems. These instructors brought with them a tradition of encouraging excellence and hard work, including preparing young women as well as men for higher education and employment. As in segregated schools, teachers in these institutions played a major role in shaping and supporting expectations (Slevin and Wingrove 1998). Black teachers were also role models for Black students.

Such factors contributed to the women's high level of performance in these predominantly Black high schools.

Evelyn Tucker and Allison Cross, both middle class, were in their schools' top academic tracks and participated in other school activities. In her interview, Evelyn stressed that, while she appreciated the teaching, what she valued most from her high school experience was having a typical adolescence. "Some of the teachers I had were exceptional by any standards, including my subsequent college experience. But what those years represent for me is the beginning of my self-discovery, of a confirmed and tested sense of who I was, how I was both like and unlike those around me." Surrounded by both Black and White peers, self-discovery and personal exploration were real possibilities. Friendships were built on personalities, politics, and lifestyles. At the same time, graduates of predominantly Black high schools were surrounded by caring Black teachers who worked with the resources at their disposal to provide students with a strong educational foundation. A school's climate can be a central ingredient in success.

In contrast to the experiences of Black women in majority White settings, receiving encouragement and academic support was less tied to social class in predominantly Black schools. Recognizing that the South's segregated schools were run by members of the Black middle class, some research on class has indicated that teachers disproportionately rewarded members of their own group (Frazier 1962; Gaines 1996). This pattern had implications for all southern predominantly Black schools, and it was noted by two respondents from different backgrounds. Florence Powell, who was raised in the middle class, thought she received higher grades than she earned. Wilma Jefferson, the daughter of a postal clerk, saw a bias in students' placement into the academic track. "There was a small Black middle class in my city, but I think all the middle-class kids were in the top track."

But social class was not critical in shaping educational experiences for this cohort. The experiences of the working-class respondents suggest that even if middle-class students were disproportionately rewarded, Black teachers, who were a significant presence in both environments, acknowledged talented working-class students.[8] Black working-class women did not have trouble gaining access to the college preparatory programs in their high schools. In describing her high school, Toni Brown wrote: "The academic program was divided into three basic curricula: science, classical, and business/vocational. Students were placed into these various curricula based on previous academic records and consultation with students in the latter portion of their eighth grade. Students were asked their career objectives and the curriculum that best fit their needs was assigned. The science curriculum characterized the majority of the college bound students. About forty-five to sixty percent of the students were college bound." In these majority Black schools, all the respondents were strongly encouraged by teachers and school officials to attend college. Many faculty also worked to make those opportunities possible. All the young women recounted advantages in positive self-esteem and encouragement to achieve their goals. In segregated schools, community support was also critical in helping build an educational environment that was not divisive in terms of social class. Regina Walker, raised in the working class, attended school in a rural community. She recalled that all the Black people knew each other and cooperated. Thinking about her segregated high school education, Regina wrote: "I enjoyed my high school experiences immensely! I was involved in many facets of the high school community and have very warm memories of the people and that period of my life." Regina's and other respondents' days in all-Black settings were remembered as positive and were important in giving these students the academic preparation and confidence needed to venture off to predominantly White colleges.

The experiences of the nine women in these settings are a sharp contrast to stereotypic pictures of Black youth in disadvantaged schools in the 1960s. As graduates of predominantly Black high schools in the South and border states, they recalled supportive Black teachers as well as parental and community involvement in their schools. The women had praise for their level of academic preparation; however, the schools differed in the level of state and local financial support they received. Furthermore, three middle-class women and four working-class women from this group were encouraged to plan for a career. For example, Wilma Jefferson was encouraged to think about teaching, and Toni Brown recalled, "One instructor guided me in the area of mathematics, but generally I wasn't encouraged to pursue a particular career, but to obtain higher education and to make a choice after having a chance to compare the various areas." They reported receiving stronger support for careers than women in other comprehensive high schools. Black teachers in these schools were part of the tradition of training Black women for employment and economic independence (Shaw 1996; Slevin and Wingrove 1998). The teachers knew from their own life experiences that educated Black women would very likely have to be employed to help support their families. Black teachers might be more inclined to encourage promising female students to think about careers than would White faculty, who might not expect women to be involved in paid employment in the 1960s.

Predominantly White High Schools

In the early 1960s, seven working-class and five middle-class respondents attended predominantly White comprehensive high schools. At this time, these schools had a majority of White students and often all-White faculty and staff. These twelve women faced special challenges in such settings. Black students obtained access to predominantly White comprehensive high schools either by attending their district high school or by reassignment to a high school in another district. In all cases, the failure of the schools to do more than just admit a new population made negotiating racial barriers difficult for these women. Since the majority of the students in their classes were middle class, the women from the working class had social class as an additional obstacle. These graduates proceeded to college, but both working- and middle-class women related more tales of loneliness, isolation, mixed messages from teachers, and pressures to succeed than women in other comprehensive high schools.

Six respondents (four middle-class and two working-class women) attended their district high schools, where their assignment was based upon their place of residence (Coleman and Hoffer 1987). The women lived in rural, suburban, and urban predominantly White communities, all in the North. For example, Elise King, a working-class woman, attended the high school in her small predominantly White town. She was one of a few Black students among a student population of 1,400. Elise was in the college track, and she appreciated the academic preparation she received, but race presented barriers to social integration into the school. A strong academic student, Elise also was active in extracurricular activities, but she still felt "socially isolated from social functions because of the lack of Black classmates. This was particularly the case when dating was involved."

Another six women, one middle class and five working class, graduated from urban, predominantly White comprehensive high schools that were outside of their home districts. Most were reassigned to a predominantly White high school as part of an urban desegregation plan or a citywide effort to address racial imbalance in public schools. Nancy Brooks, a working-class respondent from a mid-Atlantic city, was recommended by her junior high school teachers as a candidate to desegregate an all-White high school in a nearby community. When presented with this option, Nancy selected to bypass her overcrowded, predominantly Black district high school. She remarked: "My mother really wanted me to go to college, because she had not been able to finish. So she made the decision that I would go to Wilson High, an all-White high school. The only other choice was A. Philip Randolph High School, which was another all-Black school. So I took public transportation and went to Wilson High School. I was one of thirty Black students who started that year." While a respondent like Nancy Brooks saw this reassignment as an opportunity, there were other Black women who resented the practice of moving Black students to achieve desegregation goals. Overall, the working-class families, who were more dependent upon the public school system, had less control over schooling options than did middle-class respondents. Therefore parents were eager for their daughters to take advantage of opportunities that did arise, even if the schooling experiences were troublesome for the young women.

SOCIAL ISOLATION

The graduates of predominantly White public schools received comparable or perhaps better academic preparation than their peers in predominantly Black high schools.[9] However, while they gained in academic preparation, they lost in terms of levels of comfort with peers and teachers. All the respondents had comments about the general lack of social or emotional support for them within their schools. The women were most vocal about the social isolation of their years in high school. During these difficult years, their families provided essential social supports. Their stories illustrate the types of problems Black students faced in predominantly White comprehensive high schools during this era and identify the different negotiations of working- and middle-class women.

Graduates of suburban high schools openly discussed isolation, lack of Black peers, and the barriers to interactions with White students.[10] Both working-class and middle-class respondents had similar complaints. Not only racially distinct, but part of a small working-class community in a middle-class suburb, Karen Johnson often felt out of place. She recalled her difficulties in this environment: "Being one of four Black students in a population of two thousand students was difficult. I found no outlet for my desire to socialize. I feel that socially I was not prepared for college. My high school years seemed to me to have caused me to have feelings of insecurity in dealing with Blacks on a social level." Race was also a barrier to full participation for Rosalind Griffin, a middle-class member of her community who attended Springdale High School in a northeastern suburb. Rosalind was never close to any particular teacher, but she performed well academically. She received encouragement to proceed on to college, but the basic tone of her school years was unhappiness. She remarked, "In terms of peers, I didn't feel comfortable." She was always visible, as one of the few Black students in school, and this feeling was especially painful around social events, like school dances. While school was often a test, it became one that Rosalind consistently failed when dating and partying emerged in her preteen years. With few social outlets, Rosalind devoted much of her energy to schoolwork. She described this period of her life: "I was very proud of the kind of student I was. I enjoyed it. About all I had to do was study, I didn't have a lot of other activities. I took pride in getting on the honor roll."

While they could desegregate their suburban communities without incident, and their middle-class addresses secured access to excellent educational facilities for their daughters, the Griffin and Johnson families were not fully accepted in their communities. Socially Karen associated with the other working-class members of her community. Her mother kept all the children busy, and Karen also attended summer school and worked part-time. More socially isolated, Rosalind lacked close friends and social outlets. While these parents sacrificed to give their children the best education within their means, they were not able to grasp the unhappiness their daughters experienced in these environments.[11]

Rosalind and Karen were two of six women in such settings, and their comments are echoed in the interviews and written responses of other subjects. Suburban high schools in the 1960s offered more extensive college preparatory courses and more scholastically sophisticated programs than urban comprehensive high schools. This difference was a major motivator for Black parents to relocate to suburbs, but such a strategy placed their children in educational settings that were overwhelmingly White. Joyce Saunders initially faced difficulties and then continued to feel marginal. Often the women remained outsiders in these racially homogeneous bedroom communities. They paid dearly for the excellent academic preparation they received.

The women in urban high schools were also very likely to be token Black students in the honors or college preparatory programs, but these women benefited if there were other Black students in their schools. When the school board redistricted students to desegregate their city's high schools, Carolyn Greene and her sister, Marion, were part of a small group of Black students reassigned to a previously all-White high school. They left their predominantly Black working-class community and commuted across the city to desegregate this institution. Carolyn discussed being very sensitive to her visibility as one of a few Black students in the school. She recalled: "There was a small minority of Black students in a sea of White faces. In my high school most of the Black students were not college bound, while the majority of the White students were." Carolyn keenly felt isolated in the college preparatory program. The fact that she received little support in that program left her questioning her placement. Unlike those Black women who lived in the suburbs and small cities, Carolyn found her situation in schools to be different from her experiences in her neighborhood, where she was socially accepted.

Graduates of predominantly White high schools recalled their teachers and school administrators as ambivalent about the presence of Black students. While these women would later desegregate colleges that had not yet developed plans to address race, they initially encountered this lack of planning in high school. Specifically, these institutions failed to prepare faculty to handle the dynamics of addressing racial issues in interracial settings (Inniss 1995; Schofield 1982). Many teachers did not develop skills in addressing these issues, since they viewed themselves as teachers of academic subjects, not social matters. Only a few respondents recalled facing open hostility from teachers and administrators (like the experience of Joyce Saunders discussed in Chapter 4), but most had to endure years of social isolation because of their schools' unwillingness to acknowledge racial issues and their expectation that these new Black students would just fit in. Education scholars have identified this stance as a color-blind view of interracial schooling (Rist 1974). As Schofield (1982) notes: "From the color-blind perspective it is unfair or at least inappropriate to bring up race, since it is essentially irrelevant to one's needs and the opportunities that should be provided. Even taking note of race is seen as an indication of possible prejudice" (p. 50).[12] Addressing race was taboo for many White people, so students and teachers were not supposed to notice racial differences and were to focus instead on learning and teaching.

The lack of faculty leadership in interracial interaction meant that much of the work of adjusting fell on these Black women themselves (Inniss 1994, 1995).[13] Moreover, they were doing this integration work with few, if any, sources of social and emotional support within their high schools. Women reported feeling very visible as one of the few Black students in any setting, as though they were always on stage. Because there were no formal venues for addressing racial issues, it was up to the women to manage racial borders, and they varied in how well they did.

The respondents recalled White students as uncertain about approaching them. In cases of desegregation efforts, many White students resented the invasion of their schools by Black students, especially in East City. When Black students were not welcomed it shaped their reactions to their new environments. Marion Greene had been looking forward to attending her district high school, so the reassignment to a former all-White school upset her plans. Marion identified most of her friends as "lower-middle-class Black students" in different tracks.[14] The school had many academic programs, as well as business and general studies. Marion was in the standard academic program, so she took courses that met the prerequisites for college, but the majority of her friends were not college bound. Meanwhile, the scholars program at the school was all White. Marion's social involvement with her White classmates was minimal. She continued to associate with Black peers who commuted with her.

Francine Chambers, a working-class student who chose to desegregate her midwestern urban high school, recalled, "I attended a high school felt to be academically superior to the neighborhood high school." In her school, Francine reached out to the students in her college preparatory program and developed a mixed group of friends: "My friends were Jewish, middle and upper class and very goal oriented. They had a wide range of professional aspirations. Most have gone past college either to professional schools or for advanced degrees." While she did her best to cope, it was still hard for Francine to be one of only a few Black students in the academic program. Her visibility in the college preparatory program caused her to feel "pressured by the competitiveness of the White students and having to prove that [she] was intelligent." However, the experience did enable her to "learn the ability to think critically, verbalize thoughts logically, and speak clearly and with authority." In the end, Francine felt ambivalent about high school.[15] Making friends in majority White schools required crossing boundaries, which Francine obviously did. However, her ambivalent assessment of her high school might indicate the stress of that activity.

Social life, an important sphere for high school students, was a troublesome area for Black women in majority White schools. Janet Schofield's (1982) work on the middle school revealed that normative patterns in male-female recreational activities limited the cross-racial relationships for junior high school girls more than boys. While boys were often integrated through athletic events and formal games that required large groups, "girls tended to interact in small groups of just two or three. The membership in these dyads and triads was relatively stable from day to day" (p. 102). These patterns left Black girls more isolated. That isolation increased when young people began active dating. Schofield found that in the eighth grade, when romantic relations began to model adult patterns, the "traditional status order of our society" worked to the disadvantage of Black girls.[16] Socially, these were lonely years for Black women in predominantly White suburbs and towns.[17] The experiences of two suburban women suggest that while they participated in school activities with White peers, they did not necessarily develop close friendships. Joyce Saunders did little dating in high school and would often return to her former urban community to see friends. Rosalind Griffin was certainly lonely and did not have close relationships with White peers. While she grew up in a suburban community and went through school with the same people, she did not even know where her former classmates went to college. In these settings, the prejudices and ambivalence of many White students kept these Black women at a distance.

The suburban experience improves when there are larger populations of Black students. While Mary Knight said there were a few Black students in her community high school of 1,500, and Marlene Turner noted that there were less than fifty Black students in her school of 1,800, they each had more Black peers than Karen, Rosalind, or Joyce.[18] Marlene and Mary were frequently either the only Black student or one of two in advanced or college preparatory courses. Both were separated from their Black friends by the school schedule. Mary noted: "Most of the time you were limited by class schedule to only running into people in your courses. So my school friends were predominantly White and Jewish, while my out-of-school friends were all Black and from varying social classes. My courses with Black friends were limited to Physical Education and Civics." Although isolated in her academic classes, the school provided Marlene with a cohort of Black students with whom she interacted. Thus, in the end, her assessment of the high school was positive. She remarked: "I enjoyed high school; it was my only social outlet outside my family."

In these high schools, the level of racial tension was exacerbated by the fact that the majority of the student body was not only White, but middle class. Thus the Black working-class students faced both racial and class biases. The class bias was a major factor in securing support for college and career goals.

SOCIAL CLASS MATTERS

All the predominantly White public high schools attended by these women had excellent academic programs. As comprehensive institutions, they also had systems for deciding the placement of individual students. Frequently high school students were assigned to a track by counselors and/or teachers who reviewed their grades and achievement test scores (Cicourel and Kitsuse 1963; Oakes 1985). Parental or student choice was not always permitted or encouraged. In the end, social class influenced the women's ability to get into college preparatory and honors programs. Spade, Columba, and Vanfossen (1997) found that in the more affluent high schools, teachers relied on objective criteria, such as test scores and grades, in assigning students to courses and programs. They were less likely to be influenced by parent and student wishes than teachers in schools with less affluent student bodies. Most of the high schools attended by these women could be considered affluent, because of their location in suburban areas and middle-class sections of the inner city. Thus the working class students, who may have lacked the cultural capital of middle-class students, could anticipate more barriers to college preparatory programs unless they could readily demonstrate their abilities on tests. However, even if these high schools wanted to minimize the demands of parents, the protest of Black parents could be very effective.

The graduates of predominantly White schools praised the level of academic preparation their schools offered, but the support they received for academic goals was inconsistent. The women's stories reveal the complexities of race and class in these urban and suburban settings. All five of the middle-class women reported receiving encouragement for the goal of attending college, evidence that class privileges were effective in these schools. As the daughters of professionals, Marlene Turner and Mary Knight were encouraged by their teachers to go to college and even to think about a career. Mary commented, "The reason I suspect that I received encouragement was that my father was on the school board." We know from Rosalind Griffin's and Joyce Saunders's experiences that support was general, in terms of the curriculum and information, but personal attention was lacking.

Support for the working-class women's college goals was sporadic. Four of the working-class women had their educational plans supported, but three did not. Carolyn and Marion Greene were reassigned to predominantly White high schools and even placed in college preparatory programs because of their previous achievements.[19] Marion noted that high school was a rude awakening. During her first week, she was shocked at how ill prepared she was for high school. Her educational preparation in both elementary and junior high was inadequate. Both Marion and Carolyn worked very hard and stayed in the college preparatory program. However, they did not receive encouragement or special attention from their teachers. The poor preparation of Black students in predominantly Black junior high schools was often interpreted by White teachers as evidence that Black students lacked abilities. As a result, these teachers were not likely to view Black students' aspirations for college as serious and so withheld encouragement.

All of these working-class women were successful in making their way into either the college preparatory or honors tracks; they thus received a solid education. However, they were not universally accepted by teachers and students in these programs. Of the six working-class graduates, only Nancy Brooks received consistent support from school officials. Because she was a high achieving student in junior high, school officials thought Nancy would fit in with the majority White population of her new school.[20] And indeed, Nancy did not suffer academically. In her high school she continued to be a diligent student, even developing a passion for mathematics. College was an important goal and attending Wilson High helped her attain it.

In retrospect, Nancy was pleased with the curriculum but troubled by the great stress on individual high achievement. Track placement also kept her isolated from other Black students. Nancy said, "I was in the highest ability groups. In the college prep program high achievement was stressed. Most of my friends were those traveling from the same junior high school and they were in the normal ability groups. In my classes, I felt out of place socially." Nancy, who identified her family as "very poor," also faced social class barriers to participation in activities. The majority of students were middle class, and money was essential for involvement in many school activities. Some of Nancy's friends were cheerleaders, but she could not afford the funds for the uniforms. Therefore she did not even try out. She enjoyed participation in the school chorus. Unlike her White classmates, Nancy took a part-time job in high school both to save money for college and to help with living expenses. Upon graduation, she was academically prepared for college and even went to an elite college, but she felt different from her classmates in terms of both race and social class.

As we will see in Chapter 7, the task of being socially mobile could be taxing on Black women in this cohort. The lack of strong academic support often meant that the women did not develop solid confidence in their abilities. It was particularly difficult when their parents' expectations for them were not supported by teachers and school officials. Janet Sheldon attended a district high school in her midsized northeastern city, where Black people were less than 10 percent of the city's population and, consequently, of the high school's. Janet's problems did not end after winning a fight to get into the college-bound track. Her mother expected her to get high grades, which she did. During Janet's high school years, her mother regularly visited the school, met with teachers, and closely monitored her daughter's progress. Not only a racial minority, Janet was one of the few working-class students in the honors program. Although she did very well in her classes, Janet did not receive encouragement from teachers to attend college or to plan for a career. She remarked, "Most of my encouragement came from home, church, and social activities."

Janet still reported that she enjoyed high school. Like many in predominantly White schools, she had two groups of friends. They were "mostly White and affluent in classes, and mostly Black and working class in social situations. Many of my [Black] friends were made in church, and they went to school in suburban areas." Her parents were strict and did not allow her to go to many dances and parties. She recalled, "I was rather shy and inhibited and somewhat unsure of myself in social situations." Another student, Francine Chambers, also worked very hard to take advantage of the educational opportunity. She noted that encouragement for college at school was mixed: "I was told by my guidance counselor that I wasn't college material. [She said] I should try junior college. My history and English teachers encouraged me to go to college and that gave me confidence. Most of my White friends were thinking about advanced degrees and professional schools."

Some teachers strongly encouraged Karen Johnson to take the commercial course like the majority of the White working-class girls in her suburban high school. It was her family's insistence that kept her in the college preparatory program. Specific interactions with teachers frequently shaped Karen's attitudes toward the subject matter they taught. For example, one year she liked history, math, biology, and especially creative writing, because those teachers were encouraging, but the next year teachers might not be encouraging. As a bright student, Karen performed well, but she only studied what she liked. Her family was her major source of support during the difficult high school years. As the youngest of three children, Karen found that her older siblings were helpful at this period of her life. They encouraged her to study and reminded her of her potential. These supports helped her combat the negative influences of the high school faculty who had low expectations of her.

Predominantly White schools were less likely to provide the solid encouragement for careers that was found in predominantly Black schools. When asked if teachers or school officials encouraged them to plan for a career, only three middle-class women said "Yes," while two middle-class women and the seven working-class women said "No." The lack of attention to careers could reflect gender socialization in the White community and the race/gendered expectations teachers had for Black women. In the early 1960s, these White educators might have assumed that women, even if they went to college, would not spend extended time in the labor market. So they could have been passing on majority culture goals for girls. It is fair to assume that these women, as a new racial group in their high schools, were neglected because guidance and counseling staff did not anticipate their unique needs.

Overall, it was not easy for these Black women to be tokens in college preparatory programs in predominantly White high schools. The lack of schoolwide preparation for desegregation made negotiating in these schools difficult for all the women, but facing a class as well as a racial divide meant more complications for the working-class women. In the end, the middle-class respondents from predominantly White high schools often had excellent chances of continuing on to college, because of the educational foundation and the reputations of their high schools. At the same time, they felt highly visible as their race made it hard for even these Black women to fit in when there was little assistance from faculty in easing interactions. The working-class women also faced issues of visibility, but they did not receive consistent support for their academic goals. Coupled with their token status, this meant that predominantly White comprehensive high schools were often rough places for these women, even though the academic preparation they received was solid. Only Nancy Brooks had relatively few doubts about her intellectual abilities; the other five working-class women did not find their high schools personally supportive of their educational advancement. Though all were in classes designed to prepare students for college, most received either consistently negative or mixed signals about their own abilities to tackle college. While they gained in terms of academic exposure, these were not confidence-building situations. In the face of mixed messages at school, the women's families, community peers, and church affiliations were far more consistent sources of support for their educational goals and careers.

Integrated High Schools

Eighteen women, eleven from the working class and seven from the middle class, graduated from integrated comprehensive high schools. Schools classified here as "integrated" are those that the respondents indicated had student populations ranging from about 15 to 50 percent Black. Many scholars acknowledge that an integrated school experience is the best setting for an education in a democracy because students are exposed to young people and faculty from different income brackets, races, ethnicities, and physical capabilities. Such heterogeneous experiences can do much to promote tolerance of differences, and an appreciation of others can build support for cultural pluralism. There is evidence in this study that such schools could achieve this goal. Yvonne Foster, a middle-class respondent, recalled that "close relationships were formed during this time and maintained through college." Surrounded by Black as well as White peers—often with Black friends who were also college bound—the women who attended integrated schools did not experience the chronic isolation found among middle- and working-class women in predominantly White high schools.

Integrated high schools were often the first choice of Black families.[21] But in the early 1960s there were few genuinely integrated high schools. As these women's experiences will demonstrate, integrated comprehensive settings were not fully successful in providing a supportive and accepting environment for all students, because social class and race continued as key dimensions of inequality, particularly as they shaped teachers' expectations of students. These expectations resulted in assignment to specific tracks and influenced the level of educational preparation the students received. As in other comprehensive high schools, the class position of middle-class Black women worked to their advantage. As they entered integrated comprehensive high schools, working-class respondents faced the major task of securing a college preparatory education. Their social class and race worked to their disadvantage in these settings. Seven of the eleven working-class women received encouragement, and four did not. However, all seven middle-class women were encouraged to attend college. Integrated schools were often positive environments for Black middle-class women because their class privilege fostered incorporation into the school. In contrast, these schools were settings of intense struggles for women from the working class.

If individual cities had educational policies that promoted integrated schools along both race and social class lines, then more school districts would be integrated.[22] During this era, public policy structured school districts that were designed to promote advantage for those already privileged and to limit opportunities for the working class. But because some comprehensive high schools were very large, they were naturally integrated. The women's comments revealed that public integrated high schools could have very different patterns of tracking with regard to race. The most common pattern, in twelve of the eighteen schools, was to have Black students screened out of the highest tracks. For example, Yvonne Foster reported that the racial balance in her high school was not reflected in the tracking for specific courses. She noted, "Students were divided into academic courses with subgroups of languages, math, or science. And then there were general and business tracks. The students in the academic group were geared to go to college. The academic track was composed of middle- and upper middle-class Whites and some very select Blacks."

Another middle-class respondent, Helene Montgomery, was one of six women who reported that Black students were well mixed within tracks. Her high school in a midwestern city was racially integrated, both in overall school composition and in the tracks. She said, "My high school had a college prep, regular academic, and then courses related to trades. There was a large percentage of college-bound students who were middle- and upper-class Blacks and Whites—mostly Whites. The school was about a third or more Black and there was proportionate representation of Blacks in all the tracks." The racial balance was an asset, but Helene's school was far from perfect. Helene's description indicates that she was not as sensitive to the fact that working-class students, Black or White, were missing among the college-bound students. Even though she recognized little racial discrimination, comprehensive high schools were designed to reproduce the social class structure (Colclough and Beck 1986). Given that the majority of Black students in many urban schools are working class, the class barriers in comprehensive high schools influence their access to channels for success.

All of the middle-class women were enrolled in college preparatory programs, while nine of the eleven working-class women were successful in getting the courses essential to meet college prerequisites. Their comments on the questionnaires and in interviews indicate that the racial balance of the tracks was an important factor. For the middle-class women in integrated high schools, the racial balance influenced their sentiments about their schools, but for the working-class women it often was a factor in the ease with which they could enter the college-bound track. Teachers were more likely to grant credence to the college aspirations of the children of Black professionals than the children of Black clerks, factory workers, postal workers, and domestic workers. Given the formalized tracking in high schools, the task of proving oneself to be college material was difficult in a milieu that neglected Black and working-class youth. Examinations, counselors, and other barriers had to be challenged to gain access. If students' grades were not solid, these doors could be closed. Aspirations of mobility were questioned when working-class students arrived from predominantly Black junior high schools, where their preparation might not have put them on par with the performance of middle-class Black and White students. Thus, while the middle-class women reported receiving encouragement to proceed on to college, the eleven working-class graduates of integrated high schools reported many struggles as they negotiated with gatekeepers to gain access to college preparatory courses and to college itself.

THE WORKING-CLASS STORY

The first step in the route to college for working-class women was to enter their school's college preparatory program. Working-class women were challenging class barriers when they wanted access to such programs, which were dominated by middle-class students. Nine working-class women were successful in getting the courses essential for entering college. Most faced barriers, and while they might have obtained the courses, they did not necessarily receive encouragement for their goals. The racial balance of the tracks was an important factor in their success.

Sylvia Mason attended a school where Black students were well integrated through the different tracks, including the honors and academic track. The school was her small urban community's only high school.[23] Not only did Sylvia find this racial balance a comfort, she was also encouraged to attend college. Furthermore, she enjoyed her social experiences and was supported in thinking about a career in foreign languages. Sylvia was typical in her praise of the social atmosphere in integrated high schools. She reported having "friends of all social classes and races, who were all planning to attend college." However, not all integrated high schools had racially balanced tracks.

If the college preparatory programs or honors tracks were overwhelmingly White, even bright Black students had difficulty gaining access to them. If a working-class Black student found Black peers in these predominantly White settings, the other Black students were most often from the middle class. Integrated high schools were places where these bright working-class Black women learned that White students were preferred over Black students and that middle-class Black students were preferred over their working-class counterparts. Therefore the experiences of working-class women in integrated high schools differed from those of their counterparts in predominantly White high schools. Students like Carolyn and Marion Greene had to overcome the poor preparation of predominantly Black junior high schools when they made the transition to high school. However, since the school was in the early stages of desegregating, the Black students were all from the same working-class neighborhood. Integrated high schools, on the other hand, attracted both working- and middle-class Black students. The middle-class students had cultural capital and better educational preparation than the working-class ones. This contrast often made it appear that the working-class Black women were just not able to succeed in these new environments. The fact that there is little national dialogue about social class means people are more likely to seek individualistic explanations than to look at students' class backgrounds and the different cultural capital they bring into schools.

Adele Lewis, who described her own family's position as "upper poor," was the most honored student in her predominantly Black junior high school. In her integrated high school, she recognized that the middle-class Black students received more rewards and verbal encouragement from teachers than the working-class students. Adele consistently did well in school and was acknowledged as very bright by most teachers. Yet she felt some social distance from the Black middle-class students in most of her classes. She recalled her experience: "At Jefferson High School I met my first aspiring middle-class Blacks, the kids who lived on the 'Hill.' I didn't even know what hill they were talking about. . . . I had good grades for college, but I didn't make honor society. I didn't hang with the Black students in the honor society. I got invited to their parties, since we were in class together, but I didn't go."

Darlene Maxwell had to compete with Black students from the middle class to be seen as college material. Her grades in her integrated junior high school and her mother's determination enabled her to enter the school's academic program, but she was basically ignored by her teachers. While many Black students were in the college preparatory program in her all-girls high school, Darlene noticed racial differences in treatment. She described the course divisions: "The academic program was about divided equally between Black and White students, but the majority of the White girls in the student body were in this division, while most Black students were in home economics or the general division. It was also very difficult to move from one division to another." Darlene only received encouragement from teachers after she took the PSAT examination. Scoring well on this national examination gave her aspirations legitimacy. However, teachers never considered her talented enough to attend a high-ranking college and did not urge her to plan for a career, even though she was president of her senior class.[24] Upon reflection, Darlene did not enjoy high school and thought it was uninspiring and quite restrictive.[25] "My best friends were very smart, but only a few attended my school. My other friends went to Best Girls High or to Catholic schools and they were all going to college."

Graduates of predominantly Black junior high schools, like Dorothy Wall, found the transition to integrated high schools difficult. Even in the face of hostility from White teachers, Dorothy had been a diligent and cooperative student in junior high school. She approached high school with the goal of proceeding on to college. Dorothy was shocked by her initial performance and discouraged by the attitudes of her high school teachers, who were quick to interpret her poor grades as accurate reflections of her abilities. "One major drawback of junior high school—the ghetto school—was it really didn't prepare you for an integrated high school. Levels of achievement which were perfectly acceptable in junior high school would earn you a D in high school. In junior high I was on the honor roll. In high school, that first semester was like a shock treatment. My A became C. There was no way over a three-month period you could become so stupid. My study habits, that had earned me As and Bs, honor roll grades in junior high, could earn me nothing but Cs and Ds in high school." Like many of the other Black students who encountered intense screening in comprehensive high schools, Dorothy did not face this crisis alone. Her parents, who had closely monitored her previous schooling, were equally concerned about her transition to high school. Dorothy spoke about that time:

> My mother came up to school and wanted to know what was going on. They told her I was not prepared. I was an A student in one school and the pride and joy of the teachers. These old [junior high school] teachers would acclaim: "Oh, she is great, a fantastic student, and can do this and that." This led me to believe that I was not stupid. I am saying this because someone [at the high school] told me and my parents that I was a bright kid, that I had it. "It is not that you have suddenly become stupid, but that you have not been prepared. You have the brains to learn and can grasp whatever you want to learn." And it was that faith that it wasn't me that kind of got me through. And I just wonder how many kids went through that crisis and didn't have someone to say, "It's not you, it is the amount of information you have been given. It is the exposure you have been given."

Dorothy received some support from a few teachers who recognized that her initial performance was the result of discriminatory treatment, but it was mostly reassurance from her parents that helped her weather this crisis. Her poor junior high school preparation meant that Dorothy had to work extra hard in high school. She did improve, received encouragement from a few teachers, and went directly to college. Dorothy was able to reach her goals, but as with other working-class Black women in integrated high schools, it was a struggle. The journey through high school was not a pleasant one for Dorothy, and at the time of the interview in 1976, these memories were still vivid and painful.[26]

Dorothy Wall was successful in overcoming the institutionalized racism of northern schools, but not all the women were successful. Gloria McDonald noted that the majority of the Black students in her high school were directed to commercial and business courses, because teachers thought they belonged there; the college preparatory program was reserved for White students. Studies have found that learning and self-esteem can be negatively affected in students placed in lower ability groups (Oakes 1985). While reflecting on her high school years, Gloria noted, "The teachers simply did not encourage Black students to go to college. They thought most of us were dumb. It took me a long time to overcome the effects of being labeled as dumb and not college material. In retrospect, high school was a lousy, traumatic experience." Neither Gloria, who graduated from high school in 1960, nor Stephanie Lawrence, a 1959 graduate, could cross the boundaries that kept their schools' academic tracks almost exclusively White. Indeed, they were actively discouraged from academic pursuits.[27] These two women entered college five and six years, respectively, after high school. During those years they worked in factory and clerical jobs and then were recruited to attend a commuter college.

As a group, these working-class women were successful despite many problems in high schools. The majority, the nine who were in college preparatory courses, did receive the education that opened college doors for them. However, two of these women were never encouraged to continue on to college while they were in high school. Only a minority, that is, four women, were ever encouraged to think about careers. Their entrance into college would be clouded by the many ways their schools failed them. Their stories demonstrate how confronting the limitations of tracking can be troublesome for high ability Black working-class students.

Blatantly missing in these stories is the special attention that talented students would have more likely received in predominantly Black high schools in desegregated urban communities near the Mason-Dixon line. We can glimpse that attention by looking at the case of Adele Lewis, who was one of the four working-class women encouraged to plan for a career. In her case, as with other Black women, it was not unilateral support from all teachers, but encouragement from a few teachers. Furthermore, Adele was one of the few graduates interviewed from a majority White comprehensive high school who reported that she was close to a teacher. Since Adele came from a working-class family, where neither parent had college experience, the realm of higher education was foreign to her. Adele's parents, who did not initially encourage her to attempt college, could not give her specific information about the world she hoped to enter. Thus the cognitive and emotional support of a teacher in her integrated school was important in helping Adele visualize her future. Even after many years, Adele was grateful for the attention a teacher showed her. She described this relationship and where it fit into her life:

> I was close to this teacher on a minimal level. I was not as close as some of my classmates, who would pour out their problems to teachers. I was never into pouring out my problems, but I did talk about what I wanted to be when I grew up. I asked questions like what is it like to be a journalist or a writer and so forth. I was encouraged in that direction. That was the kind of support that was there for me in high school, because I didn't discuss these things at home. The whole support for my going to college came out of high school. In the college prep program, we were all going to college. And after January, there were lots of preparations about where to go for SATS and different things. At school, they made sure we wrote away for materials. I never doubted that I was going to college; it was not just a dream. I just blithely thought about going to college. Then later the reality hit me that we didn't have the money and I had to do different things [from my peers]. Within the tiny environment [the world of high school] I was going to college, but I had no idea of what college was like. School was different from home, where it wasn't discussed. I wasn't discouraged at home, they just didn't get involved with it.

In many respects, all of these women can be viewed as exceptions. It took bravery to challenge teachers' and fellow students' limited expectations of them. Support from their families was very important in keeping alive educational goals and in sustaining the women as they struggled to convince school officials of their abilities. Yet their success should not detract from the fact that comprehensive high schools contained major barriers for students of color and working-class youth across this nation.[28]

THE MIDDLE-CLASS STORY

Of all the Black women in classes with White peers, the middle-class women in integrated high schools appeared to be the most satisfied with both the social and academic aspects of high school. They were most similar to the women in seg-regated and predominantly Black high schools with regard to having a well-rounded high school career. All seven of the middle-class subjects who graduated from urban integrated comprehensive high schools expressed satisfaction with various aspects of the experience.[29] They did not experience the intense pressures of being a token because they were part of a significant Black student body. They were involved in extracurricular activities, often assuming schoolwide leadership roles. This involvement meant their high school met their requirements for a full social life. Furthermore, because they were already middle class, teachers re-spected their goals of college attendance. All were in college preparatory pro-grams and received support for that goal. Two middle-class respondents, Michelle Clark and Beverly Rawlins, were typical of graduates from the integrated compre-hensive high schools where students were racially balanced in all tracks. Michelle Clark was an excellent student who was also active in various school clubs. The majority of her school friends were working- and middle-class Black Americans. She felt comfortable in her school, and it gave her the means to investigate different aspects of the world around her.

Beverly Rawlins applauded her racially mixed high school, recalling that the student body was about 50 percent Black, 20 percent White, 15 percent Latino, and 15 percent Asian American. After many years of being a token in predomi-nantly White private schools, Beverly welcomed the change. She was active in various aspects of school life and speaks with pleasure about those days. She recalled: "I did gymnastics, worked on the newspaper, and was in one of the women's service organizations. I was in student government. I was in a lot of the different clubs they have in high school."

The faculty in Beverly's school was also racially mixed; she thought about 20 percent of the teachers were people of color. Yet Beverly indicated that she never had a Black teacher: "I don't remember any of them teaching college preparatory courses." In her comprehensive high school, minority faculty members were concentrated in the commercial and vocational tracks. This pattern was typical among schools with a history of discrimination in hiring practices; racial minor-ity faculty were frequently new and not assigned what were seen by school administrators as the "best classes" (i.e., college preparatory classes) in the 1960s. Still, the presence of Black and other racial minority faculty was important to the Black students because of the perception of greater equality among the races. This atmosphere facilitated integration in the schools.

Unlike their counterparts in predominantly Black educational settings, the women in integrated high schools reported that there was less attention given to paid employment goals in their schools. The middle-class women were very positive about their academic and social experiences and not concerned about the lack of attention to their future goals. Yvonne Foster was one of three middle-class women who was encouraged by teachers to plan for a career. However, she was urged either to be a teacher or a nurse, while her own parents held higher aspirations for her. Neither Michelle Clark nor Beverly Rawlins was encouraged to plan for a career. While the neglect of occupational concerns is a contrast to the experiences of women in predominantly Black high schools, the lack of concern by these middle-class respondents may have been compensated for by strong parental support for their careers.

Praise for integrated high schools among the middle class was not unanimous. Overall, students appeared to be most pleased if they perceived their schools as well integrated, meaning that Black students were found in all tracks. However, the majority of integrated high schools had a racial bias in tracking. If a middle-class Black student was isolated in the honors or college preparatory program, like Susan Thomas was, she could very well experience some of the problems found among those who attended predominantly White schools. Susan attended a high school in the Midwest where students were tracked into "gifted, regular, and dumb" courses. Susan was critical of the school because the division between tracks constituted hurdles to interaction with other Black students. She thought that only about 10 to 15 percent of the Black students were placed in gifted classes. Most of Susan's friends were in regular classes, so she moved between two peer groups. "I socialized with middle-class Blacks who had college aspirations. Most of them were the sons and daughters of my parents' friends. Then the majority of my classmates were middle- to upper-class Whites also with aspirations of college and professional life." As a token Black student in the top classes, Susan found herself bridging a gap between the predominantly White college-bound honor students and the Black students in regular academic classes. The tension Susan experienced could have motivated her to think more critically than her White peers in the honors course. Having close friends in the regular classes gave her more than one vantage point on the school.

Susan graduated sixteenth in a class of over 400 students, the highest-ranking Black student in her class. She participated in clubs and school activities, even holding leadership roles, and was cognizant of the excellent education she received, but she was also aware of the unfair treatment many Black students received in that school. She noted that this discrimination was most evident in the guidance and counseling services, where Black students and their aspirations were not taken seriously. The guidance for Susan was poor, but her parents, both educators, were able to compensate for this failure on the part of the school.

Susan's obvervations were echoed in comments from both Michelle Clark and

Yvonne Foster. Like the other middle-class graduates of integrated schools, they were pleased with the academic and social lives they built. Yet the sharp divisions in tracks and the differential treatment of students was evident to them and tempered their praise for their schools. Having both middle- and working-class Black friends in other tracks revealed their own privileges and broadened their perspectives on their high schools.

Their college experiences would be a surprise for the middle-class women who graduated from integrated high schools. They would find themselves to be highly visible tokens in settings with an overwhelming majority of White students and faculty. Luckily, their high schools prepared them academically for college and also enabled them to make connections with peers and develop the self-assurance needed to meet the challenges of the next educational level. They also had strong parental support in the areas where their high schools were lacking.

CHAPTER 6 : ELITE HIGH SCHOOLS
The Cost of Advantages

My mother and I both thought I should go to a coeducational high school. I didn't consider Catholic schools because I was not Catholic and was tired of Catholic schools. My first cousin was at Honors High. Although we saw very little of each other, I think that [his presence] had something to do with the decision. There were so few Blacks at Honors High. I don't think I ever had another Black student in one of my classes. Imagine, I was there for four years and was never in a class with another Black student.
—*Beth Warren, working-class graduate of a predominantly White public high school*

There are many advantages of a private school that one needs as a Black person. I was not labeled as an upward bound person. At University High, I got a good education—a standardized English education. I didn't have many academic problems at the school. There were a lot of [social] class problems that people might mistake for race problems, but they didn't apply to me. The education helped me go to a prestigious college and graduate school and to get into this firm. Attending University High put me in a network of old school buddies which helped me professionally.
—*Deborah Jones, middle-class graduate of a predominantly White private school*

The seventeen Black women discussed in this chapter attended either private schools, parochial schools, or public high schools that required a certain grade point average or an entrance examination for admission. Unlike public comprehensive high schools that have to serve all students, these schools were highly selective. They also had a different mission, most focused on preparing students for college. These schools are referred to in this study as elite high schools, because of their high level of academic preparation and the fact that they sent the majority of their graduates to four-year colleges. These schools often lacked tracks, but even if there were different courses, most of the screening of students happened before they entered the schools.[1] Not only did students get an education designed to get them into college, their schools' reputations made them attractive applicants to prestigious colleges.

These women traveled different paths to their elite high schools. What the middle-class families secured with money, the working class secured by other means. As noted in Chapter 3, if middle-class parents were displeased with their district comprehensive high schools, they could bypass their residential school assignment and send their children to institutions outside the public school system. Private and parochial schools require that parents pay tuition, although fees at parochial schools are generally lower than those at private schools because churches underwrite many expenses. Often these schools offer scholarships, but rarely do they cover all expenses; instead, these funds supplement what parents can afford. Consequently, in the 1960s it was mostly middle-class Black families who could afford private schools, while both working-class and middle-class families made use of parochial schools.

A total of seven women in this study attended either private or parochial schools: one working-class woman and three middle-class women graduated from parochial high schools, and three middle-class women graduated from private high schools. The graduates of private schools had 400 or fewer students in their co-educational institutions. The women in church-affiliated schools were also part of small school populations. Katrina Charles's coeducational religious school had 500 students enrolled in kindergarten through the twelfth grade. The other three graduates of parochial schools attended relatively small, all-girls high schools that had from 500 to 600 students over all four grades. The women in Catholic schools indicated that the girls were tracked into either academic or business courses.

Tracking was rare in private schools, where all students shared a core curriculum directing them to college. Not tied to programs required by public boards of education, private schools were free to develop their own curricula. Many schools defined themselves as college preparatory schools, making them attractive to middle-class Black families who were leery about the academic preparation available in their district high schools. Many private schools assigned college level textbooks, especially for courses in the junior and senior years. Students took advanced courses for college placement and graduated with critical skills under their belts. Many wrote research papers and did other assignments that anticipated the first two years of college. For example, Irma Dennis expected college to be challenging but found it sadly disappointing. She said, "Frankly, it was not as hard as high school. I worked ten times harder in high school than I ever worked in college." Parents were willing to pay for such instruction to ensure their daughters' futures.

Many major cities offered a public school alternative to the district comprehensive high school. Such schools rivaled the level of academic preparation in private schools, but they were only open to qualified students. A student could bypass her assigned district high school by testing well and qualifying to attend a citywide school. These schools are identified as specialized high schools in this study. The area of specialization for the schools varied: the majority were academic, but there were also schools for students with musical, artistic, or dancing talents. Seven working-class and three middle-class respondents attended high schools that required examinations or high grade point averages in junior high or grammar school. When available, specialized high schools were used by middle-class Black students as an alternative to private or parochial schools. If middle-class women failed to gain access to these specialized public schools, private schools remained an option. On the other hand, specialized curricula high schools were the only nondistrict options for most working-class women. For example, Tracy Edwards, a working-class respondent, grew up in a predominantly Black community, and her district high school was predominantly Black. Tracy tested very well and was able to attend a predominantly White, all-girls academic high school with a reputation for sending its graduates to prestigious colleges.

Specialized high schools varied in size more than private or parochial schools. Cheryl Davis's arts high school had 700 students, while Katherine Howell's university-affiliated school had only 250. The other academic specialized high schools, all located in the North, had over 1,000 students each. Linda Trott and Olivia Stevens's school, Academic High, in a mid-Atlantic city, had over 2,000 girls. Beth Warren's coeducational academic high school had 2,800 students from across her eastern city. Other schools varied from 1,200 to 1,500 students. Only three graduates of specialized high schools (Cheryl Davis, Katherine Howell, and Beth Warren) attended coeducational schools; the other seven women graduated from all-girls institutions. Academic specialized high schools provided rigorous curricula designed to prepare all their graduates for college. Only two respondents reported that these schools were tracked. For example, in addition to the college preparatory course, Academic High had an advanced track for selected students.[2] Linda Trott described the system: "The entire school was academic, drawing citywide college-bound girls. Most [of the] Black students were not in the advanced track. I was, but I was never comfortable."

These elite high schools differed in size and funding, but they were most similar in their racial composition; the majority were predominantly White. Eight middle-class women and seven working-class women graduated from high schools where they were one of the few Black students in attendance. While many private high schools are currently more integrated, in the 1960s the majority located in the North were overwhelmingly White. These respondents were attracted to predominantly White religious schools, some involved in desegregation efforts at this time, because families were looking for solid academic preparation. The large northern specialized public high schools were overwhelmingly White. During the early 1960s, these women were likely to be among the ten to fifteen Black students in attendance in the school or, in the case of large high schools, in the advanced or high honors track.

Only two women, Katherine Howell and Sandra Freeman, graduated from elite schools that were either all Black or integrated. Katherine attended a segregated laboratory school for a traditionally Black university in the South where admission required either affiliation with the university or attaining a certain grade point average. Katherine was the daughter of a working-class couple with no affiliation to the university, so it was high achievement in her segregated parochial grammar school that enabled her to obtain an elite education. Sandra, from a middle-class family, graduated from an integrated parochial boarding school that was outside of the United States.

All the women, both working-class and middle-class, acknowledged the high quality of their academic preparation in the elite schools. Most also reported that they received encouragement from their schools to attend college and even to plan for careers. However, the fact that most were in predominantly White settings posed a series of problems for the women. As seen in Chapter 5, many of the Black women in predominantly White comprehensive high schools received mixed messages about academic achievement, and their schools offered few sources of social and emotional support. Elite high schools, however, were categorically different from comprehensive high schools because most students were preparing for college. Cynthia Butler said, "It was a college preparatory school, and those graduates who decided not to go to college had to pretend to apply to keep the guidance counselors from hounding them to death." Denise Larkin noted that the one student who applied to a secretarial college was accused by the teachers of ruining the reputation of her all-girls school. These high-powered schools presented some unique advantages and disadvantages for Black people at this time.

Entering these previously all-White elite high schools in the early 1960s, the women generally found most teachers, school administrators, and students ambivalent about the presence of Black students. They were admitted because of grades, economic resources, or religious affiliation, yet the institutions, like the comprehensive schools, were not prepared for the issues and problems that desegregating their student bodies posed. Money, religious bonds, and academic achievement could not shelter these women from the reality of living in a racist society. During the turmoil of the high school years, their families and the peer groups they developed provided essential social support.

In the majority White elite schools, the women struggled against a lack of human recognition, as many White students and faculty were color-blind. The differences they reported in the degree of integration into the student community meant that the tensions for middle-class students and their working-class counterparts were different, and the women developed a range of strategies for coping with racial tensions without institutional support. Class difference in cultural capital also meant varied treatment in these schools. The middle-class women had more ease in scaling social gaps because they shared a class background with White peers. Also, many were in small schools that promoted integration into the student culture. In contrast, the working-class women were more likely to be in larger public schools rather than small private facilities. Many felt a class gap between themselves and their peers in the college preparatory programs. Social class and the size of the school were barriers to genuine incorporation into the student body. However, working-class and middle-class women varied in how they negotiated those tensions—especially when color-blind perspectives meant they had to succeed in settings that did not grant them full human recognition (Feagin, Vera, and Imani 1996; Taylor 1994). This ambiguous status of being highly visible yet not recognized manifested itself differently across social class lines.

Elite High Schools for Middle-Class Women

The nine Black middle-class graduates from elite high schools were educated in various settings. Six of these women attended private and parochial schools that were similar to each other in size, although the private schools were more likely to be coeducational. Two graduates of urban specialized high schools attended all-girl environments while one attended a coeducational school; these were all large institutions. This group was most keenly cognizant of the value of an excellent education, since their schools were strong academic institutions. Katrina Charles's elite religious school was recognized as one of the best educational institutions in her city. She recalled: "There were small classes and much individualized attention. The whole school was oriented to developing the intellectual and academic potential of the best students." Wendy Anderson found her boarding school to be intellectually stimulating. She enjoyed the opportunity to attend school with smart people and appreciated the many opportunities to learn. In most cases, the high schools more than adequately prepared these students in terms of academics and encouraged them to proceed to predominantly White colleges.

However, the eight graduates of majority White schools paid dearly for their level of academic preparation.[3] Several remarked that they either did not enjoy high school or were ambivalent about those years because they felt socially isolated and traumatized. Race was still a barrier to receiving solid support for academic goals. It was usually those students who were exceptional academically who received personal encouragement from teachers. Furthermore, the social exchanges, especially with peers, were often tense, given that these women established cross-racial friendships during this era. As a group, they expressed less satisfaction with their high school days than the five middle-class women who attended predominantly White comprehensive high schools. The middle-class women in majority White private and parochial schools were also far less satisfied than middle-class graduates of integrated or predominantly Black schools. Their stories reveal that, while social class resources enabled families to scale racist institutional barriers to provide their daughters with the best education possible, in these new settings the women faced a different type of racial barrier.

ACADEMIC SUPPORT

In majority White settings, race made these Black women outsiders in their schools. Individual academic experiences tended to be more positive when teachers perceived them as very bright students. While middle-class White women received encouragement to pursue careers, Black women had to work through personal issues to be recognized as talented. Only a few Black women received special attention. By high school, Katrina Charles had become more comfortable in her small religious school and was popular with both teachers and students. She recalled:

> I was very self-conscious about the racial stuff the first year in school. There were two other Blacks in the grade. I was not ostracized, but it was due to my own stuff. It was a very supportive environment. I was a good student, one of the smart kids in the top of the class. I didn't study real hard, but it was important. I turned in papers on time and got along with the teachers. I didn't think about being studious, but I still did well. I also did other school activities like athletics, music, and the student council. Academically it was [a] great [school]. I spent ninety percent of my time with schoolmates. I still have friendships from then.

In retrospect, Katrina recognized that it was her sharp intellect that earned her this recognition: "The environment was very supportive to their chosen people. I was really one of the stars. If I hadn't been such a strong student, I might have encountered more racism." Katrina was lucky and had one of the best high school experiences of women in this cohort.

Olivia Stevens, the daughter of a physician, was also well received in her all-girls public school. She even ran for student government. Often it took having high-status professional parents or being at the top of the class to gain recognition. Not all Black women, even middle-class ones, could meet such criteria. Irma Dennis, the daughter of a public school teacher, transferred to a private school in her junior year. She received the benefits of an excellent curriculum, but very little personal attention. When asked if she was encouraged by teachers to attend college, Irma wrote, "No." Because the whole school was college bound, "no individual encouragement was deemed necessary." Yet other graduates of private schools did receive personal encouragement.

Karen Wright's experiences may be typical of Black middle-class women who were desegregating academically specialized high schools in the 1960s. The daughter of a chemist employed as a civil servant for a city hospital and a clerical worker, Karen graduated from a predominantly Black junior high school where she was one of the few Black students in the college preparatory class. Her performance on the citywide examination gave her access to Scholars High, an excellent all-girls high school. Attendance required a three-hour commute each day. Karen's parents were not affluent, so her attendance in a public high school enabled them to save funds for her college years. Along with other students, Karen was exposed to all the information essential to help her get into a good college, but she was overlooked by most teachers. Karen remembered those years as difficult, "On the whole, school was a super bummer. I didn't make any close friends. I only knew one person from my junior high school and we were not in any of the same classes. I was the only sister [Black female] in most of my classes and felt extremely isolated, vulnerable, and insecure." Karen received a good education, went on to a prestigious college, and later trained as a physician. Yet she still carries the pain of her three lonely years in high school.[4] Like others in this position, her family's strong commitment to education and the realization that such credentials would open doors to additional opportunities prompted her to make sacrifices to secure an excellent education. Karen never thought about leaving Scholars High and transferring to another school where she would have more friends. She tolerated this unpleasant situation for the sake of her future mobility and to do her part in contradicting stereotypes about Black people. Her presence in that high school was important for Black students who would come after her, but it was not an easy path to forge.

These respondents recognized the academic advantages of elite schools, even if some lacked personalized treatment, but there were many troublesome issues surrounding their social lives. When asked if they enjoyed high school, five women said yes, three said no, and one was clearly ambivalent (she checked both "Yes" and "No" on the questionnaire). Even if they had a positive response to the question, these women expressed concern about the social consequences of attending their schools. The picture of this period in the respondents' lives is not totally bleak, however. Cheryl Davis attended a specialized high school for art and music students in a northeastern city. In addition to receiving support from teachers, she found her schoolmates to be accepting. Her peer group consisted of "Black and White middle-class students who were all college bound." Cheryl made lasting friendships during this stage of her life. Even in retrospect, Cheryl was particularly moved by the "open mindedness of her fellow students." Perhaps the common interests of art and music among students in her high school encouraged more openness to developing cross-racial friendships with peers of similar interests.

Because the experience of being socially isolated in these intense academic settings was troublesome to many women, they provided more details on this time in their lives than did the women who were pleased with their high-school days. Women like Cheryl Davis did not pay a high personal cost to secure an education. However, among the middle-class women in this study, it appears that such positive experiences were rare in predominantly White elite high schools. The fact that even middle-class women had mixed receptions in the elite schools demonstrates that race was very significant in such environments. However, high academic ability, high-status professional parents, or both could mediate the racism that women found in elite schools.

NAVIGATING TWO WORLDS

Unlike the middle-class Black women in comprehensive high schools, those in elite institutions traveled outside of their communities to attend school. Many had to negotiate race relations in two different worlds. Their social lives could get quite complex, particularly for the Black women in small private schools. These women discussed traveling between two different worlds, the White world of school and the Black world of their communities.[5] Negotiations between peer groups could be intense, especially when the women faced such problems alone. In these elite schools, as in other majority White settings, school officials took no initiative to help students address issues of race.

Some middle-class families sent their children to private schools rather than relocating. These families had established networks of Black friends in their own neighborhoods and provided their children with an active Black social life. Many middle-class respondents were part of either informal or formal social groups like Jack and Jill, a membership organization of Black families with chapters in many cities and now in suburbs.[6] Jack and Jill addressed parents' need to provide their children with Black role models in an era when few were available through the majority media and schools. Chapters held weekly or monthly activities for different age groups that promoted interaction and friendships among Black age-mates who shared social values and goals of advancement. Either through formal groups, like Jack and Jill, or informal networks these women developed relationships with other members of the Black community.

At school, these middle-class daughters related to another set of young people, mostly middle-class White peers. As a consequence, middle-class women who went to schools outside of their communities often found themselves juggling two sets of peers and attempting to bridge gaps between their White middle-class schools and the mixed social classes in their predominantly Black communities. Like other respondents who negotiated two peer groups, these women found the task to be stressful. Such tensions made life difficult for Deborah Jones and tempered her appreciation of her excellent private schooling. She commented,

> There was intellectual stimulation and I was successful at academics; still, the social and racial ambiguities and tensions were unmistakable. My friends in school were primarily upper-middle-class Blacks and Jews, who were active, aggressive, and attractive in mainstream ways. They were usually inclined towards the arts. Outside of school, my friends were upper- to lower-middle-class Blacks, whom I most often saw at parties. They considered themselves to be very hip. I strongly felt the tension between the cloistered, special, White private school life and the tough, flashier, deliberately street-derived, Black social life.

Often Black students enrolled in public schools were hostile to those few Black peers who attended predominantly White private schools. Deborah Jones reported such tensions. Many of Deborah's middle-class Black friends from her community attended comprehensive high schools and had friendships with working-class Black students. Therefore Deborah often met these young people through her friends. These new working-class acquaintances often reacted negatively to Deborah because she attended a predominantly White private school. This meant Deborah and others in her situation had to work doubly hard to be considered "cool" by middle- and working-class Black peers who attended public schools. While Deborah's parents had the funds to provide her an excellent education, she had to personally bridge the gap between her Black community and the world of her private school. Although Black middle-class parents might have wanted their daughters to be comfortable in both social worlds, this goal was not easily attainable. Knowing their daughters would need good credentials to scale the racial barriers ahead of them, these parents made securing an education a priority. Therefore, any accompanying social difficulties simply had to be endured.

Like Karen Wright, Irma Dennis was intimidated by the White middle-class people in her school. After her years in a majority Black high school, Irma said, "Private school gave me a chance to catch up educationally with other college-oriented high school students." This advantage was not without social tensions, however. "There were not many Blacks, and I felt very awkward and shy around the Whites. I also felt intimidated by what I considered to be their cultural and intellectual advantages." In this setting, she dealt with White students in the classroom but did not develop strong friendships across racial lines. Her peer group was a "small circle of middle-class Black females who wanted to go away to college, but had no specific career goals in mind."

Wendy Anderson, whose family resided in the South, graduated from a northern boarding school.[7] She bridged a gap between two worlds but did not return daily to a Black community. In the early 1960s, when many southern communities were starting to desegregate schools, Black parents feared exposing their children to the turmoil. Many southern Black middle-class parents explored alternatives to local segregated and recently desegregated schools for their children. Wendy explained her parents' motivation to send her to a boarding school: "It was largely a function of time and place. There had been a whole period of gerrymandering and parents were frightened of racial upheaval and didn't want their kids to get hurt. You could say they were overprotective, but many middle-class parents from all over the South were sending their children North to attend high school." The Andersons, novices at selecting private boarding schools, chose a progressive coeducational school in the northeast. It was safe from the racial turmoil of the South, but the school presented Wendy with different social issues.

Her progressive boarding school was small and intimate, and Wendy was one of only a few Black students on the campus. Spending the day in a predominantly White setting could be very intense, and attending a boarding school in another region of the country precluded daily reunions with family for support. Wendy described her feelings about the separation and adjustment:

I had two sets of feelings: conscious and unconscious. No big deal, in terms of conscious feelings, since going away to school was the expected thing to do. On the other hand, I was thirteen, and looking back on it, it was pretty traumatic. The environments were totally different. I went to a progressive boarding school in New England, having been in a very sheltered southern Black environment. During the whole period of the 1960s it was really kind of bizarre. It probably was a really wrenching emotional experience, but I didn't know it was. I developed a facility to do what was expected of me, keeping the lid on and having everything under control. That was part of the indoctrination that Black people have to succeed in White environments. I couldn't show that I was having trouble.

Wendy appreciated the learning and support she received for academic goals, but she had to cope with major social changes. She lived in a world totally different from that of her parents. The reality of her two lives was most deeply felt when she returned to the South to visit them. Wendy recalled those times:

There were a whole series of contradictions with being away from home, but it was only difficult when I went back home. It was hard to make the transitions back and forth. In the tenth grade I had been socialized into my new environment, then went home in a dress, but [wearing] sandals with a guitar and my dirty laundry. My parents were shocked that I wasn't wearing white gloves. They never understood that I had gone someplace that was very different. They didn't know if I was a beatnik, a hippie, or had been radicalized. I was really apolitical. Making the transition between school and home was just very hard for me.

At this time Wendy would have appeared to the casual observer as if she were untroubled. She was overwhelmed but did not feel the safety to express those feelings. Instead, she handled everything just as she had been expected to by parents and teachers. Like many of these women, Wendy learned how to cope quietly with the difficulties that came with her entrance into a predominantly White boarding school.

Not all the women were involved in such negotiations. Karen Wright, who felt socially distanced from her White peers in Scholars High, did not really develop close White friends in school. Furthermore, the long commute to and from school and the demanding class schedule gave her few opportunities to connect to Black peers in her community. It would be later in college that Karen would address these issues and develop more skills.

While most women were bridging a gap between two worlds, they received very little support for their own racial identities in their elite schools. As these overwhelmingly White schools admitted Black students, they did little to prepare faculty or students to address racial differences. Thus these Black adolescents, like their counterparts in other majority White schools, endured the tensions of tokenism. However, the women recalled that they considered this stress to be one of the many sacrifices Black people have to make to survive in a White society.

In interviews with contemporary African Americans in higher education, Feagin, Vera, and Imani (1996) identify the lack of human recognition as a common form of racism in integrated settings. Often faculty, staff, and students refuse "to see and recognize African American students as full human beings with distinctive talents, virtues, interests and problems" (p. 14). The women in this study recounted how both students and teachers were often guilty of such failings. The majority of White students in these elite schools had few interactions with Black people of the same status. Consequently, the White students accepted Black students as peers but did not view their schoolmates as part of the Black community. Instead, they saw them as "exceptions" who were more akin to White middle-class people, especially since their parents were middle class. Treating their Black classmates as exceptions meant that their interactions with these intelligent Black women rarely altered White students' stereotypes of Black people. Indeed, White peers often emphasized the ways that these Black women were *not* like other Black people. While White students may have viewed such statements as complimentary, they were insulting to Black students who chose to identify with their racial group. Furthermore, statements by White peers that denied bright Black students membership in their own racial group validated a system of racial meanings and encouraged Black students to internalize these images (Collins 1990; Taylor 1994).[8]

As a consequence of such thinking, a few Black students admitted to feeling uncomfortable when race was broached. Sherri North described her peer group at her parochial school: "I had many friends I was comfortable with. Most of my friends were solid middle-class Catholics, mostly Irish and some Italians. We were all serious students; some of us were even grinds. We all aspired to go to college, many hoping to be teachers. One friend had a White mother and Black father. She was totally White in her appearance and only her close friends knew her background. Except for the racial-ethnic differences, we were all temperamentally similar. We were all good girls. My mother would describe us as wholesome." The concern with disclosure indicates some of the isolation connected with being different or the Other in a predominantly White situation. Sherri remembered her periodic discomfort whenever race was an issue: "Anytime the teachers had census forms and had to ask race or neighborhood, I always felt uptight about acknowledging that I was Negro (at the time) and where I lived, Blackville [an urban Black community]."

It was common for Black women of both social classes and in various racial settings to learn how to pull themselves together and accomplish essential tasks.

Some, like Wendy, were even cut off from their feelings of terror and doubt. Others who felt the terror, like Karen Wright, were very quiet and shy, and keenly aware of how unhappy they were at the time. As young women, they may have appeared to teachers, peers, and their parents to be on top of things or in control. Underneath these exteriors they experienced great pain, but instead of being immobilized by the pain, they survived by blocking out the feelings that would interfere with accomplishing tasks. As tokens making sacrifices to obtain a solid education, these women rarely questioned the daily pain they felt. It was experienced as just a part of being Black. Their parents were as supportive as they could be, but only a few could grasp the unique sets of barriers and tensions that composed their children's lives.

There are privileges that come with being middle class. The women secured an excellent education, and most received support for future goals that translated into a confidence about their academic abilities. However, they sacrificed social experiences, openness, and a degree of emotional well-being for these rewards. They were moving among other middle-class young people, but their Blackness was still a source of distance. Teachers and peers had their own prejudices, which made a genuine welcoming of minority students difficult. The social distance, for many of the respondents, was only reduced by a small degree during their years in these elite schools. Such stressors precluded having what could be thought of as a "normal" high school career.

Working-Class Women in Elite Schools

Eight working-class women in this study graduated from elite high schools. Attendance at these schools was part of their families' mobility strategy. Only one was a graduate of a parochial school, while the majority, seven women, were graduates of public specialized high schools. These public elite institutions functioned as major mobility channels for working-class youth because they had reputations for sending *all* of their students to college, regardless of their racial or ethnic group or social class background. Generally limited to public school options, working-class Black women studied hard to pass rigorous entrance examinations. Once they gained access to specialized schools, they knew they were closer to their goals of attending college.

The working-class women had proved that they were college material before entering these elite schools. Therefore they did not face the barriers to entering college preparatory programs experienced by their counterparts in either majority White or integrated comprehensive high schools. Yet strong support from teachers did not automatically come with admission to college-oriented high schools. Support from teachers for academic goals was often limited to the working-class students who did exceptionally well. While they were college material, the working-class women lacked the cultural capital that even Black middle-class students had in these same settings. They were less likely than the middle-class women to find support for career goals. Seven of the nine middle-class women in elite schools indicated that they were urged to plan for careers. Among the working-class women, only half, four of the eight, were encouraged to think about careers.

Except for Katherine Howell, who graduated from a small segregated elite school in the South, the women attended large institutions that were overwhelmingly White and middle class. Immersion into majority White elite schools often required adapting a new orientation to schoolwork and becoming socialized into different activities and modes of behaving. In describing her all-girls academic high school, Denise Larkin reported, "There was lots of pressure to achieve and only a few Blacks." This is an accurate picture of the state of affairs, and it reveals three important aspects of elite high schools: the degree of competition, the intense pace of academic work, and the women's high visibility as tokens. This unique educational opportunity required the development of new coping skills to learn how to reconcile oneself to the competitive environment. The degree to which working-class respondents were able to master those skills influenced their overall adjustment to elite high schools.

SURVIVING IN ACADEMIC ELITE SCHOOLS

In many respects, the working-class women's overall view of their years in elite high schools was similar to that of their middle-class counterparts, but their class background meant they traveled very different terrain. Working-class women acknowledged the tremendous advantages of attending academically rigorous institutions, even while reflecting on the pain.[9] Only two of the eight women, both of whom attended an all-girls high school in East City, said they did not enjoy high school. Even Linda Trott, who recognized that she was ignored in high school, said she enjoyed school because "it got me to college and I could see that then." The working-class women described how they kept their eyes on the prize, worked to master academic course material, and prepared for college entrance examinations. Many also struggled with social relationships in these highly competitive, predominantly White environments. Even in retrospect the quality of their schooling remains an important ingredient in their overall evaluations of life in predominantly White high schools.

Beth Warren attended a coeducational school that drew students from all over the city. Recalling her years in high school, Beth was very positive about her academic training. She noted that "Honors High showed me what a really good school could be like, giving me a concrete model." Her earlier experiences influenced how Beth, a professional educator in 1976, worked to improve educational settings. But there were also many troublesome aspects of her high school. In addition to never being in a class with another Black student, Beth never had a Black teacher. Although there was one Black teacher at Honors High, Beth never had the opportunity to be in his class. In recounting her experiences, Beth noted, "My peer group was mostly into studying. We were not a social dating group. People there thought that if you had higher marks that you were a superior person. That is one reason they couldn't understand that I took part in the boycott of the city public schools [calling attention to de facto segregation]. They said, 'What do you care about those Negroes? You are not like them, you are like us. What do you care about those people in Blackville?' I told them, 'I was born in Blackville.' "

Just like middle-class Black women, the working-class women had difficulties being recognized as members of the larger Black population. This lack of human recognition was problematic for them and tempered their ability to become close to White peers. White peers could not recognize these young working-class women as both smart and Black. Instead, they wanted to see them as different from members of the Black community. White peers, as in the example above, could not understand their Black classmates' identification with Black communities, which they most likely stereotyped (Collins 1990; Feagin, Vera, and Imani 1996). Color-blind attitudes were not designed to validate the racial identity of group members. The inability of White people to acknowledge their race was particularly difficult for those Black students who commuted daily from predominantly Black or integrated working-class neighborhoods. They strongly identified with their families and communities and wanted this aspect of their lives recognized by their White peers.

Teachers also exhibited such attitudes. Denise Larkin and Robin Washington reported that most White teachers in their school treated them as smart people who were "exceptional for their race." Being treated differently from their Black peers was resented by Denise and Robin because, in addition to denying their racial identities, these efforts were viewed as attempts to separate them from their Black friends. Their Black peers were not only good friends to Denise and Robin but were their major supports in the school. Denise and Robin interpreted their teachers' actions as racist and thought such behavior only compounded the tensions they experienced in these high-pressure schools.[10]

The lack of human recognition meant that while Black students desegregated these settings, their presence did not represent any real change. Many White people are not open to acknowledging a racially segregated past, believing instead that Black people were not admitted previously because they were not qualified. According to this thinking, these Black classmates had the same qualifications as the White students, so they must *be* the same. Consequently, White faculty and students did not recognize the unique social needs of this new population. To them, the presence of Black students demonstrated that the institutions were fine and that structural changes were not necessary since qualified Black students could enter. At the same time, there was no acknowledgment that these students would have a different perspective on the institution and possibly have something unique to contribute. Beth, Denise, and Robin were in an odd role of being visibly different, but not validated as Black people.

In fact, faculty could be disapproving when Black students operated in solidarity with their own racial community. For example, when Denise attended a Freedom School in the Black community as part of a citywide protest to demonstrate the degree of racial discrimination in the school system, her principal reacted negatively. Such demonstrations of racial identity were important for the students to display. At these times, students pushed race to the foreground and forced teachers and their fellow students to acknowledge it on their own terms.[11] This stance challenged their everyday educational experiences of being highly visible because of their color, but surrounded by people who were determined not to acknowledge race.

While most White teachers were uncomfortable acknowledging race, there were some who specifically targeted the few Black students for ill treatment. Denise Larkin and her parents had a protracted struggle with her Latin teacher over Denise's grades and achievement. It began when she arrived at Girls' High. Denise described the times:

I flunked Latin and from never having had a B, I get an F. It was crushing. The teacher was very prejudiced, as I found out later. She never gave any indication that I was failing, [but] all of sudden I failed. I came home and cried. . . . My parents went up [to the school] and spoke with her, which was an immediate kind of thing with them. She just tried to wipe them off . . . telling them that their kid doesn't have it. My father came home very angry. He said that you are going to show that woman. I know you have it. You know you have it. She is just prejudiced. You just are going to have to knock yourself out. We will get you a tutor, we'll do whatever we have to do to get you through.

Denise continued to fail Latin that year, never getting the grades she really deserved. The tension became so great between her parents and the Latin teacher that the principal had to sit in on their meetings. In the end, Denise had to go to summer school, where she earned a grade of A. She continued her account: "The guy [teacher] at summer school kept asking me: 'What are you doing here? You know more than most of the whole class.' I had no trouble with the first test he gave to see where people were at. He felt bad that I had to sit through all the basic things, which it indicated on the test that I knew how to do. There was nothing he could do. I had to go everyday, which I resented, because it took away all my social things. Everyone else was going this place and that place, and I had to go to summer school." Such experiences meant that Denise did not enjoy high school, even though she was encouraged to go to college.

In these elite schools, being smart did not exempt Black working-class women from racist treatment. Beth Warren was troubled by the often "unstated, but still felt racial prejudice." She had only one teacher who was blatant in his actions. "There was this one French teacher who ignored me. He put me in the back of the class. I can remember his face turning red when I made 98 on my French mid-term. But this [treatment] was exceptional. Even if teachers were racist they rarely took such open actions." While a few White teachers persisted in keeping their distance, most were willing to let these Black working-class students into their special schools. Academically specialized high schools are proud of their reputations for sending all their students to college, including a sizable group to prestigious colleges. Most teachers were invested in that vision and wanted to see the few Black students follow the school's traditions.

A commitment to either a color-blind or a racist stance meant that most teachers failed to appreciate the talents of their Black students, including their skills in traversing racial borders. For example, Brenda Carter was a graduate of St. Bernard's Academy, a Catholic all-girls high school that had many tracks and where a third of the students were college bound. There were only a few Black students. According to Brenda, "The Black students were all in the academic curriculum. We had to be more qualified than the average White student to even get into the school." Even though they were in the academic curriculum, the Black girls were not immediately seen as talented. Brenda, an excellent academic student, adjusted well to school, even becoming involved with student government. However, she was not encouraged to plan for a career. If the school had less racial bias, she might have been treated differently. The ambivalence on the part of teachers was very apparent to her. Brenda discussed the contradictions of her school: "I was acknowledged by my classmates as a leader and was elected school president in my senior year. The faculty were not very happy with the selection of a Black [person] as president, but could find no legitimate grounds to interfere.

The school principal spoke to the student body and very subtly showed she was not satisfied with the class's choice."

Surviving in such settings required crossing boundaries of both race and class. Brenda could very well have developed leadership skills, since she might have been a go-between or a bridge between segments of the student population. However, her teachers could not see Brenda's potential for leadership, even though many of her classmates could. Beth, Denise, and Brenda coped quite well with their circumstances. Parental support and their early lessons in self-direction and striving for excellence kept them clearly focused on their potential and long-term goals. While most of the women learned these lessons, they were not all successful in getting support in their schools. Tracy Edwards recalled her experiences in a predominantly White academic high school:

I hated [high] school, but I had to be there. Yet, I wanted to quit. I didn't study and didn't do any work. So I was not a good student. Often I was the only Black student in class. It was a radical change from my early schooling. The teachers, who were mostly Irish, were crazy. We couldn't cross our legs, you were not allowed to walk in the corridors alone, you know, crazy stuff. It was very hard to identify with the place. The guidance counselor and principal were known to be prejudiced. The teachers were okay. At that age, you do not realize that people do not really like you. When I look back, I can really see it. You could say I learned a lot and got a good education, but it was a weird place.

Linda Trott was aware of the difficulties she faced in school, but she did cope with the situation. After graduating from an integrated junior high, where she was one of three Black students in the top track, she went to Academic High, where again she was a token Black student in high honors. Linda was like many bright Black students in the North during this era who were quietly desegregating previously all-White college preparatory programs and academically specialized high schools. In her eastern city, Black parents were pressuring school officials to improve educational opportunities for Black children. Linda had been permitted and even encouraged in junior high school to be in the predominantly White college preparatory track, and she was welcomed in her senior high school. Linda's and a small number of other Black students' presence in a couple of highly visible schools made the city's desegregation record look good. But teachers and school administrators neglected to address the personal adjustment of Black students to these predominantly White settings. Linda was neglected by teachers and socially isolated from her peers. She recalled, "I was really withdrawn in high school. I sat there and did not say anything for three years. I came there with my notebook, went through the day, and then went home. In fact, I said something in class one day in the eleventh grade. The teacher was shocked; she said, 'I want to see you after class.' At that time she told me that she was really surprised to see me so enthusiastic about something. People thought I had no feelings or anything. This teacher was so shocked. I was shocked myself; I didn't realize that I had done it."

Linda did not have close friends at school and received little attention from teachers. She was a quiet participant, and few of her classmates had any sense of her as a person. Like most teenagers, Linda wanted to socialize with other young people. In her search for a peer group, she was drawn to a local church. Here she developed a close group of friends, took on leadership roles in the youth organization, and played the organ in church. Within this sphere, she was recognized for her actions and encouraged in her goals. Linda talked about how she made the decision: "I was not religious. I was tied to the church as an institution. I wanted to hang out, but I didn't want to give up the other things [her aspiration to go to college]. So hanging out at church was a compromise." Linda considered the issues and selected a course of action that satisfied several of her needs. As a Black working-class student, she was aware that college attendance was dependent upon scholarships, financial aid, and the small family savings. Linda knew that she had to walk a straight and narrow line to make her dreams a reality. Instructions from her family in self-direction helped her work through a maze of options to find a unique solution to her social dilemma. Few White students as bright as Linda would have had to reach beyond their local school for encouragement and support. But Linda's teachers and classmates could not see the intelligent and creative young Black woman in their classes.

In addition to feeling highly visible in these overwhelmingly White environments, Black students also felt pressured to contradict stereotypes about Black people. Their parents had socialized them to appreciate the existence of racism and to work to scale discriminatory barriers. Mr. Larkin, for example, did not let Denise leave Girls' High and go to another high school where she would have had excellent grades. These women knew that they were not in high school just to get an education, but also to be tested. The test was not just for themselves, but for other members of the race. It was therefore incumbent upon these students to do well, so that other Black students might follow them into these same schools. Thus, even when they felt despondent, these young women found the motivation to continue to master their schoolwork and the social scene. This pressure was certainly a heavy burden for young people.[12] Unlike many of their White classmates, who were often just going to school for individual advancement, the Black respondents did not have role models for how to handle all the demands placed upon them. They did whatever they had to do to survive, and often their own social lives suffered. These working-class women preformed well in school and tolerated the isolation, while they faced daily encounters with prejudice and color-blind people who failed to see them as human beings.

LEARNING TO MOVE IN DIFFERENT WORLDS

Academically specialized high schools were located outside of the communities where Black working-class respondents lived. Thus these women often would rise in the morning in an integrated or predominantly Black part of the city, travel by public transportation to their schools, and return to their neighborhoods in the evening. Many of them had long commutes. Like the middle-class respondents in elite schools, they had to bridge a gap between the two worlds that composed their lives. But their class position posed an additional barrier to the middle-class world of their schoolmates.[13]

The seven working-class women in majority White schools varied in how they handled the transition between the two worlds of their lives. In most cases, the struggles were internal. Because these women regularly moved between the Black and White worlds, they were conscious of class and racial differences in resources and lifestyles, while their White classmates were often oblivious to this diversity. The contrast between the two worlds was often quite stark: the world of home and community was Black and working class, while the world of school was White and middle class. Their White middle-class schoolmates were more privileged, and it showed.[14] They had more resources, including nice clothing, spending money, private bedrooms, and other items.[15] These Black working-class women lacked visible signs of privilege. Their parents might have been homeowners, but in most cases their families survived financially because either both parents were employed or their fathers worked several jobs. Because these women lacked the cultural capital of their middle-class peers, and they were not readily invited into their social world. They were also intimidated because they lacked the material resources to participate in certain circles.

Denise Larkin recalled that members of her family had what they needed, but "there were no luxuries." In the Larkin and Edwards families, sacrifices were made to enable the children to attend college. Thus they did not have the clothes and other consumer items that many of their middle-class counterparts enjoyed. Moreover, these working-class students were not protected from the financial struggles of their parents; indeed, they were keenly aware of their parents' efforts to secure necessities for them. Many women, like Linda Trott, knew that family finances were limited and that attending college would require a scholarship.[16]

Working-class students became painfully aware of their own lack of privilege and the advantages that middle-class peers enjoyed.

Financial resources gave most of their White classmates greater exposure to cultural and educational activities, so these White peers had a level of sophistication and knowledge about the world that the Black working-class women lacked. Even though Denise Larkin's and Beth Warren's families took advantage of the free cultural events in their respective cities and had visited area museums, their White middle-class peers were in another league. Linda Trott took piano lessons and participated in cultural events, but she says, "I was really overwhelmed by the people I went to high school with." Fellow students had traveled to other cities and attended expensive cultural events. These experiences were very different indeed from those of students like Robin Washington, whose mother purchased books, magazine subscriptions, and records to provide her children with the cultural background she saw as essential for educational success.

Class privilege was also evident in their White classmates' expectations for their own lives. These classmates, like the Black middle-class women in this study, spoke with assurance about their ability to attend college and even secure advanced degrees. To Black working-class women, whose college attendance was dependent upon small family savings and their abilities to secure scholarships, this sense of privilege was amazing.[17] These expectations for educational attainment and life were very different from those voiced by other Black students in the respondents' home communities. There was a serious gap between the worlds of working-class and middle-class students, but, just as racial differences within the student population were ignored, social class was also an invisible source of inequality.

Black working-class women did not embrace all the values in their elite schools. One disturbing aspect of middle-class life was the intense competition between students. Beth Warren said that her school newspaper reported grades, and that certain people with high achievement scores did not associate with students who had lower scores. To Black working-class youth who had been taught in their families to cooperate and share their resources with others, this aspect of White middle-class society was most perplexing. In fact, the preparation for combating discrimination that they learned at home stressed appreciating *all* people. For example, Linda Trott was taught that everybody was to be treated with respect because of his/her status as a human being. In a society where Black adult men and women were routinely devalued and often addressed by their first names, Black families were intent upon teaching their children to recognize the value in everyone. Thus the practice in these highly competitive elite institutions of dismissing people who did not "rate" academically was troublesome. Such value differences did not promote the conformity that institutions expected from their students. These working-class students in elite high schools have much in common with the respondents in Mary Fuller's (1980) studies in British schools. Fuller found that women of color valued what education could help them achieve, particularly economic independence, but they were not willing to conform to all of their school's practices. The women in this study were not as overt in their behaviors but were quietly critical of some of their school's social practices. In the process, they were learning what it was like to be an outsider within the middle-class world.

While the majority of Black respondents in predominantly White high schools recognized their existence in two worlds, the working-class respondents coped differently from their Black middle-class counterparts. While their struggles were rough, their class position was a barrier to entrance into the social world of school peers; thus they did not experience the degree of tension identified by the Black middle-class students in elite high schools. In many respects, there did not appear to be illusions of greater acceptance. All of these women were marginal in their elite high schools, except for Katherine Howell, where there was just the class line to cross. In her segregated elite school she shared many values with the other students. She did lack the cultural capital of her Black middle-class peers and worked to address the mobility issues she faced (see Chapter 7).

Linda Trott found it difficult to bridge that gap between school and home, so she developed a supportive peer group outside of school. She moved between her two worlds but did not bring friends from school into her predominantly Black community. Indeed, while Black students were being asked to participate in the predominantly White world, few White schoolmates ever ventured into the Black working-class world. White peers therefore did not learn about the Black students, the Black community, and other personal aspects of their lives.

Cynthia Butler's entire all-girls high school was college bound; the institution even offered "special" classes for students with grades of ninety or above in a subject. This program enabled students actually to take college-level courses in high school. Cynthia was in the special math and social studies classes. During this time, she felt connected to both her schoolmates and her community friends. She commuted daily from a predominantly Black community to attend Scholars' High. The structure of her life created difficulties, but she did not report experiencing the same level of tension as middle-class Deborah Jones. Cynthia commented:

> I had sets of friends—friends from my block, friends from elementary school who I went to high school with, old family type friends and relatives, and new

friends I made in high school. My home and family friends were Black and working- to middle-class girls. Most of them planned to finish high school and get married, but one wanted a career as a fashion designer. My new school friends were mostly Jewish, but there was a WASP and one Chinese girl. They were all upper middle and middle class and college bound. A few wanted to finish college and get married, but the majority had professional aspirations.

Cynthia recalled moving comfortably in her high school, even though she remembered her father cautioning her, "Watch out, your White friends might betray you." Navigating between these racially and socially distinct environments was not recalled as particularly troublesome for her.

Denise Larkin was part of a neighborhood peer group, where she often downplayed her attendance at Girls' High to new people. In high school, she got along well with most students. Those White students who were either upper class or working class and "who didn't really fit in anywhere else hung out with the Black folks. I joined a couple of clubs. I wrote for the paper now and then. I cannot remember any of the folks I hung with [in school]." Moving between school and community was simply a necessity of life.

Jack and Jill, the popular social outlet organized by aspiring middle-class Black parents for their children's social development, was only mentioned by one of the working-class respondents. Beth Warren attended a few Jack and Jill dances with her cousins. Color and class were clearly issues, and Beth felt out of place in those settings. She recalled: "I was too dark and not part of the group. I felt ill at ease and didn't think I could compete with fair skinned girls with straight hair." Beth's close friends were in the Girl Scouts, and she remained involved with scouting through high school.

Most of the working-class respondents in elite institutions had friends either at school or in their communities, but a few were more isolated. These women lacked Black social networks because they lived outside of Black communities. They tended to befriend classmates very much like themselves. Their peers were minorities in the school with respect to either race, ethnicity, class background, or religion. They were academically oriented students from diverse backgrounds. These were not deep friendships, but camaraderie shared with other middle- and working-class adolescent girls (because many of the specialized high schools were single sex) who had aspirations of college.

In fact, having school peers of different colors and classes, who were serious about studying and planning to go to college, was reassuring to many Black working-class youth. They may have been troubled by the intense academic competition of their schools; however, attendance in these schools meant they did not have to face the competing value systems within the Black community. In comprehensive high schools, where academics was only one route to attention and success, their academic pursuits may have made them suspect to some peers. In specialized high schools, Black working-class respondents could excel academically and gain, rather than lose, status.

For the majority of these working-class women, their friendships with White peers were temporary. As they moved on to college and adulthood, they did not keep these White friends and lost touch with acquaintances. Linda Trott did not follow the course of her classmates as they went off to different colleges. Cynthia Butler noted, "One tends to overestimate acquaintanceships as friendships at this stage in life." One indication of the transitory nature of these relationships was a retrospective comment by Beth Warren, who noted: "My grandmother thought it was a waste of time to associate with the White students in high school, because she doubted that these friendships would continue after graduation. And she was right."

Race as well as class differences often made it difficult to solidify friendships with White classmates during this stage of life and at this time in history. Race as a barrier was complicated by the color-blind perspective then fostered in schools. Students had to learn to negotiate racial borders on their own. If working-class respondents were likely to have White friends, it was with the working-class White students in their classes, students who were also a minority population in these specialized high schools. Sharing a sense of foreignness in the school and facing the challenge of mobility, working-class students of both races could discuss the critical decisions they were making at this time (see Chapter 7). Often these friendships faded after graduation, but the skills of crossing racial borders would help these women in college.

Black working-class women emerged from their prestigious specialized high schools with excellent academic credentials. They were moving on the road to college and ultimately upward social mobility. A few had encounters with racist teachers, but on the whole, their teachers and guidance counselors recognized their talents. After all, these women successfully competed with thousands of other urban students for the few select positions in specialized high schools. They had access to honors and special programs in their schools. Most received encouragement to attend college, but faculty were more ambivalent in their support of careers. What respondents recalled as most problematic about their high schools was the lack of acknowledgment that they were bright Black women. Their racial identity was not validated; instead, it was treated either as an attribute to be overlooked or as the source of discriminatory treatment. They were also more distant from White school peers, and relationships were more superficial than those friendships that middle-class respondents formed with White students in elite schools. The middle-class women had more positive academic experiences than the working-class women. While they documented tension around social relationships with White peers, the middle-class women recalled making good friends during this period of their lives. Some even indicated that they were still in touch with these friends at the time of the study. Sharing a social class background with their White classmates aided intimacy. For many working-class respondents, however, class was an additional barrier that limited the development of deep friendships with White students in these elite settings.

CHAPTER 7 : ADULT-SPONSORED AND CHILD-SECURED MOBILITY

I don't know about the White students, but Black students got very poor counseling in course and career planning. Since my parents were both in teaching careers, they advised me. As a high school teacher, my mother gave me the most advice. And they [my parents] discussed where to go to college. My mother wanted me to go to an eastern college since she felt they offered the highest quality preparation.
—Susan Thomas, middle-class graduate of an integrated high school

The guidance staff tended not to counsel Black students in the same manner as they did White students. The teachers didn't really want us there. We had to fight to get access to information. Counselors stressed secretarial schools rather than colleges for the Black students, even those [Black] students in the college preparatory program. The Black students were the last to hear about programs which would improve their chances of entering and remaining in colleges. We had to do most of the guiding ourselves.
—Dorothy Wall, working-class graduate of an integrated high school

This chapter returns to a focus on social class to examine qualitative differences in how Black women actually went from their high schools to predominantly White colleges. Chapters 5 and 6 demonstrated that high schools varied widely in their support of Black women based on the racial composition of the school and the individual woman's social class background. Faculty and school officials could either promote, ignore, or discourage the achievement of specific women. Given the variability of schools, family support was essential in helping women achieve their goals. Their families provided the support they could, but resources differed in middle- and working-class families. These variations in family support made for qualitative differences in experiences as women overcame racial barriers and attended predominantly White colleges. All of the women were advancing in terms of educational attainment, but the middle-class women were reproducing their social class positions, while the working-class women faced upward mobility. So the women differed in the tasks and the supports.

The experience of upward mobility for Black working-class women in this cohort differs greatly from many notions of social mobility in our society. Mobility, especially for White working-class males, often begins with their selection by teachers as candidates for success (Ellis and Lane 1963). Gender alters the mobility experience because many women, even after World War II, were mobile through marriage rather than through their own educational and occupational advancement (Psathas 1968). The end of blatant sex discrimination in employment and educational programs in the mid-1960s created more opportunities for women to become financially independent. Therefore patterns of mobility have significantly shifted for women beginning with this age cohort. Before the 1960s, social mobility for Black women took place within segregated educational and employment institutions, either in the public sector or in independent Black agencies (Hine 1989; Rollins 1995; Shaw 1996; Slevin and Wingrove 1998). Even as new opportunities opened, race and gender continued to operate in key ways to shape the mobility experience for Black women (Higginbotham and Weber Cannon 1988; Higginbotham and Weber 1992).

In this study, only majority Black high schools routinely facilitated upward mobility for Black working-class women.[1] In majority White high schools, Black working-class women faced class and racial barriers as they pursued advancement. Teachers and counselors expected middle-class women to pursue higher education, but they did not expect them to attend predominantly White colleges and universities. Rather than positing that all the teachers in majority White schools held explicitly racist beliefs, we can view their actions as passive acceptance of the negative racial ideology that characterized the era. Ideologically based actions constituted a form of institutionalized racism that restricted Black students' options. Teachers, especially those in urban public school systems, have been characterized as street-level bureaucrats, that is, public employees who are expected to provide services, like education, to ever-increasing needy populations but are not given the resources to adequately perform such tasks (Lipsky 1980). They have too many students, too few supplies, and insufficient budgets. Public school teachers may narrow the scope of their jobs to tasks they can accomplish. They accepted lower levels of achievement from Black students than White students, often believing their lower expectations to be in students' best interests. Such assumptions about what Black students can learn shaped teachers' behaviors and placed ceilings on students' expectations. In the end, Black students often left schools with lower levels of achievement than White students (Clark 1965).

Middle-class parents were in a position to provide their daughters with the necessary social supports: cognitive, that is, assistance in obtaining information necessary to navigate the world of higher education; material, in the form of paying at least the majority of college tuition; and emotional, that is, reassuring their daughters that they could handle college work. These parents actively participated in their daughters' decisions about where to attend college, and many accompanied them on visits to prospective colleges. Working-class parents strongly believed in their children but could not provide all types of support. If cognitive support, such as information about appropriate colleges, was not forthcoming from their schools, then the working-class women, as Dorothy Wall stated, "had to do most of the guiding ourselves." Working-class women's plans were also limited by their families' financial resources. They were more dependent than middle-class women upon scholarships to attend private institutions and often relied on public institutions. Thus social class mattered a great deal in the process of gaining access to predominantly White educational institutions.

Adult-Sponsored Mobility

Adult-sponsored mobility occurs when parents or other adults are active in providing critical assistance that positions young people for college and aids them in the transition from high school to college. The middle-class parents in this study laid the foundation for their daughters' educational success. Parents' actions supplemented schools as well as helped their daughters navigate the institutional barriers that appeared. Yet in the educational process the prerequisite actions of parents could be invisible to their daughters and school officials. The comments of Evelyn Tucker, a graduate of a predominantly Black high school, reveal the perspective of a young woman whose experiences are identified as adult-sponsored mobility. When asked about the type of encouragement she received from teachers to attend college, Evelyn replied, "For me and other students, the decision to go to college was made long ago at home. School simply gave us the skills to accomplish that goal. It was especially a foregone conclusion for anyone in the honors track. College is what we were there for, so it was only a matter of deciding upon which college."

The Tuckers moved from an inner-city community to a suburban setting to ensure that Evelyn attended the best public schools available. The family's resources meant that Evelyn selected the college of her choice with little thought about finances. These actions, viewed as the obligations of parents, can be overlooked as explicit support. When talking about her parents' educational expectations, Evelyn noted that she was expected to attend college and then pursue an advanced degree. However, it was hard for Evelyn clearly to identify her parents' role in this process. When asked what her mother and father *did* to encourage her to seek her educational goals, she wrote, "It was so implicitly understood from as early as I can remember that I can single out nothing explicit. There was never any question that I would go on in school, so she did not have to encourage me. The answer is the same for my father. They always encouraged me to pursue whatever I liked, with unquestionable confidence in my ability and judgment." Children are not born with confidence in their abilities, however. The Tuckers provided a solid foundation that sponsored their daughter's educational success, but Evelyn's comments indicate that the privileges extended to her were unseen. In addition to emotional support, her parents' middle-class standing ensured that Evelyn was recognized as college material in schools. They were available to discuss college options as well as pay for tuition. While most families were forthcoming with emotional support, cognitive and material support from middle-class parents made critical differences in the lives of these women.[2]

NAVIGATING HIGHER EDUCATION

While the Black middle-class women had more institutional support for educational goals than their working-class counterparts, parental monitoring was still necessary as these twenty-five women challenged racial barriers in their desire to attend predominantly White colleges. These women varied in how they acknowledged the assistance of parents and other adults, but they were quite explicit about the nature of confrontations with institutional and informal racism as they applied to colleges. Many of their families had been successful in sheltering them from institutional racism until the end of high school. As middle-class daughters, these women were quickly labeled as college material, and having their choice of colleges questioned was often the first clear signal that they were not like their White peers. In their senior year, many women became aware of the limits on their high school teachers' expectations for them. Not only was this fact disturbing, but the confrontations that followed signaled the end of pleasant high school days and the beginning of more conscious negotiations around racial barriers.

The issues identified in Chapters 5 and 6 as key factors in shaping middle-class women's receptions in high schools again emerge as important in the transition to predominantly White colleges. Women in majority Black high schools enjoyed advantages at this stage, as did the women in majority White schools who were viewed as exceptional students. Teachers and officials in predominantly Black high schools were supportive of students who wished to take advantage of the new educational opportunities becoming available as predominantly White colleges began actively recruiting Black students in the mid-1960s. Because they had parents who were more knowledgeable about colleges than those of their working-class counterparts, middle-class women in majority Black schools were not solely dependent upon the guidance staff. Yet the atmosphere in Black schools promoted cooperation in helping young people attain their educational goals.

Students like Evelyn Tucker and Allison Cross frequently discussed the advantages and disadvantages of different colleges with their parents and siblings. As graduates of predominantly Black high schools with demanding academic programs, they were excellent candidates for new desegregation efforts in predominantly White colleges. This new racial atmosphere enabled Allison Cross to select her college based on its academic reputation, size, and the beauty of the campus. She noted: "I wanted a traditional ivy-ish, New England school surrounded by lots of others. I thought it would be fun and offer the most varied experiences." Allison's family could provide her with the financial means to attend college, but it took the Civil Rights movement and other struggles for social change to expand her choices.

In majority White high schools, the respondents who were perceived as very bright also received favored treatment at this stage. For example, Katrina Charles thought her advisors were very helpful because she was one of the outstanding students in her church-affiliated school, but she knew her experience was rare. Teachers encouraged her to attend Whitehall College. Wendy Anderson also found the advisors in her boarding school to be encouraging. On the other hand, those middle-class Black women who were viewed as average students, like Karen Wright, received little personal attention even in elite high schools. Karen recalled, "I had very little guidance until I started scoring very high on the SATs and other exams in my senior year. Then they [the counselors] were interested in getting me into a college that would make the school look good." Irma Dennis also did not receive special attention in her private school, but her mother helped with the college admissions process.

When majority White high schools failed to provide Black students with solid and appropriate educational counseling, the middle-class parents helped their daughters sort through the maze of colleges to find appropriate schools. Encounters with racist attitudes forced the young women to look more critically at their educational institutions. To some teachers, these middle-class women were stepping out of their place or overstepping some boundary when they dared to apply to educational institutions that were the goals for White middle- and upper-class students. Prestigious, private, predominantly White colleges were seen as appropriate schools for White students, while many Black students were steered toward state colleges and traditionally Black institutions. In the end, several Black middle-class respondents shared with their working-class counterparts the pain of confrontations with insensitive teachers, counselors, and classmates at this stage. These women did not face these barriers alone.

Beverly Rawlins's experience enables us to see the way that adults can sponsor the mobility of their children. Prior to her senior year, Beverly had praise for her integrated high school, where she was genuinely excited about learning and enjoyed the relaxed social atmosphere. When planning for college, Beverly's initial choice met with her teachers' approval. Beverly described her early plans for college:

> I was in love. The young man's name was Darryl and he was at State University. I was going to go there and we were going to get married and live happily ever after. At that time you only needed a B average for state schools. The application fee was ten dollars, so it was no big thing. My mother put her foot down and said that I had to apply to more schools than State University. One of the schools I had to apply for was Whitehall College. That was one of the few times she told me to do something, outside of household chores.[3] So I knew that Whitehall College was one of the best. I figured that if she wanted to pay fifteen dollars, I would apply to the best school. I also applied to other liberal arts schools in the East and Midwest.

Beverly discussed colleges with her mother and identified several choices. Once this list of schools was completed, Beverly took it to the school counselor to begin the process of applying to these colleges. It was at this stage that she encountered difficulties, Beverly reported:

> Before this time I was very certain that my counselor, Miss Jones, really liked me. She was surprised that I was applying to Whitehall College. There were two other students applying to this school, but they were both White. It was at this point that I realized that there were problems in terms of guidance counseling. I took my SATs and got 600s and Miss Jones told me that these scores were not good enough for Whitehall College. So I went back and took them again and got scores in the low 700s. I think Miss Jones didn't believe I really wanted to apply. I do not know what she believed. Maybe she thought they [officials at Whitehall College] wouldn't take a Black student or maybe she really thought the scores were low. Since going to Whitehall College I know that they take people with scores in the 400s. Scores were not all that important. I don't know, but that whole experience made me feel a little funny about

her. But up until that point, she had been very helpful and supportive. There was never any question about my being in college prep courses and taking the classes I wanted. But I guess when it came to going to Whitehall College, there was a question in her mind.

If her mother had not intervened, Beverly's options could have been limited by high school officials to state universities. Resistance from counselors and teachers to their goals was especially shocking for the students who had assumed that there were no limits on their educational options. In their senior year, many heard teachers say, "Black people can't go to certain colleges." Therefore, middle-class parents' knowledge about colleges and their willingness to research them with their daughters was a bonus for these women. If they were working with counselors, as in the case of predominantly Black high schools, parents could supplement the advising. When their daughters faced White guidance staff with limited expectations of Black students, parents could step in and ensure that their daughters were able to take advantages of the new opportunities enabling them to go to the colleges of their choice.

Black middle-class parents were cognizant of the changes taking place at predominantly White colleges, and many directed their daughters and sons to these newly opened doors.[4] They also thought about their daughters' many concerns. Susan Thomas, who relied on her mother for guidance, decided upon an East City university where she pursued occupational therapy, a nontraditional career for Black women at that time. Deborah Jones and her parents researched colleges to suit her unique needs. Earlier her parents had helped Deborah's sister with the selection process because they found the school counselor insensitive to the social needs of Black students. Deborah's private high school did direct Black students to predominantly White colleges but recommended small colleges in the rural Midwest. Previous graduates were unhappy in such places, and many transferred to state universities in more urban settings. Dr. and Mrs. Jones were prepared to help Deborah apply to colleges that met her various needs. They looked at schools that were rigorous academically, had the solid drama program Deborah wanted, and were also in or near urban areas where she would have access to other Black college-age students.

PAYING THE BILLS

In addition to helping their daughters negotiate the college application process, most middle-class parents paid either full college tuition and fees or at least the majority of these costs. Many Black professional parents could afford to send their children to college; indeed, six families had paid tuition for private high schools. The notion that all Black students received full scholarships was a popular myth during this era. In reality, financial aid awards were limited, and full scholarships were available only to those students who were uniquely talented and graduated from high school with honors. Most of the middle-class women did not receive any financial aid, so their parents assumed the responsibilities for the cost of higher education.[5]

Some middle-class parents struggled to send their children to college, but they viewed it as part of their responsibility. They did not necessarily share their financial concerns with their children. Overall, the middle-class respondents were less concerned with financial matters than their working-class counterparts; many appeared to have left such concerns to their parents. Only two middle-class women, Marlene Turner and Joyce Saunders, remarked that they were concerned with finances. Marlene mentioned the attractive financial aid award she received as an incentive to attend Technical University. Joyce Saunders's family was less affluent than many other middle-class families because her father was still advancing in his occupation when she began college. She had much in common with many of the working-class women because she assumed a major responsibility in thinking about paying for college. She remained in East City, selecting Regional University, rather than traveling south to a traditionally Black college, which was her parents' preference.[6]

Notions that all Black students are on financial aid reflect the nation's inability to acknowledge a small but significant Black professional class that educated their children in private institutions (Graham 1999). Myths about economic assistance also mask the hard work that Black families and the individual women endured to secure higher education. Material support in middle-class families meant these women did not experience the financial constraints faced by their working-class counterparts. Middle-class parents assumed responsibility for financial concerns and freed their daughters to select the colleges that either were the most appropriate for their occupational goals or best fit their image of the college experience. In the case of Rosalind Griffin, it was the latter. She recalled thinking about her future: "I had the typical picture of a college campus in mind—and I wanted the gay college girl life of *Seventeen*. All the white girls around me were into it. I thought it would really be like that for me too. So I selected Private Women's College, because it fit my image of what a college would be like. I didn't even visit the state university, where my father wanted me to go." Rosalind spent one year at a private women's college in New England, where she found much of the social scene of her high school reproduced. She then transferred to East City University, a coeducational institution with a larger Black population. Her family's economic resources gave her the ability to seek one type of college and then transfer to another as her image of the ideal college experience changed.

When asked about selecting a college, several middle-class women indicated that their choices were primarily dictated by the quality of the education available at the school and the assets of the particular region. Many were attracted to a particular prestigious college in East City. They were aware of status issues and the value of attending "the best school." As a group, the middle-class women applied to more colleges and were less tied to their native regions than were the working-class women. Middle-class women were more likely than those from the working class to go away to college; twenty-four of the twenty-five women did so. For the middle-class women, thoughts about college included going away to school and learning independence from their families, as well as taking advantage of the opportunities in East City. Many parents prepared their daughters for leaving home. For example, a respondent who grew up on the East Coast recalled, "I wanted to go away from home. My parents always expected me to go, but not too far. Therefore, East City was an obvious choice." Several women noted that East City appeared sophisticated and exciting, and they looked forward to living in the city. The women drew their images from novels, magazines, and the media, as well as accounts related by family members.

In their first year of college, all the middle-class women lived separately from their parents, while many of the working-class women from East City continued to live at home. Generally, middle-class families' financial resources enabled their daughters to seek their optimal college environment. The women varied in their goals for the college years. Katrina Charles wanted a larger coeducational setting because it was important to her to develop a social life, which had been difficult in her small high school. At the same time, Katrina wanted to go to a college with a solid academic program. She recalled her thinking at the time: "I was interested in meeting bright young Black people. I didn't want to continue apologizing for my academic and intellectual interests." Katrina applied to several prestigious colleges in urban areas, because she also cared about the reputation of the college and its location. While her parents encouraged Katrina to consider different schools, in the end it was her decision, and they trusted her judgment. Katrina finally selected Whitehall College because it gave her access to a coeducational environment, it was prestigious, and East City offered many opportunities for interacting with other Black college students.[7]

Other women chose to focus on the potential for an active social life, making East City attractive because of the large college-age population in the area and the greater likelihood of having Black peers. Helene Montgomery recalled her image of the college life: "I was influenced by Nancy Drew books. I wanted a college campus with rolling hills. I thought I would have fun, but also do school work." College for middle-class participants was an opportunity to expand their experiences, and they approached this time with eagerness.

Middle-class women faced the transition from high school to college without the major concerns of finances. Their parents helped if their high schools failed to provide appropriate guidance. Adult-sponsored educational mobility strategies provided Black middle-class women with essential social supports as they set their sights on attending White colleges. Given the reality of the limitations in counseling for Black students in majority White schools, we can see that having informed and resourceful parents was an advantage. Parents either acted as buffers or armed their children with the knowledge to advocate for themselves when they faced institutional barriers. The concept of adult-sponsored mobility lets us explore some of the ways that Black middle-class students were privileged, not only within predominantly Black settings, but in integrated and predominantly White ones as well. Parents' knowledge about educational institutions and financial resources, along with emotional support, helped their daughters scale the institutional barriers that presented themselves in high schools.

Child-Secured Mobility

The future was not so certain for working-class women, because their parents had limited financial resources and few knew about the world of higher education. The educational experiences of most of the working-class women could be characterized as child-secured mobility.[8] In these cases, parents provided emotional support, as they strongly believed in their children's abilities and instilled the dream of attending college. These parents had often advocated for their young people in elementary and secondary schools. However, working-class parents' abilities to provide both financial and cognitive support varied tremendously. Unlike middle-class parents, most lacked personal experience with higher education and were dependent upon teachers and counselors in high schools to help their daughters identify routes to colleges (Cicourel and Kitsuse 1963). If the schools were not supportive, young people had to initiate actions to get information about colleges and the application process, including the necessary prerequisites for specific college programs. The self-direction that parents instilled was a key factor in helping young women negotiate in an adult world.

Nancy Brooks had to overcome the limitations of her high school, where even as a bright student she was not initially directed to any private prestigious colleges. Mrs. Brooks had wanted her daughter to desegregate a public high school because this institution promised to lead to the future she wanted for her. At Wilson High, Nancy was exposed to a variety of material in the curriculum, and all of her friends were college oriented, but she did little thinking about actual colleges. While she was a good student, she was not close to any teachers, and there were few supports for her in the school. Nancy recalled, "I thought about college when I took the PSAT and I participated in those activities. But I was not really thinking about it until my senior year when I saw the counselor. She suggested a public university in the city as a safe school, but I needed a break from home, so I wanted to go away." Nancy had her PSAT scores sent to the National Scholarship Service and Fund for Negro Students (NSSFNS), an independent agency working to match Black students with colleges.[9] This agency sent Nancy's scores to several colleges, and Nancy received brochures from many of these schools, including Roosevelt University. Her school counselor "only suggested city schools [public institutions] and glossed over the other options." Nancy, who was working in high school to help her family financially, needed a scholarship to attend a private institution. With new information in her hands, Nancy made the case for applying to private colleges. In the spring of her senior year, she was accepted at three private colleges. With a scholarship from Roosevelt University and a National Defense Student Loan, she was able to leave home and attend college in East City.

In contrast to middle-class parents like the Tuckers, for example, where did Nancy's parents figure in this scenario? Mr. Brooks expected his daughter to finish high school and did not think about colleges until she was a senior. While Mrs. Brooks had college as an initial goal and monitored Nancy's schooling, she had grown up in the South and was not familiar with northern colleges and their new outreach to Black students. She primarily provided emotional support. "My mother wanted me to have what she didn't have, especially education. She didn't push, but tried to help and was encouraging. Often I was motivated to do things and then she would help me. She helped me convince my father [who was very protective] to let me go to Roosevelt University."

As members of the working class, these women entered high school more dependent upon school officials for cognitive support. Yet schools varied in the level of support they provided. Women in majority Black high schools had supportive teachers, while most in majority White settings had faculty whose aspirations for the women were lower than their own. In such settings, only prized students received help in unraveling the world of higher education. Working-class women had to seek out information about specific colleges, analyze it, assess their own abilities, and decide where to apply. Aware of family finances, they knew their selections had to be economically feasible.

Cognizant of their parents' support, working-class women had to conquer many barriers to make attending college a reality. Long before they began to learn about their many educational options, the women knew that money was limited. Therefore they had to be excellent students, since scholarships were awarded to those whose performance had been exemplary. Many women assumed a high level of responsibility at a young age. For example, Linda Trott internalized her parents' desire for her to attend college but knew that her own actions were the key to securing that goal. In the second grade, Linda was the observer of a behavioral incident in school, and the principal told all the children that he would put this incident on their record.[10] Linda recalled, "I was so upset because I thought that meant I could not go to college. So I cried and cried." Linda's mother had to reassure her that her dreams were not dashed at this early age. This experience, remembered after many years, is indicative of the tension and stress about academic success and college goals found among working-class women.

CREATING AND DECIPHERING EDUCATIONAL OPTIONS

Unlike adult-sponsored mobility, where young people experience a level of freedom because adults are "watching out" for them, child-secured mobility means that these young students are pressured to decipher what they must to do to achieve their goals. This stance might mean that they are pushed into addressing adult concerns while they are still children. It might mean a "lost" childhood. The circumstances of the working-class women varied with regard to the actual levels of emotional support from families and the degree to which cognitive and material support were found in the home. Overall, most of the working-class women did what they could and hoped that their years of hard work would be rewarded by receiving scholarships and financial aid.

The nature of their high schools was also a factor in the extent of work on their part. Like the middle-class women, the working-class respondents in predominantly Black and segregated institutions received strong support in their high schools for their educational goals. College attendance was a goal uniformly shared with family, teachers, and other community members. But even though the working-class women found support in their schools, there were many issues they had to face alone, especially that of paying tuition. Their high schools did provide assistance in learning about specific colleges and, when possible, helped in addressing financial issues.

Many working-class women in majority White schools faced discriminatory treatment as they reviewed college bulletins and thought about the next educational step. Discouragement from attending predominantly White colleges was not uniform for this population; some women did receive support, especially, as noted earlier, those who were viewed as "stars." The school counselors in Girls' High, for example, steered most of the Black students toward traditional Black institutions, but Robin Washington was pushed toward predominantly White colleges. Validation of her abilities was comforting, but her strong self-direction was the key to her decision-making process. She recalled: "Advisors even talked me into applying to Whitehall College. I was not really interested, since I wanted a more free and open environment. I was accepted at Whitehall College, but I didn't go there." Years spent in an environment that denied her racial identity had an impact on Robin. She was looking for a rigorous but more open setting. Her elite high school provided her with tools to make that decision. In addition to exposing her to information about colleges, the high school had former graduates return to talk about their experiences in college. Robin was impressed with the description one graduate gave of Roosevelt University. She knew it was highly ranked but learned that it lacked the intense pressure to succeed in prescribed ways that Robin associated with most elite schools. She resisted counselors and made the decision to attend Roosevelt University because she sensed that it was an open place where she could learn about herself.

While attending an Ivy League school was inappropriate for Robin, it became a goal for Beth Warren with the encouragement of teachers in her high school. Beth, who had scored very well on a citywide examination to enter her high school, recalled: "In my freshman year, my high school advisor had recommended I apply to Whitehall College. I never seriously considered any other school. It had a strong reputation for academic excellence. The school was small with a great teacher/student ratio and all the advantages of the varied courses and resources of a large university." However, not all Black women in majority White high schools were viewed as gifted. Many, especially those in comprehensive schools, faced both race and class discrimination. Students like Dorothy Wall had to research college options on their own and advise themselves. The combination of a lack of cognitive support from school and little information about economic options often kept working-class women in East City. While Robin and Beth had suggestions from counselors, Dorothy had to battle with teachers to get information. It was also up to her to make sure she met all the deadlines for required tests. She had to work to create options for herself. After graduation from high school, Dorothy attended a state college in East City. The respondents' experiences were different, but each path demanded that the young woman do much of the work on her own.

Support from school can assist child-secured mobility, but it is still the young person who has to assume responsibility for making adult decisions. The experiences of Katherine Howell enable us to see how child-sponsored mobility operated. Even in a supportive high school, Katherine faced many issues alone. Her family's early teachings helped her to tackle these situations. Like many other Black parents in this era, Mr. and Mrs. Howell did all they could for their two daughters. They were very involved in their children's lives and inspired them to do well. Katherine said, "My parents were very supportive of me. They would bend over backwards to help me do things. When I wanted to take art lessons, my mother made me a smock and drove me to and from my lessons. My father made me an easel. I could never do something simple. It was always a big production and I got everyone involved." However, there were limits on what the Howells, a Black working-class family in the South, could provide. Mr. Howell's work as a carpenter was unsteady. "He would be working some days and then not others," recalled Katherine. Her father worked very hard, often on weekends, to provide for his family.

Katherine attended parochial school for her first nine years of schooling. Her grades gained her access to the Black University Lab School for her secondary education. In this elite high school, Katherine was different from her peers, mostly the sons and daughters of Black University faculty, but she did not articulate this difference in terms of social class. Frequently she noted that her classmates could not figure her out. However, she did acknowledge that this was a Black middle-class school, where all students were expected to attend college. While Katherine received solid support, she felt like an outsider: "I often felt I was not totally integrated into the student body. There were a few of us who were eccentric." Unlike most of the other girls in her high school who were socially oriented, concerned with being cheerleaders and attending parties, Katherine was academically oriented. She competed in the statewide math contest and edited the yearbook.

Black University Lab School provided Katherine with avenues to the wider world. She scored well on a test and was one of two students from her school selected to attend a United Presbyterian Church Summer Program for Minority Studies in another southern city. She spent the summer before her junior year away from home in this skills-building program with other students of color from around the nation. She was close to the program director who, during her junior year, called and asked her to apply for a summer program at an eastern preparatory school. Minority students who had participated in the United Presbyterian Church Summer Program were strong candidates for this new program, which was going to be integrated. Katherine agreed to apply.

Katherine recalled that she and her school peers knew that their segregated high school was wonderful, and they appreciated the solid support given by teachers, but "we were also somewhat insecure about our ability to compete in the larger world." Participating in the Northern Preparatory School Summer Program was a way to address such concerns. Indeed, Katherine was very scared for the first two weeks, until she received positive feedback on her written work. The program faculty did not know what she had to fear, yet Katherine needed this experience to build her own confidence.

With input from teachers, Katherine began making her own educational decisions in high school. Making such decisions required a clear assessment of her skills and needs. Her parents, who were not familiar with this territory, had nevertheless prepared Katherine for such a role by stressing self-direction. Their support was in part a response to her personality. Even as young child, Katherine always had grand plans: "I was always announcing that I was going to be a doctor in New York or an artist in Paris. So my family got used to thinking about me as the one who would go out and do something big." Her parents, especially her father, promoted a great deal of independence. "From an early age, my father let me make my own decisions. It was never 'Daddy knows what is best for you.' I could do what I wanted as long as it seemed reasonable. When it was time to go to college, he did not say anything. He hated to see me leave, but could see my reasons for doing so. I had made the decisions about the summer programs. While he had misgivings, since he would not see me as often, he was supportive of me doing what I wanted to do."

Teachers at that Northern Preparatory program suggested that Katherine apply to Whitehall College. Katherine had never before even considered attending a prestigious, predominantly White college. During her senior year, her high school teachers supported her goal. "At Black University Lab School, every teacher wanted someone to get into Whitehall College." Her parents were unaware of the significance of such a choice. Katherine recalled the time:

The choice [of Whitehall College] was more encouraged by some of my teachers than my parents. My parents were willing to go along with it, but they were more concerned with where I was going to be happy. They wanted me to do something successful. But to them, if I went to college that was a big step. Because my parents were not into the ranking of colleges, they did not perceive that this [going to Whitehall College] was so much different from staying at home and going to Southern State University. They were all colleges, but this was a cut above the others. My parents did not know that in the eyes of most of the world attending such a school would make much of a difference."

Katherine thus had solid support from her high school teachers and counselors as well as emotional support from her parents and their lessons of self-direction. It was with these skills and support that she negotiated this juncture. As Katherine noted, "I always made up my own mind."

Four other working-class students from segregated institutions left the South with the help of teachers, brochures supplied through NSSFNS, and even summer programs on college campuses. Proceeding to a college in East City depended upon receiving a scholarship that was earned by grades. The fact that their daughters had literally earned these opportunities might have contributed to a pattern where working-class parents let their daughters make decisions on their own schooling. Furthermore, to many of the working-class parents, like the Howells, a college was a college.[11] They were not versed in the status differences between schools, so they let their daughters do what they thought was best. The values of self-direction and striving for excellence, as well as the strong commitment to education, that they had stressed in their families meant that parents could trust their daughters to make appropriate decisions. The downside of this situation was that family members did not really grasp the significance of the choices that their daughters were making at the time. If they had, they might better have appreciated the nature of the sacrifices young women were making as they left the South to secure such a fine education.

When young women lacked supportive teachers, they had to plot their own routes to colleges. The NSSFNS was very important when schools failed to encourage women to go beyond "safe" schools. By enabling young people to bypass high school counselors and receive information, financial aid forms, and applications directly from colleges, this agency helped women like Nancy Brooks consider schools that counselors might not bring to their attention. Furthermore, the recruitment process communicated that schools were potentially interested in these students. This interest could counter the skepticism of teachers and build students' own confidence.

Even though she was in the elite course in her all-girl academic high school, Linda Trott was not viewed by teachers as a candidate for a private college. All the graduates went to college, but Linda was advised by her counselor to apply to local state institutions. Like many working-class women, Linda advised herself.[12] Her best sources of information about colleges came from outside her high school. After receiving information from the NSSFNS, Linda selected schools she thought were appropriate, applied, and was accepted at a private college in East City. When she told her counselor where she was going, the high school officials took credit for Linda's accomplishment. Upon reflection, Linda was bitter about her school's attempt to claim her success, since such statements denied the work that she put into the process. Her school did little to support her belief in her own academic abilities and was not a source of either cognitive or emotional support for the transition to college. The school's action in claiming her success not only denied Linda's researching skills but masked the efforts of outside agencies designed to counter the racial bias found among high school counselors in the mid-1960s.

Even with support and assistance from the high school, child-secured mobility still meant thinking about college for many years with the hope that your best effort would enable you to gain admission and receive a scholarship. Parents' untested beliefs in their children were often what enabled young women to keep moving toward their goals. Summer programs were important in giving these young women, especially those from segregated schools, real-world settings to test their abilities. Peer groups also played a critical role in helping them think about colleges. Most working-class women had friends who shared their goals of going to college, and they spent hours discussing the value of attending specific colleges. Cynthia Butler recalled sharing college catalogs and talking about schools with her friends at lunch and on the daily commutes to high school. Older siblings who were either in college or graduates also helped during this transition. Karen Johnson found advice from her older brother and sister invaluable in helping her think about colleges. Their suggestions helped Karen combat poor advice from her guidance counselors. Tracy Edwards also looked to her older brothers for aid in deciphering the situation, reviewing catalogs, and identifying colleges with appropriate programs for her.

When parents had limited information about colleges, more work fell on the young women themselves. They had to rise to the task and figure out a future that was attainable. This task was very complex for those who lacked support for their academic goals in high schools. Neglect and/or hostility undermined the confidence the women should have been developing in high school. Therefore family support and the values they learned at home were essential in helping them push forward, even without positive signs from teachers and counselors. It is clear that the working-class women valued the strong emotional support and wisdom of their parents, because it gave many the courage and stamina to persist in the face of discriminatory treatment. Dorothy Wall recalled those lessons: "I grew up with the knowledge that yes, I am Black, but I am also valuable. That has come from my family, because they were full of pride, strength, and determination. So you grew up acknowledging that some people hate the fact that you are Black, but it did not matter. You were able to endure and keep going. You know that there are a lot of brick walls out there, but you also know that there are a lot of things which can break the walls down."

A critical dimension of child-secured mobility is the way that young people assumed economic responsibilities. While most of the middle-class women left paying for college to their parents as they sought the perfect college, working-class women addressed this issue themselves. In fact, economic concerns were primary factors in working-class women's decisions on whether to attend a specific college. Because most working-class families could not finance their daughters' college educations, many of these young women began to confront money issues at an early age. Karen Johnson had learned early in her childhood that she would need a scholarship for college; thus she had to study and achieve excellent grades to qualify for financial support. Karen also saved her own money for college, including earnings from small jobs she began in elementary school and gifts given at holidays and birthdays. Even though she was not yet in junior high, she was insistent upon saving her money and not spending it on "childish" things. In the end, she attended East City University and lived at home. She had a small grant from the school, which she combined with her savings, loans, and earnings from part-time jobs to finance her education.

When asked "Why did you choose to attend a college in the East City area?," ten of thirty-one working-class respondents wrote that they selected their colleges because of the financial aid award, scholarship, or low tuition fees. For example, Darlene Maxwell said, "I attended Regional University because I received a scholarship and could not afford to go out of state." The young women were aware of the economic constraints on their choices. In some cases, women did not have a vision of "going away to college" but limited their goals to institutions in East City where they could live at home and minimize expenses. They also relied on in-state tuition at public institutions to make the cost of college affordable. Cooperative programs were particularly attractive because they enabled women to resolve financial difficulties. In these programs students alternate between periods of study and periods of work, so they spend five years completing their bachelors' degrees. These programs, at least in the mid-1960s, attracted a mixed student population, including middle-class students who were not eager to rush through college and into professional schools or employment as well as working-class students who paid for their own educations.

Finances dictated the actions of several working-class students. Thirteen women remained in East City for college. Ten of these women, like Adele Lewis, never thought about "going away to college." Adele applied to two colleges in East City. As a very bright student, she was accepted at both institutions. She recalled how she decided between the two schools: "I got more personal treatment at Regional University than at East City University. Also East City University did not give me any real money. Even the financial aid package at Regional University was not enough. My mother went to the university and told them they had to give me more money, which they did. I really couldn't pay for it." In Adele's case, the cooperative program at Regional University helped to make college attendance financially feasible, since she was able to work some quarters and graduated in five years.

In her elite high school, Denise Larkin was one of the few Black students urged to go to a prestigious college, but she elected to attend Regional University. Denise was not very interested in the status rankings of schools. Furthermore, she was committed to easing some of the financial burden on her parents, which made the cooperative program very attractive. She recalled her thinking at the time: "There were three children in the family who would be in college at the same time. We were not poor enough to get real scholarships, because our need wasn't super great. My grades were all right, but they were not fabulous. You had to either have great grades or be really needy to get funded, but I didn't fall into either category. I did get an NAACP scholarship. I thought my parents could not afford to send me away to college. Even now I hate to take something if I really don't need it. It was guilt that kept me in East City." Denise had witnessed how her parents struggled to send her older sister away to college. The cooperative program at Regional University gave her the opportunity to contribute something toward her own education instead of having her parents work harder. Although her parents would have gone into debt to secure an education for her, Denise took financial responsibility for her own schooling.

Eighteen women came from outside the East City metropolitan area to attend college. They all had significant scholarships, but they also took out loans, and most worked part-time. They lived in dormitories and had "traditional college experiences." The majority of those from the East City area lived at home, at least for some of their college years, and commuted to their schools. Their parents' limited finances kept all the working-class women focused on paying the bills.

Race, Class, and Securing Schooling

The high schools of the 1960s were complex institutions for this cohort of Black women to navigate. The type of school and its social class, gender, and racial composition meant different obstacles and supports for these middle- and working-class Black women. They were amazing young women who faced the advantages and disadvantages of different schooling environments with a stamina that is to be applauded. The stakes were really quite high in comprehensive high schools, because their mission was to identify students' talents and direct them toward appropriate futures. A woman might be seen as college material, as the middle-class women were, or pushed toward either the commercial or business track and then forced to challenge the school's class bias, as several working-class women reported. Many working-class women struggled to be recognized as college material. Negotiations were often most intense in integrated schools, where they competed with White and middle-class Black students for attention from teachers. Elite schools offered advantages in terms of curriculum and pathways to colleges. However, Black women, across social class lines, were relatively new populations in these schools, and not all the women were well received. Yet the cultural capital of middle-class women gave them an advantage and fostered their integration into most elite schools.

Black women who moved from majority to minority educational settings generally experienced less individualized support for educational goals. In desegregated schools Black women were not tokens, and racial balance helped create a climate where students could make friends across racial lines. Majority Black schools also offered greater social ease. The women who attended segregated schools did not negotiate interracial relations, but they did obtain the self-confidence needed to face those challenges in college. In predominantly White and integrated schools, Black students were involved in more racial negotiations. In general, these women were either isolated in their schools or in the college-bound tracks. Few women, even in integrated schools, reported having experienced racially balanced college preparatory courses. As a result, many graduates of majority White schools had separate Black and White peer groups. In these settings, Black women did much of the work of integrating. Respondents from integrated schools made fewer social sacrifices, but the respondents in the college-bound tracks felt the same pressures as their counterparts in predominantly White high schools because they were representing their racial group. They knew they were being tested, even if this fact was not acknowledged. Despite the pressures, many women said they did their best to enjoy high school.

These different schools also varied in supporting the women's transitions from high school to college. Majority Black environments were generally supportive, but the majority White schools had a mixed record. Some were supportive, particularly of very talented young women, while others were clearly discriminatory or simply failed to consider the varied needs of young Black students. If solid support in selecting a college was not forthcoming from schools, then the women were dependent upon family. Again social class was a factor.

Middle-class women benefited from adult-sponsored mobility at this juncture, where parents provided cognitive and material support as well as expressions of belief in their daughters' abilities to handle college. These interventions helped the women resist biased guidance and supplemented counseling short-comings in majority White schools. While the lack of support was part of a familiar pattern of neglect and hostility for many working-class women, the middle-class women were surprised to find racism manifested in these same institutions where they had previously been comfortable. Having their teachers question their plans for college was a painful experience for these relatively privileged students. At the time, the women wondered if their teachers, the recognized experts, were making rational decisions, but most decided that racism was involved. This conclusion was reinforced when they gained acceptance to the colleges of their choice. As a group, young middle-class women graduated from high school with a great deal of confidence in their abilities. Parental support and the generally favorable environments paved the way to success in college.

Like their middle-class counterparts, the working-class women also had strong parental support for college. In order to meet the goals their parents had set for them, the working-class women were pushed into early maturity as they made realistic assessments of their abilities and opportunities. Following a strategy of child-secured mobility, these young women did much of the actual work of identifying colleges and locating funding for tuition. Many felt pressured to work hard in school in order to win college scholarships, since they knew their own families' finances were limited. Child-secured mobility strategies involved assessing situations, making decisions on their own, and then frequently educating their parents. This work was necessary to get an education that would enable them to be upwardly mobile in a racist and classist society. They varied in how they met this challenge, but as a group, they did not emerge from high school with the level of confidence of their middle-class peers.

Working-class women in majority White elite and comprehensive high schools faced this transition differently. Graduates of elite high schools were generally more confident in their abilities to attempt college. Some measure of encouragement from teachers in comprehensive high schools seemed necessary for women to launch a college career. If we remember that few people in this nation learn to think in structural terms before college, we can see why many high school students were not likely to identify social class as a source of differential treatment. Instead, students and teachers alike tended to view differences based on personality. Parental lessons gave many women a race lens, but they could not fully explain their schools' actions. In the end, many working-class students held questions about their abilities to win teachers' confidence. These doubts affected the visions they developed of their potential. After graduating, many carried scars from combating a tracking system through junior high and high school. Most fought the system so that institutional barriers did not push them to end schooling with high school.

Women who attended elite high schools, and a few from comprehensive high schools, were more successful in navigating this territory. They used all the resources available to them and held steadfast to the educational goals instilled by their parents. They often were successful in getting scholarships to advance their education. Their child-secured mobility strategies taught them many skills in navigating the adult world, but fully appreciating these skills was complicated. First, many high schools took credit for college acceptances of such students, even when school officials had little to do with the outcomes. Moreover, only a few working-class parents were clear about the significance of their daughters' college selections; this knowledge might have come from their daughters' teaching them the importance of aiming for elite colleges. Yet these navigating skills would serve the women well in college, where learning to appreciate them would be the foundation of stronger confidence in their abilities.

Fortunately, the women who did not receive solid encouragement from their high schools resisted counselors' suggestions and sought external sources of information. Their clusters of support varied by social class but directed them on to new challenges. For the women who had been in majority White institutions, the lessons about negotiating in mainstream institutions would help with college. Graduates from segregated schools and predominantly Black high schools would learn many new lessons in college, but their schools had equipped them with the confidence that they would need at this next stage.

CHAPTER 8 : COLLEGE
Expectations and Reality

Socially, my expectations were that I was uptight about the prospect of going to school with boys. But the main expectation that I wanted from it [college] was academic. [I wanted] To find out the answers to all the big questions about life. Starting with—what is life now? I expected that was college. It would be the place where I would sit around and think about stuff and talk about stuff with people who were smarter than me. The only two expectations I can remember; the fear expectation and the positive [academic] expectation.
—Robin Washington, respondent from working-class background

The summer before I went to college, I started worrying about how difficult this "best school" was going to be. I was concerned that it might be hard. The social thing, I expected that there would be a number of Black men at college. As is true of a lot of middle-class Black parents, I was told, "Things would be great when you go to college. That is where you will meet young Black men who will appreciate you, who will appreciate your intelligence." A number of brothers did not appreciate it in junior and high school. In fact, they made it very clear that they wished we would shut up. Those were my expectations. In terms of what actually happened, the work was not hard. . . . Socially, it was kind of abysmal for awhile.
—Beverly Rawlins, respondent from middle-class background

Working- and middle-class women had different expectations as they planned and prepared for college. One group was involved in social mobility, while the other was reproducing a middle-class position. These qualitative differences were reflected in their initial expectations and in the lives they built in college. However, both groups were challenged as racial pioneers who faced various forms of institutional and informal racism and sexism.

As the first generation in their families to attend college, the working-class women were forging new paths, and their expectations and images of the terrain before them were vague. As a group, working-class students focused mostly on the academic aspects of college and held few expectations for a social life. Katherine Howell thought she was very naive: "I thought everyone would be very heavy intellectually and that I would have to work my ass off to get through." But she had not given any thought to the nonacademic side of college: "I had no way to visualize what social life was going to be like." To working-class women, securing a college education could make them mobile and expand their employment options. Perhaps the focus on future employment was a reason why many women attended most to the academic aspect of college. This low level of concern with social activities was reported in James Hedegard and Donald Brown's (1969) comparative study of first-year students in a large public university. They found a vision of a "more study-oriented life, more restrictive in breadth of activity" among first-generation lower-middle-class Black students than they did among White students (pp. 138–39).[1] Their population could be similar to the working-class women in this study.

In contrast, the middle-class women here had more specific academic and social expectations for college. College was a setting for gaining knowledge and securing the credentials that would enable them to duplicate their social class position. In addition to stressing the importance of education for employment, their families also communicated that college meant active social lives and developing friendships that would last through their adult years. For example, Sabrina Powell grew up hearing her mother talk about what was going to happen to her in college, including learning a lot, dating, and meeting the man she would marry. But Mrs. Powell had graduated from a traditionally Black college. There was little awareness of how the middle-class women's social experiences would be shaped by the fact that they would be part of a small group of Black students on predominantly White campuses. They approached college with goals of achieving a balanced student life but quickly realized how complicated that would be at these institutions.

These fifty-six women all attended predominantly White colleges that did not make institutional changes to ease their adjustments. However, these schools varied in some critical ways. Size was important, since women were more quickly integrated into smaller institutions, while large schools contained a critical mass to develop Black peer groups. Schools also varied in their academic rigor, or in perceptions of the level of challenge in this arena. Both factors were key ones in the women's initial adjustment to being a "minority" on campus and mastering the academics required to succeed.

Different Educational Contexts: Elite and Non-Elite Colleges

While all nine colleges attended by the women had national reputations, there were significant differences in their educational programs. To examine routes to college and patterns of adaptation, we can divide these colleges into elite and non-elite institutions. Elite institutions were generally recognized as prestigious and had rigorous entrance requirements, accepting only students with high SAT scores and excellent high school grades. These schools might demand a high level of academic performance from students, often including honors projects during their senior year.[2] The five non-elite schools also had high standards but were less selective in admissions. Most important, these colleges provided very different environments for the women. In this study, twenty-seven women graduated from colleges identified as elite and twenty-nine from schools identified as non-elite. The women from different social class backgrounds were divided almost evenly between elite and non-elite institutions: fifteen working-class and twelve middle-class women were in elite colleges, while sixteen working-class and thirteen middle-class women were in non-elite schools.

When we look at the high schools the women graduated from we can see some patterns in college attendance. These observations are only suggestive of barriers that faced Black women in specific high schools in the 1960s. Furthermore, the women's goals for college varied. Some women did not want to attend elite colleges because they did not see them as ideal settings for themselves. So, while the paths to either elite or non-elite colleges were complex, a few specific patterns are evident.

First, there was a track from elite high schools to elite colleges for women of both social classes; twelve of the seventeen women from elite high schools followed this path (see Table 3). Of the eight working-class graduates of elite high schools, five went to elite colleges, while seven of the nine middle-class graduates did so. When elite colleges sought to increase their enrollment of Black students, graduates from private and specialized public schools were strong candidates. There were several reasons why some graduates of elite high schools did not follow this path. The lack of support from high school teachers could be a factor in why Irma Dennis and Brenda Carter did not apply to elite colleges. The type of elite high school could also be a factor. Cheryl Davis graduated from an arts high school that had college preparatory courses, but not all the advanced and high honors programs found in academic specialized high schools. Her institution, which sent many graduates to fine arts programs, lacked the direct channels to elite academic institutions.

Other factors informed the working-class women's decisions, particularly

TABLE 3. COLLEGE ATTENDANCE BY SOCIAL CLASS AND TYPE OF HIGH SCHOOL

ELITE COLLEGES	NON-ELITE COLLEGES
Working Class	*Working Class*
Cynthia Butler	Brenda Carter
(Elite high school)	(Elite high school)
Katherine Howell	Tracy Edwards
(Elite high school—segregated)	(Elite high school)
Linda Trott	Denise Larkin
(Elite high school)	(Elite high school)
Beth Warren	
(Elite high school)	Stephanie Lawrence
Robin Washington	(Integrated comprehensive)
(Elite high school)	Adele Lewis
	(Integrated comprehensive)
Joanne Bell	Darlene Maxwell
(Integrated comprehensive)	(Integrated comprehensive)
Carla Jenkins	Gloria McDonald
(Integrated comprehensive)	(Integrated comprehensive)
Gwen Johnston	Jennifer Taylor
(Integrated comprehensive)	(Integrated comprehensive)
Sylvia Mason	Dorothy Wall
(Integrated comprehensive)	(Integrated comprehensive)
Crystal Robinson	
(Integrated comprehensive)	Regina Walker
	(Predominantly Black comprehensive)
Toni Brown	
(Predominantly Black comprehensive)	Francine Chambers
Margaret Cooke	(Predominantly White comprehensive)
(Predominantly Black comprehensive)	Carolyn Greene
Wilma Jefferson	(Predominantly White comprehensive)
(Predominantly Black comprehensive)	Marion Green
Natalie Small	(Predominantly White comprehensive)
(Predominantly Black comprehensive)	Karen Johnson
	(Predominantly White comprehensive)
Nancy Brooks	Elise King
(Predominantly White comprehensive)	(Predominantly White comprehensive)
	Janet Sheldon
	(Predominantly White comprehensive)

their own thinking about their needs. Tracy Edwards was looking for an institution that had an allied health program, since she had a specific career goal. Denise Larkin was encouraged to attend an elite school, but she did not find this option attractive: "I knew I didn't want to go to any of the Ivy League schools, because I couldn't stand all those White people. And the Black folks I met when I went to

TABLE 3. CONTINED

ELITE COLLEGES	NON-ELITE COLLEGES
Middle Class	*Middle Class*
Wendy Anderson	Cheryl Davis
(Elite high school)	(Elite high school)
Katrina Charles	Irma Dennis
(Elite high school)	(Elite high school)
Sandra Freeman	
(Elite high school—outside U.S.)	Michelle Clark
Deborah Jones	(Integrated comprehensive)
(Elite high school)	Kimberly Davis
Sherri North	(Integrated comprehensive)
(Elite high school)	Yvonne Foster
Olivia Stevens	(Integrated comprehensive)
(Elite high school)	Helene Montgomery
Karen Wright	(Integrated comprehensive)
(Elite high school)	Rebecca Nelson
	(Integrated comprehensive)
Beverly Rawlins	
(Integrated comprehensive)	Sabrina Powell
Susan Thomas	(Predominantly Black comprehensive)
(Integrated comprehensive)	Florence Powell
	(Predominantly Black comprehensive)
Evelyn Tucker	
(Predominantly Black comprehensive)	Rosalind Griffin
Allison Cross	(Predominantly White comprehensive)
(Predominantly Black comprehensive)	Mary Knight
	(Predominantly White comprehensive)
Marlene Turner	Brenda Reed
(Predominantly White comprehensive)	(Predominantly White comprehensive)
	Joyce Saunders
	(Predominantly White comprehensive)

those schools were all 'bourgeois.' They asked, 'Where did you come from?' and 'What does your father do?' And I couldn't stand that kind of talk."

Second, six of the nine women who graduated from comprehensive segregated or predominantly Black high schools went to elite colleges. The high concentration of women from segregated and predominantly Black high schools in elite colleges can be explained by the solid encouragement offered by high school teachers and the recruitment patterns of colleges at this time. Middle- and working-class women in these schools had parental and teacher support, encouraging them to seek out new opportunities. The four working-class women received funding, as it was often elite colleges that provided full scholarships to attract high-ability students from the South. A few of these colleges operated summer programs for minority high school juniors, and segregated high schools were very cooperative in identifying potential students for such programs. These programs gave the students an opportunity to test being on a northern predominantly White campus. For example, Natalie Small, a working-class student from a small southern city, attended a summer program at Private College after her junior year. She did well that summer and enjoyed her time on the campus. In her senior year she was urged by college representatives to apply and subsequently received a full scholarship.

Third, the majority of graduates of predominantly White comprehensive high schools went to non-elite colleges. Black women from both social class groups in these schools had less solid support and exposure to educational options than women in other high schools. These schools were more likely to be ambivalent about the achievement of their highly visible Black students. Their years in these fairly hostile high schools had an impact on the women's decisions. The middle-class women were looking for a college experience that differed from the social isolation of their high schools and believed they could most likely find more Black peers in the non-elite colleges of East City. Since high schools had not provided the working-class women with many opportunities to build confidence in themselves, few made the effort to overcome their financial limitations and attempt to attend an elite school. In fact, many of the working-class women from East City remained in that community, because they thought they could secure employment there to help finance their educations. Only two of the twelve graduates of predominantly White high schools went to elite colleges. Nancy Brooks and Marlene Turner, from the working class and the middle class respectively, both had more solid support from teachers than the other women at such schools.

Fourth, the integrated comprehensive high schools had a mixed record; seven of the eighteen graduates went to elite colleges. However, while only two middle-class women went to elite colleges, five working-class women did. Again, biased patterns of advising could have been a factor, since the two middle-class women who proceeded to elite colleges, Susan Thomas and Beverly Rawlins, were both advised by their mothers. In terms of plans for colleges, rather than focusing solely on schooling, many of the middle-class women were also looking for colleges that enabled them to shape a life that balanced academics and social activities. The working-class women were not necessarily strongly encouraged by school personnel but were able to overcome barriers through the NSSFNS, which put them directly in touch with colleges. Their potential was often recognized by college recruiters, even if they had been overlooked by their own teachers and counselors.

All of these predominantly White colleges were nationally ranked and provided students with a solid education. In fact, the majority of graduates from both social classes went on to secure advanced degrees. Yet we cannot ignore the status rankings among colleges, expectations of performance, and how some institutions were able to provide their graduates with enhanced access to people and information as they planned for professional careers. These institutions also represented different contexts within which individuals shaped their educations, developed relationships with faculty, thought about careers, made friends, and looked for life partners. In this study the context relates to the academic challenge, which translates into the work and stamina needed to pass courses, as well as to the academic goals of an institution. The amount of effort necessary for an adequate academic performance influenced the time women could devote to other activities, particularly their social lives and paid employment. Thus the academic context influenced how they balanced their lives as college students.

The Reality of a Predominantly White Campus

When they arrived on their campuses, these middle- and working-class women initially were surprised by the majority White settings. They had underestimated the intensity of the struggle and the personal price they would pay as participants in this national desegregation experiment. They had been actively recruited by predominantly White colleges because they met the regular admissions requirements. They had grades, tests scores, and records of extracurricular activities that were similar to those of White students at the same institutions. Like most college students, they faced academic pressures, identity crises, social adjustments, and career and life decisions while in school. Their experiences were ordinary, like those of other college students, but also unique because they faced them as Black students. They would have to resolve the ambivalent stance about race that typified many institutions at this time. They were visibly different from the majority of students and were treated as such, but there was no public acknowledgment of differential needs. They were supposed to fit into the existing system. As a consequence, they mastered the academic work and made the adjustments necessary for survival and success. They mustered whatever resources they had and whatever networks they could develop to complete college.[3]

The changes in recruitment policies were clear when all at once a handful of Black students appeared on small campuses and 100 or 200 were enrolled at larger institutions. For the faculty, this change might mean routinely having one or two Black students in a large lecture course. While some faculty genuinely welcomed the increased diversity on campus, as a group, they were ill prepared to handle the many issues involved with introducing Black students into formerly all-White classrooms.[4] Other faculty, particularly those who associated the prestige of the institution with its exclusive racial composition, viewed increasing Black enrollments as the lowering of standards (Thomas 1992; Willie and Cunnigen 1981). As a result of these circumstances and attitudes, many Black respondents had to work to be recognized by faculty as legitimate students, especially the working-class women from comprehensive high schools.

Interacting with college peers also required some adjustments on the part of the women. While some White students had gone to high schools with Black people, others had not. So these few Black students were a new population for many of their White peers. In the mid-1960s, many White high school students might have expected Black students in their urban high schools. However, college was another stage in the educational process, and White students were often surprised to find Black students on campus, especially at elite colleges. As the women recalled, some students were welcoming, whereas others were distant and hostile. In fact, some White students openly questioned the qualifications of Black college students (Feagin, Vera, and Imani 1996; Thomas 1992). Even if these Black women were determined to live in an integrated world, they had to cope with the ambivalence of many White students and faculty about their presence on campus.

Because the majority of the women had had experiences in either predominantly White or integrated educational settings, they were familiar with the role of the token. In fact, their socialization had prepared many to act as a "stand-in" for all Black people. Yet college brought new social pressures on them as racial pioneers in higher education. They knew they had to do well here to pave the way for other Black students. However, many had to face these pressures without daily support from family and kin. Women who were mobile often had difficulties communicating these subtle pressures to their parents. It was important that they develop new support networks, but often these institutions made that task difficult.

Small private colleges in the late 1960s might typically have only twenty to fifty Black students on a campus of 2,000 to 6,000 students. For example, Katherine Howell arrived from the South in 1966 ready for the challenge of college, but she recalled: "My first days there [at Whitehall College] I had not seen any Black people. There were none in my classes and I was the only Black person in this dorm filled with White women. Finally, there was a big gathering, where the Dean spoke to all the freshmen. I was looking around for the other Black women. There were only five in my whole class. This was the first time I had seen them and I was too shy to approach them." The small number of Black students did not change much over time. Katrina Charles also attended Whitehall College and remarked that when she graduated in 1970 there were only twenty Black women at the college.[5]

Coming to grips with being a Black student on campus could be particularly rough for women at small colleges. Because their campuses lacked the critical mass of Black students to build informal race-based peer groups and organizations, college meant an immersion into White social activities. In high school, on the other hand, even respondents who graduated from integrated or predominantly White high schools had gone home at the end of each day and had affiliations in their communities and churches. Since she graduated from an integrated high school, Susan Thomas was accustomed to dealing with White people. As a member of the middle class, she had much in common with her new classmates, but she had difficulty adjusting to the social scene in college. She said: "There were few Black students on the Private College campus. One had to leave campus for contact with other Black students. The White students at Private College usually had not been around Black persons. I found that I was disproving stereotypes for White students. White students also did not readily accept Black students in social activities." While Susan made friends with middle- and upper-class White students, she was never very comfortable with the overall social setting, even though she did well academically.

Adjustments on large campuses were also difficult. Even women from large public high schools were accustomed to seeing other Black students in their schools, whether or not they were in their academic programs. But many now found themselves in colleges of 8,000 to 12,000 students with only 150 to 200 Black people. They might be the only Black student in a lecture hall with 200 or more students. Irma Dennis commented that she was initially shocked by the numbers of White students as she went about her day on the campus of East City University. This scene was a major change from her tiny, private, predominantly White high school. Women often felt isolated and uncertain in these new settings; at the same time many, particularly those who were away from home, found themselves separated from their sources of support.

Karen Johnson was initially overwhelmed by the size of East City University, but she was able to connect with a group of Black students: "The first day I met this girl, who is still my best friend. We saw each other and we both grinned. We were the only Blacks in a sea of White people. I met some other Black girls. The three of us used to hang together all of the time: Regina, Carolyn and myself. During those days I was very turned off by White people and had very little to do with them." Even if their percentage was small, the number of Black students at big universities allowed the women to develop a social life. However, many continued to feel the isolation and pressures of their minority positions in their daily academic activities.

Sensitivity to the imbalance of the races and the new social pressures that came with challenging stereotypes were troublesome to many Black women. The women had to reach into their inner cores to survive in these settings and make their own places on their campuses. With few informal or institutional supports to address their unique needs, these women developed their own survival strategies.[6] Some mastered the system but still maintained a critical stance toward it; others accommodated more to the values of the system, and still others moved beyond individual survival to create new structures that would speak to the needs of Black students. The day-to-day pressures of being a token Black woman student at a majority White college were anticipated neither by the women nor by anyone else on campus before their arrival.[7] The tensions they experienced often led to feelings of uncertainty. In the face of these tensions, many Black women students felt they had to develop strategies not only for their personal survival but also to keep attendance at such colleges open as a viable alternative to Black students in the future.

Academic Performance

Mastering the academic work was not only essential for graduating, it was a priority for these women. They knew that college would dramatically influence their futures, so most worked hard to do well. Many initially drew upon their high school experiences for a picture of academic college life. They found college to be far less structured than they anticipated. As students, they had to adjust to this newfound personal freedom. They also faced the task of succeeding academically on these predominantly White campuses. About 54 percent of the women reported cumulative grade point averages of 3.0 or above. Therefore only a slim majority did B-level work or better in college. Yet, grades are not the most accurate reflections of learning. Many of the women with below B averages appreciated their academic experiences in college. In fact, a majority of the respondents were pleased with their academic experiences: 22 percent (or twelve women) rated their experiences as excellent, and 50 percent (a total of twenty-seven women) indicated they were good. Not as pleased were fourteen women (25 percent) who indicated their experiences were fair and two women (or 3 percent) who thought the academic programs in their colleges were poor.

When asked about their academic experiences, the working-class women rated them slightly higher than their middle-class counterparts did. This is not of statistical merit but does demonstrate again that the working-class women in this study were not overly critical about their educational experiences. Perhaps these women recognized that a college education, regardless of the struggles and sacrifices, was a route to a very different life. They might also have been aware that scholarships, especially to elite schools, made that education possible. The middle-class women, whose parents were primarily funding their educations, maybe with some supplements from other sources, perhaps felt the liberty to be more critical about their academic experiences. Because the prestige of the school was important to their assessments, we will look at the academic experiences of women from each social class by prestige of college.

ACADEMIC PERFORMANCE IN ELITE COLLEGES

Four institutions, Private College, Roosevelt University, Whitehall College, and Technical University, identified as elite, were reputed to require high standards from students. The middle-class women, many from private or specialized high schools, were in fact ready for these challenges, if not more. Thus their academic performance might have been affected by other factors. In contrast, the working-class women fared differently depending upon their level of high school preparation and ability to use the universities for their own purposes.

Middle-Class Women

Eleven of the twelve middle-class women in elite colleges found the academic side of their schools generally to their liking, rating the experiences either excellent or good. Many found that college was not as hard as they had anticipated. The common experience was for middle-class women to adjust to college work within their first year. In the words of Deborah Jones, "Having an extremely good standardized education [in high school] paid off in college because the expectations of poor performance by Black students, which is really a class effect, did not apply to us." On the whole, this student population was well prepared for college-level work. They could readily address the academic aspects of the adjustment to college. Wendy Anderson thought she initially received some terrible advice about scheduling that made her first semester difficult, yet she had the skills to overcome:

> I was taking all my lower-level courses that first year. Which was a bummer, because they were all survey courses which required some depth, yet you could not bullshit your way through it. Nobody told me that it was not wise. On the other hand, I was not used to large lecture courses. And my high

school experience was good enough so I was kind of bored. I got very depressed, didn't go to classes and did miserably. I came very close to ending up on probation. So I had to figure out how to get through. I forced myself to go to classes, scheduled them as early as I could on Mondays, Wednesdays, and Fridays only, and got a job which paid money. I got the job because my parents cut off my allowance. I discovered that I learned best by osmosis, so I sat in the first row; it would sort of seep in, and I did better and better. Also there was a reading period, which is great. This system worked for me.

Coming from a public school, Beverly Rawlins had to overcome her initial fears. She recalled, "I thought it [college] would be harder than high school. I found out that the work was not that hard. I didn't do much work and put things off until the reading period." Beverly was a B student, and like other middle-class women, she found college well within her capabilities. Nine of the ten middle-class women in elite colleges who reported their grade point averages indicated that they had a B or better average. However, nonacademic factors did influence performance. Katrina Charles reported that she did not do well, but she attributed her performance to the pressures of family problems while she was in college. Furthermore, while she had initially wanted a large college, in the end she found the institution to be too impersonal. Katrina is the only woman in an elite school who rated her academic experience below good—in her case, poor.

While education was valued by these women and their parents, being in these high-powered schools did have a downside. The middle-class women had been pushed by their families and the demands of the society to perform well and challenge stereotypes. Being very visible Black students in elite colleges meant more of the same demands. However, this was a time when the women had to find their own way of coping with the stresses of academic life. Wendy Anderson talked about such pressures: "Whitehall College always impressed me as being a highly competitive place, and I was just tired of performing. I didn't like competing. . . . I was very conscious of the fact that you had to do well, and I just felt, 'Oh no, not again.' Then, at the same time, I was motivated to do well. I had been too well programmed by then to really throw it all away. It was a rough year; I guess the first year of college is rough for everyone." After a summer abroad, Wendy began dating in her sophomore year. She got married at the beginning of her senior year, which meant she had more support for facing academic pressures. In the end, she graduated magna cum laude. Wendy, like five other middle-class women in elite colleges, was more disappointed with her social rather than her academic experiences.

Deborah Jones had worked hard in high school without special attention from teachers, and she repeated this pattern in college. However, she had the skills and an interest that enabled her to do well at Roosevelt University. She recalled: "Due to the pushiness of students, I developed a nervousness about speaking out in classes that I had never had in high school. This was okay, since most classes, even small ones, were lectures. So I just concentrated on exams and writing. You do the work and you get the grades, and I always got As and Bs." This commitment to scholarship was important to her academic success. It was also a way for Deborah to cope with the poor social scene in college. She continued: "In my freshman year, I decided to be an English major, which made the most sense, since then I could do more fine arts if I wanted. It was really literature that got me through all the considerable personal depressions and unhappiness, which were surely no more than any other student in college, but that is where I was at. At that time I took more poetry courses than anything else, even though I do more prose now. I had a number of very interesting professors who were really passionate about what they were teaching." However, except for one professor, Deborah did not have personal relationships with faculty. She spoke with her theater professor once after class, and they got along quite well. In fact, he later wrote a letter of recommendation for Deborah when she applied to an advanced degree program.

Many of the middle-class women at elite institutions were employed during the academic year. Nine of the twelve women reported that they worked at some point during their college careers. Some, like Wendy Anderson, worked for spending money, while others varied in their reasons for working. Their jobs were not too demanding, and often involved working either as research assistants or in clerical positions on campus. Like other middle-class students, they were well prepared by their previous schooling for the scholarly demands of college. Therefore adjustments to college for this group related more to the individual woman's personal issues and ability to gain comfort on these predominantly White campuses. Overall, the middle-class women did well in college and were generally pleased with their academic preparation.

Working-Class Women

The fifteen working-class women in elite colleges varied widely in their assessment of their academic experiences: five reported that they were excellent, six noted that they were good, and four thought their experiences were only fair. In their questionnaires and interviews, the working-class women in general reported more academic difficulties and social adjustments. Women who excelled in comprehensive high schools had to learn new study habits, improve their writing skills, and adapt to a more competitive atmosphere. Adjusting to the immersion in another social class, most crucial in elite colleges, was also on the agenda. Prior to college, the working-class women spent limited time in middle-class institutions, since they returned to their communities every evening. Now they were away from home, living in dormitories and participating in many aspects of campus life. Engaging in these activities involved crossing both social class and racial lines. Many felt as if they were set adrift on these new campuses. In contrast to the middle-class respondents in these environments, the working-class women had many new social tasks to learn. Often it was difficult to relax until they could come to grips with the middle-class atmosphere and the inevitability of mobility. Indeed, some women never seemed to relax and were ready to retreat to old social class connections once they finished their degrees. Yet others used elite colleges for what these schools could do best, that is, prepare them academically for a middle-class future.

The fifteen working-class women varied in their level of academic preparation for elite colleges as well as in how they made the social adjustments necessary for academic success. Mastering the academic work, which was often required to maintain scholarships, was a priority, but achieving this goal in nonstructured and highly competitive environments was difficult for some of the women. Many from comprehensive high schools found elite colleges to be rigorous educational settings that were a challenge to master. Nancy Brooks had a difficult adjustment and in the end evaluated her academic experiences as fair. Unlike the middle-class students, Nancy was not prepared for the nature of college life. "I didn't know what I was getting into. I was completely taken by surprise when I arrived at Roosevelt University. It was like I had sleepwalked through the whole process of getting in and when I got there, I had to finally ask myself, 'What was I getting into?' I was intellectually oriented but not that much into studying. I was not prepared and it took me two years to get adjusted." The transition from a comprehensive high school to an elite college was hard, particularly when one was a visible minority and there were no institutional supports. Like Nancy, Sylvia Mason did not think she made the most of the educational opportunity. "I was not emotionally ready for college. I should have had more outside experiences and then gone to school." In the face of little institutional support, but with the requirement that students maintain grades to keep their funding, working-class women often had to work out ways to succeed on their own.

Natalie Small, a graduate from a southern segregated school, had a rough, but ultimately more successful, transition. She rated her academic experiences as good and commented, "I was unused to strong academic pressures. I got off to a rough start, having fair to poor grades. But as I became adjusted to the academic environment, my grades became very good. My academic average could not reflect this, because of my poor start." In the end, Natalie finished college with a

2.7 grade point average. Wilma Jefferson, another graduate from a southern segregated comprehensive high school, did very well at Whitehall College, even making the dean's list. However, it was more often the case that those women from comprehensive schools, like many college students, had to adjust to the expectations and demands of college-level work.

The working-class women who graduated from elite high schools were more similar to the middle-class women in their level of academic preparation. They might have had fears, but they were more likely to find that they were well prepared for college work. Robin Washington adapted to the academic side of Roosevelt University more quickly than to the social aspects of college. Upon reflection, she rated her academic experiences as good. "The first day I got terrified and wanted to run back home. I thought that I had bitten off more than I could chew. I was really intimidated. . . . I had been a big fish in a little pond, [and] now I was in the ocean. Quickly, I got my bearings—socially, in terms of girls on my floor, and intellectually, in terms of seeing that I could perform as well as anyone else." Other elite high school graduates, like Beth Warren and Cynthia Butler, similarly did not have the long adjustments more common among comprehensive high school graduates.

College life was somewhat complicated for members of this group because of the demands of paid employment. Only one of the fifteen women, Sylvia Mason, was not employed during the school year. The majority had positions on campus, working in laboratories, libraries, assisting faculty, or in other academic of-fices. Most of these women had sufficient funding that work demands did not compromise their schooling. However, a few, like Nancy Brooks, also had off-campus jobs and worked full-time during holidays and breaks when their col-leges were closed.

Succeeding in these elite institutions was facilitated by a woman's acceptance of academics as a priority. If a Black woman focused on these goals and either postponed other concerns or was willing to look beyond the campus to meet her social needs, she could shape a successful strategy. Linda Trott wanted a White school for many reasons, but particularly for the academics. "I knew that if I went to a Black school, I would not get educated as well [as in a White school]. This message was clear to me from my own education. There was a big difference between predominantly White classes and predominantly Black classes from junior high school on. I realize now that this [attending a White college] is how [Black] people get isolated from their communities, but at the time I was looking for schooling, not socializing, a husband or the other reasons why other people were choosing Black colleges." Linda had a rough adjustment in college but was able to use the skills of self-direction and chart her own course.

Focusing on scholarship, Linda made the most of her years at Roosevelt University. While she had been ignored by teachers in high school, she thrived in college. "In small classes I was noticed. In high school, I had gotten no feedback, except for grammar on my papers. Therefore, in college I had to learn how to write. By the junior year I was doing very well." College was a place where Linda learned how to learn, so by her third year she was ready to shape her own learning. She made maximum use of the opportunities available. In her senior year, she was interested in community schools. While Roosevelt University did not have an urban site, she developed her own placement in an urban school. During that year she lived off campus, worked in the Black community of East City, took courses, and completed an honors thesis. She noted: "I used those years to test out ideas. I decided I wanted to be a teacher because of my own college experience." While she praised the academic experience, she knew it did not come without costs. Linda remarked, "I was very isolated from my community. It was the price I paid for the education."

Beth Warren also made education a priority and rated her academic experiences as excellent. She loved all the opportunities at Whitehall College, including seminars and independent study courses. In the end, she thought she had received "good training in writing, research methods, and discussion." Like other working-class women raised in Black communities, she felt the social isolation and was weary of the stereotypic treatment she received. These circumstances motivated her to branch out from the campus. Beth was raised in a family where political action was a way of life. Therefore, in addition to her part-time work, Beth volunteered in the Black community of East City. She worked on voter registration and educational programs. The social class differences within the Black student population at Whitehall College were clear: while some students were working, others were hanging out. Beth said, "It was essential [for me] to work, since the university was such a rarified atmosphere. I couldn't relate and needed to have at least one foot in the real world." Moving beyond the campus enabled her to achieve the balance she wanted in her life.

Among the twelve working-class women who reported their grade point averages, eight had averages of B or better. As they met the academic demands and social adjustments that were necessary for survival, many women did very well. Their own personal goals of upward mobility helped to keep them on track.

ACADEMIC PERFORMANCE IN NON-ELITE COLLEGES

Five institutions were identified as non-elite: Melville College, State College, Regional University, East City University, and Music College. They were all sites where a woman could get a fine education as well as clarify her career goals and proceed to advanced degree programs. Again high school preparation, often linked to social class, shaped the women's abilities to do college-level work without much adjustment. In general, the schools did well by the women who made academics a priority. To a greater extent than in elite schools, the individual agendas of women influenced their academic performance and adjustment in non-elite institutions.

Middle-Class Women

The thirteen middle-class women in non-elite colleges approached these institutions with different agendas: training in a specific field, socializing, or gaining clarity on career goals. Rebecca Nelson, Sabrina Powell, and Yvonne Foster all picked their colleges because of specific programs: music, speech therapy, and occupational therapy, respectively. These women, even if they changed majors, were generally pleased with their academic experiences. Rebecca thought the academic programs at East City University were excellent. "I learned a tremendous amount and was given opportunities based on merit and competition. I had small classes and concerned teachers." Yvonne also thought she learned a great deal and was well prepared in her profession.

Another group of middle-class women were attracted to the metropolitan area of East City rather than to a specific school. They were motivated by a desire to address both the academic and social sides of college life. For example, Mary Knight recalled, "At the time there were few [predominantly White] colleges with a significant Black student population. The East City area had so many colleges that collectively there was a significant Black population. The same factors were true for Mid-Atlantic City schools, but I didn't want to live at home." Because they were selecting the area, rather than the university, some women were not pleased with their academic experiences. Irma Dennis did not really have much information about East City University but knew people who had gone there or who were going to other schools in the East City area. However, after her private high school Irma found East City University relatively easy: "Except for philosophy courses, which I liked and attended, and did well in, much of the curriculum was boring and easy to pass courses without much work. I seldom attended classes." After majoring in philosophy and government, Irma went to law school, which she found more interesting. Michelle Clark was also drawn to the area rather than Regional University. In the end, she was disappointed because of what she saw as "poor academic standards and instruction." However, Michelle did well and proceeded to medical school.

These middle-class women, like their counterparts in elite colleges, were well equipped to handle the academic side of college. Only a couple of women raised issues of academic preparation, and these concerns were course specific. Evaluating the academic side of college, three women rated their academic experiences as excellent, five reported good, four noted fair, and one rated her experience as poor. Those who were disappointed in their academic programs mentioned the lack of challenge as the problem. These middle-class women varied widely in their performance, with five women reporting they did B or above academic work and seven women reporting below B-level work. Overall, the performance of the middle-class women was related not to their level of academic preparation but more to their goals for the years in college.

A few women noted that the lack of academic challenges enabled them to have the social lives they desired. So while some women were disappointed in their classes, it was also possible to let huge classes, which they could easily pass, work to their advantage. Helene Montgomery selected her school for a variety of reasons. "My parents both attended Stewart [a predominantly Black college] and I briefly thought about following in their footsteps. However, I didn't think I was going to live in an all-Black world, so I was not attracted to an all-Black school. It might have been better, but at the time I felt socially inferior to Black peers, so I didn't know if I would have 'come out' at Stewart. . . . My parents stressed that college was a time of important social development. So I wanted a large university, with high academic standards, that had a number of Black students in a city with a Black community." Helene, a C student at East City University, said, "I discovered that it took a minimum of work to stay in and that is what I gave it. It was a big difference from high school." Rating her experiences as fair, Helene noted that her priority was building a rewarding social life. Later, when she went to graduate school, Helene realized that she could have gained more from her courses if she had put in more effort.

Other middle-class women used their college years to clarify educational goals and generally had praise for their academic preparation. Cheryl Davis had friends who had gone to East City University and was also drawn to the area. Her academic experiences were good, but she did have a rough start. "In the beginning I was in the wrong field for me [math], but when I changed to Sociology, I enjoyed it very much and therefore learned a great deal." Joyce Saunders started Regional University interested in majoring in biology because she was considering attending medical school. Her job placements helped her clarify her career goals. Joyce did very well in the social sciences and proceeded to graduate school. Overall, Joyce thought her university's academic program was excellent.

Like those middle-class women in elite colleges, solid secondary preparation paid off for this group, as by and large most could readily handle their schools' academic work. While the large classes and less than rigorous standards made it easy to survive without much effort, those who did apply themselves profited from the settings. Perhaps because many middle-class women were raised with the expectation of getting an advanced degree, ten of the thirteen graduates proceeded from these institutions to graduate programs or professional schools.

Working-Class Women

The majority of the sixteen working-class women in non-elite institutions had praise for their schools: two rated their academic experiences as excellent, nine reported good, and four reported fair (one person did not rate her experience). These women, especially those from comprehensive high schools, spoke about the adjustment period as they learned new habits to master college-level work. For Adele Lewis the transition from an East City public high school to Regional University was surprising. As an honor student in high school, she did well with little effort, but college required that she learn new study habits. Yet she always found the "college competition to be very trying." Succeeding in college meant spending time on the campus studying in the library, in science laboratories, study groups, and in other education-related activities. Brenda Carter also talked about adjusting: "It took me two years to settle into a study routine, so the last years were much better." The lack of structure in college, particularly compared with fairly rigid high schools, required such adjustments.

While mastering habits to survive at college was more easily attempted when one lived on campus, the women who resided with their families also had to establish new patterns. Karen Johnson commuted to campus, but she still had to learn to pace and motivate herself. She said, "The first year was a waste. I was so taken by the fact that I could just float around all day. I didn't study and was on probation. Then the second year I started to study, and then the last two years I did well. I think I got a good education there. I wasn't very serious until the last two years; then I had decided that I'd better do something with my life." This was a common pattern for many college students. In the face of all the adjustments, the working-class women varied in academic performance. Six women reported having done B-level work or better, while ten women reported their work was below B-level.

Academic success was not just a matter of adjusting. For many of the women, college was a positive environment, yet a few reported racism as a factor in academic life. The freedom of movement in college, whereby students could drop and add courses as they desired, gave many the ability to avoid hostile faculty. However, some pockets of the university were more welcoming than others. Francine Chambers began her time at East City University in the fine arts college. She had faced ambivalent teachers in high school, but the drama department at her university was deeply problematic. These encounters forced her to change majors. "I started as an acting major, but switched because of the oppressive racist attitudes in that college. I transferred to liberal arts and majored in Political Science. Prior to that I was the only Black female in drama. Others had left previously." Francine did very well in her new major and viewed this new program and her academic experiences as excellent.

In addition to adjusting to the demands and pace of college work, several working-class women worked part-time while attending college. Rather than juggling school and a social life, like their middle-class counterparts in the same schools, these women were integrating paid employment with their academic careers. For example, Carolyn Greene held jobs as a sales clerk, telephone correspondent, office machine operator, and floor manager while in college. She noted that "I had to work and could not devote complete attention to my studies." As a group, the working-class women in non-elite schools were quite serious about their studies. Yet the fact that some of the women were also engaged in paid work hindered how much time they could devote to academics.

Many of the women selected non-elite colleges with specific career goals, while others were vague about their futures and saw college as a place to explore career options. That process could be stressful in cases where women were not in organized programs. The women who lacked clear guidance had to sort out their own lives, just as many had investigated colleges while in high school. Janet Sheldon thought her academic experiences were only fair because of the courses and counseling. "In retrospect, the education courses that I took were most interesting. Courses in my major field [math] became less interesting in my last two years as they became more abstract. Poor career planning prevented me from learning ways of using my major."

As in high school, these working-class Black women varied in their connections with faculty. While a few had close relationships, others just used the resources of the institution to sort out their futures. However, most were genuinely appreciative of the opportunities that college gave them. In retrospect, Dorothy Wall thought that she went to college for her parents. Yet the experience radically changed her vision of what she could do. "I thought I would go through college and finish. I knew that I could be a teacher and hoped that I would come up with an alternative while in college." Dorothy majored in English and education. She did her student teaching but was not very excited about the classroom. In considering her future, she began to talk with an advisor about education administration. However, it was a concrete experience that helped her identify a career plan. Dorothy explained: "I talked about the lack of advising for students at State College who were considering graduate programs with Professor

Avallone. There was no place to help students get organized and to get advice. So I read up on it and then worked with Professor Avallone to organize a library. I realized that I liked education administration and decided to go to graduate school [in this field]. I found out about financial aid and applied to eight schools and was accepted at seven universities." Unlike her experience in high school, where she was not given special attention, Dorothy was strongly encouraged in college to pursue graduate programs. She was working on her doctorate at the time of the interview in 1976. While she began in a non-elite institution, she attended advanced degree programs in elite institutions. Dorothy was like twelve of the other working-class women in non-elite institutions who continued their schooling beyond college.

While Dorothy identified a career at her university, the world of work helped other students clarify careers options. Darlene Maxwell was very aware of all the dead-end jobs that were available, so she used her cooperative jobs while at Regional University to gain experience in the communications field. After her elite high school, Denise Larkin found Regional University to be very easy, but her employment experiences helped her plan for the future.

> I just did stuff and got As and learned the knack of getting good grades [at Regional University], like make yourself known to the professor and stuff like that. I was on Dean's List most semesters. I liked the working. I started off in an insurance company, and I did what I was supposed to do. I sort of learned other things; I'd get my work done and then see what someone else was doing. I switched all over; then I did secretarial kinds of stuff and was working in another area of the insurance company. Then I was a teller and ended up training bank tellers. I was not sure if I wanted to teach, so I seriously considered working in banking. . . . I had a great student-teaching experience, so I decided to be a teacher.

Like their counterparts in elite colleges, these working-class women were getting an education to prepare for a career. Attending non-elite schools, where there was less scholarship money, often meant heavier employment commitments for students. Yet even within these settings working-class women learned profound lessons. Jennifer Taylor thought the program at East City University was excellent. She wrote on her questionnaire: "The classes and instructors were very good and the students were alert. Being a large private school, East City University had a wide range of academic resources. . . . The course work was not as important in and of itself as learning how to be an independent, thinking individual as opposed to be being a spoon-fed one." These working-class women made the necessary adjustments, rough at times, to their colleges and survived.

Many achieved their goals and balanced schooling with strong commitments to paid employment, while others had more freedom to focus on the academics.

Summary

Like previous generations of African American women, these fifty-six women continued a tradition of valuing education. In addition to providing skills and credentials to achieve economic independence, college enabled some women to become upwardly mobile and others to reproduce their parents' middle-class positions. Attending a predominantly White college presented some unique challenges, as all the women were shocked by the realities of life on their campuses. Their new environments demanded many academic and social adjustments, especially when there were few institutional supports. Social class position stamped both the women's expectations and their transitions to college. The middle-class women reported less trouble with the academic aspects of adjustment than their working-class counterparts. Economic advantages enabled middle-class women to balance social and academic goals, and in a few cases, to make developing a social life a priority in college. Adult-sponsored mobility gave the women the freedom to enjoy a well-rounded student experience. Most still had an eye on college as a path to either employment or advanced schooling.

The working-class women, often employing child-secured mobility strategies that involved both continually searching out information and a high level of responsibility for financing college, had more narrowly focused expectations. Their transitions varied, as those from elite high schools were better prepared for college-level work than some of the women from comprehensive high schools. Even if social adjustments were troublesome, the requirement of maintaining a grade point average to keep their scholarships determined their priorities. Many women also felt a strong sense of responsibility as one of the first in their families to attend college. After getting their bearings, the women did the work required to succeed. Some women, like Linda Trott and Dorothy Wall, found college more supportive than their high schools had been and were able to shape new career goals with a more accurate sense of their abilities. The values initially nurtured in their families helped the women make the most of what their schools could offer. These women from both social classes were up for the challenge of the day and made the most of the academic opportunities that class and talent opened for them.

CHAPTER 9 : SURVIVAL STRATEGIES
IN COLLEGE

Compared to high school, I was more involved in politics in college. I didn't join many
clubs in college. When I was in college, I realized that I didn't really want to go to college.
What I wanted was a degree and I have said more than once that I wished I could take a
giant capsule and be over with this [experience]. It was good in that it gave you time to get
to know people and grow up, and especially at that particular institution [Whitehall
College], there were some very interesting people. At the same time, it seems like it was too
much like a day camp. People would sit around and mope and talk. Not that much
learning took place, except for people who were in the physical sciences. . . . My major was
sociology. I didn't really have any idea of what I wanted to do with it. It seems like a
versatile, well-rounded major. It was the closest thing to general studies. Since I was only
interested in the degree, it didn't make too much of a difference.
—Beverly Rawlins, respondent from middle-class background

The flavor of it [college] was misery. At the time I was pretty miserable, and it was only
that I was so docile that it never occurred to me to leave. The guys could not leave because
of the draft. I could not leave because it was beyond me to even think about it.
—Robin Washington, respondent from working-class background

Mastering academic course work was just one of the tasks these fifty-six
women faced in college. As noted in Chapter 8, the working-class women frequently began college with a sharp focus on getting an education that could be
translated into future employment. The middle-class women were also groomed
to prepare for the labor market, but many had expectations for the college years
that included a social life and perhaps meeting a mate. Yet as all the women
arrived and settled in at their institutions, it was clear that college was a special
place and time in their lives. Writing about women in college, Shirley Angrist and
Elizabeth Almquist (1975) noted that "it is here [in college] that choices of values,
field, friends, and a mate will occur, producing consequences that will last for a

lifetime" (p. 8). Regardless of the priorities the women entered with, they had to wrestle with the challenges that the college experience presented. It was a time of many choices and decisions.

College was also a place where these women met new people and were challenged in various ways. In dormitories and lunchrooms as well as classrooms, they discussed many issues with peers. Evelyn Tucker, who was raised middle class, said, "I got to know a wide variety of people [at Whitehall College] and I also discovered a lot about myself." These colleges, especially the small schools, gave the women many opportunities to learn about others. In the process they rethought their own social positions, developed new aspirations, and modified their career plans.

This chapter explores two issues: peer groups and the women's thinking about their futures while students in college. How did they create rich social lives on the campus, both to garner support from others and to balance the academic pressures? How did they envision their futures, particularly in regard to paid employment? How did they bridge the gap between gender socialization of family and school? How did they juggle their commitments to the multiple roles of worker, wife, and mother that most Black women were socialized to assume?

Creating Spaces on White Campuses

It was incumbent upon these racial pioneers to build their own informal supports, because college administrators in the mid-1960s did little to anticipate the realities of desegregation. The practice then, as now, was a "one-way assimilation process in which black students [were] forced to adapt to white views, norms, and practices" (Feagin, Vera, and Imani 1996, p. xi). While other Black women may have attempted the process at these institutions and left for other schools, and still others might have dropped out of college, as many young people did in the 1960s, these women stayed and graduated. Their strategies are therefore important in understanding how Black women coped without the institutional supports that would be available to later cohorts.

It is clear that many women in this cohort created spaces to gather together and reaffirm their racial identity. It is this population of Black students, those admitted to many predominantly White colleges in the mid-1960s, who initially formed African American student organizations on their campuses in the late 1960s (Willie and Cunnigen 1981). Toni Brown was part of a small group that organized social activities for Black students at Private College and other schools in East City. She was also one of the founders of her university's African American Society. Denise Larkin was instrumental in organizing the Black students at Regional University. Nationwide, Black students took the initiative on many campuses, demanding that administrators assume responsibility for structural inequality, admit more minority students, and even establish programs to remedy the deficient secondary educations of many students of color (Van Deberg 1992). After such student actions, some administrations developed recruitment programs, hired more Black faculty and staff, and provided additional services for minority students.

These women survived in college without formal institutional supports, however. To explore the social aspects of their college years, the women were asked to evaluate their social experiences in college. Generally speaking, the majority of the women enjoyed their social experiences and were pleased with their social growth. Most respondents (61 percent) built social lives that they viewed as excellent or good. Most of the women took the initiative to satisfy their social needs. Others were not as pleased, but only a few noted poor social experiences.[1] The respondents were also asked to characterize the social class, racial composition, and aspirations of their peer groups. The twenty women interviewed talked at length about this aspect of their college years. Developing a peer group as a racial pioneer was a challenge. As part of a small Black population on their campuses, these women were very different from each other. In addition to coming from different social class backgrounds, they came from East City and other regions of the country. Many women sought to make close friends in college but had to do so within the context of their campuses. They were surrounded by White students who had different experiences with Black peers and varied in their desire to befriend Black classmates. The failure of many White students and faculty to see Black students for themselves, including their racial identity, was a persistent problem. This lack of human recognition of Black students persists in education today (Feagin, Vera, and Imani 1996; Tatum 1997b).

The women had to build supportive networks for themselves in order to thrive in college, especially when they were separated from family and friends. As racial pioneers in the 1960s, these women had basically two choices, either integrated or predominantly Black peer groups. The majority of the women had integrated friendship groups. Fourteen women indicated that they had predominantly Black peer groups at some point in college, and three respondents discussed either feeling socially isolated or being too busy working to have had a social life in college. Some women had two groups of friends, and a few shifted networks during their years of college.[2] There are no neat patterns to their choices that fall along social class lines or the types of institutions. The different schools presented various options, but the actions of the women reflected their own particular needs at the time. In integrated groups, the women were in many respects cultural envoys, teaching White students about their racial group. However, these Black women also needed reciprocal relationships to satisfy their own needs, so many continued a practice established in high school of moving between two groups. Other women used the college years to retreat into pockets of Black peers, which became a common pattern on predominantly White campuses when there were larger cohorts (Tatum 1997b; Willie 1995). At this time, these peer groups were important in solidifying racial identities for women who had often been racial pioneers in other educational settings.

PREDOMINANTLY BLACK PEER GROUPS

Fourteen women, five from the middle class and nine from the working class, described the people they spent time with in college as a majority Black group. Most of the women just reported the composition of their peer groups on the questionnaires, but some provided commentary to explain their choice of friends. Thus, rather than imagining that those who made this choice were young women opting out of integration, we can see the purposes that such groups served for college-age youth. As racial pioneers these women were committed to integration, and most of their time on the campus was in majority White settings. Peer groups were different. These were the places that women shared intimacies, spent their free time, and perhaps created the pool from which they sought mates. Women developed Black peer groups for many reasons. Some replicated a pattern they had learned from their own families. Some women, especially those from the South, had little experience socializing across race and frequently encountered White classmates who were equally parochial. Majority Black peer groups represented a level of safety in an educational setting where women took risks every day. For a few women raised in predominantly White neighborhoods, college was their first opportunity to socialize with Black peers. They used these spaces to explore and affirm their racial identities.

Being a racial pioneer was not easy. Students faced racism from both teachers and the institution at large, mostly in their failure to address student needs. Therefore majority Black peer groups were spaces and places for recuperating from the assaults suffered in desegregating these schools. Enduring the direct and subtle racism of these institutions took a toll on the women, and they needed places to receive support for being a Black student, regroup, evaluate their circumstances, and prepare for continuing to attend classes and seminars. If they did not transfer out of these predominantly White schools, they needed an antidote to survive in them.[3]

An article on East City University calling it the Howard University of East City caught the attention of a few middle-class students. That label identified the university as having a significant number of Black students, making it as attractive as the historically Black university in Washington, D.C. Attending East City University thus enabled women who had primarily socialized in Black circles in high school to continue that practice while in college. Irma Dennis grew up in a Black community, and her social life had revolved around her Black friends. She was among the small group of women who selected East City University because the pool of students ensured that they could attend a White college but still be socially active with Black peers. To meet the other Black students, Helene Montgomery joined an informal group that held activities such as parties and dances. Helene could easily balance her life between academic and social activities, because she was not employed during the school year. She even met the man she would later marry. Other middle-class students like Helene "partied" and made close friends with Black students at their own colleges as well as at other schools in the area. For women like Rosalind Griffin, who had endured years of isolation in the predominantly White suburbs, East City University meant the opportunity finally to meet a variety of young Black people. Rather than consistently being the only person challenging racial stereotypes, Rosalind now had Black friends to support her and opportunities to explore Black cultural activities. Her friends were middle-class and working-class Black students who were aspiring professionals. She noted, "I felt accepted and a part of things."

Most of the predominantly Black groups were mixed across social class lines. These were spaces where working-class students were socialized into a Black middle-class subculture. As a member of the working class, Karen Johnson had scaled both race and class barriers in her predominantly White suburb to enter college. After years with White teachers and students who were ambivalent about her, Karen welcomed the opportunity to have a Black peer group at East City University. In college, she socialized exclusively with Black students and limited her interactions with White students to the classroom. She was like many Black students who immersed themselves in an African American subculture on their college campuses and used the time to resolve identity issues (Tatum 1997b). At the time of the interview in 1976, her friendship network was integrated, but she had needed the time in college to talk openly about racial issues with Black peers.

While some women were beginning to develop links with Black peers, others were coping with new interactions with White students, many of whom failed to appreciate their Black peers. Majority Black groups provided these women a place to heal and gain the support they needed. Adjusting to Whitehall College was difficult for Katherine Howell. While her new college peers were welcoming, they saw her as an exception and did not affirm her racial identity. Because she had fair skin, her roommates questioned her racial identity. To Katherine, who grew up in the South, this situation was unreal. She described an early encounter: "They [her White roommates] were nice, but they kept asking me, 'What do you mean you are Black?' They told me that I looked White and could easily pass for White. I had never been challenged like that before, so I did not even know how to answer the question. I told them that my parents are Black, that I grew up in a Black community, went to Black schools and Black churches, and that I just was Black. I had never thought about being White." Perhaps these White students' queries were grounded in an acceptance of the myth of Black inferiority, but they failed to appreciate that Katherine was proud of her culture. As a Black woman at Whitehall College, Katherine routinely challenged accepted stereotypes and con-tradicted students' and teachers' expectations. She learned a great deal, prepared for the future, and made friends in college, but she continued to face social hurdles as a racial minority. As a result, Katherine said, her first two years were horribly lonely. As a junior, she met some Black people and had a better social life. Her predominantly Black peer group for the last two years of college was composed of middle-class and career-oriented students.

It was not only student interactions, but also experiences with academic programs that motivated Black women to seek refuge. Working-class respondent Francine Chambers had an integrated peer group in high school, but her college experience was different. She was troubled by the racism at East City University and spent much of her time with other Black students. This peer group choice was critical to her enjoyment of the college years. She socialized with Black middle-class students who wanted to become part of the upper middle class, but they were also committed to helping other Black people.[4] These students did what was required to survive, including creating safe spaces on their predomi-nantly White campuses.

INTEGRATED PEER GROUPS

Most women in both elite and non-elite institutions had integrated peer groups. Large institutions gave Black women many opportunities for interaction. Women could have racially balanced peer groups as well as majority Black ones. Jennifer Taylor, a working-class graduate of an integrated high school, described her peer group at East City University as "equally Black and White." She wrote: "They were intellectually acute and fun. The White students were securely middle-class, while the Black students were working to be so. The White students thought in terms of being the heads of agencies, while the Black people thought about secure professional jobs in government or private industry." After college, Jennifer pursued an advanced degree and then worked for the government.

Brenda Carter, a working-class graduate of a parochial school, welcomed the size of East City University. Brenda's college peer group was well integrated. Her friends were mostly working-class Black students similar to Brenda, the daughter of a postal clerk, but her friendship circle also included middle-class White students. Brenda indicated that she only knew a few middle-class Black peers. Her friends all aspired to finish college and get good jobs; only a few talked about advanced degrees. After college Brenda entered a master's program.

In elite schools, women established peer groups that were not as well mixed in terms of racial composition as those in non-elite schools. Yet for some women these groups were places to grow and receive support. Even students from urban areas appreciated the opportunities for growth and exposure that came from getting to know many different people. One middle-class respondent spoke directly to this issue. Marlene Turner, who attended Technical University, saw her social experiences as excellent. She wrote: "To this day I have strong feelings about the warm openness of the students and faculty at Technical University which was further enriched by the ethnic and national multiplicity of people and the large number of social and cultural events on campus."

Linda Trott, a working-class graduate of a predominantly White elite high school, also commented that meeting a range of different people was important for her growth. She thought Roosevelt University gave her the opportunity to meet people who were very different from her. While the college appeared to be homogeneous, Linda associated with poor White students, Black students, Jewish students, and foreign students. This exposure meant that Linda, a very private person, learned many new skills. She recalled, "I learned that it was valid to think about yourself. I didn't take it to extremes, but I opened up." Two White women and one Black woman, who were initially in the same dormitory, were Linda's close friends. While all her good friends were middle class, they were very different from each other in many respects. These friendships were ways of learning about dimensions of class and race in the society, because Linda's friends were coping with different issues. She said, "We never talked about aspirations, because people did not know what they wanted to do. Separation from family was not difficult for me, but my friends spent much of their first year in college confronting this issue. What was hard for some of my friends was not hard for me. I was struggling with other issues. There was a great deal of learning on all sides. I think that knowing these different women helped me affirm strengths I did not know I had." College was a place for Linda to gain perspective on those early family lessons of self-direction and independence. Her skills in navigating adult environments had paved the road to Roosevelt University but had not been validated by teachers. Her friendships with middle-class women helped Linda appreciate what she had achieved, and these insights enhanced her confidence.

While some women developed friendships with people from varied backgrounds and lifestyles, other respondents were drawn to students with whom they shared an outlook. A few women with integrated peer groups noted that politics was an overriding factor in bringing a diverse group together. During the late 1960s, a time of turmoil and change in many nations, Beth Warren at Whitehall College socialized with students from this country and abroad who were concerned with issues of social change. Beth also had friends off campus.

Participants in integrated peer groups might have faced the same battles of challenging stereotypes that pushed some women into majority Black groups. These were days of experimentation, and while most of the Black women had integrated experiences before, their classmates did not necessarily have such exposure. Some women who had integrated peer groups on campus also spent time with friends in majority Black settings. This bicultural pattern is common among contemporary Black professionals who might compartmentalize friendships. In her research on Black women managers, Ella Bell (1990) found that many had one set of friends in the predominantly White workplace and other friends outside of work. In this study a few women mentioned that they had two friendship groups, an integrated one, mostly women from their dormitories, and another group that was majority Black. It was the latter group that they socialized with most in college.

Margaret Cooke, who had a diverse social experience, spoke directly about a bicultural pattern. In her predominantly Black high school, her peer group included Black, White, and Asian American students. She developed a different style in college. In the dormitory, Margaret had White friends with whom she spent time. She also pledged with a Black sorority off campus to widen her contacts with Black college students in the area. Like some of the other Black women on campuses with small Black cohorts, Margaret had to leave her campus for connections with Black peers. The few Black students at her university did not socialize on a regular basis. Margaret remarked that she was the Black student whom most White students on her campus knew. In her emissary role, she was advancing her group by her achievements in the classroom and in student groups (Tatum 1997b). In this role she learned much about the White world, while her White friends, who never knew many Black students during their years in college, learned little about Black people. Margaret's experiences were similar to those of respondents in Kathleen Slevin and C. Ray Wingrove's (1998) study of retired Black American professional women, who saw being bicultural as necessary. One respondent noted to the researcher: "We've [Black Americans] had to under-stand you. We've had to figure out your world and what made you tick as White people, but you've never done that for us. You've never tried to figure out what is special about us, what is our uniqueness" (p. 113). As long as the assimilation was one way, Black students did more of the accommodating, and some women sought refuge from the tensions this created.

Mary Knight, who attended East City University, also established a bicultural pattern. She recalled, "On campus I spent time with White and Black folks looking to get through school. Their social classes varied. Off campus, my friends were mostly Black folks trying to make it, usually through the academic route, from many different social class backgrounds." Mary, Margaret, and other Black students in college at this time were able to establish social relationships with White students, even if these affiliations were uneasy. But they also moved within majority Black groups. In Chapter 4, Deborah Jones talked about moving be-tween two worlds in high school and being confused about what was appropriate in each setting. If they had not done so in high school, as racial pioneers, many of these women learned to be bicultural in college. They shifted between the two worlds, able to interact in educational and social settings. These skills would help them later in graduate school and professional work. Yet while they learned important skills, there was a cost, as women did not always have their own social needs met in majority White groups.

Most of the respondents were successful in building a life on their predomi-nantly White campuses, even though it was not easy. The women would have benefited from more institutional support, rather than having to take respon-sibility for doing much of the reaching out across racial lines themselves. Stu-dents created their own spaces because administrators did not recognize the racism that Black students experienced and their need for peers as a respite from the tensions of their token roles. At this stage, the women's socialization helped them achieve their goals because they took charge of the situations they found themselves in and used their own standards to chart a course.

Considering Their Futures

As many scholars have noted, college attendance does not ensure achievement for women (Angrist and Almquist 1975; Holland and Eisenhart 1990). A college education was a step toward economic independence, but mobility through mar-riage was often the norm for women in the 1960s and 1970s. However, patterns of dual-spouse employment were common in both working- and middle-class

Black families. Therefore Black women were raised to value economic independence and to anticipate long-term paid employment (Billingsley 1992; Shaw 1996; Slevin and Wingrove 1998; Taylor 2000). Research on Black women in college in the 1960s and 1970s has indicated that this population was more likely than their White counterparts to see marriage, children, and full-time employment in their futures (Fichter 1967; Mednick and Puryear 1975; Turner and McCaffrey 1974).

Like other Black college women in this age cohort, these fifty-six women were socialized to link securing higher education with future employment (Fichter 1967; Higginbotham and Weber 1992; Mednick and Puryear 1975; Turner and McCaffrey 1974). The majority of the women (82 percent) had specific career goals in mind when they were planning for college. Like most college women, their initial choices shifted and were modified over time as they turned general aspirations into concrete commitments. Yet the fact that the majority had career goals in mind when they selected a major and when they graduated from college is evidence that they were continuing a tradition. How did they think about future employment? What were the major influences on their attitudes? Were there social class differences in their orientations to future work?

In the 1960s, many White women entered college expecting to marry and spend little time in the labor market, while these Black women were very employment oriented (Angrist and Almquist 1975). Joseph Fichter (1967) gave special attention to Black women's strong work orientation in *Graduates of Predominantly Negro Colleges: Class of 1964*. The author saw Black women as "not as ready as white women to say that it [marriage and family] would interfere either with post graduate study or with their occupational careers" (pp. 100–101). Getting an education was a priority for all, but many women were also thinking about marriage and children. What were their priorities? If they planned to marry, how did they consider integrating paid employment into their lives?

Exploring both their thoughts on employment and how these women envisioned their futures reveals differences across social class lines. All these women valued employment, but they varied in their abilities to picture a career within the context of a lifestyle. They were faced with different problems while in college, so that immediate mobility tasks took priority over finding a mate for most working-class women. In contrast, the middle-class women, many of whom had social goals as well as academic ones, varied in how they ranked family and career.

EDUCATED FOR EMPLOYMENT

In the late 1960s, society continued to undergo many racial and gender transformations. As they listened to peers and teachers and watched the social changes, many Black women refocused their initial goals. As young women they were cognizant of new opportunities and made career choices they had not anticipated earlier. To explore their attitudes about education and employment, the women were asked: "During your senior year, how important did you feel it was for you to have knowledge and/or skills to *make* you employable?" Fifty-four percent of the women (eighteen who were raised working class and twelve who were raised middle class) indicated that it was very important. Twenty-eight percent of the respondents (ten raised working class and six raised middle class) thought it was important. Only 18 percent of the women (seven raised working class and three raised middle class) replied that having knowledge and/or skills to make oneself employable was either not very important or not important at all. Many respondents who marked these latter answers indicated on their questionnaires that they anticipated securing skills in graduate and/or professional school. For example, Kimberly Davis replied that having knowledge and/or skills to make one employable was not important at all, "because I had always planned on going to graduate or professional school." Their answers to these two questions indicated that preparing for paid employment was a concern for the majority.

Economic pressures translated into a strong career orientation, especially among many of the women from working-class backgrounds. When they entered college, Tracy Edwards and Natalie Small had their eyes on specific traditionally female occupations, physical therapy and education, respectively. They trained for these occupations in college and entered them upon graduation. Elise King, a graduate of Regional University, recognized the need to be self-supporting. Aware of the student loans she had to repay, Elise wanted to achieve the necessary standard of living. She went directly from college into law school and was a practicing attorney in 1976.

Although women from working class families were conscious of the need to work, some of them were uncertain about employment options. The cooperative program at Regional University helped many women identify areas in which they wanted to work. However, six of the working-class women were vague about specific occupational aspirations even when they graduated. For example, Marion Greene wanted interesting work and knew that attendance at State College would enable her to avoid clerical positions. Upon graduation, she found employment in higher education, a challenging work setting with opportunities for advancement. As a group, though, working-class women were working toward future employment while in college. Like Tracy, Natalie, and Elise, they were more likely to have specific goals in mind than their middle-class counterparts.

A concern with employment options crossed social class lines, as middle-class women were also raised to secure employment. However, more of the middle-class women were unclear about the specific work they would do after graduation than the working-class women. In fact, this group was more evenly split among those with specific occupational goals (thirteen women) and those who did not have clear aspirations (twelve women). Middle-class respondent Susan Thomas had clear goals and entered a professional program in occupational therapy because she wanted to be self-supporting after getting her bachelor's degree. Olivia Stevens decided in college to become an attorney. She majored in government and upon graduation from Whitehall College went directly to law school. Eleven other middle-class women focused on future employment while in college and made sure they had the requirements for that work or the prerequisites for graduate study.

There were also middle-class women who did not know what waited for them beyond the degree. Wendy Anderson, who married while in college, was unclear about a specific career while at Whitehall College, but she was committed to employment. Wendy noted: "I had no models for not working. I had large doses of the Protestant ethic throughout my life." After working in various jobs, she became a television producer. Deborah Jones was initially attracted to Roosevelt University because she wanted a solid liberal arts education and also wished to pursue the arts. Her parents, who were concerned about their daughter's career opportunities, made sure she thought about bread and butter issues as well as the romanticized life of an actress. Roosevelt University gave her that balance, but as a senior Deborah no longer had clear aspirations. After graduation she worked in the arts and later received a degree in journalism—not a career she had in mind while in college.

Like many undergraduate students, these young women shifted aspirations while in college. Much of the confusion for the middle-class women was brought on by the reality of integrating employment into a lifestyle (Angrist and Almquist 1975). Because middle-class Black women were more directly socialized to marry than the working-class women, they were more likely to be flexible about future employment while in college (Higginbotham 1981). The lack of clear aspirations in college meant their own plans were dependent upon the actions of their significant others. Marriage considerations influenced thinking about career commitment. Helene Montgomery talked frankly about how a career became less important while she was in college. When planning for college and when selecting a major, she was looking toward a career in "big business," but at graduation she wanted a well-paying job that allowed for a personal life. She majored in economics and, as one of the few Black women in the field, thought she had an edge on the job market. She thought being employable was very important. The reality of racism in the society, as discussed by her parents, meant that Helene knew she had to be "overqualified." Even with her eye on marriage, she was still committed to her education. She remarked: "It never occurred to me to marry before I had finished my education and my [future] husband had finished his education. I was taught that. If you did not [follow that plan], then it would put too much strain on the marriage." Helene did not marry until she had her master's degree and her husband had completed his law degree. While Helene and other women were exposed to mainstream gender expectations, their choices were grounded in their own race and class locations. They had no illusions about Black women retreating from the labor market.

Whether they were unclear about aspirations or waiting on a potential spouse to complete his schooling, the flexibility of middle-class women is another qualitative social class difference between these graduates. Their parents' resources gave middle-class women a degree of control as they faced the transitions of their senior years. Women like Helene and Deborah knew that they could still anticipate some material support from their parents while they were establishing their own careers. Few working-class women had that luxury.

Class, like racial privilege, is often obscure to those who possess it. But close interactions with middle-class people influenced how some working-class women thought about their futures. By observation of her middle-class peers, Katherine Howell learned to have similar expectations of control. In reflecting on her college years in 1976, Katherine was keenly aware of the differences between herself and most of her counterparts at Whitehall. All but a few of them were White, and the majority were also middle and upper class. These students were raised with the expectation of attending a very prestigious college, while Katherine had to display her talents before she even heard about such schools. In the process of becoming middle class, Katherine learned two central principles: the importance of attending the best schools and the need to plan your life. She noted, "I wasn't very organized about planning for college.[5] I thought it really is a northern phenomenon or at least someone else's phenomenon. It rubbed off on me when I came North. I felt very much more that I needed to plan my life. I knew when I left college that I was going to go to law school and what I was going to do afterwards, because these were important decisions." Katherine had to become self-supporting immediately. She also needed to recuperate from years of isolation in college. While she was unclear about her immediate future, in her elite college she had learned to have an expectation of control. There were many such subtle lessons in elite schools.

Women faced thinking about future employment as best they could. Most women had resolved racial identity issues at this stage and were comfortable with a racial identity and a network of friends who could support them either in a new career or advanced degree program. Yet there were also social class differences at this juncture. Having a sense of control of their lives, based on parental resources, gave some middle-class women the space to be flexible and the freedom to be unclear about their futures when they were seniors. Like their working-class counterparts, they were committed to spending much of their adult life in the workforce, but they varied in their determination to select a specific career. In contrast, the working-class women were more career focused and more likely to plan for future work while in college.

LIFE PLAN PREFERENCES IN COLLEGE

In college women prepare for many adult roles. The challenge for the women in this cohort was to get these roles to work together. Black women from the middle and working classes broached this task in different ways. The middle-class women were more likely to focus on how to achieve that integration in college, while the working-class women often delayed the challenge. While marriage was a priority for some women, especially those from the middle class, some focused on careers that would be integrated into family life, some were flexible about careers until they had a fiancé or spouse, and others were firmly set on their careers, so that marriage had to fit into that lifestyle. In contrast, many of the working-class women postponed dealing with the question of how work and family would fit together.

To explore the women's images of their futures, the questionnaire presented them with seven options for a life plan preference. These ranged from "marriage only," an option that none of the fifty-six women selected, to "career only."[6] The women were asked to select the life plan preference that came closest to their expectations during their senior year in college. The most popular choice, "marriage, children, and full-time career," was selected by 43 percent (or twenty-four women) of the total group (see Table 4). Another five women selected "marriage, children, and periodic employment." A majority of the women (52 percent) planned to integrate employment with marriage and children, a finding consistent with the results of earlier comparative research (Fichter 1967; Mednick and Puryear 1975; Turner and McCaffrey 1974). Only one woman, Carla Jenkins, selected "marriage and children." She had married in college and was most influenced in this choice by her husband. Ten women (six raised working class and four raised middle class) selected "marriage and career." Many of these women, like Adele Lewis, were either already married or planning on marriage. Eleven women (eight raised working class and three raised middle class) chose "career only." Finally, five women, the majority (four) of whom were raised working class, reported that they did not have expectations.

These Black women were different from most White women in college in the

TABLE 4. LIFE PLAN PREFERENCES DURING SENIOR YEAR IN COLLEGE BY SOCIAL CLASS

| | Social Class | | |
Life Plan Preference	Working Class (N=31)	Middle Class (N=25)	Total* (N=56)
Marriage and children	3%	0%	2%
	(1)	(0)	(1)
Marriage, children, and periodic employment	3%	16%	9%
	(1)	(4)	(5)
Marriage, children, and full-time career	35%	52%	43%
	(11)	(13)	(24)
Marriage and career	19%	16%	18%
	(6)	(4)	(10)
Career only	26%	12%	20%
	(8)	(3)	(11)
No expectations	13%	4%	9%
	(4)	(1)	(5)
Total**	99%	100%	101%

*Percentage of the total group
**Totals do not always come out to 100% because of rounding.

1960s. In their study of White college women, Shirley Angrist and Elizabeth Almquist (1975) found support for the traditionally female pattern of women leaving the work force when they had children. They followed 188 women in a class entering a private university in 1964. When asked questions each year about their goals, the majority of the eighty-seven women who graduated did not see themselves as employed when their children were young. There were shifts from year to year, but only a minority, 16 percent, consistently viewed career and family as equal priorities.

Family socialization to contend with the realities of racial oppression shaped these Black women's expectations of adult roles. Unlike White women, they saw themselves as committed to paid employment. But the expectations of combining work and family life were not uniformly shared among these Black women while they were in college. The majority of the women raised in the middle class (68 percent, or seventeen women) expected to integrate marriage, children, and paid employment, while only 38 percent (or twelve women) of those who were raised in the working class had such expectations while seniors in college. When they began college, middle-class women were attending to both social and academic matters. Therefore, they had experience in thinking about a balanced life after college. Many working-class women also thought of integrating marriage, children, and employment, but there was a sizable population that focused just on the immediate goals of completing college and securing employment. Their responses of "career only" or "no expectations" indicated a delay in sorting out how employment would be integrated into the rest of their lives.

Respondents were asked to rank the persons most influential in their choice of a life plan during the last year in college. Among the fifty women who had life plans (six had no expectations) there were class differences in their reports of parental influences. Twelve of the twenty-three middle-class women who had plans noted parents and family as a major influence (ranked either first or second). A common pattern was boyfriend first and then parents and family. These twelve women selected either marriage, children, and employment or marriage and career. Three other middle-class women ranked parents and family as influential, but not first or second. Eight middle-class women did not rank family as an influence; instead, their rankings included male and female peers, professors, advisors, and work associates. When compared to the working-class group, these women were more influenced by parents and family, their same source of information and support as they made the earlier transition from high school to college.

Mobility meant that many working-class women were charting territory that their own parents had never seen. Yet parental encouragement for economic independence and education were constants. Among the twenty-seven working-class women who reported life plans while in college, nine ranked their parents and family as major influences, and two more included them among other influences. In both of these cases, spouses and male peers were ranked before parents and other family. These eleven women selected life plans that ranged from "marriage, children, and full-time career" to "career only." But sixteen working-class women did not include parents as influences in their life plans at this stage. These women were diverse both in their selection of life plans and in their identification of other influences. Four women were self-guided and reported no outside influences. The other twelve women identified boyfriends, peers, professors, and work associates as helping them construct a vision of a lifestyle. There were limits on the help that parents could offer them, because as college seniors many of the women were about to achieve the major goal their parents had supported. However, critical family lessons on self-direction were helpful as the women continued to be upwardly mobile. Many were resourceful and either explored their own options or looked to other people to help them make decisions.

The interviews showed how the middle-class women were more actively socialized by parents to anticipate an adulthood that included marriage and employment than the working-class women (Higginbotham 1981). The experiences of Irma Dennis reveal this parental teaching and the daughter's expectations. When she was growing up, her mother conveyed that there was no question that she would complete college, but her mother also talked about marriage. Irma recalled: "My mother wanted me to marry someone who was rich, ambitious, super polite, someone like a Greek god. She wanted me to be rich and famous." As a college senior, Irma thought she was uninformed about marriage. "I was in love with a man, he proposed, and later we broke up. I really wanted to get married." When her plans changed, Irma proceeded to law school because she wanted a job that would be challenging. She knew she had to support herself. Yvonne Foster had similar expectations; however, she integrated her goals differently. Yvonne recalled, "I wanted to be independent and financially able to take care of myself. A married woman should be able to support herself and family if needed." In college, Yvonne trained to be an occupational therapist, a career she could integrate with family roles.

How women juggled employment and marriage varied within this middle-class group. Helene Montgomery lost interest in a specific career as she anticipated marriage, while Irma Dennis focused on a career when her plans of marriage changed. As a group, these women were planning to integrate paid employment and marriage, but they did so in various ways. Parental encouragement for the women to pursue education first was important in their plans, and parental insistence that they be economically independent often had priority over marriage plans. Kimberly Davis also wanted to be married, have children, and have a full-time career. These were her own goals, for which she had parental and family support. Through college and law school she dated and was then engaged to a man. However, he did not support her aspirations, so she broke off the engagement. She met her future husband after law school.

While in college, eleven of the working-class women thought they would marry, have children, and work full-time. A few of these women were seriously dating men or already married, like Crystal Robinson. For others, this lifestyle preference was more of an ideal than a concrete reality. In 1976, six of these eleven women were single, among them Robin Washington. When asked about the source of the vision of marriage, children, and full-time career while in college, Robin said, "That image came from books and what I thought I should be doing. As a senior in college, I could not really picture myself with a husband and children."

A common pattern among working-class women was to focus on education and employment goals and delay thinking about marriage. We see more evidence of this in looking at the women who selected the option of "career only." A total of eleven respondents (eight raised working class and three raised middle class) selected "career only." Rather than speaking for a preferred lifestyle, these responses indicate the confusion about adult roles that plagued mobile women in college. Six of the eight women who preferred "career only" in college were married, cohabiting, or in committed relationships in 1976. While in college they lacked a clear vision of how to integrate employment and interpersonal relationships. Further, their own parents were not as explicit in pushing marriage. Many Black working-class parents assumed that there were sufficient messages about marriage in the culture, but not enough about the importance of education for women (Higginbotham 1981; Higginbotham and Weber 1992). Just as they entered college with few visions of a social life, working-class women did not expect to graduate and immediately marry. This study demonstrates that the expectation of assuming multiple roles was not shared by all Black college women. Mastering the academic work, sorting out the social dynamics of college, and identifying and clarifying career objectives took priority over other interpersonal goals for many working-class women in predominantly White colleges. Linda Trott, single and working as a professional in 1976, explained her preference of "career only" while in college: "I did not exclude the other choices, but had not thought about them. I didn't feel I would never get married. In college I thought about one thing [work/career] and my choice reflects that ideal." Later Linda would marry, have a child, and work as a full-time professional.

Even at the same institutions, the working- and middle-class women faced different pressures with regard to sorting out careers and relationships. The majority of the middle-class women entered college with both marriage and career on their minds. However, mastering the academic work in college and thinking about translating these skills into paid employment were priorities for women from the working class. Thus the working-class women were less likely to be consciously or unconsciously juggling thoughts of marriage and careers. Many of the working-class women postponed dealing with men and relationships until college was completed. Only a few settled into relationships early, like Carla Jenkins, who made marriage a priority, and Adele Lewis, who married in college and was mobile with her spouse as they both pursued professional careers. For this group, being comfortable with their mobility, both in personal and employment terms, was a critical goal.

The reported life plan preferences reflected the women's own visions, which incorporated parental expectations. Investigating the link between work and personal life is thus an ideal vehicle for exploring the social class differences in educational mobility. The middle-class women were duplicating their social class position, which often included marriage. In contrast, those from the working class were intent upon upward mobility. With these differences in mind, in the final chapter we can look at where the women were six to eight years after their graduation from college and explore some of the consequences of the educational strategies they employed.

Social class again becomes critical as the women reflected on their thinking about their futures. Like generations of Black women before them, these women were in college to gain credentials that could be translated into employment opportunities. However, the middle-class women were more poised in college to figure out futures that would involve marriage, employment, and children. While some working-class women also had broad expectations for their lives, many were not able to think about marriage and children in college. The demands of mobility kept them focused on identifying and clarifying their career options.

All of these women achieved their goal of college graduation. In 1968, 1969, and 1970, as their parents, other family, and friends watched them receive their degrees, these women were highly visible because there were few African Americans in caps and gowns on those occasions. The experience of successfully completing college would prepare them to be racial pioneers in new settings.

CHAPTER 10 : STRUGGLING TO BUILD A SATISFYING LIFE IN A RACIST SOCIETY

Being an Afro-American in a White company, like existing in the society, has advantages and disadvantages. I am constantly dealing with stereotypes. People are unsure about how to relate to me. I'm a novelty, which can sometimes give me an edge over people. But there are also disadvantages, since I have to overcome automatic prejudice. It is better here [present job] than my old job in Chester, where I was not taken seriously. That made the job very tense. Douglas is better. People here had more experience with Black women.
—Sabrina Powell, respondent from middle-class background employed as an attorney

I interviewed with the principal of the Jefferson School [in the suburban community of Dexter] and he really made me angry. I asked him if special accommodations were made for the Black students [who were bused from East City]. He got an attitude. He also assumed that Dexter was my first choice. I said that it wasn't. At that time I was waiting on the Douglass School in East City. He said that I was lucky that they were even interviewing me, because I had no experience. I told him I could not work for him and then he tried to get real social like. He told me about the Black women that partied with him and stuff. Then he asked me if I would be able to offer the children dancing, typing, and other stuff after school hours. I told him that all my qualifications deal with during school hours. I told him that I did not want that job and that I could not work for him. Earlier I had talked to the superintendent of personnel, who had been really good. He told me not to sign anything [a contract] until I had talked with him. I [called him back and] told him that there was no way I could work for the Jefferson school principal. He talked about how there were other principals, so I worked in Dexter, but at the Crawford School.
—Denise Larkin, respondent from working-class background
    employed as an elementary school teacher

There are many myths about the success of educated African American women. These myths come from powerful images of a dozen or so Black women who are very visible in the media because they are elected officials, media personalities, independent entrepreneurs, public school administrators, or directors of social service programs. Yet these women are truly unique. Most Black women with college degrees are more likely to work in public sector government jobs than as elected officials; to work behind the scenes rather than in front of the camera; to work for others rather than control their own businesses; and to be teachers or social workers rather than principals of schools or social service directors. In reality, the majority of educated Black women, even those educated after the Civil Rights movement, work in traditionally female occupations. Those women who enter formerly predominantly male fields often do so within the public sectors of urban areas and increasingly in not-for-profit agencies and organizations (Higginbotham 1987, 1994; Sokoloff 1992; Woody 1992). The achievements of all these Black women are significant, but only a minority are among the highly visible examples typically seen in the media. These popular images obscure the costs of educational and occupational mobility for Black women. Most women's expectations for their lives are hard to meet, and membership in a racially oppressed group complicates that quest.

When contacted in 1976, these fifty-six women had moved well beyond their college days. They were employed in a range of occupations. A few women worked in majority Black settings, where Black women have always had a place (Shaw 1996; Slevin and Wingrove 1998). After getting her master's degree in education in the North, Toni Brown returned to the South to work at a traditionally Black university. The majority of the women were racial pioneers in graduate programs and employment settings. These paths were not easily traversed. Like Sabrina Powell, many respondents were race and gender tokens battling to be seen as individuals in traditionally male professions in predominantly White settings. Black professionals in such positions enjoy a high level of pay, but there are many stressors that come with the job (Davis and Watson 1982; Feagin and Sikes 1994; Higginbotham and Weber 1999). Respondents employed in traditionally female fields also encountered racism, especially those working in integrated settings. Denise Larkin's mixed experiences with administrators in the predominantly White suburb of Dexter would be followed by occasional incidents with parents. A few White parents made racial slurs about her when they complained to the principal about a sex education unit she taught to fifth graders. She recalled, "One father came and told me that I was perverted. He said that everyone knows that Black people are prostitutes." Although the principal supported her, since Denise was teaching the school board–approved curriculum, she was still hurt by the remarks. While Black women had been teaching in public schools for decades, Denise was crossing into new territory by working for a suburban rather than an urban school system.

The task of finding work can be troublesome. Karen Johnson was conscious of her limited employment options. She noted that "being Black often makes it difficult to get a job. In some areas, especially anti-poverty programs, they want to hire a minority person. So finding those jobs is easier. I think I should be more aggressive about finding a job, but I sell myself short by working in areas where Black people are welcome." The availability of antipoverty funds in the 1970s masked the difficulties that even educated Black Americans faced in the job market. Many Black people with college degrees found work in various urban antipoverty programs and agencies that received government funding, but their salaries were relatively low compared with those of similar positions in the private sector. When Black women attempted to secure jobs in the predominantly White private sector, they often found few opportunities, and consequently many remained employed in the public sector (Higginbotham 1994). Economists acknowledge the gains made by educated Black women in the 1970s but note that "relative wages of young African American women fell by almost ten percent from 1976 to 1991. Relative wage declines were especially significant among college graduates" (Bound and Dresser 1999, p. 63). These data might be tracking the decline of public sector jobs, where many Black women with college degrees found employment. Yet these patterns indicate that rather than disappearing, racism continues as a factor in Black women's lives.

The need to confront stereotypic images of African Americans and beliefs of racial inferiority did not stop when these women received college degrees and even advanced training. Being middle class does not shield people of color from informal or institutionalized racism (Anderson 1990; Feagin 1991; Feagin and Sikes 1994; Higginbotham 1994; St. Jean and Feagin 1998; Sokoloff 1992). The commitment these women learned in primary and secondary schools to work hard to demonstrate that members of their race could succeed continued to motivate them as they moved beyond college into advanced training and professional employment. Employment was not their sole motivation in life, however. They also had personal needs and commitments to shape satisfying lives.

The late 1960s and the early 1970s brought significant changes in both race relations and gender roles. The stories of the women reveal the challenges faced by Black women with college degrees from predominantly White colleges. Race, social class, and gender were key dimensions that shaped the context within which these women built lives that included paid employment as well as intimate relationships. Building a satisfying life in a racist society is not an easy task, even though these respondents were aware that they enjoyed many social class privileges. College degrees, especially from predominantly White institutions, enhanced their options both for continued schooling and for employment. As they left college and pursued adult roles, many continued to negotiate their own visions of their identity within integrated settings where their perspectives were not shared by the majority of White people. Just as they had battled limited or even negative visions of themselves by others in predominantly White and integrated educational settings before and during college, they faced many of the same struggles after college. These continued negotiations formed part of the backdrop against which they built their lives.

Life beyond College

The majority of these women had established their careers and a few were considering career shifts when contacted six, seven, or eight years after their graduation from college. Eleven of the fifty-six women were involved in graduate or professional training, including two about to begin medical internships. Four women had left paid employment to devote their time to raising children.[1] In terms of residence, the majority of the women in the study had left East City to pursue further education, return to their native regions, or begin their careers in new cities. Of the twenty-five women remaining in East City, most were native to the area and had begun to work full-time in East City. After attending college in the area, several other women adopted East City as their home. Of those still living in East City, seven women were in graduate school, many of them working part-time in their chosen fields.

Most respondents were employed in occupations or preparing for careers they did not anticipate while in college. In 1976 only 30 percent of the women were employed in the occupations they identified as what they were aspiring to during their senior year. The women employed full- and part-time were evenly divided between traditionally male and traditionally female occupations. Table 5 is a simple listing of their occupations in 1976. Class of origin was not related to employment in either traditionally male or traditionally female occupations. There are public school teachers and lawyers from both the working and the middle class.

At the time of the study, the majority of the women had been or remained married (eighteen from the working class and eighteen from the middle class).[2] Twenty respondents (thirteen raised working class and seven raised middle class) had never married. See Table 6 for a complete breakdown of marital status by social class background. While marriage rates were higher among the women from the middle class, so were divorce and separation rates; one woman raised working class had a divorce, while four women raised middle class had ended

TABLE 5. WOMEN'S OCCUPATIONS IN 1976 BY SOCIAL CLASS BACKGROUND

Working Class	Middle Class
Attorney (2)	Architect
Bank officer	Attorney (5)
Communications consultant	Educators
Educators	Administration—primary
Administrator—college	Teacher—college (2)
Consultant—primary	Teacher—high school
Counselor	Homemaker (3)
Teacher—college (5)	Journalist
Teacher—primary (2)	Manager—business
Filmmaker	Occupational therapist
Government official (2)	Physician (3)
Homemaker (2)	Research consultant
Hospital administrator (2)	Student—undefined
Librarian	Television producer
Research analyst (2)	Writer
Scientist	
Social worker	
Television producer (2)	
Urban planner	

Note: Students were placed in the occupations that they were in training to pursue.

TABLE 6. WOMEN'S MARITAL STATUS IN 1976 BY SOCIAL CLASS BACKGROUND

	Social Class		
Marital Status	Working Class (N=31)	Middle Class (N=25)	Total* (N=56)
Single	42%	28%	36%
	(13)	(7)	(20)
Divorced/separated	3%	16%	9%
	(1)	(4)	(5)
Married			
Childless	32%	20%	27%
	(10)	(5)	(15)
With children	23%	36%	28%
	(7)	(9)	(16)
Total	55%	56%	55%
	(17)	(14)	(31)
Total	100%	100%	100%

*Percentage of the total group

their first marriages. We cannot generalize from this study about employment options and marriage patterns of Black women college graduates of predominantly White colleges.[3] The women's experiences can help us to understand the costs as well as the advantages of educational and occupational attainment for Black women. In line with the focus of other chapters, we will look at the paths of the women from middle- and working-class families, because the differences in their socioeconomic origins played a role in their lives beyond college. Understanding these differences can help clarify the class, gender, and racial barriers that we still have to address before we have a nation of equals.

Middle-Class Women Reproducing Middle-Class Lifestyles

The paths traveled by two of the women from middle-class backgrounds, Rosalind Griffin and Sabrina Powell, illustrate some of the challenges that faced this group as they sought to combine advanced schooling, employment, and a personal life. Rosalind Griffin, the only child of professionals, used college to recuperate from years of isolation in a predominantly White suburb by affirming her racial identity and developing strong bonds with other young Black people. While her college environment supported her social transformation, Rosalind was less positive about how East City University prepared her for a career. Growing up, Rosalind watched her father and mother build careers, in health and education respectively. She had role models for parenting and advancing one's career. When asked her life plan preference when she was a senior, Rosalind, like many others, noted marriage, children, and full-time career, but on her questionnaire she added that "this was my plan for after my children were in school." When asked in the interview to clarify her thinking, she said, "I had always intended to marry, have children, and work. My parents expected me to do just that. My mother often told me she wanted me to go to college, become a teacher, and get married. She never pushed marriage, so she was not upset when I graduated from college and was not engaged, the way some parents were. Education was very important, and when I was ready I'd get married. I knew I did not want to teach, but at that point [senior in college] I had not thought about a career. Maybe I thought about a job. I was under the illusion that with a college degree, I could get any job."

Rosalind had held the typical summer jobs for women college students: camp counselor, youth worker, and clerical worker. In her senior year she decided to pursue a career in personnel. Career planning at East City University was not very helpful; advisors could not even tell Rosalind how to prepare for the career she had selected. Rosalind continued: "I didn't know what I was going to do. I was waiting for someone to tell me. My mother had always told me what I could do, so I was used to that. I guess I was waiting for someone to give me choices, but that never happened." Not only does this comment reveal the dependence on family, but it also highlights how little assistance her college provided. Her parents and family remained the major influences on Rosalind as she thought about her life after college. However, their aspirations could not help her resolve the dilemma of how to integrate a career and her desire for a family. She was caught between the gender expectations of her parents and those of a predominantly White university that did not take career counseling for women seriously. Among the graduates of both elite and non-elite schools, only nine women from the middle class mentioned professors or school advisors as influential in helping them think about a life plan.

After graduation, Rosalind discovered that she could not get a job in personnel without additional training. She found a job as a group worker in a settlement house for one year.[4] After working for six months, she began graduate school to pursue a master's in guidance. She initially went to school part-time but then quit her settlement house job to attend full-time. During this time Rosalind was dating and planning her wedding. Two years after graduating from college, when she had received a master's degree, Rosalind married.

With an advanced degree in counseling education, Rosalind accepted a position in higher education. She had to leave that position after one year when her husband, John, took a job on the West Coast. Rosalind worked in the field of personnel while they lived there but was able to resume her career in higher education when they returned to the East. At that time she was committed to starting a family, so she worked part-time until she was pregnant. After the birth of her first child, she found it hard to keep her part-time job because it was very demanding. She also lacked the funds for child care, which made it difficult to maintain professional commitments that required travel. Rosalind eventually left paid employment when she was pregnant with her second child.

Rosalind was pleased with her marriage and planned to combine family and career when her children were older. John's earnings as an attorney were more than adequate, but a second income would make a difference in their daily lifestyle and enable them to save for their children's college educations. When interviewed in her home, Rosalind revealed that her life had been different from her expectations: "I expected to have a career set with a few years of experience behind me by the time I had children." She was still considering her options and trying to define her career objectives eight years after graduating from college. While her children were young, she planned to explore advanced degree programs. John was supportive of her goals. In reality, as Rosalind's experience demonstrates, shaping a satisfying life that balances work and family is not an easy task in America, even for a Black middle-class woman (Gerson 1985).

Rosalind appears to have had more clarity on marriage and family goals than she recognized in college. One might argue that Rosalind was more similar to White college women at that time because her parents' material resources gave her the leverage to be concerned about a career, but not panicked (Angrist and Almquist 1975). She had the time and space to sort it out as she discovered that creating this preferred lifestyle was more difficult than holding an aspiration. Other scholars have written about how many women may juggle their own career goals until they find the appropriate mate. Under these circumstances, women are less likely to commit to a specific career goal and pursue it, since it is incumbent upon them to remain flexible about work objectives (Angrist and Almquist 1975; Holland and Eisenhart 1990). While these are the circumstances many young adult women face, some of these women's reconsiderations were also responses to new opportunities as racial and gender barriers to graduate programs and careers were lifted.

One can also attribute some of the failure of Rosalind's career planning to her attendance at a large, non-elite, predominantly White university that typically failed to prepare women for specific careers. In the 1960s women graduates were expected to marry, so career counselors were not attentive to career planning for this group. Furthermore, counseling staff were not aware that Black women's orientations toward employment were different from those of the majority of White women at that time. Just as high school counselors in majority White high schools had not been very helpful with the transition to college, the lack of attention from college career counselors forced Black women to look elsewhere for assistance at this point in their lives.

Sabrina Powell, the middle of three daughters raised in the South, made her occupational choice a priority as she built her life. Sabrina's father was a minister and her mother an elementary school teacher. Her parents were the first in their families to secure higher education, and they stressed achievement to their daughters. While in elementary and secondary schools, Sabrina did a little bit of everything: music lessons, music camp in the summers, science clubs on the weekends, and of course, many church activities. Sabrina was socialized to re-create the type of middle-class family in which she was raised. Her mother did not talk explicitly about careers but focused more on marriage and children. Sabrina remembered her mother's priorities: "She expected that I would marry and become an extension of that man's life. If I had a career, since we [the daughters] were all expected to do something other than just marry, it would not come first." Sabrina's father was more career oriented and thus talked little about marriage and family life. Instead, Sabrina learned about her father's own development, his interests, and the importance of getting an education. She identified closely with her father in his independence and aggressive personality. Mr. Powell, rather than Mrs. Powell, was really the role model for Sabrina's adult development.

Like the majority of the respondents from middle-class families, Sabrina's life plan preference in college was marriage, children, and full-time career. During the interview, Sabrina reflected on her own thinking about marriage while she was in college: "When I grew up I did not think very much about marriage, but thought I would get married. I felt I would marry late, not right after college, which is what I actually did. I did not think I would emphasize marriage, children, or career any [one] more than the other." Sabrina actually gave much thought to her future employment. She had an interest in the law, partially because her father, as a minister, was involved with the Civil Rights movement. But she was dissuaded from a legal career when she was in high school. Career day was a common event in many Black segregated high schools. Sabrina listened attentively for information about careers. She recalled, "One day Black men who were attorneys spoke about law and legal activities. They were not doing well and had sad stories about the profession. So I got into speech. I had done a lot of extra speaking as a child, because I was the preacher's child, and I thought about speech therapy. It was on that basis that I selected my college."

In college, Sabrina realized that she did not want to be a speech therapist because she did not like clinical work. In order to teach in the field, she would need a doctorate. She therefore reevaluated her commitment to that field. She was dating a pre-law student, her future husband, so they talked about legal careers.[5] The legal field was changing, and her fiancé presented a more positive vision of employment prospects for African Americans.[6] Black attorneys were involved in making significant changes in the system. Sabrina reconsidered her initial decision and prepared for law. School advisors played no role in her decision, so she did not face the same difficulties as Rosalind Griffin. Like many Black women, she sought alternative sources.

Many of these young women discussed careers with male and female peers; boyfriends seemed to be particularly influential. Although Dorothy Holland and Margaret Eisenhart's (1990) comparative study, *Educated in Romance*, found that boyfriends were distractions from studying and pursuing careers for Black women in a traditionally Black university, the women in this study spoke of Black men as supports. While this study, unlike Holland and Eisenhart's work, was limited to Black women who completed college, it does illuminate another role of

Black men. Many men were recognized as supportive of their future or current wives. These Black men were raised in families where their mothers were employed outside the home, an experience that shaped their own models and expectations of Black women.

Upon graduation from college, Sabrina married, and she and her husband, Richard, went directly to law school. In 1976 Sabrina and Richard worked full-time as attorneys. Over the years, their careers have taken them across the country and then back to East City. In 1976 Sabrina had been working for a major corporation for two years and had recently been promoted to the legal department. In her previous position she had traveled regularly, so this new position fit better with her family commitment. As the only Black attorney in the legal department, she was a racial pioneer, but this position was better than one with a previous employer, where she experienced more sexism. She noted that there were no other Black people in upper-level middle management.

Sabrina identified Richard as a supportive and encouraging partner. Committed to marriage, children, and a full-time career, Sabrina was a new mother in 1976. After seven years of marriage, she and Richard had their first child. Their daughter was in full-time child care while both parents continued to work. Sabrina presents a different model of reproducing one's social class position. She consistently thought about and prepared for a career. Even though she changed directions, establishing a career was a priority over beginning a family. Sabrina's goal was to balance a career and family, in contrast to her own mother, who worked to enable the family to survive economically but made family a priority.

In terms of career development, Sabrina took the commitment to work from her father and shaped other aspects of her life around her occupation choice and career. While she married early, even earlier than Rosalind Griffin, Sabrina still worked toward her career objectives. Furthermore, she and Richard delayed having a child until they were at a particular point in their careers and marriage. Sabrina notes that both she and Richard felt emotionally ready to be parents and could afford the type of child care that enabled them to continue working full-time.

Parental expectations, internalization of priorities, class advantages, and the shifting gender and racial opportunities in the society influenced Rosalind's and Sabrina's life courses. Both women were comfortable with their lives, even though they were leading very different ones. Their patterns of developing careers and personal lives illustrate some important trends in the life chances and choices of Black women from the middle class. More positions in new sectors of the economy enabled these educated women to be racial pioneers in new settings. The expansion of professional opportunities in the 1970s meant new employment options for African American professionals both in the public sector and in the predominantly White private sector (Sokoloff 1992). Some families achieved a degree of economic success that supported family functioning, and Black mothers like Rosalind were able to remain home with their children.[7] In addition to Rosalind, four other women of the fifty-six in the sample identified their occupations as homemaker (two raised middle class and two raised working class).[8] All of these women planned to return to paid employment when their youngest child was school-age. By contrast, few middle-class Black women of previous generations had had the freedom to remain home with their children for an extended period of time (Shaw 1996; Slevin and Wingrove 1998).

In the late 1960s, when many White middle-class daughters sought new occupational avenues, many Black women also pursued demanding careers in spheres that had traditionally been male dominated (Higginbotham 1987, 1994; Sokoloff 1992; Woody 1992). However, in the case of this cohort of Black women, many entered settings that were predominantly White (Higginbotham and Weber 1992). Thus these respondents are representative of many middle-class Black women who are building both traditional and innovative careers in new racial settings. They faced many obstacles to acceptance in the workplace, in addition to the challenge of integrating work and family life.

Charting a New Course: Working-Class Women Face Mobility

As noted earlier, women from working-class backgrounds were disadvantaged in their educational pursuits by a lack of funds, but they also emerged from families with limited visions of their futures. These women charted different courses from those of their families. They were less certain about the nature of their futures and had fewer role models within their families and communities. In college they were often focused on resolving issues of employment, even though some women were still vague about their futures in their senior year. Most of the working-class parents wanted some of the same goals for their daughters as the middle-class parents did, but they socialized their daughters differently. Rather than encouraging them to marry, working-class parents were more likely to stress educational goals. Parents knew that marriage was already a salient goal in their communities, so they put more emphasis on getting into and through college (Higginbotham 1981). Among some respondents who were raised working class, remaining single came to be part of a successful mobility strategy, since early marriage and childbearing could jeopardize the educational futures of women with few economic resources (Albelda and Tilly 1997; Scott

1991). For example, Karen Johnson recalled her parents stressing education. She stated: "They wanted me to go to college. When we passed East City University on the bus, my mother would tell me I was going to go there. In contrast, they never really talked about my getting married." Therefore Karen was quite surprised when, after her graduation from East City University, her parents asked many questions about whom she was dating and her plans for the future. They had never mentioned marriage when she was growing up, but as an adult Karen realized that her parents always assumed she would marry. Rather than hearing descriptions of life in which employment and interpersonal relationships were integrated, the women from working-class families heard their parents stress getting a college degree or even more schooling. It would be up to the women to figure out how their educational attainment would work with other aspects of their lives.

Social mobility means entering a world that your parents could not completely prepare you to enter (Higginbotham and Weber 1992; Strauss 1971). A college education often meant that these women would establish careers, but the women from working-class backgrounds were less likely to have parental or family role models for building such careers. Their own parents had jobs rather than careers; that is, they worked from 8:00 A.M. to 4:30 P.M., 9:00 A.M. to 5:00 P.M., or even 10:00 P.M. to 6:00 A.M. Their parents wanted them to do cleaner, more interesting work and to have the respect of the community. Many of these women initially thought that college would open doors to cleaner and more interesting work, but while they were in college many learned that their education was to prepare them for careers rather than jobs. Most would enter occupations that do not routinely end at 5:00 or 6:00 P.M. For these women the strategy of child-secured mobility including mastering many of the subtle aspects of middle-class life that were often obscure to their working-class parents. They learned how middle-class people were highly identified with their occupations and that establishing those careers required bringing work home and strategizing how to advance in one's profession.

Working-class parents did not realize that their daughters were entering a credentialing process that could result in different social relations at work. As new members of the middle class, these daughters might supervise or plan work for working-class subordinates like their own parents (Vanneman and Cannon 1987). Others might teach school and play a role in deciding which working-class children would be candidates for upward mobility. Not only did these women have to overcome obstacles to obtain these positions, they also had to come to some resolution about these class transitions (Cuadraz and Pierce 1994). Finally, unlike previous generations of educated Black people, their social mobility, like their higher educational experiences, would mean crossing racial as well as class barriers (Higginbotham and Weber 1992). Looking at the experiences of Denise Larkin and Katherine Howell will illustrate how the women from working class backgrounds faced these critical mobility issues and integrated their new educational and occupational attainment into their lives.

Like Rosalind Griffin, Denise Larkin was at home with her young daughter at the time of the interview in 1976, but she was still a woman with employment issues on her mind. A native of East City, Denise was the second of four children in a working-class home. Her father left his position in the post office to begin a career in real estate when Denise was eleven. Uncertainty characterized his new position, so when Denise was thirteen, her mother took a position in the post office. Denise recalled that her family had the basics, but no luxuries. As noted in Chapter 7, Denise selected Regional University because it had a cooperative program that enabled her to work and help pay for her education. When asked about her life plan preference as a senior, Denise chose marriage and career, since she was dating her future husband while in college. She explained this choice:

> I felt very strongly that it was important for me to keep my independence. Robert and I were the type that when we went to a party, we both went off in our own directions and sought people; if we wanted to be with just ourselves, we would be home. He, to some extent, recognized that I needed an interest and needed to do this [a career] for me. My parents have always felt that people stay together because the wife has no other options. Their feelings were that you [the daughter] wanted to have as many options as possible. My mother was also concerned with security. It was important that I have something that I am interested in and could be happy [doing]. Marriage was not necessarily related to the thing, but I needed a supportive person. Robert is very supportive, [and] he helps me make decisions.

Denise was initially unclear about employment plans, but her university's cooperative program provided her with opportunities to explore different employment avenues. After graduation she went directly into teaching elementary school in a suburban school district. Many women who were first-generation college graduates entered traditionally female occupations directly after college. These women were less likely than those from middle-class homes to have the funds to immediately pursue an advanced degree. Furthermore, depending upon how the women financed college, many graduates were eager to gain economic rewards for their education before securing additional schooling. This was Denise's situation. But in the process, she also found her calling. Denise married two years after graduating from college, while she continued to build her career.

Even though she taught in a suburban community, Denise had a racially balanced classroom because of African American children participating in a regional busing program. Denise put a great deal of energy into her teaching. She taught language arts for three years and then science and social science. In the social science classes, she taught a unit on Africa and discussed major African American leaders with her students. She was an excellent teacher who enjoyed working with colleagues as well as the children. In her second year, Denise was nominated by the Dexter Teachers' Association for an award. She thought her life was balanced.

Denise and Robert were committed to starting a family and building a life in East City. Talking about these issues, Denise noted that she did not want to be the only one making sacrifices to have children. Having children would mean a change in both of their lives. She did not appear to be a reluctant mother, as were the women who were ambivalent about integrating children in their lives in Kathleen Gerson's (1985) *Hard Choices*. Instead, she had a career in place before entering motherhood. Furthermore, asking one's spouse to share household and child rearing tasks was common in African American families (Baca Zinn 1990; Billingsley 1992; Taylor 2000). Denise and Robert were committed to her remaining at home while their children were young. It would mean going without some luxuries, but they could already see the benefits in their first child, Karin, who was very bright and outgoing.

Staying at home with her daughter gave Denise time to get into writing and other projects. Denise and Robert shared many parenting tasks. "When he [Robert] comes home, he takes Karin bike riding or they do something else together. She is equally at home with both of us. If he is sitting here and she needs a change, she will go to him and not automatically come to me." Their daughter had added much to their lives, and they were planning for additional children. Denise was considering preparing to work in her father's real estate firm while her children were young.[9] She planned to return to teaching when they were school-age.

For all the women from working-class backgrounds, college meant the opening of many new doors. Denise tried several doors until she found a comfortable career. Many women were simply overwhelmed with their choices and therefore decided not to choose. Meanwhile, others were primarily focused on future employment while in college. Both patterns were found among the women from working-class families. Remaining in East City rather than going away to college shaped Denise's mobility experience. Living at home made the college years affordable but also kept Denise close to her family. This arrangement enabled her to share her upward mobility with her family. Denise slowly altered her relationship to the larger Black community as she progressed through college. She and

Robert bought a home, so seven years after college graduation she was raising her family in the same community where her parents lived.

Confronting mobility issues could be rough for women who came to East City from other states and were temporarily disconnected from family support at a critical time in their development. These were times of major resolutions that women addressed differently. Some were very clear about goals, while others were confused. The uncertainty about the future among those women from the working class was qualitatively different from the lack of decision making among the middle-class women. The former group's inability to decide was not explicitly related to the priority of identifying a marriage partner. Instead, their uncertainty was often related to the challenges of being mobile, particularly to resolving their relationships to family, kin, and community. These difficult issues are illustrated in the life of Katherine Howell.

From the South, Katherine traveled north on a full scholarship to attend Whitehall College. Katherine did well in college, finishing with over a B average. She confessed that college was not an easy time. "I found the Whitehall College experience challenging, but then at other times the whole mystique was disappointing." While she was single in 1976, Katherine's life plan preference as a college senior had been marriage, children, and a full-time career. She explained her thinking at that time: "I was a victim of the American Dream. I was in a liberated women's institution where careers were strongly promoted. Yet I think I had accepted that [life plan] before college. Also I had a very traditional side that still wanted family and the very traditional things that I knew women had done or wanted to do."

Katherine was still committed to the goal of marriage, children, and a full-time career in 1976. Six years after graduating from college, she saw herself as finally in the position to seek a partner. In college she could not decide upon a career, and even though she dated, she could not focus on getting married. While the majority of her peer group, mostly middle-class Black students, were eager to pursue careers, Katherine found that her vision of her own future was vague. It was hard for her to see where she could fit in the society with a degree from Whitehall College. Integrating this isolated academic experience into the rest of their lives was a challenge for many women raised in the working class, especially those at elite colleges. Isolated from her family and her supportive southern Black community, Katherine remembered this period as a time of pain. "I had adjustment problems; there was just too much imposed on me at once." She dealt with many issues: separation from her family, adjusting to the racial dynamics of northern living, serving as a cultural envoy to White students, reassessing her religion, and mastering the academic work required at an elite college. During this adjustment period, Katherine did not feel she could confide in her family. She felt so miserable that she did not go home the first summer. She did not want her parents to see that college, which should have been building her esteem, was a very painful place. It would have been hard to share with them that their long-time goal for her, going to college, was in reality a lonely and miserable experience.

Katherine's lament is similar to Katie Cannon's experience, as told by Sara Lawrence-Lightfoot (1994) in *I've Known Rivers*. Union Theological Seminary felt rich, strange, and hostile to Katie. The cultural norms were so different that she found herself alienated, but she could not communicate this pain to her family. Lightfoot described Katie's plight:

> How could she write home and complain about her lonely and depressed life at Union, when by any objective measures anyone could name, Katie was leading a relatively privileged existence? When she would occasionally break down and reveal her frustrations and anguish to her mother, Corine would respond with the inevitable litany: 'Katie, if you're unhappy, you can always come home and work in the mill.' By now, Corine must have know that the choice was no longer a real alternative for her daughter. It was merely used as a reminder that Katie should not indulge in self-pity when most of her family and her people had far, far less. (Pp. 103–4)

In reality, social mobility meant distance from family as well as confronting the many challenges of survival in a new middle-class social environment (Higginbotham and Weber 1992; Strauss 1971). Counseling helped Katherine through this time. Speaking about those days she said, "I was miserable and really considered suicide. I was with friends who were all suffering, but we did not admit it. Therefore we couldn't be supportive of each other. This was a very sad time for Black people in predominantly White universities." Katherine began to remedy her suffering when she got involved in the Black community. She initially did so by working the summer after her sophomore year in a community center on the West Coast. The invitation came from a high school friend who attended college in the West. This work experience helped her see how the skills she was learning could be put to use. When she returned to Whitehall College she majored in the social sciences and also began doing volunteer work in East City. She thought about going into social services but did not begin looking for a job until March of her senior year. In her senior year, Katherine knew that she would eventually go to law school, but she was not ready to make that commitment in 1970.

While some working-class women were influenced by professors or school advisors in thinking about their life plans, Katherine was not. She had often kept her own counsel when growing up, and at this juncture she also charted her own course. Katherine wanted to put some distance between herself and the academy. After college she moved to a mid-Atlantic city and looked for work. "I felt as if I'd been in an unreal environment for four years." She was eager to reenter the real world and test herself. By midsummer, she found a position in a comprehensive community organization and worked there for three years. Her job involved a range of social service activities, liaison with other agencies, and organizing health programs for the community. She did public relations, direct service, and community organizing. She gained confidence in her abilities and realized that she could be upwardly mobile but not dramatically change her values and personality. Her predominantly White college had not been able to give her that reassurance. Upon reflection she said, "I did not see myself as self-assured or self-directed in college. This has come more recently. I'm not sure of what I want to do with my life, but I am beginning to know what will make me happy. . . . I am sorting out that decency in people is what is important. I'm still similar to that person in South City." This centering was critical for her development. After reconnecting with the Black community and working for three years, Katherine applied to law schools and relocated to another state. While she admitted that her law school, which was predominantly White, was "isolating, competitive, and difficult in many respects," Katherine coped better than she had as an undergraduate. She had a clear sense of direction, confidence in herself, and the skills to both build and rely on a support network in law school.

When interviewed in 1976, Katherine was beginning to practice law with a private firm. She had moved back to the mid-Atlantic city where she had worked for three years. She was eager to start her new career and thought very differently about this transition. Higher education had created a gap between Katherine and her working-class parents, but personal growth enabled her to bridge that gap and involve them more fully in her life. With this move, unlike her previous moves, Katherine involved her parents in an important change in her life. They traveled from South City to help her relocate from one northern city to another and get settled into her new apartment. While Denise Larkin never lost touch with her family and community, those women, like Katherine Howell, who went away to school often had to reintegrate their families into their middle-class lives.

African Americans have been mobile for decades, but the context of mobility for this generation was different from earlier cohorts in terms of their educational training and employment options. Among previous generations, most African Americans received their high school and college educations in traditionally Black institutions in which they were systematically taught a commitment to using their knowledge and skills to make a living and work for racial uplift (Shaw 1996; Slevin and Wingrove 1998; Walker 1996). They were exposed to faculty who exhibited this commitment. The situation was quite different in predominantly White high schools and colleges, where learning an ethic of socially responsible individualism was not part of the curriculum. Instead, Black students were exposed to White peers, the majority of whom were already middle class. Even the White working-class students were not seeking an education to work for the betterment of their communities but rather viewed mobility as the means to achieve personal goals. However, many White working-class youth can also be troubled by the gap that education introduces within families (Steinitz and Solomon 1986).

In predominantly White colleges, Black women often had to find their own supports for a more African American orientation to mobility, particularly one that stressed commitment to the broader Black community. Many of these women were isolated from Black communities at this time in their lives, although a few were tied to the local Black community either by employment or volunteer work. Because their own parents were limited in their ability to help, as a group these women were more dependent upon external help. Five of the women in elite schools and eight of those in non-elite schools indicated that professors or school advisors were influences on their life plans. A few ranked these influences as major, often along with either family or peers (since some women did not list family). Yet these same faculty might not have understood the broader commitments these women shared as members of an oppressed racial group. Goals shaped by commitments to their racial group could be seen as deviant by faculty and advisors, as well as by White students.[10]

While all Black women in predominantly White colleges needed supports to remain connected to the Black community, it was most critical for the working-class women because they were coping with mobility issues. The marginality that has often surrounded upward mobility is complex when race and gender are involved (Higginbotham and Weber 1992; Strauss 1971). Working-class women did not grow up with parents who modeled professional roles, and predominantly White colleges were institutions that promoted individual achievement. Many Black women from the working class, whose families and communities have been major supports for their own educational attainment, have had to reconcile their personal goals with group purposes (Higginbotham and Weber 1992). Black women could often find support among peers at large colleges or through community work, and a few found a circle of friends in small colleges.[11] Negotiating the changes that come with moving up in social class often requires time as well as situations where women can demonstrate to themselves and perhaps others that their educations have not separated them from their communities. These negotiations do not end with college and early adulthood.

The working-class women shared with their middle-class peers participation in a cohort that was distinct from previous generations of educated Black Americans in that they were more likely to work as professionals in predominantly White or integrated settings than within Black communities. There was no preparation for this role in their colleges, unless they had Black faculty in their fields. A few women noted this advantage, particularly Margaret Cooke and Linda Trott, who both had strong support from a Black faculty member. These predominantly White institutions had few Black faculty at this time, however. In fact, while these women's very presence in college was connected to a legacy of working for racial uplift, this fact was not acknowledged. College itself became a setting to prepare the women for the additional burdens of being a token in the workplace. While in college they had to face the daily challenges of racial barriers and learn to define their plight as a protracted struggle. Again support groups were critical, but it appears that women were not as likely to discuss openly the pain and constant pressure of proving themselves. The early values of self-direction and having confidence in yourself helped keep them committed to their goals in these settings. But there is a way that being overlooked, neglected, and misread for years in college can lower one's self-esteem. Some women, like Katherine Howell, needed employment to regain that confidence.

Employment after college graduation was not the only pattern of development for women from working-class backgrounds to resolve mobility issues. Each woman had to map her own path, and family lessons in self-direction aided them at this time. Linda Trott was recognized and rewarded in college and graduated with higher self-esteem than when she finished high school. She had done some connecting to the Black community in East City to sustain her while in college. Her excellent work in school meant she was nominated for a traveling fellowship. In the end she had to decide whether to take the prestigious fellowship or begin graduate school in education. She recalled how she made the decision: "I decided upon going to school. I didn't take the [traveling] fellowship because I didn't need to go off and travel. I needed to work on relationships with people and get established in a community. I could not do that if I was traveling around Europe and Africa. It would have meant more isolation and alienation." In contrast, after college Beth Warren decided to travel. She went to Africa and taught. This experience gave her an opportunity to use her skills for broader goals. Afterwards she returned to her home city and taught young children. While college was a rarified environment, Beth used what it did offer to expand her horizons and access the resources to help her chart an occupational course in an integrated work world.

Succeeding in majority White colleges required many complex negotiations as working-class women faced racial and social class boundaries. They varied in their abilities to build supportive communities for their growth. Meeting the challenges of such negotiations prepared them for futures in graduate programs and work settings where they would again be racial pioneers. These women had various strategies for addressing mobility issues. Their assessments of their needs confirm that self-direction remained a key survival skill. Like reaffirming their racial identity, resolving mobility issues, and remaining anchored in the Black community, was essential for progress in their careers and for enabling them to make contributions to society.

The Costs of Success

Being successful as a Black women required sustaining a self-defined perspective on one's circumstances and life objectives. As we can see, these women were quite resilient in withstanding many of the challenges to their self-esteem and plans for their lives. Yet they were still living not only in a nation where most people assessed others on the basis of their race, but also within institutions in which privileges and disadvantages were distributed by social class, race, and gender. As new research notes, being middle class does give Black people additional resources to face racial disadvantage, but it does not eliminate racism (Collins 1998; Feagin and Sikes 1994; Franklin 1991; Oliver and Shapiro 1995; Pattillo-McCoy 1999). Thus these women continued to face racial barriers that formed the backdrop against which they built their adult lives. By exploring their situations as adults in 1976, we can get another measure of the costs of the educational strategies Black women employed either to reproduce a middle-class status or to be upwardly mobile into the middle class.

Women need to have opportunities to develop balanced lives. Research on women demonstrates the key role that relationships play in their lives, especially where they seek to pioneer new lifestyles and careers (Angrist and Almquist 1975; Gerson 1985; Holland and Eisenhart 1990; Lorber 1994; Miller 1986). Of course, there will be diversity in how women elect to balance their lives, particularly when they include nontraditional paths. To see how these fifty-six women wanted to shape their lives, they were asked to select the lifestyle that came closest to their current life plan preference. The women selected from the same preferences used in the question about their future expectations during their senior year in college, ranging from "marriage only" to "career only." Twenty-three women selected "marriage, children, and full-time career" as their current preference (see Table 7). Even after the women left college and assumed adult roles,

Life Plan Preference	Social Class		
	Working Class (N=31)	Middle Class (N=25)	Total* (N=56)
Marriage and children	0%	4%	1%
	(0)	(1)	(1)
Marriage, children, with periodic employment	13%	8%	11%
	(4)	(2)	(6)
Marriage, children, with steady part-time career	13%	12%	12%
	(4)	(3)	(7)
Marriage, children, and full-time career	32%	52%	41%
	(10)	(13)	(23)
Marriage and career	23%	12%	18%
	(7)	(3)	(10)
Career only	13%	12%	13%
	(4)	(3)	(7)
No expectations	6%	0%	4%
	(2)	(0)	(2)
Total	100%	100%	100%

*Percentage of the total group

this lifestyle was still a popular choice. Only one woman noted "marriage and children," but not the same woman who made this selection while in college. What is most surprising is the increase in the percentage of women who preferred marriage, children, and either periodic employment or a steady part-time career. As college seniors, only five women had this preference. In 1976 thirteen women made this choice, which might demonstrate that they recognized the realities of integrating children, a marital relationship, and the demands of a professional career. Ten women preferred "marriage and career," which was slightly higher than the number who made this selection as college seniors. However, the composition of this group did shift somewhat.

Six to eight years after graduation, seven women indicated that they preferred "career only," which represents a decrease from eleven women who identified such a preference as seniors in college. In 1976 only two women indicated that they either held no expectations or had no plans. This was a decrease from the five women who had reported "no expectations" as college seniors.[12] These shifts in reflect how many women, especially those from the working class, were more able to envision the lives they wanted after college rather than while still students.

If we look at the number of women who were actually living their lifestyle preferences, we get a picture of the costs of strategies for many educated Black women today. Of the fifty-six women, twenty-three (or 41 percent) were living the lifestyles they wanted. In contrast, the majority of the respondents, thirty-three women (or 59 percent), were not living their preferred lifestyle.[13] The majority of these respondents were in their late twenties, so achieving the balance they wanted could have been an immediate goal. Looking at the lives that these women had established and at their remaining life goals helps to illustrate some issues that are still important in the lives of educated Black women.

LIVING THE LIFE I WANT

Those women who reported that their current lifestyle was their life plan preference represent a range of lifestyles, covering six of the seven options. Again, no one selected "marriage only." Their preferences were as follows: one for "marriage and children"; one for "marriage, children, and periodic employment"; two for "marriage, children, and steady part-time career"; eight for "marriage, children, and full-time career"; five for "marriage and career"; and six for "career only." The women varied in their social class backgrounds, as twelve were raised working class and eleven middle class. While in college, the middle-class women had been better able to conceptualize the futures they wanted. After graduation and career building many women from both the working and middle classes were able to shape lives that they found satisfying.

Beth Warren, who was raised working class, had no expectations for her future when she was a college senior, but in 1976 she was satisfied with her lifestyle. She married two years after graduation. While primarily a homemaker, she had completed her master's degree. She had children and worked periodically as an educational consultant and teacher in higher education. She was also continuing her own education. She planned to return to full-time employment and hoped to advance in the field of international education when her youngest child went to school. She spent her time rearing her children, advocating within the public school system for them, nurturing her marriage, and pursuing her own career and education goals.

Like eight other women who were raised working class, Nancy Brooks indicated "career only" as her lifestyle choice in college. Upon graduation, she returned to her home city and secured an entry-level position in a private sector firm. She remained at the same firm and advanced over the years. She married four years after college; at the time of the interview, she had two children. Other than maternity leaves, she had worked full-time. She said: "I thought it was natural for me to marry, raise a family, and work. While I can handle everything, it is difficult." When her mother retired, she offered to help with child care. Six years after graduation Nancy was proud of her children and her home and was glad that she had developed this foundation. "This is a base for me," she said. As a mother with young children, Nancy thought she faced discrimination on the job. Her firm had a policy of not promoting women in her situation. However, support from her own mother gave Nancy the flexibility to return to graduate school to expand her employment options.

Another woman from the working class, Adele Lewis, selected "marriage and career" as her preference as a college senior. In 1976 Adele worked as a television producer. She had been married for three years but had been with the same partner since college. She and her spouse shared a home, their careers, their cats, and a commitment to personal growth. In her late twenties, Adele was planning to return to school to develop her creative writing skills. It was not a necessity for her job, but she wanted to see if she could write professionally. With a strong foundation she could work toward this new goal.

Deborah Jones, who was raised middle class, selected "career only" as a senior and remained committed to that goal as she worked as a journalist in 1976. "I would like to avoid falling into a nuclear family," she noted. Friends played an important role in Deborah's life, helping her to develop both personally and in her career. Her personal goals were nontraditional in many respects. She was involved in Black feminist thinking and organizations, and her opinions reflected those influences. She said: "I want to find a better way of incorporating 'romantic love' into my life. I do not want it to contradict friendship or feminism. . . . I do not want to actively live with anyone. I always want to keep my own apartment." Deborah was clearly single by choice, while other single women were merely resigned to accepting their status.

Susan Thomas had selected "marriage, children, and periodic employment" as a college senior, but in 1976 her choice was "career only." She noted, "I still would like to be married and have children. I have no marriage prospects and try to accept myself as a single person." In line with that goal, Susan was working on an advanced degree in the medical field at the time of the study. Since 1970 the number of African American women who do not marry has increased. Yet we see that those with higher education face this alternative with varying attitudes (Higginbotham 1981; Tucker and Mitchell-Kernan 1996a). In the additional comments section of the questionnaire, Susan wrote: "I see myself as a happy person. I live one day at a time and do not make long-range plans."

Women raised middle class who were married and working, like Sabrina Powell, were pleased with the shape of their lives. Among this group were also women who were combining marriage, children, and part-time careers. Sherri North graduated from Whitehall College in 1970 and married at the time of her graduation. After working in a range of fields, including the arts and publishing, she became a freelance writer. While her preference in college was "marriage, children, and full-time career," her current plans reflected the reality of integrating work and children. She selected "marriage, children, and steady part-time career" but noted: "Part-time isn't an appropriate word. I write and work in different segments of the day, averaging four to eight hours." She had remained very professionally active since the birth of her first child, but she wondered about the future. Like many women in this cohort, she had concerns about integrating work and children. She wrote: "Having more children will complicate my professional life. Writing as steadily as I've been doing now makes me reluctant to have the second baby."

The twenty-three women in this group were living their lifestyle preferences, even when it meant some tension and disappointments—which are all a part of life. Like other women in this age cohort, they still had issues to resolve in their lives. Employment was a sphere of concern. Additional degrees were often necessary to advance in their careers. Their strategies were shaped by the racism and sexism in the workplace in the mid-1970s. Mothers were particularly concerned about schooling options for their children. As parents, they debated the prospects of educating their children in either predominantly White suburban or inner-city schools where children of color were quickly becoming the majority. These dilemmas were not very different from those of middle-class parents of the previous generation. Yet one can see that, even as they voiced their concerns, these women had built a foundation for a satisfying life.

STILL STRIVING

Thirty-three women reported life plan preferences that were not their current lifestyles. The group was mixed in marital status and class background. Seven women were married and planned on children to achieve their life plan preferences. These respondents were between the ages of twenty-seven and twenty-nine at the time of the study; thus in most cases they could expect that children would come with time. Four women were stay-at-home mothers who planned to return to a full-time career or periodic employment in the future. They were not unhappy with this stage of their lives but knew that the balance they wanted would come when their children were school-age. Their plans also reflected the realities of raising a family in our current economy. As a college senior, Carla Jenkins thought her life would involve only marriage and children. While in college, she married the man she had dated since high school. A year after graduation from Whitehall College, Carla gave birth to their first child. In college she expected to be financially dependent upon her husband, but six years after graduation economic realities had changed her preference. She had taught for awhile when she only had one child but left paid employment before the birth of her second child. With the youngest child approaching school age, Carla wanted to return to paid employment. She planned to help the family meet financial goals, especially homeownership. Economic concerns had pushed her to change the domestic relationship she had envisioned.

Other women's responses indicated that the task of integrating family and career was complex. Many married women in the study who initially wanted to integrate work and family found themselves planning on decreasing their level of employment from full-time career to either a part-time career or periodic employment. Child care and the need for time to raise a family were concerns. We can see that the shifts in racial barriers created some new opportunities for African Americans, like the choice of a parent to remain home while her/his children are young. However, this group, like much of the U.S. population, found that two-wage-earner families were the only way most middle-class Americans could survive (Danziger and Gottschalk 1995; Pattillo-McCoy 1999).

Two respondents wanted marriage, children, and full-time career and were living with a partner at the time of the study. One respondent was planning her wedding, while the other, Allison Cross, was in a committed relationship. Yet her case demonstrates the difficulties of even planning on integrating work and family. Allison, raised middle class, went into law school directly after graduation from Private College. She worked in the legal field and resettled in her native mid-Atlantic city. She had been living with a partner for more than two years. Her goal was for marriage, children, and a full-time career. In terms of her career, she wanted to combine law and psychology and do more writing and teaching. These career aspirations were hard to reconcile with her plans to start a family. She noted that the financial difficulties of furthering her education conflicted with the desire not to delay children much longer. Yet she noted strong support from her partner and friends in achieving her goals.

Seventeen of the women were single, including three who had been married and were separated or divorced at the time of the study, but most of these women wanted another lifestyle. Of the twenty-five unattached women in the entire study, only six indicated that remaining single was their life plan preference; others were interested in marriage and career or marriage, children, and some level of paid employment. Achieving their preferred lifestyle was not a easy task. Ten of the single women (six raised middle class and four raised working class) wanted to be married, have children, and work full-time. In 1976 Wendy Anderson was recently divorced and pursuing her career. In her interview, she discussed how she was still committed to the ideal of integrating a career with marriage and children. With regard to a spouse, she planned to be more selective the next time. She did not have children in her first marriage but anticipated them in the future. In talking about her life she said, "I like children and feel that there is a whole side of my personality which is not developed. Raising a child would help me develop that side. I don't want to miss anything and raising children is a whole realm of experiences." Wendy was confident about attaining her goal, but she acknowledged that integrating children into a demanding career as a television producer was difficult. "I've seen friends hassle with feeling guilty about neglecting their children, so I know it is not easy. But there are also many rewards," she said.

Three single women (one raised middle class and two raised working class) wanted to be married, have children, and work part-time or periodically. While they were single, they anticipated that marriage and children would mean a reduced commitment to paid employment. For example, eight years after her college graduation, Francine Chambers, who was raised working class, had moved to a different city and had a stable career in the private sector. Her aspirations for herself were inspired by her mother, who was a single parent. Francine wanted to be "an intelligent and self-sufficient woman," but the cost for that was being single. So as she approached thirty, she still had other aspirations that were not fulfilled.

Finally, five of the single women (one raised middle class and four raised working class) wanted career and marriage (or a stable relationship). After years of taking advantage of opportunities as they developed, Robin Washington, raised working class, was clear about her career objectives. Like some other single women, she wanted to share her life with someone but was unwilling to commit to children. Karen Johnson, another raised working-class respondent, also indicated that she was primarily interested in a committed relationship. "I don't want to get married. The older I get, the more marriage seems like a difficult thing. It is beyond me to see why people get married." Karen had lived with a man for two years. Her thinking was not focused on marriage or even on living with someone again, but on having a stable relationship with a man who was a lover and a friend. In the interview, Karen commented, "I really love being single. I know that I can go anywhere and do anything, without depending on someone. I have been dating. . . . I may get married, but it is not in the plan. So many of my friends are divorced now or they are unhappy and they have two or three kids. I don't want to have to deal with all that." Karen's focus was on being more assertive and getting her career in place.

Singlehood can be viewed as a lifestyle that gives people freedom to maximize potential growth (Stein 1981). But this perspective is evident in the comments of only a minority of the women in this study, like Deborah Jones and Karen

Johnson. The majority of the twenty-five women who were unattached preferred to be part of a couple, and a significant segment also wanted children. Thus we have to look at singlehood within the population of Black women carefully. Viewing it as a mobility strategy can often be problematic, because many of these women did not focus on finding a spouse until they had established their careers. They did not anticipate nor were they all pleased with singlehood as a long-term lifestyle (Higginbotham 1981). Their search for a partner was complicated by a skewed sex ratio in which there were more Black women in the population than Black men (Tucker and Mitchell-Kernan 1996b). Indeed, the majority of the women who had married had Black mates.[14] The search for a mate was further complicated by educational and income gaps within the pool of Black men and women eligible for marriage (Staples 1981; Tucker and Mitchell-Kernan 1996b). As these single women approached their thirties, securing mates might have become difficult. The sex ratio worked against them, especially if they limited themselves to Black men as mates. It is possible that some of the women with a strong interest in raising children might have opted in the future for single parenthood (Collins 1990). Given the renowned homophobia in the Black community in the 1970s, there was little discussion by the women of homosexuality. None of the women indicated a sexual orientation other than heterosexual in either the interviews or on the questionnaires.

As a group, these single women employed their social support networks, self-direction, and resilience to help them continue to strive for the lives they wanted. Perhaps their struggles were not very different from those of other women in this age cohort. Many women did think that while their educational experiences helped in the arena of careers, their social lives in college, especially at elite colleges, did not help in the area of meeting potential mates.

FACING THE FUTURE

In 1976 many women were not where they wanted to be with regard to their personal lives. Other women were pleased with their lifestyles. These fifty-six women appeared to be cognizant of the resources and privileges they had. Lessons of an earlier age continued to aid them at this stage. They were socialized for survival, diligently taught to strive to be self-directed, independent, and caring individuals. They were aware of the role that race, and frequently gender, played in shaping and placing barriers to their options and chances for happiness. Yet they still persisted in the face of these obstacles.

As Black women moved into traditional male and White positions, they faced different tensions from those experienced in traditional female occupations. Women in these nontraditional positions were often challenged to display their right to hold such occupations. For example, Tracy Edwards had worked as a clinician in her health field for years. Like many at this career stage, she was seeking a change. She was retraining to teach and was involved in part-time instruction while in graduate school. As she proceeded to teach students, Tracy faced new race and gender barriers and resistance that complicated this transition. Students could not easily trust her judgment. As a single woman, she had to nurture herself in ways that were different from the recuperating she did when employed in clinical work. In 1976 she appeared to be very flexible about other aspects of her life. When discussing her lifestyle preference, she noted, "I have no expectations and that doesn't bother me. I plan up to a limit, but there are things you just cannot plan. . . . I'm not sure if marriage is an experience I would not like to have. If I met somebody who I thought had the qualities I like in a person and I thought I would form a permanent relationship, I would probably marry him. . . . If marriage comes, it comes. Children? Today no, but who knows what I will think next year."

Building a life requires continued evaluation and personal negotiations as women shift priorities at key stages in their lives. Compromises are necessary. Yet on the whole the women in this group appeared to be clear on how far they had come. Most also had a level of personal satisfaction with their lives. The majority had made a transition from working-class families, a few from actual poverty, to lifestyles where they had a measure of economic security unknown to their parents. They also had an education that could continue to create opportunities for them, since this asset was something that no one could take away from them. Other women built upon the foundation of a middle-class background to construct solid lives for themselves.

Along the way racial and social class barriers, and in many respects people's limited visions of women, had been obstacles. These women had scaled many barriers, but they still faced others in their futures. Most of the respondents were proud of the women they had become but were also clear on the costs of building their lives. Deborah Jones was pleased with her life, which she says came "from a lot of thinking and developing on my own." Her response when asked about the major area of failure in her life showed that she was cognizant of the costs. She said, "Building my life has cost me too much. I am too depressed and discouraged, which means defeated, at any small setback. I waste a lot of time—not years, but days, weeks, months mount up. I waste a lot of time recuperating [from racial assaults and disappointments]. That is a form of cowardice. It takes different forms and that is a problem."

We all face costs, but for many White and middle-class people in this society they are directly related to personal attributes. For these Black women, who all have different personalities, talents, and work styles, there were costs directly related to their racial identification. Their membership in an oppressed racial group means confronting ideological and structural limitations throughout their lives to achieve specific goals. If they did not accept these external limitations, then it was incumbent upon them to develop a perspective to challenge the dominant cultural influences that shaped those limitations. This task involved remaining clear on their own plans (Collins 1990). In many respects, their success can be attributed to how well they were prepared by their families and how well they developed ways to nurture and shield themselves from the impact of racism in their lives. But because the constant correcting for external distortions took a great deal of energy, their success was not without costs. Many people of color have viewed such costs as necessary for life in a racist society. But others are beginning to question why they have to pay so dearly for basic rights. As Black women and men enter positions of power they can foster institutional changes so that future generations do not have to pay so dearly in their quest for education and occupational success.

EPILOGUE

The women in this book graduated from predominantly White colleges, and many then proceeded to predominantly White graduate programs and/or professional schools and into majority White workplaces in the 1970s. As a group they have clearly achieved and advanced to new places. The women from working-class homes have been upwardly mobile, but many of the middle-class women have moved to majority group, private sector employment and surpassed their own parents' occupational achievements. How do we talk about that progress? Such achievement could be taken as evidence that racial barriers no longer exist, that we are now a meritocracy, and that when people from disadvantaged groups work hard enough they can assimilate into the larger society. This epilogue highlights how this study questions these approaches and pushes for a more nuanced appreciation of the achievements of educated Black women, and consequently of Black men.

First, social class matters. It shapes different routes to college and professional jobs for Black women. Even if Black women from working-class and middle-class worlds go to law school and become practicing attorneys, they travel different paths to this occupation. A perspective that addresses critical issues in Black mobility sheds new light on these achievements. Usual approaches fail to acknowledge the many informal and formal racial barriers that exist within integrated and predominantly White settings. In these settings, people of color frequently confront stated and unstated assumptions of their inferiority. These assumptions have consequences for their lives, as Black people may be omitted from networks essential for advancement. We can anticipate that working-class and middle-class women may face different constellations of barriers that can mean different track records in schools and other institutions.

Second, an assumption that new groups will accommodate to established patterns fails to acknowledge that Black people enter these educational and employment settings with values and goals that have been nurtured in families and formed in cultures of resistance. There is no uniformity in objectives, as working-class and middle-class women can have some shared and some different values. Because these women are continually challenging stereotypes as they scale barriers, their objectives can extend well beyond the individualistic goals that most majority group members see as rationales for educational and career attainment. Again, these values make for complex negotiations on the part of the women as they seek to achieve for a range of reasons that are often lost on members of the majority group.

It is clear from my discussions with women in 1976 and my knowledge of some women's careers over the years that they continued to be pioneers who worked to make a difference in the new worlds they inhabited. They were propelled in this effort because of their early socialization, and the support networks they developed to succeed remained important to their identities. In their employment settings, their differences were not always acknowledged by members of the majority group, particularly as many White people were eager to move beyond Civil Rights struggles and pronounce the racial problem solved. Many people and organizations in this nation assume a color-blind stance. But thinking that racial problems are behind us does not mean that they are solved. As Cornel West (1993) clearly states, race matters. For these women and other Black women in U.S. society, race remains a key life issue, one they wrestle with daily.

In new settings, as through their educational careers, Black women's survival is based on continued negotiations with coworkers, supervisors, neighbors, and other people in different social institutions. These negotiations change as the external racial and gender boundaries shift. Furthermore, negotiations vary depending upon a woman's own social class, parental status, sexuality, and response to the racial composition of the workplace, as well as other intangible and immutable characteristics and factors. Yet what is consistent is that life will be marked by daily negotiations with external barriers and controlling images as well as by an internal propulsion from one's own identity, goals, and aspirations. Understanding the nature of these daily negotiations can provide a key to the complexity of race in contemporary society. In particular, such understanding would highlight human agency and illuminate much about cultures of resistance.

As long as racist ideologies persist and depict Black women in demeaning ways, there will be counterimages from the Black community. These conflicting images of Black women are defined and nurtured within different contexts, but they must be reconciled if women are to move between these two worlds. Black women in this study were raised in families that believed in their abilities and shaped expectations of high achievement. Then they entered majority White settings where people held mainstream stereotypes about Black people. Teachers, school officials, and even peers might have expected these Black women to have minimal goals and to do little work. When parents like Mrs. Maxwell believed in their children and insisted that they be in the college preparatory program, teachers may have indulged them but not have been able to see beyond their own stereotypes of Black people. Such teachers were unaware of how Darlene and other young Black women were being socialized to survive in a hostile environment, which included excelling in school. Instead, teachers may have worked under the assumption that Mrs. Maxwell and other Black parents were mistaken about their own children. Such assessments might have been challenged by a score on a standardized test, as in Darlene's case, or they might never be changed.

After years of strong messages via the media and most teachings, even the most liberal White person can still harbor some beliefs in racial inferiority or, more important, in White supremacy. Such beliefs, especially if below the level of consciousness for the White people themselves, complicate interaction for Black people who are part of a cohort that was raised to achieve excellence and not give themselves much margin for error. This clash of expectations can be harsh, as Black women want to get somewhere, but White people block their way—and view such actions as appropriate. In fact, they might even see themselves as saving Black people from disappointment. For Black women, this clash is constant and unrelenting, as barriers have to be scaled with each new teacher and each new educational or employment setting.

A further complicating factor in interactions is the common White practice of seeing race but not acknowledging it. While race might not be stated, a Black woman is very clear about the unstated fact, particularly when she is a test case, and might feel more rather than less pressured to meet her own expectations for herself. Meanwhile, these very different assumptions and expectations can make for a chilly climate. White people are acting on their own assumptions, which can be stifling to Black women who are working under a different set of rules. Yet the lack of understanding about those assumptions means that those in charge, usually White people, are not taking the appropriate measures to work to improve the climate for the members of disadvantaged groups.

Most people who attend school or work with others are involved in complex negotiations. Yet Black women often enter into such exchanges with people who have negative images or low expectations of them. Therefore they often face the task of having to prove themselves in order to accomplish their work. The educational experiences of the majority of these fifty-six women illustrate this point. Given this landscape, it is hard for Black women to believe in the meritocracy, to assume barriers do not matter, and to embrace assimilation. Even when they have achieved, Black women remain the Other and carry the badge of a historical legacy. Attention to the detailed negotiations people engage in when moving within racial boundaries and crossing racial borders will help advance scholarship on race relations.

This study explored the complex negotiations of Black parents who worked to advance their children through a web of networks and resources within the constraints of the limited legal status of Black citizens. Writing about another era, Stephanie Shaw (1996) documented how newly freed men and women worked hard to create new options for their sons and daughters, brothers and sisters, cousins, and others. To these Black citizens, "formal education, *and* the people who made it possible, were 'highways' around those [racial] limitations" they faced (p. 1). The families of the women in this study had similar goals, but the paths were no longer limited to traditionally Black colleges and a few liberal colleges in the North. In the 1950s and 1960s, when the stable Black working-class population was significant, the mobility of their children was more of a family than a community pursuit. The smaller number of middle-class families could more effectively shape their children's educational futures. These two class groups were raising their families in an era of racial change that meant new educational as well as employment opportunities for their children. Yet, even in the 1960s, their goals were not achieved without challenging the status quo. The questions raised about this era can also be addressed to the post–Civil Rights era decades.

As we begin a new millennium, many scholars and public spokespersons are reflecting on our progress and charting a course for the future. Addressing the racial inequality that remains today necessitates acknowledging the progress and putting the difficulties that Black middle-class people experience in perspective. I do not want to overlook the increased poverty and precariousness of the Black working class. Yet scholarship can still address the lives of Black Americans who have credentials to compete in the postmodern United States. Much can be learned by examining how this middle-class group copes in the face of increased class polarization.

We need to be cognizant of how different dimensions of oppression and privilege create various lenses to reflect on one's life. Their socialization, support networks, and politics keep this cohort of Black American women's attention on race. Discussing the intersection of different dimensions of analysis, such as race and class or race and gender, may shape different frameworks within various social contexts. Patricia Hill Collins (1998) reminds us that "institutionalized racism constitutes such a fundamental feature of lived Black experience that in the minds of many African-American women, racism overshadows sexism and other forms of group based oppression" (p. 208). What are the critical factors that shape the lens for subsequent generations in the post–Civil Rights decades? What are their experiences in integrated and desegregated institutions? Are they agents for change in these settings, as many of these Black women pushed for institutional changes in their colleges?

As members of families and as individuals, the fifty-six women whose stories are told here were shaped not just by the reality of racial restrictions and stereotypes that may have influenced gatekeepers' perceptions of them, but also by the work necessary to overcome those barriers. In the course of their advancement, the necessity of this work meant additional hurdles to overcome in getting an education, finding friends to play with, securing employment, and developing a personal life. Such life tasks are not easy for anyone, but racism complicates getting them accomplished. In a society where those with privileges are often blind to their own advantages and oblivious to the concerns of subordinate groups, majority group members might not recognize what members of those new groups must do to enter predominantly White places. Once they arrive, the members of new groups must then begin intense negotiations with the more privileged individuals.

Recognizing the work that negotiating entails is not just a matter relevant for those women who entered predominantly White colleges in the mid-1960s. Such recognition is important for other investigations today. As scholars ponder the gap in achievement scores between Black and White students who are all middle class, they can learn from students' own perspectives. What energy is required for Black students to cope in today's high schools, whether they are predominantly White, integrated, or predominantly Black? Rather than attributing differences to parental involvement, scholars can ask students about the nature of the supports and difficulties in their schools. With whom are these students negotiating? What characterizes the nature of such negotiations in different schools in this new millennium? What about the circumstances of contemporary poor and working-class youth? How do these young people see the opportunity structure? What do they see as the path to upward mobility? What supports do they have and what strategies do they develop to achieve? We need more investigations of human agency in the face of continued informal and institutionalized racism.

Looking at race in contemporary U.S. society also means acknowledging progress. The fact that Black and White people, as well as members of other racial and ethnic groups, are negotiating in common spaces is itself evidence of progress. Just as these Black women were socialized to shed the subordinate role and not accept a "place" predetermined by White people's expectations, Black people today are facing White people and negotiating new places for themselves. More and more they are doing what Mr. Larkin instructed his daughter, Denise, to do when she started high school. Black people are not letting White people tell them where they belong. Indeed, this era is complex and uncomfortable because Black people are no longer paying deference to White people's expectations of them. Instead, Black women and men are asserting new identities and negotiating to change places rather than fit in.

In contemplating the new racial dynamics, I keep thinking about the lines from the Langston Hughes poem that opens, "I, too, sing America."

> I am the darker brother.
> They send me to eat in the kitchen
> When company comes,
> But I laugh,
> And I eat well,
> And grow strong.
>
> Tomorrow,
> I'll be at the table
> When company comes.
> (Rampersad and Roeseel 1996, p. 46)

Around this nation, many people of color are taking seats at the table. Yet you do not just walk in and take your seat at the table. It is a long path to the table. And you are aware of all the steps from the kitchen to the dining room, and of that careful walk on the carpet. You have to attend to your step, so you do not trip, and then gently pull out the chair and sit down. And you need to know the appropriate way to use the array of forks, spoons, and knives. Which is your bread plate and in what direction do you pass the food? As you eat the meal, these considerations make for hard work.

There are many new people at the table, many who are there but often not seen. They know who helped them get to the table, and of their own personal efforts to reach their seats. If you enter school with cultural capital, prepared for block building, schooled in being quiet to listen to stories, you may not be aware of how these skills are the first lessons for some children. Sorting out what you have to learn and then doing the learning requires energy. These tasks begin early in your schooling, but as you advance there are always additional skills, and more barriers to achievement. The invisibility of these hurdles to members of privileged groups means they rarely acknowledge that barriers have been scaled. They do not ask why you were not sitting at the table before. It is as if it were only your reluctance that kept you in the kitchen. Maybe they do not want to talk about your earlier absence because they think it is about them. Yet their denial makes the being here, and the effort surrounding eating, all the more painful.

The Black women here, perhaps like many other people of color who succeed in majority White settings, are not victims. Many did struggle, but they found themselves to be powerful people. They had strong internal controls and an awareness of what they could not control. Those were the barriers that they had to confront. When asked if she was a powerful person, Tracy Edwards said, "I never considered it that way, but I was determined. I was not easily intimidated. I am not aggressive, but assertive." Like others in her cohort, Tracy developed expectations in her family and pushed against racial and class barriers to achieve her goals in the world. After years practicing in a health field, she contemplated a career shift to make teaching her specialty. When interviewed in 1976, she had found herself pushing against new racial barriers. When Black women face new obstacles, just as in primary and secondary schools and college, they find support from family, peers, and plain old self-determination. Yet they are often confronted with people who deny that there ever was a problem. If we do not acknowledge that barriers on many levels still exist and that the doors of opportunity are just cracked, not wide open, then we cannot really have that discussion about race.

As I sit at the table I want to contribute to the conversation. I want my views to be heard and not just work to pick up the ongoing discussion. I want to talk about how I got here, why it took me so long, and what we need to do to put more leaves in the table and get my brothers and sisters out of the kitchen. Then we can all sing America.

NOTES

CHAPTER ONE

1. To protect the privacy of the respondents, all subject names in this book, as well as names of East City and other cities, communities, neighborhoods, schools, colleges, and universities, are pseudonyms. Respondents are categorized as working class or middle class according to their social class background, although at the time they completed the questionnaires all had achieved middle-class status.

2. Most public and private schools in the 1950s were segregated, either legally (de jure) or in fact (de facto), since public school district boundaries reflected existing patterns of residential segregation.

3. The role of token is not a choice but rather is determined by the objective characteristics of the situation (Kanter 1977). As one of only a few Black students in their schools, these women were often seen as representatives of their racial group. As stand-ins for all Black people in these predominantly White settings, they knew they had to make a good impression.

4. The nine Black women from the South in this study all graduated from segregated high schools, whereas the respondents from the North were more likely to be graduates of either integrated or predominantly White high schools.

5. Many of the respondents, especially the middle-class women, talked at length about their parents' involvement with their schools. Such involvement was not only an expression of how parents valued education, it was also evidence that they did not instinctively trust integrated and predominantly White primary and secondary schools. They carefully watched for evidence of racism in these schools and either acted to confront it or instructed their children to do so when problems arose (see Chapters 4, 5, 6, and 7).

6. In the 1950s and early 1960s, Aid to Families with Dependent Children (AFDC) required that the custodial parent stay home to rear her/his children. If a parent worked, the earnings were deducted from the welfare payments, and there was no allowance for child care or work-related expenses. Thus, during this period of time, single mothers on welfare were dependent solely on the state (Polakow 1993).

7. In the 1960s many college preparatory high schools in eastern cities were same-sex institutions. Such high schools gave young women opportunities to excel and assume leadership roles without competing with boys.

8. Over 14 million Americans were eligible for benefits under the Serviceman's Readjust-

ment Act of 1944. An estimated 2.2 million attended college, including about 70,000 African American veterans or family members (Kiester 1994).

9. The figure for Black males was 3.4 percent of that age group. In 1980 the figures would increase to 4.3 percent and 5.6 percent for males and females, respectively (McGhee 1983, table 14).

10. Transcribed from the tape of a news segment that included an interview with Johnnetta Cole broadcast in 1990 on *All Things Considered*, National Public Radio Tape #900308.

11. Unfortunately, the stories that my current Black American students at the University of Delaware tell me about their own high school experiences also contain many of the same themes as those of earlier cohorts.

12. Two respondents who were born before World War II (in 1941 and 1942) were part of this college cohort; they did not go directly from high school into college. The other respondents, who went directly into college from high school, are considered baby boomers; one was born in 1945, nine in 1946, twenty-four in 1947, seventeen in 1948, and three in 1949.

13. Since I was a graduate student, there were limitations on my ability to travel, but I was able to interview women residing in East City and three other major metropolitan areas.

CHAPTER TWO

1. The other eight women talked about their families as working class, lower class or poor. It is very possible that when they were growing up several of the thirty-one working-class respondents thought their families were middle class, since they were likely to use the unique categories employed to discuss status differences within the Black community. Dorothy Wall said that her father was working class, but his values were middle class. In cases where the working-class parents were homeowners and pillars in their own communities, it is likely that some daughters saw them as middle class. However, the women's greater exposure to mainstream U.S. lifestyles could have altered their earlier views on class placements. It is also possible that as college-educated women, they would have a deeper appreciation for the span of social class in the nation, and this knowledge could modify their earlier visions of their own past.

2. In his study *The New Black Middle Class*, Landry (1987) includes *all* white-collar workers, small businessmen, and a number of service occupations in the middle class. His analysis does not include the skilled and unskilled working class.

3. *The American Perception of Class* by Reeve Vanneman and Lynn Weber Cannon (1987) builds on the class divisions as specified by Nicos Poulantzas (1974) and then uses quantitative analysis to explore their validity with respect to the American public.

4. Vanneman and Weber Cannon (1987) compared three objective class divisions and status factors (middle mass, white-collar/blue-collar, and professional-managerial class). Their examination reveals that the division between mental and manual labor reflected in the professional-managerial class and working class dichotomy most closely captures the class divisions perceived by Black women and men.

5. As noted above, many stable working-class families are included in studies of the Black middle class because scholars used a middle mass model or designated all white-collar workers, including people in clerical and sales positions, as middle class.

6. The denial of access to many occupations made college and other advanced education

the primary route out of low-wage occupations for Black Americans. This option will be explored below in the discussion of the Black middle class.

7. Dual labor market theory as conceptualized by Michael Piore is used here, but there are several theoretical positions that recognize segmentation in the labor force. Such theories are direct challenges to orthodox economic views that link increases in education, skills, and other human capital variables with increased wages, occupational positions, and improved working conditions. Researchers of urban labor markets in the late 1960s and early 1970s found depressed economies with limited employment options for Black people. Instead of finding support for the human capital model, scholars found that "the determinants of labor force status—whether a worker happened to be employed, unemployed, or out of the labor force—sometimes appeared to be relatively random" (Gordon 1972, p. 45).

Researchers of such structural barriers consistently identify a labor market principally composed of people of color, women, and young workers that differs sharply from the stable market, in which jobs primarily go to White males. Yet researchers attend to different aspects of the firms involved (core or periphery) and the resulting labor force (Bluestone, Murphy, and Stevenson 1973; Gordon, Edwards, and Reich 1982). Recognizing this segmentation is critical to grasping the roots of poverty and economic hardship in the Black community. Two parents can be equal in education, work experience, skills, and level of motivation, but one will be located in a marginal firm making low wages, while the other is on the way to developing some security in a unionized, core industry or a primary labor market job.

8. Four of the women did not know how many years of education their fathers had, often because they were raised by their mothers.

9. Reginald Clark (1983) also found that high achievers from single-parent families often received much encouragement to do well in school from mothers who had not completed high school when they were young. In the study here, single-parent mothers faced major obstacles to achieving economic stability in the labor market without a diploma or higher education. They were often limited to low-wage jobs, so that even steady employment did not enable them to reap major economic rewards.

10. Of the eight women who were middle children, only two had parents who were in their thirties when they were born; most of these women were born when their parents were in their early twenties. The women who were the youngest children had the oldest parents; all were in their thirties at the time of the birth of their last child.

11. These scholars used a more expansive definition of the Black middle class than employed in this study; however, one can still gain insights from their research. Primarily their work counters the portrait that Frazier left in the field, in terms of the lifestyles of members of the Black middle class.

12. One respondent did not report her parents' levels of education. However, her father, an entrepreneur, owned a business and a farm.

13. Most of the college-educated middle-class parents had attended predominantly Black colleges and universities, although a few had attended public majority White institutions in their regions.

14. This number includes a woman whose parents divorced when she, the youngest child, was in college.

15. In the case in which a woman lost her mother, her father remarried and she was then raised by her father and stepmother.

16. One of these large families was a blended family, since the subject reported the final family size after her father remarried.

CHAPTER THREE

1. Overwhelmingly an urban population in the 1960s, Black Americans have slowly been moving to the suburbs. During the 1950s and 1960s, restrictive covenants and discriminatory housing practices limited the number of Black Americans who could access suburban communities. Even though suburbanization has increased among the Black population, their rates lag behind those of White Americans (Massey and Denton 1993; Tatum 1987). Furthermore, the suburbanization of African Americans, especially in northern cities, often means the expansion of urban Black communities across city lines or into segments of suburban communities that are diverse (Pattillo-McCoy 1999).

2. In many instances, Black community residents have difficulties getting newspapers delivered, securing a diaper service, and obtaining other private sector services that other urban residents take for granted, such as having pizza delivered.

3. In this case, I wanted to use the language of the 1960s and 1970s, when people talked openly about ghetto schools. These schools were a major social problem for many African American families at that time. Yet the descriptions of ghetto schools from the 1960s and 1970s are still applicable to many inner city schools. One significant difference between the 1950s and 1960s and contemporary schooling is that significant numbers of teachers and administrators are now people of color, especially Black Americans. In the earlier era, a few cities, like Chicago, hired substantial numbers of Black teachers for predominantly Black schools, but elsewhere Black Americans had to fight for public sector professional jobs (Anyon 1997; Kozol 1991).

4. The complex series of political, economic, and social events that results in urban decline for racial-ethnic communities is beyond the scope of this book; see Hirsch (1983), Massey and Denton (1993), Sugrue (1996), and Wilson (1987, 1996) for in-depth treatments. Whereas Wilson sees middle-class African Americans escaping deteriorating inner city areas, Massey and Denton note that even middle-class Black residents operate within a dual housing market. Data reveal the dominance of race over class in the search for housing; high degrees of residential segregation persist as income increases. While Wilson paints a picture of affluent African Americans leaving inner city communities for life in the mainstream, this population is small. It is very likely that the many clerical and sales workers who make up the majority of the African American middle class as Wilson classifies it were still living in predominantly Black middle-class communities, waging battles for resources and services in central cities as well as suburbs, in the 1980s and 1990s. Mary Pattillo-McCoy's (1999) ethnographic study demonstrates how white-collar workers in a predominantly Black suburban community contend with crime, problems with services, and other issues of inequality. They are continuing a struggle very similar to that waged by previous generations, even if the site of the struggle has changed.

5. The real estate field was dominated by White entrepreneurs. The few Black agents were

denied membership in the National Association of Real Estate Boards. Although Black people in the business developed a parallel organization in 1947, the National Association of Real Estate Brokers (Blackwell 1985), Black brokers remained marginal in the field. Many Black prospective homeowners thus had to deal with White agents, who frequently discriminated against them (Massey and Denton 1993).

6. The National Association of Real Estate Brokers led to the development of the United Mortgage Bankers of America, which organized institutions that granted loans to Black Americans. If a city had a Black-owned mortgage bank, there was greater likelihood that Black Americans would be granted loans. But the capital investment of these banks remained small when compared to the major banks and lending institutions of that era.

7. In *The Black Community*, Blackwell (1985) assessed the role of the federal government. He noted: "Historically, the federal government has been a major perpetrator of housing discrimination. The historical antecedent for present-day conditions and inequities can be found in policy mandates promulgated by federal and local agencies, as well as a policy of calculated inaction or benign neglect. It should be noted that restrictive covenants preceded the Federal Housing Administration (FHA) by several years. But the government set the original standards that began and fostered residential segregation that effectively prevented blacks from having equal access with whites to decent housing" (p. 203).

8. The heterogeneity of many metropolitan Black communities has dramatically changed in the last three decades. Now many urban Black communities are more class-stratified than in the past. Upper-middle-class Black residents have greater access to integrated and predominantly White urban and suburban areas and also have greater resources to establish and maintain their areas. However, a more modest Black middle-class population resides in urban and suburban communities where they face more problems (Landry 1987; Pattillo-McCoy 1999). And many poor and working-class Black people live in inner-city neighborhoods that have been devastated by the loss of jobs and resources (Anderson 1999; Wilson 1987, 1996). However, as scholars like Feagin and Sikes (1994), Franklin (1991), Oliver and Shapiro (1995), and Massey and Denton (1993) note, even Black middle-class homeowners pay a racial tax in terms of the neighborhood, resale value of their homes, and other housing issues. Thus race, across social class, continues to be a major factor in securing a home.

9. This observation reflected the lack of options on the part of northern urban Black people in the center city. Although many parents recognized that schooling with White children would have its costs, they traded their children's social lives for access to improved educational facilities and well-trained teachers.

10. This observation is in line with other research that shows that during the 1960s "non-whites in the highest occupational categories became slightly less segregated from whites of all occupational categories" (Simkus 1978, p. 90). Meanwhile, White and non-White laborers became more segregated from each other, perhaps due to the expansion of suburbs for the White working class. Yet by the 1970s "nonwhite professionals were clearly less segregated from whites of all occupations than were other nonwhites" (p. 90).

11. Black suburbanization would become more prominent by 1980, but as Massey and Denton (1993) noted, this did not mean integration. In fact, "suburban blacks experi-

enced considerable segregation and isolation, both of which tended to be quite high in suburbs where blacks were represented in larger numbers" (p. 74).

12. Social science researchers generally use the census tract as the unit of measurement when analyzing residential segregation. However, block-level data is better for demonstrating the level of concentration and how racial segregation is a major structural feature of metropolitan areas (Massey and Denton 1993). In the case of the Turner family, the census tract would appear integrated, but there was a level of segregation within that tract that would only be captured by block-level data.

13. The feeling of discomfort with her own race was not a permanent state. Many young people raised in these isolated settings, where they do not receive uniform support for their racial identities, come to an acceptance and pride in their race in other settings (Cross 1991; Tatum 1997b). In her interviews with Black suburban residents in the early 1980s, Beverly Daniel Tatum (1987) also found isolation and identified how such communities could complicate the matter of racial identification for African American children.

14. Drawing on reports from Detroit area studies, Massey and Denton (1993) discuss the preferences for diverse communities among Black and White Detroit area residents. While Black people express preferences for racial parity and for neighborhoods that are well integrated, even fifty/fifty, White residents strongly prefer predominantly White areas. Surveys in Milwaukee, Omaha, Cincinnati, Kansas City, and Los Angeles confirm these findings. They all "show that blacks strongly prefer a 50-50 mixture and that whites have little tolerance for racial mixtures beyond 20% black" (p. 93).

15. It is in the past three decades that public housing projects have become ghettos of women and children. Data from 1978 indicated that 73 percent of the households in public housing were headed solely by women (Freeman 1980). By 1987 that figure was as high as 81 percent, and of the 718,000 families with female household heads, 94 percent were living with related children under the age of eighteen (U.S. Bureau of the Census 1989).

16. This figure excludes the women who recalled living in public housing projects during either their preschool or grade school years, because their families later lived in their own homes or private rental units.

CHAPTER FOUR

1. Now there is much talk about cultures of opposition, where Black community members advance values that challenge accepted mainstream ones. In *Code of the Streets*, Anderson (1999) found both decent and street families in an inner-city Philadelphia community. The decent families uphold mainstream values and teach children to respect authority, while street families, alienated from most U.S. institutions, disregard those values and lack consideration for others. In contrast, cultures of resistance accept many mainstream U.S. values, such as education, hard work, family, and achievement, but reject notions of White supremacy. Many might also question some middle-class values, such as individual career pursuits, that overlook collective gains for one's community (Higginbotham and Weber 1992). Most critical here is the rejection of White supremacy and actions that follow from this premise.

2. The exploration of values in this chapter is based primarily on the interviews with the subgroup of twenty respondents. Comments from the other thirty-six women, who only answered the questionnaires, are used when detailed discussions were included in their answers.

3. Family research in this nation generally begins with the experiences of White middle-class families as the norm and compares Black and other people of color to these standards (Coontz 1992). It also focuses on family functioning as a product of culture. There is little attention to identifying specific parenting tasks that accompany racial oppression. Pioneering work such as that by Maxine Baca Zinn (1989, 1990), Andrew Billingsley (1992), Bonnie Thornton Dill (1980, 1988), and Leith Mullings (1997) reveals the impact of social structural factors (i.e., labor market patterns, educational opportunities, social policy, and family composition) on family structure and functioning. Culture also plays a role in family patterns. For example, African American families have often had wives and mothers employed rather than requiring that the children leave school to contribute to the family income. Black families have been willing to invest in the next generation. Also, extended families are a tradition in the African American community, in both rural and urban settings, where limited occupational access necessitated many wage earners contributing to family economic well-being and grandparents and other kin helping with child care. As Black families advance economically, they often assume the nuclear family form, but they still have a strong kin network, and wives continue to be employed (Billingsley 1992).

4. Jennifer Taylor's father, who was employed in a stable public sector job, had higher educational aspirations for her than did her mother. Neither parent had completed high school, which was the goal that her mother held for her. However, her father, she noted, expected her to go "as far as I would like, as long as I finished an undergraduate degree."

5. Respondents were asked two questions to differentiate between their parents' educational expectations, but the results for both parents are presented in Table 2.

6. As noted in Chapter 3, seven of the working-class women were only children. This status enabled families to maximize educational options for their one child.

7. Much of the research on Black women in college in the 1960s and 1970s highlighted how these women expected to combine marriage, motherhood, and either part-time or full-time employment. These goals set them apart from the majority of White women in college at this time.

8. Denise's older sister graduated from college and become a teacher.

9. The possession of family libraries is an interesting and important regional difference. The Powells lived in a mid-sized southern city, where, as in many cities in the South, the public libraries were segregated until the 1960s. In larger cities there was typically one branch for the Black citizens, while in smaller communities Black residents often had to rely on the library in the local predominantly Black high school. These resources were not funded as well as the White facilities. If resources were limited in their city, it was very important for families to compensate in any way that they could. An important way was to have a family library and expose children to as many books as possible.

10. Cynthia's mother did not work outside the home for pay until Cynthia was thirteen;

thus this was not a two-income family. However, Mr. Butler worked for the municipal transit authority, so he had a unionized working-class job that enabled him to support a family.

11. There was no item on the questionnaire about music or dance lessons, but a few middle-class women mentioned lessons in their interviews. It was less often the case for the working-class women to mention private lessons, but many did learn an instrument in school. In addition to early lessons, two of the middle-class women developed careers in music. Further exploration of this topic might address the links with religious participation, since music and its performance are a central part of the Black church, and learning to play the piano was a way to prepare for certain church roles. Joyce Saunders, who came from an extended family with ministers on both sides, could have been being groomed for a role in the church.

12. Only one respondent did not indicate a religious affiliation.

13. In *I've Known Rivers*, Sara Lawrence-Lightfoot (1994) explored this theme. Her six male and female subjects were similar in age to the cohort represented here. Both those raised middle class and the upwardly mobile Black men and women from the working class expressed a strong obligation to the community, but the sources of this commitment were different. The ideology was explicitly taught in middle-class homes, while the subjects raised in the working class felt strong obligations to family members and friends who were still working class. Yet these professionals all felt the tensions of being a token Black in predominantly White settings and took on the role of advocating for the members of the Black community who did not have such access.

14. It should be noted that the majority of Black middle-class parents in this study were often the first generation in their own families to achieve middle-class positions. While the middle-class respondents were duplicating their own social class position, the majority were raised by parents who had themselves been upwardly mobile from the working class. Thus many parents were very serious about working for the larger Black community. As scholars study the stratification of the Black community in more detail, we might begin to understand the ways that the mobility experience for different cohorts influences how individuals raise their own children.

15. In a comparative study of Black and White professional and managerial women in the Memphis area, an age cohort similar to the women in this study, Higginbotham and Weber (1992) found a strong sense of obligation to kin and community among the Black women, both those raised in the working class and those from the middle class, that was less pronounced among the White women. Also, the Black women were more likely to be involved in church and community organizations, continuing to work for racial uplift, while the White women were more likely to be involved in professional organizations. More research is needed to examine the complex ways in which a professional ethic or tradition that is developed in majority Black settings is sustained, modified, or relinquished as Black women work in integrated and majority White professional settings.

16. Traditionally, racial ghettos have consisted of poor yet stable working-class and middle-class Black residents (Massey and Denton 1993; Taueber and Taueber 1972). Because a dual housing market made it difficult for middle-class Blacks to find housing in the predominantly White housing market, for much of this century, prior to local, state,

and national fair housing legislation, Black people had neighbors from different social class positions who could supply a range of role models.

17. Eighteen of the middle-class women reported that all or most of their friends went on to college, while five reported that some of their friends did, and two women did not know. These latter two women were in predominantly White high schools and did not have close friends in their schools, so they did not necessarily keep up with their classmates. Twenty-one of the working-class women said that all or most of their friends went to college, and four women said some attended, this latter group including women whose peer groups were mixed. Six women reported that only a few friends attended college, including the two women in the study who were in the commercial track in high school. These two women, born before World War II, did not attend college directly after high school. This group of six also includes women who were closer to working-class students who planned to work after high school, even if the subject herself was in the college preparatory program, and one woman who was in a small southern rural school, where everyone knew each other. On the whole, most of the women were surrounded by young people who also valued education and had aspirations of attending college.

18. The 1950s and 1960s were times of optimism about race relations. Therefore, while Black students faced competing values system, they still had hopes for a positive future if they followed their parents' advice. Also, in these mixed social class Black communities there were Black doctors, teachers, and nurses who served as models for professional aspirations. In the 1980s and 1990s the struggles became more intense as youth with aspirations of college attendance contended with greater peer pressures (Suskind 1998). Black youth are now less likely to have successful professionals in their communities, and there is a greater sense of alienation in the Black community from mainstream American life (Anderson 1999).

19. One of the working-class women reported that she became pregnant in high school. At that time she received special counseling, independent of her comprehensive high school. After having her baby, she proceeded to college because this independent agency saw her as a bright and articulate person and considered securing a college education the best route to enable her to care for her child successfully. This approach is a contrast to current treatment of pregnant teenagers, many of whom do not complete high school, much less continue to college.

20. This statement is not meant to indicate that the Black community is not achievement oriented. On the contrary, there is widespread support throughout the Black community for educational goals. At the same time, however, job ceilings and blocked opportunities promote a highly visible and frequently vocal street culture that rejects many mainstream American values, so that growing up, particularly in the Black community, Black youth confront challenges to their values of educational achievement and legitimate employment (e.g., Williams and Kornblum 1985).

21. The teacher's vision of Karen's future as a seamstress or a cook is obviously related to her gender as well as her race. Some teachers thought her brother was stupid and should go into the army. However, like many of the Black women interviewed in 1976, Karen focused on race and did not express concerns with regard to gender. There was an obvious racial bias in her suburban school. Karen was also clear about social class,

because she was close to the other working-class students, many of whom did not attend college.

CHAPTER FIVE

1. Spade, Columba, and Vanfossen (1997) examined high schools that were between 94 and 98 percent White in student composition, since social class was the factor under investigation. However, their research findings about climate are important since they speak to the abilities of segregated schools to do much with few resources. Segregated schools were limited by funding, so they often lacked extensive course offerings, equipment, and opportunities to enhance student learning. Yet teachers were very involved with the students and pushed them to take advantage of what the schools could offer (Walker 1996).

2. It should be noted that this finding only reflects perceptions of some women who were successful in predominantly Black schools and went on to predominantly White colleges. Other graduates and dropouts of these same schools may have very different tales to tell. But the focus here is on the experiences of successful college graduates who attended different types of secondary high schools and then went on to predominantly White colleges.

3. This position is an example of Du Bois's early thinking on the matter. Although he was later committed to segregated education and advocated increased funding for such facilities, his early characterization of southern Black schools remained correct throughout the 1950s (Kluger 1977).

4. A seventh woman, Katherine Howell, graduated from a small southern segregated high school that was affiliated with a traditional Black college. This school offered a curriculum superior to those in public comprehensive high schools, and both high grades and an examination were required for attendance. Thus Katherine's experiences will be discussed in Chapter 6 with those of the other graduates of elite high schools.

5. The means by which Black communities united to structure positive segregated schools is detailed in the recent study by Walker (1996). Part of that formula was racial pride and a strong achievement orientation. The students were taught an awareness of race in a historical and contemporary context. This vision was a sharp contrast to the color-blind orientation that many integrated and predominantly White schools were likely to take (Schofield 1982). Further, Slevin and Wingrove's (1998) study of retired African American women demonstrates the level of commitment of teachers in segregated schools.

6. The U.S. Census Bureau identifies the South as beginning with Maryland, Delaware, and the District of Columbia and working its way south to include Florida and west to encompass Oklahoma and Texas. Thus it includes Virginia and West Virginia, North and South Carolina, Kentucky, Tennessee, Georgia, Alabama, Mississippi, Louisiana, and Missouri. The border states and the District of Columbia have had higher per pupil expenditures and teachers' salaries than the states in the Deep South. Teachers' salaries in border states, like the District of Columbia, Maryland, and Delaware, were above the national average, while salaries from Deep South states were *all* below the national average.

7. Both here and later, in assessing life circumstances in general, the working-class women

were less critical than those from the middle class. They could very well be aware of the limitations that existed and of how teachers and parents worked within them to do the best they could. Rosario Ceballo has posited that such views were a sign of maturity as these women developed coping skills. The new research that looks at resiliency to survive poverty also identifies the supports or protective factors that mediate risk factors and sustain achievement. It is very likely that we are looking not at a romanticization, but at a genuine appreciation of an educational setting that gave women a level of confidence to cope later in more hostile environments, particularly in colleges. These women might also develop skills at getting what they need from environments. Middle-class women, who would enjoy more class privileges in all settings, might not be as cognizant of the efforts expended by others to help them. Having both working- and middle-class women from segregated schools provides different perspectives on the environments and enables us to see what others might take for granted as well as what some view as lacking (Ceballo 1999). The critical assessments from middle-class women are important in filling out the pictures, while the praise by working-class women helps us see what the schools did provide.

8. Given that all the respondents were high achievers, it is possible that the brightest students received disproportionate benefits. Nevertheless, the stories of these schools in the Deep South (Mississippi, Georgia, South Carolina, and Texas) reveal how Black communities resisted oppression and could create institutional support for young Black people.

9. The financial support for northern high schools meant that in terms of academic preparation of students, the predominantly White high schools would have been on par with the predominantly Black high schools but comparably better than the southern segregated high schools of the women in this study.

10. There is a small but growing body of research on the experiences of Black youth growing up in predominantly White suburbs. Beverly Daniel Tatum (1987, 1997a) interviewed middle-class young people about their suburban experiences. While her cohort is much later, coming of age in the 1980s, they made comments similar to those made by women in this study. However, her group was in fact more integrated into the social scene, since Black residents represented about 2 percent of the population of these suburban communities in the 1980s, while the number of Black residents was well below 1 percent in the 1950s and early 1960s. Also see Lawrence Otis Graham (1999) for a more journalistic account of the life of Black professionals in the suburbs.

11. In the 1960s Black parents focused on educational gains and did not make their children's social lives a priority. We can also look to the parents' ages for insights into their thinking. Karen's father was born in 1906 and her mother in 1910. Their youths were shaped by World War I and a short period of prosperity that was followed by the Depression. Rosalind's parents were a little younger. Mr. Griffin was born in 1911 and Mrs. Griffin in 1919, so their own youths were shaped by the Depression and World War II. These parents could not anticipate the centrality of a social life to their daughters, who were part of a new baby boom cohort. Socializing was especially an expectation in middle-class suburban communities, where many young people were freed from employment responsibilities.

12. Janet Schofield (1982) studied a northeastern middle school that opened in 1975 as

a model of integration and education. Her observations revealed that many of the teachers defined their job as teaching and avoided dealing with the social relations of Black and White students unless such actions directly affected their authority or disrupted the learning environment. Thus students did not get much help in learning how to interact across racial lines. Many teachers, Black and White, had the color-blind viewpoint and thought they could let integration proceed naturally. Rather than expecting the structural inequalities to be replicated in the classroom and taking actions to address them, the more recent way of addressing diversity (Cannon 1990), the teachers saw the classroom as removed from those inequalities. Schofield concludes: "The image of the classroom as a world of its own, functioning according to rules and regulations quite different from those of the outside world, also contributed to the development of the taboo by leading teachers to be comfortable with discouraging all reference to race in spite of its obvious importance in many nonclassroom situations" (p. 64). Such attitudes were common in the 1960s and 1970s, when integration was just supposed to happen.

13. Leslie Inniss's (1995) work addresses the aftermath of southern high school desegregation, but what is relevant here is her documentation of the lack of accommodation to the Black students doing the desegregating. These practices were not as dramatic as southern strategies that used "powerless children as a catalyst for changing entrenched racist and discriminatory practices" (p. 148). However, northern strategies were often implemented "without regard for the high emotional and psychological price these children would eventually pay as adults" (p. 148). Not as prominent in Inniss's work, but again very relevant here, is her placement of such actions within a context that was more optimistic about race relations. Thus Black families and often the young people themselves elected to participate because they were "doing" the work of advancing the race. Yet they found themselves doing that work with little institutional support, since schools were uncertain about how to proceed beyond granting access to their spaces. Upon reflection, I think that my junior high school administrators were forward thinking. Rather than have the one Black woman in the honors course in the seventh grade continue in that status for two more years, she was joined by two other bright Black students, who had not been identified by their elementary school as promising but had performed well in the seventh grade. Being one of three in an honors course was not as tense as being alone. But strategies that involved curriculum, open discussion about diversity, and other advances would have to wait for a later cohort.

14. In this study these students would be identified, like Marion Greene, as working class.

15. In response to questions about receiving encouragement and enjoying high school, Francine marked both "Yes" and "No." Although she was ambivalent about the whole experience, Francine appeared to have had better social relations with classmates than other graduates of predominantly White high schools, and she kept up with White peers through college. Such relationships might speak to the go-between role that Linda Grant (1984, 1994) identified among Black female students in elementary schools.

16. In the Wexler middle school that Schofield (1982) studied, the Black boys were attracted to the White girls, and many White girls pursued Black boys, since girls often develop romantic interests earlier than boys. Black girls were not successful in pursuing White

boys, however. They did not engage in early "attempts at expressing romantic interest, such as hitting and poking, [since these actions] would be misunderstood and would serve to scare rather than attract" boys (p. 150). The competition over Black boys drove a wedge between Black and White girls and generally was a source of frustration for the Black girls. In the cases of the suburban communities in this study, there were not the steep cross-class contacts that Schofield found in an urban school. And there was no genuine mix of the races. In these cases, for most of these women in high schools in the 1960s, there either were no Black boys or, if there were, given the tense racial climate, these boys dated Black girls. So the presence of Black boys contributed to a more positive atmosphere. However, Schofield's finding does indicate how the lack of Black male peers meant Black girls were not likely to date at all, since they did not date White boys.

17. The social isolation of Black women in suburban and small-town communities is a theme in other writing about the Black middle class (Tatum 1987, 1997a). Orlando Bagwell, a filmmaker, who was interviewed by Sara Lawrence-Lightfoot (1994) for *I've Known Rivers*, recalled the consequences of his family moving to New Hampshire to get their children out of the streets of Baltimore. Bagwell, also a baby boomer, is close in age to the women in this study. The family's relocation in 1965 was very difficult for the social lives of the children, especially Bagwell's sister. Bagwell still recalls his sister's feeling of being a social outcast at a time when she could have been very successful in the social realm. The implications of the family move were neither anticipated by the parents nor discussed with the children. While, as parents, the women in this study think about the social implications of moves for their children, their own parents did not. In fact, these respondents go to great lengths to talk with friends who have moved to sections of suburbs with high percentages of Black children in schools; they do research to find well integrated sleep-away camps. But this earlier cohort of middle-class parents did not anticipate the social costs of integration for their children.

18. The exploratory data here suggest that the geographic location of schools is a factor in students' experiences that merits greater investigation. The question of whether or not Black respondents lived in the same community as their predominantly White high schools presents a unique set of issues and problems. Therefore the research on Black youth in suburban communities needs to be very cognizant of historical developments in residential segregation trends. Douglas Massey and Nancy Denton (1993) identified distinctive patterns of Black suburbanization. Residents can be clustered in suburban Black enclaves that are either separate or adjacent to predominantly Black urban areas, or they can be widely distributed throughout suburban communities. These residential patterns can structure different social lives, especially for young people who are limited in geographic mobility until they can either use bicycles or drive a car.

19. The difference in soliciting volunteers for desegregation or assigning students without their consent reflects differences in education policies across cities. Francine Chambers and Nancy Brooks lived in cities where it was the policy to ask students, at least in the early stages of desegregation, while the Greene sisters were residents of a city that did not ask parents or students. Being forced to attend a high school where they were not welcome and where there were no institutional preparations for integration was viewed

as a burden by some women. Having the opportunity to choose gave individuals more of a feeling of power and control over their lives. This sense of control could play a role in the women's modes of adjustment and their attitudes toward the experience.

20. Such attitudes reflected the nature of even progressive thinking about race at the time. If Black students were studious and performed well in their studies, many White teachers assumed that they were "less Black" than other Black students and more akin to White students. The general expectation was that Black students were indeed inferior and not adept at academic work. This type of thinking made it easier for administrators to place Black students who preformed well in school in predominantly White settings with little thought about their social adjustment.

21. It should be noted that a few families who had previously depended on private and/or parochial schools for elementary or junior high school education sent their children to integrated public high schools.

22. An example of such planning efforts is John F. Kennedy High School in the Riverdale section of the Bronx in New York City. Designed to draw a heterogeneous student population with regard to both race, ethnicity, and social class, this school opened in 1972. It is described in Sara Lawrence-Lightfoot's (1983) *The Good High School* and is a model of administrators, faculty, and students working to preserve a diverse school where high school tracking better reflects the abilities of students rather than their racial and ethnic backgrounds or social class positions.

23. The population of Sylvia's small city in 1960 was about 38,000; about 10 percent of the population was Black (U.S. Bureau of the Census 1967).

24. The assumption of leadership roles by Black women in integrated settings is an arena ripe for more study rather than immediate celebration. Darlene Maxwell, who had been in integrated public schools prior to high school, might very well have had more experience negotiating between races than other Black or White students. In "Sisterhood as Collaboration," Weber, Higginbotham, and Dill (1997) posit that the election of women of color and working-class women to student offices and leadership roles in high school might actually be expressions of their marginality. Marginal women often develop border-crossing skills to cope on the edges. This marginality brings to mind the go-between role, identified by Grant (1984), among Black girls in the first grade.

25. All-girls high schools had broader districts than coed comprehensive high schools; in fact, some were citywide schools. Black women often selected them because they offered better college preparatory courses than their coed district schools. Furthermore, in the 1960s these schools were often praised for the opportunities they afforded women, especially in gaining leadership and academic skills. Yet the cases of Darlene Maxwell and Dorothy Wall (discussed below) demonstrate that these schools were not free of racial and class biases. Indeed, race might have been most pronounced in these cases, since the schools also served White ethnic women from the working class, although they often directed them to traditionally female occupations.

26. All the women who were interviewed in person were asked about sexism in high school, but most did not respond to the question. However, Dorothy Wall talked about how the math preparation offered in her all-girls high school was not adequate. Also, the girls were not encouraged in the direction of math or the sciences. This observation was made in retrospect, since Dorothy admitted she was not cognizant of gender issues

at the time. It does direct our attention to how we might want to attend not just to the gender composition of a school, but to the attitudes toward and expectations of women.

27. In the commercial or business track Gloria and Stephanie did not receive all the prerequisites for college and were basically prepared for clerical positions. Their class-mates, both Black and White, were mostly members of the working class. Gloria entered college in 1965. When she returned her questionnaire she had earned her doctorate and was a college professor. Stephanie was teaching part-time in a university and working on her doctorate.

28. As we will see in Chapter 7, the working-class women did not always have parents who were knowledgeable enough about what they needed to compensate for the ways that schools failed them.

29. It is important to note that the majority of these families had the resources to seek alternative schooling if the integrated district high school was not viewed as adequate. Therefore it is not by chance that this is the population most pleased with their schooling situation in high school. Nevertheless, their stories reveal the advantage of being middle class in a comprehensive high school, even for Black Americans.

CHAPTER SIX

1. Only large Catholic high schools had non–college preparatory tracks. The business track in parochial high schools prepared girls for traditional female occupations in the business environment (e.g., bookkeeping or secretarial positions). However, Black parents used Catholic schools for the academic courses.

2. These tracks could be equivalent to the college preparatory, accelerated, honors, or advanced placement courses found by Spade, Columba, and Vanfossen (1997) in their investigation of comprehensive high schools. However, the climate in college prepara-tory schools is distinctly different. It is not a question of whether or not students are college material, but of which college they will attend.

3. Sandra Freeman was an exception to this pattern and is not included in this discussion. She attended an integrated parochial high school outside the United States, where she received much support for continuing on to college and even beyond.

4. Karen was not interviewed in person, but she provided detailed comments on her questionnaire about the difficulties of high school, which was more troublesome than her predominantly White college, where she could find a peer group that was support-ive. Her isolation in high school was complicated by lengthy commuting and by the demands of studying, which often did not enable young women attending predomi-nantly White schools outside their communities to find the time to compensate for what their schools lacked.

5. One respondent, Brenda Reed, who went outside of her community to attend a com-prehensive high school, had problems similar to respondents who attended private or academically specialized high schools because she traveled between two communities. Yet Brenda's school was not as affluent as those attended by women here. In a com-prehensive school there were many working-class students, while the student popula-tions in these elite schools were overwhelmingly middle class.

6. Jack and Jill of America was founded in 1938 by Black parents who were entrepreneurs,

business people, lawyers, doctors, and other professionals. Their goal was to create a national Black organization with chapters in cities across the country. As stated in the by-laws in 1946: "The object of this organization is to create a medium of contact for children and to provide a constructive educational, recreational, and social program for children and their parents" (Whitted 1960). Lawrence Otis Graham (1999) writes in detail about Jack and Jill in *Our Kind of People*, an account of the Black upper class. His own family was invited to join Jack and Jill when he was young. The organization was critical to his survival in a majority White suburban community and a private school. Membership was also important for many affluent Black youth in urban Black communities where they might not immediately gain acceptance by their neighborhood peers.

7. Wendy is one of two middle-class women who graduated from a boarding school. The other, Sandra Freeman, went to a school outside the United States.

8. For a full discussion of how controlling images of Black women operate in everyday life, see Patricia Hill Collins (1990), *Black Feminist Thought: Knowledge, Consciousness and the Politics of Empowerment* (pp. 78–82).

9. Assessments of schools by working-class women were not as critical as those of the middle-class women. Perhaps their lack of privilege and the knowledge that this schooling may have profoundly changed their lives tempered any negative comments they may have had.

10. In independent interviews, both women shared these perceptions. Initially Denise and Robin wondered what signs they gave off that indicated they were "less Black" than their peers, but in the end they came to see this behavior as originating with their teachers. Both women resented being viewed in this way and being placed in such a position with regard to their peers.

11. Otherwise, when race was introduced in the traditional curriculum in the early 1960s it was around issues of slavery, reconstruction, and the establishment of segregation in the South. Such presentations often confirmed the status quo and perhaps highlighted the "Negro problem," as did the social science of that era (McKee 1993).

12. As noted in Chapter 4, all the respondents were socialized to take responsibility for the image of the race. This theme can be found in much of the writing by Black Americans (see, for example, McClain [1986]), yet there are class differences in their perceptions of the task. Black Americans raised in the middle class are contradicting mainstream images of their group, while those intent upon mobility are from the very families (that is, poor and working-class) that are maligned in the popular culture. It is possible that working-class students living in predominantly Black communities were hypersensitive about challenging majority group images of Black people. As I have talked about my research over the years, even well-meaning White people have found it hard to believe that poor and working-class Black people had high aspirations for their children and were more than willing to make sacrifices to ensure their futures. I can only think about the plight of young Black Americans today who face this challenge on a daily basis.

13. Personal narratives have discussed how race complicates the mobility process (Cary 1991, McDonald 1999). Such tensions were not unique to Black women. Sara Lawrence-Lightfoot's (1994) subjects who were mobile described similar tension, including the need to reconcile their two worlds. John Edgar Wideman (1984) also writes about moving between the world of school and home and the tensions involved in growing

up in Pittsburgh. He describes how his mobility experiences were complicated by his racial identity.

14. White middle-class families preferred to send their children to public academically specialized high schools because they would get an excellent education. If children were not accepted, these parents would make the financial investment in private schools. But if the first strategy was successful, parents could save funds for college tuition and also give their children more luxuries, such as clothing, vacations, and cars.

15. Dress was not an issue in Catholic schools, where everyone at this time wore the same uniform. Yet Brenda Carter's school appeared to be more diverse along social class lines than the specialized high school. This pattern could be attributed to the fact that her parochial high school was comprehensive, offering college and non-college tracks.

16. Mobility was a more collective and shared enterprise in racially oppressed communities than in the majority culture. This perspective has been missing in social stratification research, which assumes that all people are mobile for individual reasons. Issues related to race and gender implications of social mobility are explored in Higginbotham and Weber Cannon (1988) and Higginbotham and Weber (1992).

17. As predominantly White colleges reached out to Black students who could meet their institutions' regular admissions requirements, there would be some funding for these women's college attendance. However, when these same women began high school in the early 1960s, there was no evidence that financial assistance would be forthcoming from such colleges and universities. Thus when these women thought about attending college, they considered combining small savings with loans, the few existing scholarships colleges offered, and part-time employment.

CHAPTER SEVEN

1. It is possible that these schools responded to the educational goals that parents had instilled in children. Yet there is enough evidence to suggest that many southern segregated schools took the mission of educational advancement seriously (Shaw 1996; Walker 1996).

2. Later in their lives, as many of these women take actions to promote educational attainment for their own children, they might be able to place their own parents' activities in another perspective. We do see here how privileges are often invisible to those who are advantaged.

3. This comment is also evidence of self-direction as a key value in Black families. Beverly generally made her own decisions about schooling and social activities. However, she had a middle-class parent to step in and direct her when necessary. Like many adolescents, Beverly initially approached thinking about college without a full grasp of the implications of her decision.

4. Surely the middle-class women took national examinations, scored well, and were contacted by the National Scholarship Service and Fund for Negro Students (NSSFNS), but they did not mention this agency as a source of information about colleges or as critical in helping them make decisions. They were more likely to discuss the activities of their parents or family friends. Many other parents in their families' social circles faced the same issues, so they shared information through these informal networks. As the first generation in their families to attend college, the working-class women were

more dependent upon outside agencies if information was not forthcoming in their high schools.

5. Black middle-class families were frequently less affluent than the families of middle-class White students applying to private colleges, since this was an era when educated Black people did not reap the same rewards from their education as White people. While their sample was all male, Althauser, Spivack, and Amsel (1975) documented the differential earnings of Black and White men from comparable institutions of higher learning. A few of the middle-class women in this study qualified for some financial assistance and received scholarships. These students' excellent secondary educations also made them attractive candidates for aid. Colleges were taking very few risks investing in such students. This arrangement also helped their parents pay the bills and offset some of the expenses of going away to college, which was a reason these middle-class women were not terribly troubled by financial considerations.

6. Self-direction remained an important value even for middle-class women. These young people had been socialized to review their options and their goals and make informed decisions about their lives in many arenas. Thus they approached this major decision with critical skills. It also explains why many parents respected their daughters' careful deliberations.

7. Female students at Whitehall College also took courses at the Ivy League male college adjacent to their campus. Thus, for the most part, classes were coeducational.

8. The concepts of adult-sponsored and child-secured educational mobility were derived from an analysis of the data. One might define child-secured mobility as occurring when a young woman was required to initiate more than one type of support for herself. For example, parents might provide cognitive and emotional support, while the young women needed to work hard for the scholarship. However, we are looking at a different situation when a young woman in her teens has to navigate the adult worlds for information about colleges, the necessary examinations, and the finances that would make college attendance a reality. Both adult-sponsored and child-secured educational mobility require the individuals to be good students, but there was often more pressure on the working-class women or any woman who fit the pattern of child-secured mobility.

The study was not designed to test for these concepts and relate them to a dependent variable. All of these women reached their goal of attending college, but those who were child-secured, especially the working-class women who went directly from high school into college, may be exceptional as a group. While a complete analysis is outside the scope of this study, the findings here also suggest that not all efforts at child-secured mobility are initially successful. For example, Gloria McDonald and Stephanie Lawrence were in the labor force for several years before pursuing higher education. The fact that these women were not even in college preparatory programs in high school was too much of a structural obstacle to overcome. The problem was more than a lack of emotional support, since their schools did much to undermine their confidence, in addition to not giving them the courses to prepare for college. Thus the barriers to college attendance directly from high school were too enormous for young women to scale. However, we can think about these concepts as a continuum with varying levels of emotional, cognitive, and material support for college attendance and explore them in new research.

9. This agency helped connect talented Black students with predominantly White colleges interested in admitting Black students. The NSSFNS identified promising Black students based upon their scores on college entrance examinations. Upon receipt of a questionnaire indicating the student's preferences with regard to the size and location of colleges, the agency directed the name of that student to specific colleges. The colleges then sent information and application forms directly to the potential candidate; many institutions had financial aid packages available. Working with the NSSFNS enabled colleges to bypass counselors and communicate directly with the student and her or his parents. The strategy developed by this agency was very effective in communicating to Black families that the national picture on admission policies in many predominantly White colleges had changed.

10. In the interview, Linda could not recall the specific incident she witnessed, but she clearly remembered her reaction and her mother's support.

11. This perception might not be true for working-class parents today, since more people are familiar with the status rankings of American colleges. However, the majority of the working-class women, in interviews and on the questionnaires, indicated that their parents knew little about the status of colleges. Thus most women made the decisions about where to attend on their own—perhaps sharing information with classmates. But few Black students had this information, since only a tiny fraction of Black Americans had attended predominantly White colleges at this time and there was little data, given high levels of employment discrimination, on how attending an elite, predominantly White college would translate in the labor market. Today there is not only greater mass media attention to the status rankings of schools, but within family networks there might also be more information about how graduating from high status colleges could be an advantage in the search for employment.

12. Self-guidance was especially the case for the seven working-class respondents who were only children (e.g., Linda Trott, Nancy Brooks, and Dorothy Wall) and the women who were the oldest in their families (e.g., Adele Lewis, Darlene Maxwell, and Jennifer Taylor). However, the other working-class women, like Karen Johnson and Tracy Edwards, had older siblings at home to help them navigate the world of higher education.

CHAPTER EIGHT

1. Here, as in other studies, various measures were used to assess social class placement. Many of those families identified as lower middle class by Hedegard and Brown (1969) would be labeled as working class in this study.

2. To distinguish elite from non-elite colleges, I examined college handbooks. I also asked fifteen college-educated colleagues in Massachusetts and Pennsylvania to rank the schools. Their assessments agreed with the objective differences reflected in the handbooks.

3. This pattern has been identified in other research on Black students in predominantly White colleges during this era, especially Jewelle Gibbs (1977) and Jacqueline Fleming (1985).

4. Many advances have been made in recent years on the subject of teaching to a diverse student population, but college faculty in the late 1960s had few lessons on how to address the racial tension in the classroom, particularly when White students openly challenged the presence of Black students at their college. Thus the classroom was not a place where racial issues were discussed. Also, the curriculum did not change to include information about African Americans and other people of color. If questions of race did come up, for example, in social science courses, faculty often let Black students serve as experts on their racial group. Black students were called on and expected to speak for their group (Thomas 1992; Van Deberg 1992). Faculty did not consider learning new material to enable them to address these issues; instead, many let Black students serve the role of informal teacher. However, this practice put students at a disadvantage, because they lacked the legitimacy of the faculty role. The colleges' failure to alter the curriculum and teach faculty how to handle classroom dynamics often heightened the Black students' feelings of isolation in the classroom, where there were rarely more than two or three of them. It also meant that problems of racial tension were often resolved in social settings, without the supervision of faculty or advisors.

5. The male Ivy League college paired with Whitehall College generally had about twice as many Black males as Whitehall College had Black females. So this total made for a somewhat larger Black peer group on campus.

6. The neglect of special services for African American students at this time was part of a liberal color-blind ideology, where officials did not see these students as having special needs. Instead, because these students, who had the same educational profiles as White students, did not fit administrators' stereotypical notions of Black people, they were viewed as exceptions. These officials were also insensitive to what it meant to desegregate their schools and to how the racist ideas held by many faculty and students could shape their interactions with Black students. At this time, there were few if any African Americans either on the faculty or in student life to inform school officials that they would have to attend to the social and emotional aspects of this great social experiment (Van Deberg 1992).

7. These women, who entered college between 1963 and 1966, were different from Black women who would enter these same institutions in the years that followed. Interviews with Black college-senior women in 1974 revealed that the lonely plight of Black women on predominantly White campuses was well publicized by the late 1960s (Higginbotham 1974). Thus many of those Black women who entered predominantly White colleges by 1970 knew that there would be little dating and socializing in their school years. Yet many still elected to attend such schools because the need for educational credentials outweighed their concerns for a social life. Or, in the case of many of the working-class women, they did little thinking about the nature of social life in college and selected the college that offered the best financial-aid package (Thomas 1992).

CHAPTER NINE

1. Two respondents, Carolyn and Marion Greene, were commuter students combining college with paid employment. Their schedules left no time to develop peer groups.

2. For example, Karen Wright felt socially isolated in college and also had an integrated peer group, where she was doing much of the integration. Katherine Howell socialized

with a small group of White students from her dorm for about two years before she had a majority Black peer group.

3. It is an error to assume that these women would seek to re-create the same type of peer group in their adult lives. College was very much a time of experimentation and seeking solutions to immediate needs; one need was to solidify one's racial identity. Black psychologists identify stages of racial identity (Cross 1991; Tatum 1997b). Once a young person is aware of race and its significance with regard to inequality, it is important for him/her to have role models and a knowledge of history and social studies that counters the blame-the-victim explanations that were plentiful from the majority group in the 1950s and 1960s. Parents were often able to provide many of these lessons, but young people also needed the support of peers. Support was critical for these young women, who were often themselves the contradiction to stereotypes. They needed to be able to get support for such actions and also talk about race in their lives. At this time in our nation's history, just as today, few White people were able to have these discussions (Tatum 1997b). Once Black people were comfortable with their racial identity, they could enter into other friendships. Therefore the friendship patterns the women reported in 1976 reflected their own preferences as well as community dynamics, occupational niches, and individual life circumstances.

4. As noted before, the ethic of social responsibility was still prevalent in the Black community. This ideology played a large role in the socialization of a Black professional class that was attentive to the overall status of the Black community (Shaw 1996). The selection of a majority Black peer group, in addition to meeting these students' social needs, could have helped them keep this ethic alive on a predominantly White campus where the focus of educational and occupational attainment was for self only.

5. Such an observation on her part was relative to the people she met in college. Katherine attended two summer programs and appeared to be more organized about college than many working-class respondents. We could learn more about child-secured mobility, since it involves a great deal of work on the part of the participant, but we know little of the participant's perception of these efforts. The fact that many middle-class people can plan because they have the financial resources to control more of their environment might also have been lost on Katherine. Yet her actions after college enabled her to secure the economic resources to follow her plan.

6. In a more recent comparative study of Black and White college-educated women, there were differences in parental expectations about marriage. Those women, born between 1945 and 1960, were employed in professional and managerial positions in the Memphis area in the mid-1980s. The sample included women from working-class and middle-class families. When asked, "Do you recall your mother or father emphasizing that marriage should be your primary life goal?," the majority of the women responded that they did not get that message. Very few of the Black respondents noted that their parents stressed marriage as a primary life goal, only 6 percent of the working class and 4 percent of the middle class, while 22 percent of the White working-class respondents and 18 percent of the White middle-class respondents said they received this message from their parents (Higginbotham and Weber 1992). Thus these respondents were not socialized to find security in marriage, but to assume some level of economic responsibility for their well-being.

1. Much of the research on educated Black women either explores the lives of women while in college or looks at Black women in specific occupations. This study was designed to explore the diversity of choices for Black women with a college degree; thus it includes four women who were not in paid employment. These women planned to resume paid employment in the future, but at the time of the study they were home with children while their husbands supported the family.

2. Two women who were living with a partner and planning to marry were treated as married in this study.

3. Further communications with a subset of the respondents and news of them through alumni publications indicate that many women continued to advance in their occupations and that some developed careers in new fields. Because this study explored their status very early in their careers, it cannot be used to draw links between social class background, colleges attended, and occupational outcomes. Table 5 and Table 6 are for informational purposes only. This study's strength is in exploring the issues women have to address in order to build careers and families.

4. The War on Poverty had an impact on the employment options of many women graduating from college in the late 1960s. Funds for a range of social service occupations made such employment readily available to graduates with a bachelor's degree. The fact that such jobs were plentiful was also a reason that many women did not think that specialized knowledge and/or skills were necessary. While these positions provided initial jobs, few women considered developing life-long careers in these social service agencies.

5. Holland and Eisenhart (1990) note that peers are important in helping each other confirm their initial plans or change plans about careers. In this study, many of the women who either married in college and/or dated men in college they would later marry talked about how these men were involved in their thinking about their future careers. In the case of Black men, there was the expectation that these women, as their current or future spouses, would make careers a priority in their lives. This illustrates a different orientation on the part of this cohort of Black men, in expecting women also to make a commitment to a life of doing interesting work, rather than making family the priority and being flexible about their work roles.

6. Practicing law in the South was indeed problematic for Black attorneys because they were not respected in the courts. Many Black clients therefore preferred to have White attorneys represent them in southern courtrooms. This situation changed dramatically in the late 1960s and 1970s, however, and law became an attractive occupation for many people of color.

7. These women were interviewed in 1976, prior to major national economic problems. The recession has had a tremendous impact on members of the Black middle class (Pattillo-McCoy 1999). Since the mid-1980s, it is less likely that married women can stay home until their children are school-age. For this cohort, who were graduates of predominantly White universities and professional schools, more women had the option than prior generations, when only elite professional Black men could support their families on one income (Graham 1999).

8. Two other respondents were working part-time while they made caring for children a

priority in their lives. Beth Warren, who was raised working class, worked part-time in educational consulting. Sherri North, raised middle class, was a freelance writer, spending four to eight hours a day writing at home, while she also tended to her children. Unlike the other four women, these two women were routinely involved in paid employment and saw themselves as pursuing careers.

9. Denise's father, who had been a postal clerk and then gone into real estate when Denise was young, had his own real estate firm by 1976.

10. When looking for respondents for this study, I was discussing the project with a faculty member at my university. He told me that some of the Black women who graduated from Whitehall College were wasting their educations, because he knew of one woman, Beth Warren, who was home raising children. He did not recognize Beth's commitment to family and to her children's education, and to the larger issues of the education of Black children in public schools. Many of the White women who graduated from Whitehall probably were also primarily raising children, but their actions were not viewed as deviant. Yet, as a Black woman graduate of an elite college, Beth was expected to go on to greatness, rather than be given the right to live the life that she wanted. So there is the possibility that faculty might not be willing even to listen to the many factors that Black women considered when making career and life decisions. Perhaps some women were able to find faculty who were supportive and aware of the many challenges they faced.

11. Black sororities also served this function, because they were primarily service as well as social groups. Thus Margaret Cooke at Technical University was able to join an East City–wide branch of a Black sorority, and her participation helped address many of her needs.

12. These two women held orientations in which they did not have expectations, both as college seniors and in 1976.

13. This total group includes seven women who were married but did not have the children they wanted at the time of the study, one woman who was married but wanted career only, and four women who were currently at home with children but planned to return to some level of paid employment when their children were school-age. We can assume that these twelve women had some measure of control over their futures, but there were nineteen who needed marriage to begin to address the life plan they wanted.

14. There was a total of thirty-seven marriages among these women, including those who had divorced and/or were engaged at the time of the questionnaire or interview. Only seven women married a non-Black man. This includes one woman who had remarried. Her first husband was Black, but the second was White. There was no social class difference here; three middle-class and four working-class women had married White men.

BIBLIOGRAPHY

Albelda, Randy, and Chris Tilly. 1997. *Glass Ceilings and Bottomless Pits: Women's Work, Women's Poverty*. Boston: South End Press.

Althauser, Robert P., Sydney S. Spivack, and Beverly M. Amsel. 1975. *The Unequal Elites*. New York: John Wiley and Sons.

American Council on Education. 1990. *Fact Book on Higher Education, 1989–90*. Compiled by Cecilia A. Ottinger. New York: Macmillan.

Amott, Teresa, and Julie Matthaei. 1991. *Race, Gender and Work: A Multicultural Economic History of Women in the United States*. Boston: South End Press.

Anderson, Elijah. 1999. *Code of the Streets*. New York: W. W. Norton.

———. 1990. *Streetwise: Race, Class, and Change in an Urban Community*. Chicago: University of Chicago Press.

Angrist, Shirley, and Elizabeth Almquist. 1975. *Careers and Contingencies*. New York: Dunellen.

Anyon, Jean. 1997. *Ghetto Schooling: A Political Economy of Urban Educational Reform*. New York: Teachers College Press.

Baca Zinn, Maxine. 1990. "Family, Feminism, and Race in America." *Gender and Society* 4:68–82.

———. 1989. "Family, Race and Poverty in the Eighties." *SIGNS: Journal of Women in Culture and Society* 14:856–74.

Bell, Ella Louise. 1990. "The Bicultural Life Experiences of Career-Oriented Black Women." *Journal of Organizational Behavior* 11:459–77.

Berry, Mary Frances. 1983. "Blacks in Predominantly White Institutions of Higher Learning." In *State of Black America, 1983*, edited by James Williams, 295–318. New York: Urban League.

Billingsley, Andrew. 1992. *Climbing Jacob's Ladder: The Enduring Legacy of African American Families*. New York: Touchstone Books.

Blackwell, James. 1985. *The Black Community: Diversity and Unity*. 2d ed. New York: Harper and Row.

Blackwell, James, and Philip Hart. 1982. *Cities, Suburbs and Blacks: A Study of Concerns, Distrust and Alienation*. Bayside, N.Y.: General Hall.

Blauner, Robert. 1972. *Racial Oppression in America*. New York: Harper and Row.

Bluestone, Barry, William M. Murphy, and Mary Stevenson. 1973. *Low Wages and the Working Poor*. Ann Arbor: Institute for Labor and Industrial Relations, University of Michigan–Wayne State University.

Bound, John, and Laura Dresser. 1999. "Losing Ground: The Erosion of the Relative Earnings of African American Women during the 1980s." In *Latinas and African American Women at Work*, edited by Irene Browne, 61–104. New York: Russell Sage Foundation.

Bowles, Samuel, and Herbert Gintis. 1977. *Schooling in Capitalist America*. New York: Basic Books.

Braverman, Harry. 1974. *Labor and Monopoly Capital*. New York: Monthly Review Press.

Bullock, Henry Allen. 1964. *A History of Negro Education in the South*. New York: Praeger.

Cannon, Lynn Weber. 1990. "Fostering Positive Race, Class, and Gender Dynamics in the Classroom." *Women's Studies Quarterly* 18:126–34.

Carter, Stephen L. 1991. *Reflections of an Affirmative Action Baby*. New York: Basic Books.

Cary, Lorene. 1991. *Black Ice*. New York: Alfred A. Knopf.

Ceballo, Rosario. 1999. "Negotiating the Life Narrative: A Dialogue with an African American Social Worker." *Psychology of Women Quarterly* 23:309–21.

Cicourel, Aaron V., and John Kitsuse. 1963. *The Educational Decision-Makers*. Indianapolis: Bobbs-Merrill.

Clark, Kenneth. 1965. *Dark Ghetto*. New York: Harper and Row.

Clark, Reginald. 1983. *Family Life and School Achievement: Why Poor Black Children Succeed or Fail*. Chicago: University of Chicago Press.

Colclough, Glenna, and E. M. Beck. 1986. "The American Educational Structure and the Reproduction of Social Class." *Sociological Inquiry* 36:456–76.

Coleman, James S. 1966. *Equality of Educational Opportunity*. Washington, D.C.: U.S. Office of Education.

Coleman, James S., and Thomas Hoffer. 1987. *Public and Private High Schools: The Impact of Community*. New York: Basic Books.

Collins, Patricia Hill. 1998. *Fighting Words: Black Women and the Search for Justice*. Minneapolis: University of Minnesota Press.

——. 1990. *Black Feminist Thought: Knowledge, Consciousness and the Politics of Empowerment*. Boston: Unwin Hyman Press.

Collins, Sharon. 1997. *Black Corporate Executives: The Making and Breaking of a Black Middle Class*. Philadelphia: Temple University Press.

Coontz, Stephanie. 1992. *The Way We Never Were: American Families and the Nostalgia Trap*. New York: Basic Books.

Cose, Ellis. 1993. *The Rage of the Privileged Class*. New York: HarperCollins.

Cross, William E., Jr. 1991. *Shades of Black: Diversity in African-American Identity*. Philadelphia: Temple University Press.

Cuadraz, Gloria H., and Jennifer L. Pierce. 1994. "From Scholarship Girls to Scholarship Women: Surviving the Contradictions of Class and Race in Academe." *International Migration Review* 17:21–44.

Danziger, Sheldon, and Peter Gottschalk. 1995. *America Unequal*. New York: Russell Sage Foundation; Cambridge: Harvard University Press.

Davis, Angela Y. 1974. *An Autobiography*. New York: Random House.

Davis, George, and Glegg Watson. 1982. *Black Life in Corporate America*. New York: Anchor Press/Doubleday.

Dews, C. L. Barney, and Carolyn Leste Law, eds. 1995. *This Fine Place So Far from Home: Voices of Academics from the Working Class*. Philadelphia: Temple University Press.

Dill, Bonnie Thornton. 1988. "Our Mothers' Grief: Racial Ethnic Women and the Maintenance of Families." *Journal of Family History* 13:415–31.

———. 1980. "The Means to Put My Children Through: Childrearing Goals and Strategies among Black Female Domestic Servants." In *The Black Woman*, edited by LaFrance Rodgers-Rose, 107–23. Beverly Hills, Calif.: Sage Publications.

Drake, St. Clair, and Horace Cayton. 1970. *Black Metropolis: A Study of Negro Life in a Northern City*. Rev. ed. New York: Harcourt, Brace and World.

Edin, Kathryn, and Laura Lein. 1997. *Making Ends Meet: How Single Mothers Survive Welfare and Low-Wage Work*. New York: Russell Sage Foundation.

Ehrenreich, Barbara, and John Ehrenreich. 1979. "The Professional and Managerial Class." In *Between Labor and Capital*, edited by Pat Walker, 5–45. Boston: South End Press.

Ellis, Robert, and W. Clayton Lane. 1963. "Structural Supports of Upward Mobility." *American Sociological Review* 28:743–56.

Ellwood, David T. 1988. *Poor Support: Poverty in the American Family*. New York: Basic Books.

Essed, Philomena. 1990. *Everyday Racism: Reports from Women of Two Cultures*. Claremont, Calif.: Hunter House.

Farley, Reynolds. 1984. *Blacks and Whites: Narrowing the Gap?* Cambridge: Harvard University Press.

Feagin, Joe R. 1991. "The Continuing Significance of Race: Anti-Black Discrimination in Public Places." *American Sociological Review* 56:101–16

Feagin, Joe R., and Melvin Sikes. 1994. *Living with Racism: The Black Middle-Class Experience*. Boston: Beacon Press.

Feagin, Joe R., Hernan Vera, and Nikitah Imani. 1996. *The Agony of Education*. New York: Routledge.

Fichter, Joseph. 1967. *Graduates of Predominantly Negro Colleges: Class of 1964*. Washington, D.C.: U.S. Government Printing Office.

Fields, Barbara. 1990. "Slavery, Race, and Ideology in the United States of America." *New Left Review* 181:95–118.

Fleming, Jacqueline. 1985. *Blacks in Colleges: A Comparative Study of Student Success in Black and White Colleges*. San Francisco: Jossey-Bass.

Forman, Robert. 1971. *Black Ghettos, White Ghettos and Slums*. Englewood Cliffs, N.J.: Prentice-Hall.

Franklin, John Hope, and Alfred A. Moss, Jr. 1994. *From Slavery to Freedom*. 7th ed. New York: Alfred A. Knopf.

Franklin, Raymond S. 1991. *Shadows of Race and Class*. Minneapolis: University of Minnesota Press.

Frazier, E. Franklin. 1962. *Black Bourgeoisie*. New York: Collier Books.

Freeman, Jo. 1980. "Women and Urban Policy." *SIGNS: Journal of Women and Culture in Society*, 5 (suppl.): 4–21. Special Issue: "Women and the American City."

Fuller, Mary. 1980. "Black Girls in a London Comprehensive School." In *Schooling for Women's Work*, edited by Rosemary Deem, 52–65. London: Routledge and Kegan Paul.

Gaines, Kevin K. 1996. *Uplifting the Race: Black Leadership, Politics, and Culture in the Twentieth Century*. Chapel Hill: University of North Carolina Press.

Gans, Herbert J. 1962. *The Urban Villagers: Group and Class in the Life of Italian Americans*. New York: Free Press.

Gates, Henry Louis. 1994. *Colored People: A Memoir*. New York: Alfred A. Knopf.

Gerson, Kathleen. 1985. *Hard Choices: How Women Decide about Work, Career, and Motherhood*. Berkeley: University of California Press.

Gibbs, Jewelle T. 1977. "Black Students in Integrated Colleges: Problems and Prospects." In *Black/Brown/White Relations*, edited by Charles Willie, 35–57. New Brunswick, N.J.: Transaction Books.

Ginzberg, Eli. 1967. *The Middle-Class Negro in the White Man's World*. New York: Columbia University Press.

Glenn, Evelyn Nakano. 1992. "From Servitude to Service: Historical Continuities in the Racial Division of Paid Reproductive Labor." *SIGNS: Journal of Women and Culture in Society* 18:1–43.

Goings, Kenneth W. 1994. *Mammy and Uncle Mose*. Bloomington: Indiana University Press.

Goings, Kenneth W., and Raymond Mohl, eds. 1996. *The New African American Urban History*. Thousand Oaks, Calif.: Sage Publications.

Goldberg, David Theo. 1998. "The New Segregation." *Race and Society* 1:5–32.

Gordon, David M. 1972. *Theories of Poverty and Underemployment: Orthodox, Radical, and Dual Labor Market Perspectives*. Lexington, Mass.: Lexington Books.

Gordon, David M., Richard Edwards, and Michael Reich. 1982. *Segmented Work, Divided Workers*. Cambridge: Cambridge University Press.

Graham, Lawrence Otis. 1999. *Our Kind of People: Inside America's Black Upper Class*. New York: HarperCollins.

Grant, Linda. 1994. "Helpers, Enforcers, and Go-Betweens: Black Females in Elementary School Classrooms." In *Women of Color in U.S. Society*, edited by Maxine Baca Zinn and Bonnie Thornton Dill, 43–63. Philadelphia: Temple University Press.

———. 1984. "Black Female's 'Place' in Desegregated Classrooms." *Sociology of Education* 57:98–111.

Handlin, Oscar. 1965. *The Newcomers: Negroes and Puerto Ricans in a Changing Metropolis*. Cambridge: Harvard University Press.

Harding, Vincent G. 1987. "Wresting toward the Dawn: The Afro-American Freedom Movement and the Changing Constitution." *Journal of American History* 74:718–38.

Harris, William H. 1982. *The Harder We Run: Black Workers since the Civil War*. New York: Oxford University Press.

Hedegard, James, and Donald Brown. 1969. "Encounters of Some Negro and White Freshman with a Public Multiversity." *Journal of Social Issues* 25:131–44.

Higginbotham, Elizabeth. 1994. "Black Professional Women: Job Ceilings and Employment Sectors." In *Women of Color in U.S. Society*, edited by Maxine Baca Zinn and Bonnie Thornton Dill, 113–31. Philadelphia: Temple University Press.

———. 1987. "Employment for Professional Black Women in the Twentieth Century." In *Ingredients for Women's Employment Policy*, edited by Christine Bose and Glenna Spitze, 73–91. Albany: State University of New York Press.

———. 1985. "Race and Class Barriers to Black Women's College Attendance." *Journal of Ethnic Studies* 13:89–107.

———. 1981. "Is Marriage a Priority?: Class Differences in Marital Options of Educated Black Women." In *Single Life: Unmarried Adults in Social Context*, edited by Peter J. Stein, 259–67. New York: St. Martin's Press.

———. 1980. "Educated Black Women: An Exploration into Life Chances and Choice." Ph.D. diss., Brandeis University.

———. 1974. "Contemporary Black College Women in Predominantly White Colleges: A Pilot Study." Paper presented at Berkshire Conference on the History of Women, Cambridge, Mass.

Higginbotham, Elizabeth, and Lynn Weber. 1999. "Perceptions of Workplace Discrimination among Black and White Professional-Managerial Women." In *Latinas and African American Women at Work: Race, Gender, and Economic Inequality*, edited by Irene Browne, 327–53. New York: Russell Sage Publications.

———. 1992. "Moving Up with Kin and Community: Upward Social Mobility for Black and White Women." *Gender and Society* 6:416–40.

Higginbotham, Elizabeth, and Lynn Weber Cannon. 1988. "Rethinking Mobility: Towards a Race and Gender Inclusive Theory." Research Paper #8, Center for Research on Women, University of Memphis.

Hine, Darlene Clark. 1989. *Black Women in White: Racial Conflict and Cooperation in the Nursing Profession.* Bloomington: Indiana University Press.

Hirsch, Arnold. 1983. *Making the Second Ghetto: Race and Housing in Chicago, 1940–1960.* New York: Cambridge University Press.

Hochschild, Jennifer L. 1995. *Facing Up to the American Dream: Race, Class, and the Soul of the Nation.* Princeton: Princeton University Press.

———. 1993. "Middle-Class Blacks and the Ambiguities of Success." In *Prejudice, Politics, and the American Dilemma*, edited by P. Sniderman, P. Tetlock, and E. Carmines, 148–72. Palo Alto: Stanford University Press.

Holland, Dorothy C., and Margaret Eisenhart. 1990. *Educated in Romance: Women, Achievement, and College Culture.* Chicago: University of Chicago Press.

Hollingshead, August. 1949. *Elmstown's Youth.* New York: John Wiley and Sons.

Holt, Thomas C. 1995. "Marking: Race, Race-making, and the Writing of History." *American Historical Review* 100:1–20.

Hunter-Gault, Charlayne. 1992. *In My Place.* New York: Farrar Straus Giroux.

Inniss, Leslie Baham. 1995. "The Legacy of School Desegregation Pioneers." In *The Bubbling Cauldron: Race, Ethnicity, and the Urban Crisis*, edited by M. P. Smith and J. R. Feagin, 142–62. Minneapolis: University of Minnesota Press.

———. 1994. "Desegregation Pioneers: Casualities of a Peaceful Process." *International Journal of Contemporary Sociology* 31:253–72.

Jarrett, Robin L. 1995. "Growing Up Poor: The Family Experiences of Socially Mobile Youth in Low-Income African American Neighborhoods." *Journal of Adolescent Research* 10:111–35.

Jaynes, Gerald D., and Robin M. Williams. 1989. *A Common Destiny: Black and American Society.* Washington, D.C.: National Academic Press.

Jones, Jacqueline. 1985. *Labor of Love, Labor of Sorrow: Black Women, Work and Family from Slavery to the Present*. New York: Basic Books.

Kanter, Rosabeth. 1977. *Men and Women of the Corporation*. New York: Basic Books.

Kiester, Edwin, Jr. 1994. "The G.I. Bill May Be the Best Deal Ever Made by Uncle Sam." *Smithsonian* 25 (November): 128–39.

Kluger, Richard. 1977. *Simple Justice*. New York: Vintage.

Kohl, Herbert. 1967. *Thirty-six Children*. New York: New American Library.

Kotlowitz, Alex. 1991. *There Are No Children Here*. New York: Doubleday.

Kozol, Jonathan. 1991. *Savage Inequalities: Children in America's School*. New York: Crown.

——. 1967. *Death at an Early Age*. Boston: Houghton Mifflin.

Kronus, Sidney. 1971. *The Black Middle Class*. Columbus, Ohio: Charles Merrill.

Kushnick, Louis. 1999. "Responding to Urban Crisis: Functions of White Racism." In *A New Introduction to Poverty: The Role of Race, Power and Politics*, edited by Louis Kushnick and James Jennings, 147–66. New York: New York University Press.

Landry, Bart. 1987. *The New Black Middle Class*. Berkeley: University of California Press.

Larkin, Ralph. 1979. *Suburban Youth in Cultural Crisis*. New York: Oxford University Press.

Lawrence-Lightfoot, Sara. 1994. *I've Known Rivers: Lives of Loss and Liberation*. Reading, Mass.: Addison-Wesley.

——. 1983. *The Good High School: Portraits of Character and Culture*. New York: Basic Books.

Leacock, Eleanor Burke. 1969. *Teaching and Learning in City Schools: A Comparative Study*. New York: Basic Books.

Lee, Frank. 1961. *Negro and White in Connecticut Town*. New York: Bookman Associates.

Levine, Daniel U., and Allan C. Ornstein. 1981. "Education, Socialization, and Sex." *High School Journal* 64:337–42.

Lipsky, Michael. 1980. *Street Level Bureaucracy*. New York: Basic Books.

Lorber, Judith. 1994. *Paradoxes of Gender*. New Haven: Yale University Press.

Lucal, Betsy. 1994. "Class Stratification in Introductory Textbooks: Relational or Distributional Models?" *Teaching Sociology* 22:139–50.

McAdam, Doug. 1982. *Political Process and the Development of Black Insurgency, 1930–1970*. Chicago: University of Chicago Press.

McAdoo, Harriette Pipes. 1997. "Upward Mobility across Generations of African American Families." In *Black Families*, 3d ed., edited by H. P. McAdoo, 139–62. Thousand Oaks, Calif.: Sage Publications.

McClain, Leanita. 1986. *A Foot in Each World: Essay and Articles by Leanita McClain*. Edited by Clarence Page. Evanston, Ill.: Northwestern University Press.

McDonald, Janet. 1999. *Project Girl*. New York: Farrar, Straus and Giroux.

McGhee, James D. 1983. "The Changing Demographics in Black America." In *State of Black America, 1983*, edited by James Williams, 1–44. New York: Urban League.

McKee, James B. 1993. *Sociology and the Race Problem*. Urbana: University of Illinois Press.

Malcom, Shirley Mahaley, Paula Quick Hall, and Janet Welsh Brown. 1976. "The Double Bind: The Price of Being a Minority Woman in Science." AAAS Report No. 76-R-3. Washington, D.C.: American Association for the Advancement of Science.

Marks, Carole. 1991. "The Urban Underclass," *Annual Review of Sociology* 17:445–66.

———. 1989. *Farewell—We're Good and Gone: The Black Labor Migration*. Bloomington: Indiana University Press.

Massey, Douglas S., and Nancy A. Denton. 1993. *American Apartheid: Segregation and the Making of the Underclass*. Cambridge: Harvard University Press.

Mednick, Martha, and Gwendolyn Puryear. 1975. "Motivational and Personality Factors Related to Career Goals of Black College Women." *Journal of Social and Behavioral Scientists* 21:1–30.

Miller, Jean Baker. 1986. *Towards a Psychology of Women*. 2d ed. Boston: Beacon Press.

Mingle, James R. 1981. "The Opening of White Colleges and Universities to Black Students." In *Black Students in Higher Education*, edited by Gail Thomas, 18–29. Westport, Conn.: Greenwood Press.

Morris, Aldon D. 1984. *The Origins of the Civil Rights Movement*. New York: Free Press.

Morton, Patricia. 1991. *Disfigured Images: The Historical Assault on Afro-American Women*. New York: Praeger.

Mullings, Leith. 1997. *On Our Own Terms: Race, Class, and Gender in the Lives of African American Women*. New York: Routledge.

National Center for Educational Statistics. 1989. *Digest of Education Statistics, 1989*. Washington, D.C.: U.S. Government Printing Office.

Nelson, Jill. 1993. *Volunteer Slavery: My Authentic Negro Experience*. Chicago: Noble Press.

Noble, Jeanne. 1956. *The Negro Woman's College Education*. New York: Teachers College, Columbia University.

Oakes, Jeannie. 1985. *Keeping Track: How Schools Structure Inequality*. New Haven: Yale University Press.

Oliver, Melvin, and Thomas Shapiro. 1995. *Black Wealth/White Wealth: A New Perspective on Racial Inequality*. New York: Routledge.

Omi, Michael, and Howard Winant. 1994. *Racial Formation in the United States from the 1960s to the 1980s*. 2d ed. New York: Routledge.

Osofsky, Gilbert. 1971. *Harlem: The Making of a Ghetto*. New York: Harper Torchbooks.

Palmer, Phyllis M. 1983. "White Women/Black Women: The Dualism of Female Identity and Experience in the United States." *Feminist Studies* 9:151–70.

Parker, Gwendolyn M. 1997. *Trespassing: My Sojourn in the Hall of Privilege*. Boston: Houghton Mifflin.

Pattillo-McCoy, Mary. 1999. *Black Picket Fences: Privilege and Peril among the Black Middle Class*. Chicago: University of Chicago Press.

Payne, Charles M. 1995. *I've Got the Light of Freedom: The Organizing Tradition and the Mississippi Freedom Struggle*. Berkeley: University of California Press.

Piore, Michael J. 1975. "Notes for a Theory of Labor Market Stratification." In *Labor Market Segmentation*, edited by Richard Edwards, Michael Reich, and David Gordon, 125–50. Lexington, Mass.: D. C. Heath.

Pohlmann, Marcus. 1990. *Black Politics in Conservative America*. New York: Longmann Press.

Polakow, Valerie. 1993. *Lives on the Edge: Single Mothers and Their Children in the Other America*. Chicago: University of Chicago Press.

Poulantzas, Nicos. 1974. *Classes in Contemporary Capitalism*. London: New Left Books.

Psathas, George. 1968. "Towards a Theory of Occupational Choice for Women." *Sociology and Social Research* 52:253–69.

Quadagno, Jill. 1994. *The Color of Welfare: How Racism Undermined the War on Poverty.* New York: Oxford University Press.

Rampersad, Arnold, and David Roeseel. 1996. *The Collected Poems of Langston Hughes.* New York: Alfred A. Knopf.

Reagon, Bernice Johnson. 1982. "My Black Mothers and Sisters or on Beginning a Cultural Autobiography." *Feminist Studies* 8:81–96.

Rist, Ray. 1974. *The Urban School: A Factory for Failure.* Cambridge, Mass.: MIT Press.

Roediger, David. 1991. *The Wages of Whiteness.* London: Verso.

Rollins, Judith. 1995. *All Is Never Said: The Narrative of Odette Harper Hines.* Philadelphia: Temple University Press.

Roof, Clark Wade. 1979. "Race and Residence: The Shifting Basis of American Race Relations." *Annals of the American Academy of Political and Social Sciences* 441:1–12.

St. Jean, Yanick, and Joe R. Feagin. 1998. *Double Burden: Black Women and Everyday Racism.* Armonk, N.Y.: M. E. Sharpe.

Sampson, William, and Peter Rossi. 1975. "Race and Family Social Standing." *American Sociological Review* 40:201–14.

Scanzoni, John. 1971. *The Black Family in Modern Society.* Boston: Allyn and Bacon.

Schafer, Walter, Carol Olexa, and Kenneth Polk. 1970. "Programmed for Social Class: Tracking in High School." *Transaction* 7:39–46.

Schofield, Janet Ward. 1982. *Black and White in School: Trust, Tension or Tolerance?* New York: Teachers College Press.

Scott, Kesho. 1991. *The Habit of Surviving: Black Women's Strategies for Life.* New Brunswick, N.J.: Rutgers University Press.

Shaw, Stephanie J. 1996. *What a Woman Ought to Be and to Do: Black Professional Women Workers during the Jim Crow Era.* Chicago: University of Chicago Press.

Sidel, Ruth. 1994. *Battling Bias: The Struggle for Identity and Community on College Campuses.* New York: Viking.

Simkus, Albert A. 1978. "Residential Segregation by Occupation and Race in Ten Urbanized Areas, 1950–1970." *American Sociological Review* 43:81–93.

Slevin, Kathleen F., and C. Ray Wingrove. 1998. *From Stumbling Blocks to Stepping Stones.* New York: New York University Press.

Sokoloff, Natalie. 1992. *Black Women and White Women in the Professions.* New York: Routledge.

Spade, Joan Z., Lynn Columba, and Beth E. Vanfossen. 1997. "Tracking in Mathematics and Science: Courses and Course-Selection Procedures." *Sociology of Education* 70:108–27.

Spear, Allan. 1967. *Black Chicago: The Making of a Ghetto.* Chicago: University of Chicago Press.

Stack, Carol. 1973. *All Our Kin.* New York: Harper and Row.

Staples, Robert. 1981. *The World of Black Singles.* Westport, Conn.: Greenwood Press.

Stein, Peter J., ed. 1981. *Single Life: Unmarried Adults in Social Context.* New York: St. Martin's Press.

Steinitz, Victoria Ann, and Ellen Rachel Solomon. 1986. *Starting Out: Class and Community in the Lives of Working Class Youth*. Philadelphia: Temple University Press.

Strauss, Anselm. 1971. *The Context of Social Mobility*. Chicago: Aldine.

Sugrue, Thomas J. 1996. *The Origins of the Urban Crisis*. Princeton: Princeton University Press.

Suskind, Ron. 1998. *A Hope of the Unseen*. New York: Broadway Books.

Takaki, Ronald. 1993. *A Different Mirror: A History of Multicultural America*. Boston: Back Bay Books.

———. 1989. *Strangers from a Different Shore*. Boston: Little, Brown.

Tatum, Beverly Daniel. 1997a. "Out There Stranded?: Black Families in White Communities." In *Black Families*, 3d ed., edited by Harriette P. McAdoo, 214–33. Thousand Oaks, Calif.: Sage Publications.

———. 1997b. *"Why Are All the Black Kids Sitting Together in the Cafeteria?" and Other Conversations about Race*. New York: Basic Books.

———. 1987. *Assimilation Blues: Black Families in a White Community*. New York: Greenwood Press.

Taueber, Karl E., and Alma F. Taueber. 1972. *Negroes in Cities*. New York: Atheneum.

Taylor, Charles. 1994. "The Politics of Recognition." In *Multiculturalism: A Critical Reader*, edited by David Theo Goldberg, 75–106. Cambridge, Mass.: Blackwell Publishers.

Taylor, Ronald L. 2000. "Diversity within African American Families." In *Handbook on Family Diversity*, edited by David Demo, Katherine Allen, and Mark Fine, 232–51. New York: Oxford University Press.

Thomas, Daphyne B. 1992. "College in the 1970s—Climbing Mountains." In *Black Women in Higher Education: An Anthology of Essays, Studies, and Documents*, edited by Elizabeth Ihle, 327–32. New York: Garland.

Timmer, Doug A., D. Stanley Eitzen, and Kathryn D. Talley. 1994. *Paths to Homelessness: Extreme Poverty and the Urban Housing Crisis*. Boulder, Colo.: Westview Press.

Tucker, M. Belinda, and Claudia Mitchell-Kernan. 1996a. "Marital Behavior and Expectations: Ethnic Comparison of Attitudinal and Structural Correlates." In *The Decline of Marriage among African Americans*, edited by M. Belinda Tucker and Claudia Mitchell-Kernan, 145–71. New York: Russell Sage Foundation.

——— 1996b. "Trends in African American Family Formation: A Theoretical and Statistical Overview." In *The Decline of Marriage among African Americans*, edited by M. Belinda Tucker and Claudia Mitchell-Kernan, 3–26. New York: Russell Sage Foundation.

Turner, Barbara, and Joanne McCaffrey. 1974. "Socialization and Career Orientation among Black and White College Women." *Journal of Vocational Behavior* 5:307–19.

Turner, Jonathan, Royce Singleton Jr., and David Musick. 1985. *Oppression: A Socio-History of Black-White Relations in America*. Chicago: Nelson-Hall.

Tushnet, Mark. 1987. *The NAACP's Legal Strategy against Segregated Education, 1925–1950*. Chapel Hill: University of North Carolina Press.

Tyack, David B. 1974. *The One Best System: A History of American Urban Education*. Cambridge: Harvard University Press.

U.S. Bureau of the Census. 1989. "Poverty in the United States: 1987." Current Population Reports, Series P-60, no. 163. Washington, D.C.: U.S. Government Printing Office.

———. 1983. *Statistical Abstract of the United States: 1984.* 104th ed. Washington, D.C.: U.S. Government Printing Office.

———. 1967. *County and City Data Book, 1967: A Statistical Abstract Supplement.* Washington, D.C.: U.S. Government Printing Office.

U.S. Department of Labor. Employment and Training Administration. 1977. *Dictionary of Occupational Titles.* 4th ed. Washington, D.C.: U.S. Government Printing Office.

Valentine, Bettylou. 1978. *Hustling and Other Hard Work.* New York: Macmillan.

Van Deberg, William L. 1992. *New Day in Babylon: The Black Power Movement and American Culture, 1965–1975.* Chicago: University of Chicago Press.

Vanneman, Reeve, and Lynn Weber Cannon. 1987. *The American Perception of Class.* Philadelphia: Temple University Press.

Vose, Clement E. 1959. *Caucasian Only: The Supreme Court, the NAACP, and the Restrictive Covenant Cases.* Berkeley: University of California Press.

Walker, Vanessa Siddle. 1996. *Their Highest Potential: An African American School Community in the Segregated South.* Chapel Hill: University of North Carolina Press.

Wallace, Phyllis Ann. 1982. *Black Women in the Labor Force.* Cambridge, Mass.: MIT Press.

Weber, Lynn. 1998. "A Conceptual Framework for Understanding Race, Class, Gender, and Sexuality." *Psychology of Women Quarterly* 22:12–32.

Weber, Lynn, Elizabeth Higginbotham, and Bonnie Thornton Dill. 1997. "Sisterhood as Collaboration: Building the Center for Research on Women at the University of Memphis." In *Feminist Sociology: Life Histories of a Movement,* edited by Barbara Laslett and Barrie Thorne, 229–56. New Brunswick, N.J.: Rutgers University Press.

West, Cornel. 1993. *Race Matters.* Boston: Beacon Press.

Whitted, Burma. 1960. *History and National Program Manual of Jack and Jill of America, Incorporated.* N.p.: Jack and Jill of America.

Wideman, John Edgar. 1984. *Brothers and Keepers.* New York: Holt, Rinehart and Winston.

Williams, Bruce. 1987. *Black Workers in an Industrial Suburb.* New Brunswick, N.J.: Rutgers University Press.

Williams, Juan. 1987. *Eyes on the Prize: America's Civil Rights Years, 1954–1965.* New York: Penguin Books.

Williams, Patricia J. 1991. *The Alchemy of Race and Rights.* Cambridge: Harvard University Press.

Williams, Terry, and William Kornblum. 1985. *Growing Up Poor.* Lexington, Mass.: Lexington Books.

Willie, Charles V. 1981. *A New Look at Black Families.* 2d ed. Bayside, N.Y.: General Hall.

———. 1976. *A New Look at Black Families.* Bayside, N.Y.: General Hall.

Willie, Charles V., and Donald Cunnigen. 1981. "Black Students in Higher Education: A Review of Studies, 1965–1980." *Annual Review of Sociology* 7:177–98.

Willie, Sarah Susannah. 1995. "When We Were Black: The College Experience of Post–Civil Rights Era African Americans." Ph.D. diss., Northwestern University.

Wilson, William J. 1996. *When Work Disappears: The New World of the Urban Poor.* New York: Alfred A. Knopf.

———. 1987. *The Truly Disadvantaged: The Inner City, the Underclass, and Public Policy.* Chicago: University of Chicago Press.

———. 1978. *The Declining Significance of Race.* Chicago: University of Chicago Press.

Winters, Wendy Glasgow. 1993. *African American Mothers and Urban Schools*. New York: Lexington Books.

Woody, Bette. 1992. *Black Women in the Workplace: Impact of Structural Changes in the Economy*. New York: Greenwood Press.

Wright, Gwendolyn. 1981. *Building the Dream*. New York: Pantheon.

ACKNOWLEDGMENTS

When one works on a project as long as this book has been in the making, there are many people to thank. For the initial dissertation work I am grateful to the wonderful faculty at Brandeis University who pushed my thinking on matters of class, gender, and race, especially my committee, Kristine Keese, Gordon Fellman, and Morris Schwartz. The National Fellowship Fund, the American Sociological Association for the Sydney S. Spivak Minority Dissertation Fellowship, and Brandeis University offered fellowship support for my education. The opportunity to do graduate work is a privilege, and I am grateful to the foundations, organizations, and universities that make it possible to bring working-class voices to the academy. I also had the support of fellow graduate students both on and off the campus; many have continued to be part of my network. Acting as both role models and supporters, people like Alvia Branch, Suzanne McClain Litner, Brenda Venable Powell, and Linda Sharpe gave me the courage to be the type of scholar that I am.

I am forever appreciative of Bonnie Thornton Dill and Lynn Weber, who in the face of many demands at the Center for Research on Women at the University of Memphis never let me forget the value of this manuscript. Between other research projects, curriculum transformation workshops, editorial responsibilities, and professional obligations, as well as teaching undergraduate and graduate students, it has always been nice to sit down and work on this book. Support over the years, including reading various versions, came from Margaret Andersen, Maxine Baca Zinn, Patricia Hill Collins, Joe Feagin, Martha Foschini, Cheryl Townsend Gilkes, and Ruth Zambrana. In the last few years, I have profited much from careful readings and suggestions from Arlene Kaplan Daniels, Kenneth Goings, Allison Graham, Larry Griffith, Gwendolyn Lewis, Christopher Peterson, Abby Stewart, and Sarah Watts.

Academics could not write books if it were not for institutional support. Over the years, the University of Memphis and the University of Delaware have provided support, particularly in the form of clerical assistance and graduate students to help me manage this manuscript. An invitation, via Abby Stewart, to spend a year in Women's Studies and the Center for African American and African Studies at the University of Michigan in Ann Arbor gave me the opportunity to move the manuscript to its final phase. Graduate students who helped in the last few years are Patrice Dickerson, Lucy Hancock, Amy Hill, and Michelle Meloy. They helped me with library research and tables, but mostly I benefited from their suggestions to add material for readers who do not necessarily know the history of this era.

I am pleased that the manuscript found a home at the University of North Carolina

Press. Years ago at a dinner in rural Mississippi, Nell Irvin Painter voiced an interest in seeing it. Her assessment was a welcome relief, since previous reviewers were pushing me to advance race in the analysis and drop social class. Nell's ability to look at the intersection and encourage me to voice it more clearly helped guide me through further revisions. In the process, I gained much from the insights and suggestions from two anonymous readers for the Press, as well as from Caroline Hodges Persell and Thadious Davis. Kate Torrey is a delight to work with, and I am grateful for the professionalism and support of the Press.

Finally, I am appreciative of the fifty-six women who took time out of their busy lives to answer a questionnaire, and of the subgroup of twenty whom I was able to meet in person and interview. They trusted me with the details of their lives, and I hope that this book does justice to that trust.

INDEX

African Americans. *See* Black Americans

Aid to Families with Dependent Children (AFDC), 30, 241 (n. 6)

American Perception of Class, The (Vanneman and Cannon), 22, 242 (n. 3)

Anderson, Wendy: academic performance of, in college, 173–74; adult-sponsored mobility experienced by, 145; career goals of, 196; education of parents of, 36; employment of, during college, 175; high school experience of, 51–52, 120, 125–26, 128, 256 (n. 7); lifestyle of, 228–29

Attorneys, Black, 262 (n. 6)

Baby boomers, 1, 9–10, 11, 33

Bagwell, Orlando, 253 (n. 17)

Bell, Ella, 192

Bell, Joanne, 27

Billingsley, Andrew, 30, 76, 247 (n. 3)

Black Americans: in contemporary segregated settings, 1–2, 13; geographic mobility of, 8; urban population of, 43, 244 (n. 1); as veterans, 8–9, 241–42 (n. 8). *See also* Black community; Black men; Black women

Black Bourgeoisie (Frazier), 34

Black community: class divisions in, 20; competing value systems in, 248–49 (n. 16), 249 (n. 20); cultures of opposition in, 233, 234, 246 (n. 1); heterogeneous, 47, 245 (n. 8); obligations of Black people to, 75–76, 83, 248 (nn. 13, 14, 15), 256 (n. 12); and racism, 14; social and cultural values of, 14; social responsibility supported by, 261 (n. 4); as source of resilience for Black women, 15; and value of education, 66. *See also* Black Americans

Black Community, The (Blackwell), 245 (n. 7)

Black Feminist Thought (Collins), 2, 63

Black men: occupations available to educated, 12–13; support women's careers, 212–13, 262 (n. 5)

Black women: economic contributions of, 23, 28, 29–30, 247 (n. 3); and full-time employment, 193–94; gender bias against, 12–13; negotiate between races, 254 (n. 24); negotiate in White settings, 2–3, 11, 14–15, 234–36; as Other, 2, 13, 235; stereotypes of, 64, 80; and struggle against racism, 3–4, 18–19, 224–32; studied by author, 2–3, 17–19, 241 (n. 1), 242 (nn. 12, 13); support networks for, 239; as representative of all Blacks, 241 (n. 3)

Blockbusting, 45–46, 56

Bourgeoisie, Black, 34–35, 36

Braverman, Harry, 3

Brooks, Nancy: child-secured mobility experienced by, 150–51, 156, 259 (n. 12); college experience of, 168, 176, 177; and dating, 79; and housing, 57; lifestyle of, 225–26; high school attended by, 97–98, 103–4, 105, 253–54 (n. 19)

Brown, Toni, 95–96, 186–87, 205

Brown v. Board of Education, 4, 9, 10, 92

Butler, Cynthia: academic performance of, 177; college goals of, 157, 259 (n. 12); and education stressed by family, 68, 70; high school experience of, 119, 137–38, 139–40; and parents' occupations, 27, 247–48 (n. 10); and private lessons, 71–72, 247–48 (n. 10); and youth groups, 73

Career. See Occupation
Carter, Brenda, 60–61, 132–33, 165, 181, 191, 257 (n. 15)
Central High School (Little Rock), 11
Chambers, Francine: lifestyle of, 229; and mother's occupation, 30; college experience of, 181–82, 190; high school experience of, 101, 104, 252 (n. 15), 253–54 (n. 19)
Charles, Katrina, 20; academic performance of, in college, 174; adult-sponsored mobility of, 145; Black students at college of, 171, 260 (n. 5); college chosen by, 149, 258 (n. 76); educational strategies of, 53; high school experience of, 117, 120, 121–22; and parents' occupations, 38; and private lessons, 71; self-direction stressed by family of, 78
Children, 207, 214, 227, 262 (n. 1), 262–63 (n. 8), 263 (n. 10)
Civil Rights movement, 9, 10, 11, 25
Clark, Kenneth, 60, 70
Clark, Michelle, 86, 113, 114–15, 179
Clark, Reginald, 79–80, 243 (n. 9)
Class: and bias in educational system, 10; and Black access to majority White colleges, 7; and Black Americans, 20; and college attendance, 87, 141, 143, 165–68; and dating, 79; definition of, 3, 21–23, 242 (n. 2), 242 (n. 3); and educational strategies, 21, 23–24, 42, 61–62; and employment goals, 195–98; and high school, 88, 102–6, 159–60; and housing, 244 (n. 4), 245 (n. 8); and mobility, 233–34; and navigating in White settings, 21, 62; and obligations to Black community, 75, 248 (nn. 13, 14, 15), 256 (n. 12); and occupation, 21–22; as perceived by Black Americans, 22, 242 (n. 4); and power, 3;

22, 242 (n. 4); and private lessons, 248 (n. 11); and racism, 12, 16, 40, 62; and reading, 70; significance of, 23, 233; and status and affluence, 21; and travel, 72; and underclass, 20, 24; and values, 21, 242 (n. 1). See also Middle class; Working class
Code of the Streets (Anderson), 246 (n. 1)
Cole, Johnnetta, 16
College attendance, Black: 1960, 9–10; 1970, 10; and access to social circles, 41; and achievement for women, 193; and class, 87, 141, 143, 165–68; at elite colleges, 165–67, 168; and families' economic stability, 10; and high school preparation, 7, 86, 102–6; of men, 242 (n. 9); middle-class, 12, 142–42, 143–44, 148–50, 160–61; at non-elite colleges, 168; of peers, 77, 249 (n. 17); and veterans of World War II, 8–9, 241–42 (n. 8); of women, 10, 242 (n. 9); working-class, 12, 141–42, 143, 150–52, 161–62
Colleges
—elite: academic performance of middle-class women at, 173–75; academic performance of working-class women at, 175–78; determination of, 165, 259 (n. 2); track from high schools to, 165–69
—non-elite: academic performance of middle-class women at, 178–81; academic performance of working-class women at, 181–84; determination of, 165, 259 (n. 2)
—White: academic challenges at, 169; academic performance of Black students at, 172–84; adjustment of Black women to, 164, 169–72, 184; Blacks attending, in 1960s, 9–10, 170–71; Black students recruited by, 10, 145, 169; Black student organizations at, 186–87; and class, 7, 165, 184; faculty reception of Black students, 169–70, 260 (n. 4); middle-class attendance of, 12, 141–42, 143–44, 148–50, 160–61; middle-class expectations of, 163, 164; race tensions at, 169, 259 (n. 3), 260

(n. 4); social isolation in, 171–72; social spaces created at, 186–93, 260 (n. 1); special services for Black students neglected at, 169, 172, 260 (n. 6); rank of, 156, 259 (n. 11); transition from high schools to, 144–45, 151, 152, 160, 161, 162; and White peers' reception of Black students, 170, 260 (n. 4); working-class expectations of, 163–64

Collins, Patricia Hill, 2, 13, 63, 66, 80, 236

Competition, 5, 77, 136–37

Congress of Industrial Organizations (CIO), 25

Cooke, Margaret, 93–94, 192, 222, 263 (n. 11)

Cross, Allison, 5–6, 7, 35, 145, 228; high school experience of, 95, 145

Dating, 77, 79–81, 249 (n. 19); in White high schools, 97, 98, 101, 252–53 (n. 16)

Davis, Cheryl, 71, 118, 123, 165, 180

Davis, Kimberly, 195, 201

Declining Significance of Race, The (Wilson), 21

Dennis, Irma: Black community described by, 51; college experience of, 165, 171, 179, 189; education of parents of, 36; extended family of, 39; high school experience of, 51, 117, 122, 125, 145; life plans of, 201

Desegregation: and Black women negotiating between races, 254 (n. 24); in education, 1–2; in North, 4, 241 (n. 3); social costs of, for Black students, 100–101, 252 (n. 13), 253 (n. 17)

Dill, Bonnie Thornton, 247 (n. 3)

Dual labor market theory, 243 (n. 7)

Du Bois, W. E. B., 92, 250 (n. 3)

Educated in Romance (Holland and Eisenhart), 212

Education: and access to majority White colleges, 7; broad definitions of, 71–73; desegregation in, 1–2, 234; and employment, 194–98; as escape from low-wage occupations, 243 (n. 7); linked to hous-

ing, 42; of middle-class parents, 5–6, 36, 243 (nn. 12, 13); and opportunities for Blacks, 8–10; and optimism in Black community, 11; racism in, 10, 14, 15–16, 87, 88–89, 90–91, 159–60, 241 (n. 2), 242 (n. 11); and segregation, 241 (n. 2); as stressed by parents, 13, 66–70, 244 (n. 5), 247 (n. 5); as valued in Black community, 66; of working-class parents, 5–6, 26, 243 (n. 8). See also College; Educational strategies; High schools

Educational strategies, 21; in integrated schools, 47–48, 245 (n. 9); middle-class, 48, 49–54; working-class, 54–55, 62, 112, 255 (n. 8), 257–58 (n. 4)

Edwards, Tracy, 20; career goals of, 195; child-secured mobility experienced by, 259 (n. 12); and college, 166; college goals of, shared with peers, 157, 259 (n. 12); extended family of, 32; high school experience of, 118, 133, 135; lifestyle of, 231, 239; and parents' occupations, 26, 27; self-esteem for, 239; values taught by family of, 64–65, 68

Elmtown's Youth (Hollingshead), 88

Employment: dual-spouse, 193–94; education for, 194–98; and mobility, 222; in racist society, 15, 204–7; and social class goals, 195–98. See also Life plans; Occupation

Fair housing, 46, 48

Families: college education of, 5–6, 26, 36, 243 (nn. 8, 12); complex environments in, 64; dual-spouse employment in, 193–94; educational strategies of, 7, 21, 236; education stressed by, 13, 66–70, 244 (n. 5), 247 (n. 5); extended, 32, 39–40, 247 (n. 3); gender beliefs in, 89–90; obligations to Black community stressed by, 74–76, 83, 248 (nn. 13, 14, 15); positive self-esteem nurtured in, 2, 13, 64; as product of culture, 247 (n. 3); resistance to racism nurtured in, 3–4, 13–14, 18, 63–65, 81–83, 84–85, 233, 234; self-direction stressed by, 76–79, 84, 85, 200, 248–49 (n. 16), 257 (n. 3), 258 (n. 6); striving for excellence taught in, 73–74, 76, 84; values stressed in, 13, 14, 64–65, 73–79, 84, 244 (n. 2); and White college chosen for daughters, 38–39. *See also* Family, composition of; Middle class; Parents; Working class

Family, composition of: and access to majority White colleges, 7; and family functioning, 30; middle-class, 39, 40, 243 (nn. 14, 15), 244 (n. 16); and poverty, 30; and single mothers, 29–30, 243 (n. 9); and size, 33, 40, 244 (n. 16); working-class, 29

Feagin, Joe, 21–22, 127, 245 (n. 8)

Federal Housing Administration (FHA), 245 (n. 7)

Fichter, Joseph, 194

Foster, Yvonne, 106, 107, 114–15, 179, 201

Frazier, E. Franklin, 34, 35, 243 (n. 11)

Freeman, Sandra, 119, 255 (n. 3), 256 (n. 7)

Friends. *See* Peers

Fuller, Mary, 137

Gender, 15; beliefs about, in Black families, 89–90; bias in education, 10, 254–55 (n. 26); and economic support of family, 23; and hidden curriculum in high school, 89; and mobility, 142

Gerson, Kathleen, 217

Ghetto: definiton of, 47; protective setting of, 51; staying in, 57–58

Ghetto schools, 44, 244 (n. 3)

G. I. Bill, 9

Girl Scouts, 73

Good High School, The (Lawrence-Lightfoot), 254 (n. 22)

Graduates of Predominantly Negro Colleges (Fichter), 194

Grant, Linda, 89, 90, 252 (n. 15), 254 (n. 24)

Greene, Carolyn, 30, 182, 260 (n. 1); high school experience of, 99, 103, 109, 253–54 (n. 19)

Greene, Marion, 30, 195, 260 (n. 1); high

school experience of, 99, 100, 103, 109, 252 (n. 14), 253–54 (n. 19)

Griffin, Rosalind: Black peer group of, in college, 189; college selected by, 148–49; and middle-class lifestyle, 209–11; and parents' occupations, 38; social life of, in high school, 98–99, 101, 102, 103, 251 (n. 11); in suburbs, 49, 50–51; and travel, 72

Hankenson, Aretha, 16

Hard Choices (Gerson), 217

High schools: and Black women negotiating between races, 254 (n. 24); classism, racism, and sexism in, 14, 16, 87, 88–89, 90–91, 159–60, 242 (n. 11); and college attendance, 7; college preparation during, 86, 102–6; courses offered in, 88–89, 250 (n. 1); negotiations necessary for survival in, 237; same sex college preparatory, 241 (n. 7); social experiences in, 86; suburban, 99; track from, to elite colleges, 165–69; urban, 99

—Black, 91–96, 250 (n. 2); class bias in, 95–96, 251 (n. 8); college preparation in, 95–96; desegregated, 93–94, 250 (n. 6); and elite college attendance, 167–68; experience of middle class in, 144–45; and mobility for Black working-class women, 142, 257 (n. 1); parental goals supported in, 90; positive, 92–93, 250 (n. 5); segregated, 92, 94, 96, 250 (nn. 4, 5), 250–51 (n. 9); and transitions to White colleges, 144–45, 151, 152, 160, 162; women encouraged in, 96; working-class experience in, 151, 152

—elite: and academic performance in college, 177, 184; academic preparation in, 116–17, 119, 120–23, 128–29, 255 (n. 2); Black students in, 119–20, 127, 130–31, 160, 256 (n. 11); career goals at, 129; class differences at, 135, 136, 140, 257 (nn. 14, 17); competition at, 136–37; and Black students navigating two worlds, 123–28, 135–40, 255 (n. 5), 256–57 (n. 13); and

elite college attendance, 165–67; experience of working class in, 117, 120, 128–40, 256 (n. 9); experience of middle class in, 117, 120–28, 140, 160; parochial, 116, 117, 255 (n. 1); private, 116, 117; public alternative, 116, 118; racial composition in, 118–19; racial identity not validated at, 127, 130–31, 139, 256 (n. 11); and social costs of attending, 121, 122–28, 123–28, 134–35, 255 (n. 3); stereotypes at, 134–35, 256 (n. 12); tracking in, 116, 117, 118, 255 (n. 1), 255 (n. 2); and transitions to White colleges, 161
—integrated, 106–15; academic preparation in, 115; and elite college attendance, 168; as first choice of Black families, 106, 254 (n. 21); middle-class experience in, 106–8, 112–15, 160, 255 (n. 29); occupational goals in, 113–14; by race and class, 107, 254 (n. 22); racial negotiations in, 160; social life in, 113, 115; tracking in, 107–8, 114, 115, 254 (n. 22); and transitions to White colleges, 160; working-class experience in, 106, 107–12, 253 (n. 28)
—segregated, 91–92, 250 (n. 1); and elite college attendance, 167–68; and transitions to White colleges, 162
—White, 97–106; academic preparation in, 98, 251 (n. 9); attitudes about Black students in, 100, 142, 251–52 (n. 12), 254 (n. 20); careers not encouraged for Black women in, 105; class obstacles in, 97, 102–6, 142; and non-elite college attendance, 168; pressure to contradict stereotypes at, 134–35, 256 (n. 12); racial negotiations in, 160; social isolation in, 97, 98–102, 251 (nn. 10, 11), 253 (nn. 17, 18); social life of Black boys in, 101, 252–53 (n. 16); suburban, 101–2; and transitions to White colleges, 145–47, 160, 161; working-class experience at, 151, 152–53
Hochschild, Jennifer, 21–22
Hollingshead, August, 88
Housing: integrated, 55–57; linked to education, 42; middle-class, 48, 245 (n. 10);

public, 58, 246 (nn. 15, 16); and race and class, 244 (n. 4), 245 (n. 8), 246 (n. 14); segregation in 1950s, 42–47; working-class, 54–59
Housing Act of 1954, 59
Howell, Katherine, 250 (n. 4); Black students in college of, 170–71, 190, 260–61 (n. 2); career goals of, 197, 261 (n. 5); and expectations of college, 164; extended family of, 32; high school experience of, 60, 118, 119, 129, 137; and mobility, 154–56; 197, 216, 218–20; and parents' occupations, 24; self-esteem for, 222; values stressed by family of, 75, 76, 78
Hughes, Langston, 238

Individualism, 75–76
Integration, 11. See also Desegregation
I've Known Rivers (Lawrence-Lightfoot), 219, 248 (n. 13), 253 (n. 17)

Jack and Jill of America, 124–25, 138, 255–56 (n. 6)
Jefferson, Wilma, 95, 177
Jenkins, Carla, 69, 73, 198, 202, 227–28
John F. Kennedy High School (New York City), 254 (n. 22)
Johnson, Karen: academic performance of, in college, 181; adjusts to college social scene, 171; Black peer group of, in college, 189; child-secured mobility experienced by, 259 (n. 12); college goals of, 157, 259 (n. 12); and dating, 79; education financed by, 158; education stressed by family of, 69, 215; on employment options, 206; high school experience of, 98, 99, 104–5, 251 (n. 11); housing situation of, 56–57; lifestyle of, 229; and parents' occupations, 31; and resisting racism, 81–82, 249–50 (n. 21); and singlehood, 229–30; values stressed by family of, 69, 70, 81, 82, 215
Jones, Deborah: academic performance of, in college, 173, 174–75; adult-sponsored mobility experienced by, 147; career goals

of, 196, 197; cost of success for, 231; high
school attended by, 51, 116, 124, 137, 193;
housing situation of, 52; lifestyle of, 226;
and parents' occupations, 38; and private
lessons, 71, 72; and singlehood, 229–30;
and stereotyped Black middle class, 35;
values stressed by family of, 63, 75, 77

King, Elise, 27, 97, 195
Knight, Mary, 37, 68, 179, 193; high school
attended by, 101–2, 103
Kronus, Sidney, 34–35, 65

Labor market, 243 (n. 7)
Landry, Bart, 21–22, 34–35, 242 (n. 2)
Larkin, Denise, 238; college chosen by, 159,
166–67; cultural resources of, 72; education stressed by family of, 69; encounters
racism in occupation, 204, 205; high
school experience of, 1, 119, 129, 130–31,
135, 136, 138, 256 (n. 10); on housing situation, 42; mobility issues and career
choices for, 216–18, 263 (n. 9); parents'
recognition of potential of, 2; as representative of all Blacks, 2, 241 (n. 3); self-
direction stressed by family of, 77; college attended by, 1, 183, 187
Lawrence, Stephanie, 28, 111, 255 (n. 27),
258–59 (n. 8)
Lawrence-Lightfoot, Sara, 219, 248 (n. 13),
253 (n. 17), 254 (n. 22), 256–57 (n. 13)
Lewis, Adele: academic performance of, in
college, 181; blockbusting recalled by, 56;
child-secured mobility experienced by,
259 (n. 12); college chosen by, 158–59;
education stressed by family of, 67, 69,
247 (n. 8); father's work recalled by, 32;
high school experience of, 109, 111–12;
life plans of, 202; lifestyle of, 226; and
marriage, 198
Libraries, 70–71, 247 (n. 9)
Life plans, 198–203; and commitment to
racial group, 221, 263 (n. 10); and parental expectations, 200–201, 202, 261 (n. 6);

and peer input, 221, 263 (n. 11); preferences in 1976, 223, 263 (n. 12); working-
class, 221
Little Rock Nine, 11

McDonald, Gloria, 59, 111, 255 (n. 27), 258–
59 (n. 8)
Marriage, 198; in 1976, 207, 209, 262 (n. 2);
to Black men, 230; and class, 196; to
White men, 263 (n. 14); and working-
class women, 214
Mason, Sylvia, 28, 108, 176, 177, 254 (n. 23)
Maxwell, Darlene, 235; and career planning
at college, 183; child-secured mobility
experienced by, 259 (n. 12); college
chosen by, 158; high school experience of,
109–10, 254 (nn. 24, 25); and parents'
occupations, 24, 28
Meritocracy, 233, 235
Middle class, 3, 35–40; academic performance of, at elite colleges, 173–75; academic performance of, at non-elite colleges, 178–81; alternatives to public
schools chosen by, 51–53; and Black
bourgeoisie, 34, 35; Black clients of, 38; in
Black high schools, 144–45; Black women
in, 35–40; bourgeoisie, 36; and class
polarization, 236; college attendance of,
12, 141–42, 143–44, 160–61; college costs
paid by, 147–50, 258 (n. 5); colleges
chosen by, 148–50; commitment to relatives of, 39–40; contemporary, 20; assessments of life circumstances by, 173, 250–
51 (n. 7); defined, 21–22, 34–35, 242
(n. 2), 243 (n. 11); educational strategies
of, 48, 49–54; in elite high schools, 117,
120–28, 140, 160; expectations for daughters of, 40–41, 67–68; expectations of
college, 163, 164; family size and composition in, 39, 40, 243 (nn. 14, 15), 244
(n. 16); and financial aid, 148; hard work
by, 37–38; housing available to, 48, 245
(n. 10); in integrated high schools, 106–8,
112–15, 160, 255 (n. 29); navigating higher

education, 144–47, 257–58 (n. 4); in 1950s and 1960s, 21; obstacles faced by daughters of, 41; occupations of, 33–34, 67–69; professional, 34, 36–37, 67–69; racism challeged by, 34–35; and recession, 262 (n. 7); reproduces middle-class lifestyles, 209–14; resources of, 3, 40, 61–62; and White world, 33, 34, 35. *See also* Class; Families; Mobility: adult-sponsored

Mobility: adult-sponsored, 143–50, 160–61, 184, 257–58 (n. 4); and Black institutions, 220–21; for Black women, prior to 1960s, 142; child-secured, 150–59, 161–62, 184, 258–59 (n. 8); and class, 233–34; and college education, 184; and employment goals, 222; and gender, 142; and middle-class women, 236; and race, 256–57 (n. 13), 257 (n. 16); and socially responsible individualism, 220–21; through marriage, 193; and White institutions, 221; for White working-class males, 142; and working-class women, 194, 214–23, 236

Montgomery, Helene: academic performance of, at college, 180; Black peer group of, in college, 189; career goals of, 196–97; college attendance expected of, 6–7; college chosen by, 149–50, 180; education of parents of, 36; high school experience of, 7, 107; life plans of, 201; as viewed by high school teachers, 7

Myths: of educated Black women, 204–5; of equality of education, 87

National Association for the Advancement of Colored People (NAACP), 82

National Scholarship Service and Fund for Negro Students (NSSFNS), 10, 151, 156, 168, 257–58 (n. 4), 259 (n. 9)

Nelson, Rebecca, 179

New Black Middle Class, The (Landry), 242 (n. 2)

New Deal, 8, 9, 25

North, Sherri, 53–54, 127, 226–27

NSSFNS. *See* National Scholarship Service and Fund for Negro Students

Occupation: in 1976, 207, 209, 262 (n. 3); and class, 21–22; combined with marriage and motherhood by Black women, 247 (n. 7); for educated Black women in 1950s and 1960s, 35; and higher education of children, 23; and integrated high schools, 113–14; middle-class, 33–34, 67–69; and Blacks negotiating in White settings, 234; of parents by social class, 26–28; and peer input, 212, 262 (n. 5); and primary and secondary labor market, 25–27; and segregation, 245 (n. 10); and War on Poverty, 262 (n. 4); working-class, 24–27, 31–32, 68–69, 243 (n. 7). *See also* Employment

Our Kind of People (Graham), 255–56 (n. 6)

Parents: ages of middle-class, 40; ages of working-class, 33, 243 (n. 10); Black colleges attended by, 243 (n. 13); education of, 36, 243 (n. 12); and involvement with schools, 4, 241 (n. 5); occupations of, by social class, 26–28. *See also* Families

Pattillo-McCoy, Mary, 244 (n. 4)

Peers: Black, at college, 188–93, 261 (nn. 3, 4); and career choices, 212, 262 (n. 5); college attendance of, 77, 249 (n. 17); and life plans, 221, 263 (n. 11); and self-direction, 77–78, 249 (n. 18)

Piano lessons, 71–72, 248 (n. 11)

Plessy v. Ferguson, 91

Poulantzas, Nicos, 3, 22, 242 (n. 3)

Powell, Florence, 71, 72, 73, 80; high school experience of, 94, 95

Powell, Sabrina: and church activities, 73; college chosen by, 179; and expectations of college, 164; lifestyle of, 209, 211–13, 226; and parents' occupations, 38; and private lessons, 71; high school recalled by, 94; as token in male White occupation, 204, 205

Private lessons, 71, 248 (n. 11)
Pseudonyms, 241 (n. 1)

Race: color-blind approach to, 234, 235; and
gender, 15; and housing, 244 (n. 4), 245
(n. 8); and progress, 1, 8–10, 237–38; significance of, 15, 234
Racism, 14; and class, 12, 16, 40, 62; consequences of, 233, 237; contemporary patterns of, 15–17; costs of opposing, 3–4,
18–19; in educational system, 10, 14, 15–
16, 44, 87, 88–89, 90–91, 159–60, 241
(n. 2), 242 (n. 11); institutionalized, 236–
37; and mobility, 234–35; and other
group-based oppression, 236–37; rethinking, 12–17; skills acquired to fight, 2;
socialization against, unrecognized by
scholars, 65, 247 (n. 3); subconscious, 235
Rawlins, Beverly: adult-sponsored mobility
experienced by, 146–47, 257 (n. 3); college experience of, 168, 174, 185; and dating, 79; educational history of, 52–53;
education stressed by family of, 69–70;
and expectations of college, 163; extended family of, 39; high school experience of, 113, 114; and parents' occupations, 38; on positive self-image, 84
Reading, 5, 70–71
Reed, Brenda, 37, 255 (n. 5)
Religion, 73, 248 (n. 12)
Research methods, 17–19, 242 (nn. 12, 13)
Robinson, Crystal, 59, 201
Robinson, Lorie, 16

Saunders, Joyce: academic performance of,
at college, 180; college costs for family of,
148; high school experience of, 50, 99,
100, 101, 102, 103; and private lessons, 71,
248 (n. 11); and racism, 82–83; and travel,
72; values stressed by family of, 70, 74, 75
Schofield, Janet, 100, 101, 251–52 (n. 12),
252–53 (n. 16)
Schools: alternatives to public, 51–53; and
educational strategies, 47–48, 245 (n. 9);
inner city, 244 (n. 3); northern desegre-

gated, 241 (n. 3); parents' involvement
with, 4, 241 (n. 5); southern segregated,
241 (n. 3)
Segregation, 12; contemporary patterns of,
13, 15; in education, 241 (n. 2); and New
Deal, 8; in 1950s, 241 (n. 2); and occupation, 245 (n. 10)
—residential, 42–47, 247 (n. 3); contemporary, 47; determination of, 246 (n. 12);
disadvantages of, 45, 244 (n. 4); institutionalized, 44–45; and money saved by
cities, 43–44, 244 (n. 2); perpetrators of,
45–46, 244–45 (n. 5), 245 (nn. 6, 7)
Serviceman's Readjustment Act of 1944,
241–42 (n. 8)
Sexism, 10, 254–55 (n. 26)
Shaw, Stephanie, 13, 75, 236
Sheldon, Janet, 27, 91, 182; high school
experience of, 86, 104
Sikes, Melvin, 21–22, 245 (n. 8)
Singlehood, 226, 228, 229–30
Single mothers, 29–30, 30–31, 241 (n. 6),
243 (n. 9)
Slum: defined, 47
Small, Natalie, 28, 92, 168, 176–77, 195
Social class. See Class
Social mobility. See Mobility
Spelman College (Atlanta), 16
Stevens, Olivia, 38, 118, 122, 196
Suburbanization, 49, 244 (n. 1), 245–46
(n. 11), 253 (n. 18)
Suburbs: Black residents in, 49, 244 (n. 1),
245–46 (n. 11); inner city problems in,
44; social relations in, 49, 50–51, 245
(n. 9), 246 (n. 13)

Taylor, Jennifer: academic performance of,
at college, 183; child-secured mobility
experienced by, 259 (n. 12); education
stressed by family of, 4, 66, 247 (n. 4);
high school experience of, 4–5; housing
history recalled by, 55; and limited
parental resources, 7; peer group of, in
college, 190–91
Thomas, Susan: adult-sponsored mobility

experienced by, 147; career goals of, 196; college chosen by, 168; and college social scene, 171; education stressed by family of, 69; guidance counseling received by, 141; high school experience of, 114; lifestyle of, 226

Trott, Linda: on being an only child, 33; Black faculty support of, 222; child-secured mobility experienced by, 152, 156–57, 259 (n. 10), 259 (n. 12); and church activities, 73; college experience of, 177, 177–78, 184, 191–92; and dating, 81; high school experience of, 118, 129, 131, 133–34, 135, 136, 137, 139–40; housing recalled by, 56; life plans of, 202; and parents' occupations, 28; peer group of, in college, 191–92; and private lessons, 71; self-esteem for, 222; social relations of, in high school, 133–34, 139–40; on striving for excellence, 63; values stressed by family of, 78–79, 84

Tucker, Evelyn: adult-sponsored mobility experienced by, 143–44, 145–47, 257 (n. 2); in Black section of White suburbs, 49, 246 (n. 12); on college experience, 186; high school experience of, 95, 145; and parents' occupations, 37

Turner, Marlene: and church activities, 73; college chosen by, 168; college costs for family of, 148; high school experience of, 102, 103; housing situation of, 42, 49, 58; peer group of, in college, 191

Upward mobility. *See* Mobility
Urban renewal, 59

Walker, Regina, 96
Wall, Dorothy, 242 (n. 1); child-secured mobility experienced by, 153, 259 (n. 12); college experience of, 182–83, 184; education stressed by family of, 1, 68; extended family of, 32; family support and values of, 68, 157; high school experience of, 110–11, 141, 143, 153, 254 (n. 25), 254– 55 (n. 26); housing situation of, 58; and par-

ents' involvement with schools, 69; racial stereotypes contradicted by, 74–75; and youth groups, 73

War on Poverty, 30, 262 (n. 4)
Warren, Beth, 263 (n. 10); child-secured mobility experienced by, 153; college experience of, 177, 178, 192; and cultural resources, 72; high school experience of, 60, 116, 118, 129–30, 131, 132, 136, 139–40, 153; lifestyle of, 225; and mother's occupation, 30; navigating two worlds to attend high school, 138; and racism, 132; self-esteem for, 222; social relations of, in high school, 139–40; values stressed by family of, 74, 77; and youth groups, 73

Washington, Robin, 241 (n. 6); child-secured mobility experienced by, 7, 153; and church activities, 73; college experience of, 163, 177, 185; high school experience of, 130, 131, 136, 153, 241 (n. 7), 256 (n. 10); extended family of, 32; life plans of, 201; lifestyle of, 229; and public housing situation, 5, 59; and racism, 83; reading encouraged by mother, 5, 71; and youth groups, 73

Weber, Max, 21, 22
Welfare, 241 (n. 6)
West, Cornel, 234
What a Woman Ought to Be and to Do (Shaw), 13
White women: Black women viewed by, 83; and obligation to community, 248 (n. 15); occupational expectations of, 68– 69, 194, 247 (n. 7)
Willie, Charles, 34–35
Wilson, William J., 21, 244 (n. 4)
Women. *See* Black women; White women
Working class: academic performance of, at elite colleges, 175–78; academic performance of, at non-elite colleges, 181–84; assessments of life circumstances by, 173, 250–51 (n. 7); in Black high schools, 151, 152; Black women in, 25, 26, 27; college attendance of, 12, 141–42, 143, 150–52, 161–62; colleges chosen by, 158; contem-

porary, 20; definition of, 22, 24, 243 (n. 6); and educational mobility, 26, 33; educational options for, 7, 59–61, 152–57; educational strategies of, 54–55, 62, 112, 255 (n. 8), 257–58 (n. 4); education of parents of, 5–6, 26, 243 (n. 8); in elite high schools, 117, 120, 128–40, 256 (n. 9); expectations and resources of, 3, 7, 40; expectations for daughters of, 41, 247 (n. 6); expectations of college for, 163–64; family size and composition of, 29, 33; and financing college, 7, 158–59; and housing, 54–59; in integrated high schools, 106, 107–12, 253 (n. 28); in 1950s and 1960s, 20; occupational options open to, 24–27, 31–32, 68–69, 243 (n. 7); and parents' ages, 33, 243 (n. 10); and ranking of colleges, 156, 259 (n. 11); in ghetto, 57–58. *See also* Class; Families; Mobility: child-secured

World War I, 8

World War II, 1; veterans of, 8–9, 241–42 (n. 8)

Wright, Karen: and colleges, 145; high school experience of, 122, 125, 126, 128, 145, 255 (n. 4); and parents' occupations, 37; peer group of, in college, 260–61 (n. 2); and social tension, 126, 128;

Youth groups, 73

GENDER & AMERICAN CULTURE

Too Much to Ask: Black Women in the Era of Integration, by Elizabeth Higginbotham (2001)

Imagining Medea: Rhodessa Jones and Theater for Incarcerated Women, by Rena Fraden (2001)

Painting Professionals: Women Artists and the Development of Modern American Art, 1870–1920, by Kirsten Swinth (2001)

Remaking Respectability: African American Women in Interwar Detroit, by Victoria W. Wolcott (2001)

Ida B. Wells-Barnett and American Reform, 1880–1930, by Patricia A. Schechter (2001)

Taking Haiti: Military Occupation and the Culture of U.S. Imperialism, 1915–1940, by Mary A. Renda (2001)

Before Jim Crow: The Politics of Race in Postemancipation Virginia, by Jane Dailey (2000)

Captain Ahab Had a Wife: New England Women and the Whalefishery, 1720–1870, by Lisa Norling (2000)

Civilizing Capitalism: The National Consumers' League, Women's Activism, and Labor Standards in the New Deal Era, by Landon R. Y. Storrs (2000)

Rank Ladies: Gender and Cultural Hierarchy in American Vaudeville, by M. Alison Kibler (1999)

Strangers and Pilgrims: Female Preaching in America, 1740–1845, by Catherine A. Brekus (1998)

Sex and Citizenship in Antebellum America, by Nancy Isenberg (1998)

Yours in Sisterhood: Ms. Magazine and the Promise of Popular Feminism, by Amy Erdman Farrell (1998)

We Mean to Be Counted: White Women and Politics in Antebellum Virginia, by Elizabeth R. Varon (1998)

Women Against the Good War: Conscientious Objection and Gender on the American Home Front, 1941–1947, by Rachel Waltner Goossen (1997)

Toward an Intellectual History of Women: Essays by Linda K. Kerber (1997)

Gender and Jim Crow: Women and the Politics of White Supremacy in North Carolina, 1896–1920, by Glenda Elizabeth Gilmore (1996)

Delinquent Daughters: Protecting and Policing Adolescent Female Sexuality in the United States, 1885–1920, by Mary E. Odem (1995)

U.S. History as Women's History: New Feminist Essays, edited by Linda K. Kerber, Alice Kessler-Harris, and Kathryn Kish Sklar (1995)

Common Sense and a Little Fire: Women and Working-Class Politics in the United States, 1900–1965, by Annelise Orleck (1995)

How Am I to Be Heard?: Letters of Lillian Smith, edited by Margaret Rose Gladney (1993)

Entitled to Power: Farm Women and Technology, 1913–1963, by Katherine Jellison (1993)

Revising Life: Sylvia Plath's Ariel Poems, by Susan R. Van Dyne (1993)

Made From This Earth: American Women and Nature, by Vera Norwood (1993)

Unruly Women: The Politics of Social and Sexual Control in the Old South, by Victoria E. Bynum (1992)

The Work of Self-Representation: Lyric Poetry in Colonial New England, by Ivy Schweitzer (1991)

Labor and Desire: Women's Revolutionary Fiction in Depression America, by Paula Rabinowitz (1991)

Community of Suffering and Struggle: Women, Men, and the Labor Movement in Minneapolis, 1915–1945, by Elizabeth Faue (1991)

All That Hollywood Allows: Re-reading Gender in 1950s Melodrama, by Jackie Byars (1991)

Doing Literary Business: American Women Writers in the Nineteenth Century, by Susan Coultrap-McQuin (1990)

Ladies, Women, and Wenches: Choice and Constraint in Antebellum Charleston and Boston, by Jane H. Pease and William H. Pease (1990)

The Secret Eye: The Journal of Ella Gertrude Clanton Thomas, 1848–1889, edited by Virginia Ingraham Burr, with an introduction by Nell Irvin Painter (1990)

Second Stories: The Politics of Language, Form, and Gender in Early American Fictions, by Cynthia S. Jordan (1989)

Within the Plantation Household: Black and White Women of the Old South, by Elizabeth Fox-Genovese (1988)

The Limits of Sisterhood: The Beecher Sisters on Women's Rights and Woman's Sphere, by Jeanne Boydston, Mary Kelley, and Anne Margolis (1988)